PATIENTS, CONSUMERS AND CIVIL SOCIETY

ADVANCES IN MEDICAL SOCIOLOGY

Series Editor: Barbara Katz Rothman

Series Editor for Volumes 5–6: Gary L. Albrecht

Series Editor for Volumes 7–8: Judith A. Levy

Recent Volumes:

Volume 5:	Quality of Life in Health Care – Edited by Ray Fitzpatrick
Volume 6:	Case and Care Management – Edited by Gary L. Albrecht
Volume 7:	Emergent Issues in the Field of Drug Abuse – Edited by Judith A. Levy, Richard C. Stephens and Duane C. McBride
Volume 8:	Social Networks and Health – Edited by Bernice A. Pescosolido and Judith A. Levy
Volume 9:	Bioethical Issues, Sociological Perspectives – Edited by Barbara Katz Rothman, Elizabeth M. Armstrong and Rebecca Tiger

ADVANCES IN MEDICAL SOCIOLOGY VOLUME 10

PATIENTS, CONSUMERS AND CIVIL SOCIETY

EDITED BY

SUSAN M. CHAMBRÉ

Baruch College, City University of New York, USA

MELINDA GOLDNER

Union College, USA

Emerald

JAI

United Kingdom – North America – Japan
India – Malaysia – China

JAI Press is an imprint of Emerald Group Publishing Limited
Howard House, Wagon Lane, Bingley BD16 1WA, UK

First edition 2008

British Library Cataloguing in Publication Data
A catalogue record for this book is available from the British Library

ISBN: 978-1-84855-214-2
ISSN: 1057-6290 (Series)

CONTENTS

LIST OF CONTRIBUTORS

Paul Almeida	Department of Sociology, Texas A&M University, College Station, TX, USA
René Bekkers	ICS/Department of Sociology, Utrecht University, Utrecht, The Netherlands and Department of Philanthropic Studies, Vrije Universiteit Amsterdam, Amsterdam, The Netherlands
Cecilia Benoit	University of Victoria, British Columbia, Canada
Thomasina Borkman	George Mason University, Silver Spring, MD, USA
Ivy Lynn Bourgeault	University of Ottawa, Ottawa, Ontario, Canada
Joanne Coury	State University of New York at Buffalo, NY, USA
Eugene Declercq	Boston University School of Public Health, Boston, MA, USA
Roxana Delgado	Las Dignas, San Salvador, El Salvador
Raymond DeVries	University of Michigan, Ann Arbor, MI, USA
Ann Dill	Brown University, Providence, RI, USA
Astrid Eich-Krohm	Southern Connecticut State University New Haven, CT, USA
Jill A. Fisher	Center for Biomedical Ethics & Society, Vanderbilt University, Nashville, TN, USA

Selina Gallo-Cruz	Sociology Department, Emory University, Atlanta, GA, USA
Chris Ganchoff	Lyman Briggs College, Michigan State University, East Lansing, MI, USA
Itay Greenspan	School of Social Policy and Practice, University of Pennsylvania, Philadelphia, PA, USA
Femida Handy	School of Social Policy and Practice, University of Pennsylvania, Philadelphia, PA, USA
Kristin Holster	Dean College, Franklin, MA, USA
Carol Munn-Giddings	Faculty of Health and Social Care, Anglia Ruskin University, Chelmsford, Essex, UK
Lorna M. Ronald	Department of Sociology, Queens College, Flushing, NY, USA
Markella Rutherford	Wellesley College, Wellesley, MA, USA
Jane Sandall	King's College London, London, UK
Lee Staples	Boston University School of Social Work, Boston, MA, USA
Reva Stein	Massachusetts Clubhouse Coalition, Waltham, MA, USA
Gayle A. Sulik	Texas Woman's University, Denton, TX, USA
Edwin van Teijlingen	School of Medicine and Dentistry, University of Aberdeen, Foresterhill, Aberdeen, Scotland, UK
Meredith Vanstone	University of Western Ontario, London, Ontario, Canada
Sirpa Wrede	Swedish School of Social Science, University of Helsinki, Helsinki, Finland

INTRODUCTION

Health care systems all over the world are undergoing rapid and profound transformations. These changes are the result of a broad array of economic and social trends including neo-liberal economic policies that are contributing to the trend toward privatization, the commodification of health services and products, institutional restructuring (e.g., managed care) to contain costs in the context of technological advances, globalization and demographic changes such as population aging in post-industrial societies. Questions about the accessibility and quality of health care delivery in the face of persistent health disparities, growing numbers of medical errors, and new and uncertain risks posed by emerging infectious diseases, some of them drug-resistant, have also contributed to rethinking about health policy.

In the context of these changes, this volume explores cultural forces at work in the transformation of health care institutions, specifically shifts in our understanding about the role of individuals seeking health care and their identity as patients and/or as consumers. Growing numbers of activated and empowered health consumers and professionals are individually and collectively taking a reflexive and critical role, forming and participating in health-related service, research and advocacy organizations. These changes have contributed to the growth in the number and the role of civil society organizations engaged in shaping and responding to cultural and institutional transformations in health care. The book bridges a number of areas of interest to scholars and policymakers including medical sociology, women's health care, health policy, health social movements, nonprofit organizations and civil society.

Health social movement organizations play a critical role in forging health policy in a number of contexts. While several chapters focus on the United States, the collection includes discussions of a number of other societies including the United Kingdom, Canada, Serbia, Croatia, the Netherlands, Finland and El Salvador. Several chapters look at the cross-cultural adoption of organizational forms including Borkman and Munn-Giddings' comparison of self-help groups in the United States and the United Kingdom, as well as Staples and Stein's discussion of the

Clubhouse model which has been adopted in 28 different countries. Taken together, the chapters suggest that similar processes are occurring in different contexts: the activation and mobilization of patients and consumers is challenging institutions and the state at the micro and macro levels, and in the process are contributing to a reexamination and restructuring of health care and health policy.

The chapters address three main themes: changes in relations between patients/consumers and health care professionals and institutions in the context of increased commodification and privatization of health care; the role of a growing number of patient, disease-related and health advocacy organizations in various cultural and political contexts; and theoretical and policy implications of the rise of health consumerism and health organizations. They examine major trends influencing health policies throughout the world, some of them well understood, but others just beginning to be examined empirically.

A great deal of the public and sociological discourse about health seeking behavior assumes that "patients" became "health consumers" in the latter part of the mid-20th century. This transition has involved a profound change in the relationships between individuals, professionals and institutions. "Patients" rely heavily on health professionals for information, decision-making and care. In contrast, "consumers" actively seek optimal care by choosing providers, obtaining information, serving as their own advocates, engaging in collaborative decision-making with those who render care and participating in advocacy organizations. This change – from patient to consumer – is especially understandable since more and more health care goods and services are being sold as a commodity rendered by a "provider" rather than by a "professional."

The sources of the change to consumerism are complex and varied. They include declining trust in medical authority; the diffusion of ideas from the free speech, civil rights, women's and other social movements; and rising educational levels in the population. For example, contemporary health consumerism has its roots in the social movements of the 1960s (see Borkman & Munn-Giddings) and the women's health movement in particular. These movements drew attention to individual rights and also, by extension, to individual choice. A substantial number of articles concentrate on women's health issues, a fact that bears witness to the centrality of the women's health movement in mapping out the contours of health consumerism. At the same time, growing affluence created what Baudrillard (1998) observes is a consumer society where consumption is not simply done to fulfill basic needs, but is a major social practice and even an obligation of citizens. More recently, the contours of health consumerism have been affected by growing frustration with the "managed care revolution" and by increasing access to health and medical information and support on the Internet. According to many accounts, the shift from patient to consumer became especially evident in the 1980s with the development of AIDS and breast cancer activism. Arno and Feiden (1992) note a common view that before AIDS "the patient population never led the charge toward clinical advances" (p. 243).

Historical evidence suggests that the presence of activated patients in the United States – perhaps meriting the label of consumer – may have a longer history than sometimes described. Participants in 19th century health reform movements, tuberculosis patients in the 19th century and polio patients in the 20th century took activist and reflexive approaches toward health care actively pursuing cures, obtaining information, developing care strategies of their own and framing policies (Oshinsky, 2005; Rothman, 1994; Whorton, 2002). Recent work by Nancy Tomes (2001, 2005, 2006) shows how the consumer movement of the progressive era and the growth of medical advertising created a consumer consciousness that promoted the patient agency and activism which became especially apparent in the 1960s.

Most of the chapters in this volume challenge the view that there was a straightforward or seamless transition from patient to consumer. The patient/consumer binary, in the view of some researchers (Lupton, 1997) and several authors in this volume (Bourgeault et al.; Rutherford & Gallo-Cruz; Sulik & Eich-Krohm) may in fact oversimplify the reality. Patient activation on some dimensions, for example, interest in obtaining information, is not necessarily accompanied by high levels of patient agency in other areas, such as the willingness to challenge or even ignore physician's authority (Haug & Lavin, 1983). The apparent dichotomy of consumer or patient might be combined in complex ways in the course of an individual's lifetime or even during the course of an illness. Sulik and Eich-Krohm point out that "The social transformation from patient to medical consumer occurred as the term 'consumer' became the label of choice within health and social services and the medical system became increasingly more complex ... At the micro-level, however, individuals continually negotiate the role of patient and medical consumer in medical interactions ... and other situational contexts" (p. 4). While it might seem logical that a rise in consumerism might lead individuals to choose and even to dictate their health care, Bourgeault et al. indicate that a widely publicized view, that maternal requests are a major causal factor in the sharp rise in Caesarean sections, is not supported by data from the United States, Canada or the

United Kingdom, where rates are rising, or in Finland, where Caesarean section (C-section) rates are stable. Likewise, Dill and Coury find that self-help groups in Slovenia and Croatia do not necessarily challenge medical authority or operate in opposition to the state.

Several authors in this volume point out that the health care "market" operates differently than the economy for other types of goods (Borkman & Munn-Giddings; Holster). Greater access to information of all sorts has empowered consumers but also intersected with the commodification of health care to create consumers who are influenced and perhaps pressured by market forces promoting utilization, if not overutilization of health care, rather than autonomous purchasers who make individual choices (see Brownlee, 2007). This is true for the process of donating and buying eggs (Holster), decisions about how and where women give birth (Bourgeault et al.; Rutherford & Gallo-Cruz; Sulik & Eich-Krohm), becoming informed about medications or participating in clinical trials (Fisher & Ronald). The consumerist ideology has paradoxical implications, both empowering individuals and promoting "person-blame." As Sulik and Eich-Krohm point out, although the consumer achieves more autonomy, the role of a medical consumer is "an individualized role. The medical consumer must gather and decipher medical information, make the right choices, and take full responsibility for these choices regardless of their outcomes. While ownership can be empowering to some, it can also be a burden" (p. 22).

Several chapters point to the ways that the discourse of "empowered patient" may be utilized by corporations, specifically drug companies, to advance their own interests by enlarging the demand for medical products. The growth in medical information can be both empowering and overwhelming. Direct-to-consumer advertising and the expansion of access to clinical trials, initially conceived as benefiting patients, may have had unintended consequences. Thus, Fisher and Ronald point out that "empowered consumers, according to the discourse, would ensure drug consumption by watching advertising, visiting their doctors, requesting prescriptions, and adhering to treatment regimens" (p. 35).

The individual empowerment implied by the trope of "health care consumer" is also evident in the remarkable growth of health-related organizations, many of them engaged in advocacy. These organizations, often focused on a particular disease, attract a broad constituency. In the case of the AIDS community, for example, this includes those who are "infected and affected." This volume shows how collective action can be forged by people with a diverse set of health problems who have a shared sense of risk (Ganchoff), or by a broad coalition brought together by shared concerns about health policy (Almeida & Delgado). The role of such organizations in some contexts, most notably AIDS and breast cancer, have been amply documented (Arno & Feiden, 1992; Boehmer, 2000; Chambré, 2006; Epstein, 1996; Lerner, 2001) but our understanding of the processes of activation and mobilization is incomplete. Chapters in this volume enlarge our understanding of the nature of empowerment and its dimensions.

Over the past half century, health-related organizations have proliferated in many contexts both in sites where there is a long history of voluntary associations like the United States, Canada and the United Kingdom (Borkman & Munn-Giddings; Greenspan & Handy) and in societies where this tradition is not as strong but where such groups are growing in importance like post-socialist countries and in El Salvador (Almeida & Delgado; Dill & Coury). They are important in relatively privatized systems like the United States or more collectivist systems like Canada and former socialist countries where there is a need for information. Even though citizens in these societies have universal access to care, there are, nonetheless, gaps in service (see Dill & Coury). Greenspan and Handy note that "in Canada ... even a government-sponsored universal healthcare system does not provide sufficient services for women with breast cancer; hence, VHOs arise to supply the unmet demands for psychological and social support" (p. 157). As Bekkers points out, voluntary health organizations fill important gaps in societies with universal health care systems that are not necessarily undergoing transformation. It is striking that in a society like Holland with universal and high quality health care, one quarter of the funds raised by the Dutch Heart Association are allocated to patient care. Thus, voluntary health organizations play a critical role in both stable and changing political contexts.

Voluntary health organizations, many of them organized around specific diseases, play myriad roles in offering information and support, and serve as a venue for patient activation. For growing numbers of individuals, self-help and patient organizations play a critical role in mediating between individuals and health institutions (Borkman & Munn-Giddings; Greenspan & Handy). They may, as Dill and Coury suggest for Slovenia and Croatia, be promoted by the state in order to buffer the effects of privatization and restructuring of health care. For individuals, voluntary associations – whether self-help or mutual aid – are contexts for seeking social support or forming collaborative partnerships with professionals as an important platform for healing and recovery (Dill & Coury; Staples & Stein). In contrast to a widely held view that self-help organizations promote introspection and might blunt the development of activism, the roots of collective action and political activity often begin when people tell their stories, share information and form strong bonds with people in similar circumstances.

At the same time, health organizations play a central role in challenging and shaping policies. A wide variety of actors and a complex set of processes lead to the development of civil society organizations focused on health issues. Many voluntary organizations, like the Dutch Heart Association examined by Bekkers, focus on a specific disease and promote awareness, raise funds, disseminate information and influence policy. They attract donors who feel a connection to the issue, because of their own experience or the connection to someone affected by the disease. Other groups are brought together to fund or to lobby for scientific research. In the case of stem cell activists, the process of creating a collective identity is different than when the cause involves a single disease (Ganchoff). There, people with Parkinson's disease, diabetes and a host of other illnesses engaged in collective action to pressure the California legislature to fund scientific research given the lack of federal funding because of the controversial nature of stem cell research. In the case of El Salvador, a plan to privatize the health care system mobilized a broad range of citizens with the Salvadorian women's movement playing a central role in the successful challenge of this proposal (Almeida & Delgado). As has been the case in other contexts (Koven & Michel, 1993), women mobilized both as citizens and as mothers working as both insiders and outsiders to pressure the state to withdraw its plans.

In the first section of the book, authors explore changes in relations between patients and consumers in different health care systems. The first chapter by Sulik and Eich-Krohm titled "No Longer a Patient: The Social Construction of the Medical Consumer" examines changing relations between consumers and health care providers by looking at breast cancer and infertility. They argue that the transition from patient to consumer is an ongoing process that entails tensions between medical control and individual agency. Fisher and Ronald then explore how the pharmaceutical industry uses the discourse of patient empowerment in direct-to-consumer advertising and clinical drug development in order to convey their expectations about appropriate patient behavior. In the next chapter titled "Making Connections: Egg Donation, the Internet, and the New Reproductive Technology Marketplace," Holster examines how patients are transformed into consumers through the egg donation market on the Internet, which deals with technologically manipulated products. Rutherford and Gallo-Cruz, in their chapter "Selling the Ideal Birth: Rationalization and Re-enchantment in the Marketing of Maternity Care," then analyze hospital websites in order to depict the influence of the natural birth movement and consumer demand on hospital maternity services. Though showing evidence of the empowerment of women, they show how this is constrained by, and serve the interests of, providers. Bourgeault et al. provide evidence in "Too Posh to Push? Comparative Perspectives on Maternal Request Caesarean Sections in Canada, the US, the UK and Finland" that the growing C-section rate in Canada, the United States, the United Kingdom and Finland is not significantly influenced by maternal requests. They end their chapter speculating that "The present cost-conscious context may discourage CS consumerism as a more costly practice. It may be very likely in the future, however, that because of dwindling maternity care human resources globally (obstetricians, midwives and nurses) and the predictability that scheduled CS entails, there may be a shift in the discourse and accepted practices towards its greater use, even when not indicated medically" (p. 118).

The second section of the book turns to the role of health organizations in various cultural and political contexts. Borkman and Munn-Giddings explore how self-help groups and organizations are shaped by their country's health care system (specifically the United States and the United Kingdom) in their chapter titled "Self-Help, Consumerism and Changing Health Care Systems in the UK and the US." They find that on a community level they transform patients into consumers who challenge medical knowledge and advocate for wider participation. Greenspan and Handy ("From Discovery to Recovery and Beyond: The Role of Voluntary Health Sector Organizations in the Lives of Women with Breast Cancer") examine how voluntary health sector organizations help Canadian women cope with breast cancer by providing information, counseling and support. In addition to acting as consumers, some service recipients become empowered when they volunteer to help other women diagnosed with breast cancer. Staples and Stein, in "The Clubhouse Model: Mental Health Consumer–Provider Partnerships for Recovery," examine the international Clubhouse movement, which is designed to help people with mental illness become better integrated into their communities. The partnerships with staff are very empowering and critical to the recovery process. In "Straight from the Heart," Bekkers illustrates how individuals who know someone with heart disease, especially those in poor health, are more likely to donate to the Dutch Heart Association. Thus, there are limits to the sense of solidarity people feel with others.

The final section of the book examines theoretical and policy implications of the rise of health consumerism and health organizations both locally and globally. In "Speaking for Stem Cells: Biomedical Activism and Emerging

Forms of Patienthood," Ganchoff explores why diverse actors developed the collective identity of stem cell activist to support California's Proposition 71 in support of stem cell research. Their work is helping to redefine being a patient. Dill and Coury then examine how self-help groups interact collaboratively with health care providers in Slovenia and Croatia, while contributing to civil society, in their chapter titled "Forging a New Commons: Self-Help/Mutual Aid Associations in Post-Socialist Countries." They note that "As self-help groups engage their members in meaning-making activities, they generate trust and shared understandings that in turn build social capital. As groups generate and disseminate these perspectives through their activities and their members' own changed identities, they may also, if gradually, transform the wider culture" (p. 271). The last chapter, by Almeida and Delgado, illustrates how the Salvadoran women's movement, in coordination with a larger consumer movement and public health sector employees, resisted privatization of the public health care system in their chapter "Gendered Networks and Health Care Privatization."

Together, these 12 articles advance our knowledge by illustrating how patients and consumers, both individually and collectively, are key actors in restructuring health care systems and health policy in numerous contexts. They illustrate several global trends but, at the same time, significant differences in various societies. Our work is an invitation to other scholars as we map out what is known about these issues and hopefully provide a motivation for other scholars to both consolidate and advance our understanding of these issues.

ACKNOWLEDGMENTS

This has been a new and successful collaboration between two sociologists who became better acquainted in the course of doing this book. We were fortunate to attract a gifted and dedicated group of scholars to join this venture. And so, our first set of thanks go to all of the authors who gracefully and appreciatively responded to a series of requests for additional drafts so that this book could include original articles that expressed different viewpoints but also had a coherence that enabled us to outline a set of crosscutting issues that bring together previously disparate fields within sociology.

We also want to thank our home institutions, Baruch College and Union College, for granting us simultaneous sabbaticals – an unplanned event – that allowed us to gain momentum on the project. Valued colleagues at these institutions, including Barbara Katz Rothman – the editor of the series who gave us free reign in doing this book – as well as Robin Root and Shoshanna Sofaer provided invaluable support.

Finally, we want to express our appreciation to our families – Bob Chambré and the children and grandchildren, and Jeff Feldman and Toby Goldner – who encourage and enable us to lead rich and satisfying lives.

REFERENCES

Arno, P. S., & Feiden, K. L. (1992). *Against the odds: The story of AIDS, drug development, politics & profits*. New York, NY: HarperCollins.

Baudrillard, J. (1998). *The consumer society: Myths & structures*. Thousand Oaks, CA: Sage.

Boehmer, U. (2000). *The personal and the political: Women's activism in response to the breast cancer and AIDS epidemics*. Albany, NY: State University of New York.

Brownlee, S. (2007). *Overtreated: Why too much medicine is making us sicker and poorer*. New York: Bloomsbury.

Chambré, S. M. (2006). *Fighting for our lives: New York's AIDS community and the politics of disease*. New Brunswick, NJ: Rutgers University Press.

Epstein, S. (1996). *Impure science: AIDS, activism, and the politics of knowledge*. Berkeley, CA: University of California Press.

Haug, M., & Lavin, B. (1983). *Consumerism in medicine: Challenging physician authority*. Beverly Hills, CA: Sage Publications.

Koven, S., & Michel, S. (Eds). (1993). *Mothers of a new world: Maternalist politics and the origins of welfare states*. New York, NY: Routledge.

Lerner, B. H. (2001). *The breast cancer wars: Hope, fear, and the pursuit of a cure in twentieth-century America*. New York, NY: Oxford University Press.

Lupton, D. (1997). Consumerism, reflexivity and the medical encounter. *Social Science and Medicine*, *45*(3), 373–381.

Oshinsky, D. M. (2005). *Polio: An American story*. New York, NY: Oxford University Press.

Rothman, S. M. (1994). *Living in the shadow of death: Tuberculosis and the social experience of illness in American history*. New York, NY: Basic Books.

Tomes, N. (2001). Merchants of health: Medicine and consumer culture in the United States, 1900–1940. *The Journal of American History*, *88*, 519–547.

Tomes, N. (2005). The great American medicine show revisited. *Bulletin of the History of Medicine*, *79*, 627–663.

Tomes, N. (2006). Patients or health consumers? Why the history of contested terms matters. In: R. A. Stevens, C. E. Rosenberg & L. R. Burns (Eds), *History and health policy in the United States*. New Brunswick, NJ: Rutgers University Press.

Whorton, J. C. (2002). *Nature cures: The history of alternative medicine*. New York, NY: Oxford University Press.

Susan M. Chambré
Melinda Goldner
Editors

PART I
PATIENTS, CONSUMERS AND HEALTH SYSTEMS

NO LONGER A PATIENT: THE SOCIAL CONSTRUCTION OF THE MEDICAL CONSUMER

Gayle A. Sulik and Astrid Eich-Krohm

ABSTRACT

Purpose – *This chapter examines medical consumerism and the changing relations between patients as consumers and the medical system across two women's health contexts, breast cancer and infertility.*

Methodology/approach – *The analysis draws on two qualitative studies: The first explores the experiences of 60 breast cancer survivors through in-depth interviews and participant observation (Sulik, 2005), and the second uses in-depth interviews to analyze 18 women's experiences with infertility (Eich-Krohm, 2000).*

Findings – *The medical consumer is an individualized role that shifts attention away from the quality problem in health care and toward the quality of the person as a medical consumer who is characterized to be optimistic, proactive, rational, responsible, and informed.*

Research limitations/implications – *As medicine has become a form of mass consumption, the category of medical consumer has elevated the individual in medical decision-making. The shift from patient to medical consumer is an ongoing process that is grounded in a tension between*

Patients, Consumers and Civil Society
Advances in Medical Sociology, Volume 10, 3–28

ISSN: 1057-6290/doi:10.1016/S1057-6290(08)10002-X

medical control and individual agency, and is exacerbated by the intensity and incomprehensibility of modern medicine.

Practical implications – *The proliferation of medical information and personal illness narratives through the Internet, advice books, and self-help groups have advanced lay knowledge about preventive medicine and medical treatment while simultaneously introducing new fears and anxiety about the multitude of options and outcomes.*

Originality/value of chapter – *This study contributes to our knowledge on medical consumerism and its impact on illness experience and the synthesis of lay and professional knowledge.*

In the twentieth century's Progressive Era a newly politicized consumption emerged. The consumer movement linked consumption both to choice and access to goods and services, and to citizenship and agency within a free society (Glickman, 1999). The origins of consumerism in health are closely tied to the consumer and other social movements of the 1960s and 1970s. Individuals and lay interest groups began to challenge the authority of experts and the dominance of the medical system. As consumers, individuals who used health services would be empowered to play an active role in making informed choices about their health. The social transformation from patient to medical consumer occurred as the term "consumer" became the label of choice within health and social services and the medical system became increasingly more complex (Kapp, 1999; Hardey, 2001). At the micro-level, however, individuals continually negotiate the role of patient and medical consumer in medical interactions (Lupton, 1997) and other situational contexts. Drawing from research on breast cancer and infertility, this chapter examines the process of *becoming* a medical consumer and the changing relations between patients-as-consumers and the medical system.

Breast cancer and infertility are important sites for analyzing the role of the medical consumer as they represent a continuum of the medicalization of women's health. Whereas breast cancer is fully institutionalized within the medical system, infertility is only partially institutionalized and functions primarily within a for-profit medical market that is not typically covered by insurance. However, both are defined as medical problems and treatment is medically specialized. Information about these conditions is controversial, abstract, and incomplete. For example, breast cancer has many misunderstood causes, and known risk factors (such as age, reproductive factors, inherited genetic mutations, postmenopausal obesity, hormone replacement therapy, alcohol consumption, and previous history of cancer of the endometrium, ovary, or colon) account for less than 30 percent of breast cancer cases (Hulka & Stark, 1995; Smith-Warner, Spiegelman, & Yaun, 1998; Love, 2005). Few interventions reduce risk, and none of them prevent breast cancer. Causes of infertility are not known in 20% of all cases (NYSTF, 1998). Known causes include behavioral risk factors such as weight, age, tobacco, alcohol, and sexually transmitted diseases, as well as endometriosis and DES exposure (NYSTF, 1998). There is no guaranteed treatment for bringing a fetus to term (CDC, 2005).

Although they function within different medical markets, both depend on technoscientific diagnostics, treatments, and the *promise* of new medical–technological advances: "All of these tests are only tools that, added together, help to give us a picture ... and decide what to do ... None of this gives us absolute knowledge ... you need to be optimistic, but careful" (Love, 2000, pp. 344–345). Within the medical system, careful optimism suggests compliance with medical surveillance and intervention while making one's own choices. Because infertility treatment occurs largely in a for-profit medical market, choice is paramount and those facing infertility are generally more likely to face issues of affordability. As both are positioned within a medical system that is optimistic without making unequivocal promises, the role of the medical consumer creates a tension between the dependent/inactive patient and the independent/active medical consumer, encompassing processes of medicalization and challenges to medical authority.

Medicalization remains a powerful force within the changing power relations among the medical profession and related social institutions (Gabe, Bury, & Elston, 2004), the medical division of labor (Light, 1993; Mykytyn, 2006; Zetka, 2008); the expansion of mediated and private medical markets (Hardey, 2001; Conrad & Leiter, 2004); and cooperative relationships between doctors and patients (Mead & Bower, 2000; Thomas, 2000; Mykytyn, 2006). Professional and institutional acceptance of medical surveillance, urgent and aggressive treatment, and faith in medical science construct a medical logic that is firmly rooted in twentieth century medicine and underlies norms for the profession, the consumer, and health activism (Hardon, 2006). Breast cancer and infertility highlight the position women have assumed as medical consumers vis-à-vis modern medicine and health advocacy. Analyzing how the pressure and desire to become a medical consumer shapes women's subjective responses across these women's health contexts reveals the ubiquity of medical consumerism, its function in re-energizing medicalization processes, and the role of medicalization in women's lives.

The rules of medical consumerism come from a variety of sources, including medical staff, personal contacts, support groups, educational programs, books, medical journals, and Internet health sites. Fundamental characteristics of the medical consumer role are *personal responsibility*, *proactive and prevention-conscious behavior*, *rationality*, and *choice*. Personal responsibility is a key element of this role, reflecting the integration of professional medical systems and the broader cultural climate (Davison, Smith, & Frankel, 1991; Henwood, Wyatt, Hart, & Smith, 2003). Individuals become aware of their status as patients/consumers through public representations such as health promotion and education campaigns, public service announcements, self-help groups (Dill & Coury, 2008), health activism (Borkman & Munn-Giddings, 2008), and popular media (Franklin, 1990; Fosket, Karran, & LaFia, 2000; Landzelius, 2006b). Then, they judge these messages in light of their personal knowledge and experience (Copelton, 2006).

Many assume that being informed can help a person to get quality care (Zimmerman & Hill, 2000; Bryan, Gill, Greenfield, Gutridge, & Marshall, 2006). What is quality care? While systematic data on the quality of health care delivery in the United States are limited, the current system leaves large gaps between the care people should and do receive (Kohn, Corrigan, & Donaldson, 1999; Eisenberg & Power, 2000; IOM, 2001; McGlynn et al., 2003). The Committee on the Quality of Health Care in America concluded that care is inconsistent and dangerously inadequate, and that the health care delivery system needs fundamental change (NIM/NRC, 1999). Yet, the medical consumer is socially constructed to break through these barriers, get information, make choices, and get better care.

Similar to other politicized consumerist movements of the 1960s and 1970s, the Women's Health Movement (WHM) played a vital role in transforming how women would interact with the traditional medical system, influencing how they would understand medical care for themselves, their families, and their communities (Ehrenreich & English, 1989; Zimmerman & Hill, 2000; Morgen, 2002). As informed patients, political activists, and active participants in their health and medical care, the WHM sought to expand women's support networks and increase women's sense of control. Envisioning women as informed and self-determined, capable of making empowered decisions, the notable *Our Bodies, Our Selves*, placed women's health in a new socio-political context, helping to launch the national and international WHM (BWHBC, 1973). Identifying and collaborating with individuals and organizations that provide services, generate research and policy analysis, and organize for social change, the book urged women to *inform themselves* about health issues.

Collective mobilization works to represent and advocate for specific illnesses and medical conditions, and energizes public concern about these conditions and the people who have them (Rabeharisoa, 2006). Information and communication technologies have enabled patients to become more active in their medical treatment and care (Hardey, 2001; Clarke, Shim, Mamo, Fosket, & Fishman, 2003; Radin, 2006). Access to medical information is recognized to be a primary factor in weakening the boundaries of authority between patients and medical professionals, even enabling patients to become producers of health knowledge and services (Greenspan & Handy, 2008). Traditional doctor–patient relationships are defined as hierarchical. Physicians hold authoritative and dominant positions, with patients assuming passive roles as recipients of medical care (Freidson, 1970; Schneider, 1997; Lyman, 2000). While some prefer this arrangement rather than fully participating in decision-making (Schneider, 1997), a new model of care views the doctor–patient relationship as a cooperative partnership (Mead & Bower, 2000; Thomas, 2000; Landzelius, 2006a). Within this model, the *patient-as-consumer* suggests an active role in becoming informed, making medical decisions, and determining the course of treatment and care (Haug & Lavin, 1983; Light, 1993; Kapp, 1999; Kronenfeld, 2001; Jost, 2003).

The Internet has furthered the notion that individuals *should* have and want information. For example, WebMD Health Corporation is the leading provider of online health information services, with 12 million visitors monthly (Ebizmba.com, 2007). The site includes advertisements, information from corporate sponsors, and has an Independent Medical Review Board of four medical doctors to evaluate content. The second most visited site (with 9 million monthly visitors) is the official website of the National Institutes of Health (NIH.gov). NIH does not endorse or recommend any commercial products, processes, or services and recognizes peer review as the primary means of quality control. The third most visited health website, MayoClinic.com, is operated by the world's largest not-for-profit group medical practice and serves 5.1 million monthly visitors. The site includes advertising and sponsorship under strict guidelines, and the information is evaluated with a 43-person editorial staff, the majority of whom are medical doctors. Further consolidating its domination of the health information market, WebMD announced an exclusive, multi-year search and advertising agreement with Yahoo!, one of the most trafficked Internet destinations worldwide (WebMD, 2007).

The anticipated growth of the online health information distribution market is likely to increase medical consumption and the desire for more information. This is due in part to an erosion of trust in doctors and medicine. However, the complexity and specialization of medical knowledge continues to fortify the need for technical medical expertise (Weitz, 1999; Bryan et al., 2006). Differentiation allows physicians to maintain authority by selectively providing information, disregarding uncomfortable questions, ignoring patients' decisions when they challenge their own, and reiterating the general view that medical treatment is an ethical, and therefore nonnegotiable, commitment (Weitz, 1999). Institutionalized policies and practices also shape the types of choices available (Bourgeault, Declerq, & Sandall, 2008; Rutherford & Gallo-Cruz, 2008). Media, self-help groups, the pharmaceutical industry, and the broader health care system use *empowerment rhetoric* to create specific expectations about patient–consumer behavior (Fisher & Ronald, 2008). Within a person-blame paradigm (Fosket et al., 2000), however, medical consumers are responsible for making medical decisions and taking full responsibility for their choices.

The shift from patient to medical consumer puts the responsibility for medical decisions and their outcomes on those seeking help, guidance, and care from the medical system. The delegation of responsibility to the medical consumer supports the notion that those who do have access to the medical system will have a direct impact on their care.

METHODS

This chapter draws on two qualitative studies from two different women's health contexts: The first study explores the experiences of 60 breast cancer survivors through in-depth interviews and participant observation (Sulik, 2005), and the second uses in-depth interviews to analyze 18 women's experiences with infertility (Eich-Krohm, 2000). Participation was voluntary and unpaid. To protect confidentiality, the authors give pseudonyms to all respondents. We contextualize the interview data with self-help information from the National Breast Cancer Coalition (NBCC) and RESOLVE: The National Infertility Association, as well as public accounts of breast cancer and infertility. Commonalities across these studies illuminate the role of medical consumerism and the changing doctor/patient relationship for both groups of women.

The Breast Cancer Study

Sulik gathered and analyzed data using ethnography, interviewing techniques, and a grounded theory approach to qualitative analysis

(Glaser & Strauss, 1967; Lofland & Lofland, 1995; Gubrium & Holstein, 2002). She observed a community-based breast cancer organization in the northeast for six months. Then, she constructed an interview schedule (Reinharz, 1992) with a loose chronological order, open-ended questions, and themes that related to the diagnosis story and the impact of breast cancer on women's lives, relationships, and perspectives. Interviews ranged from 1 to 4 hours in a location of the respondent's choice.

Consistent with grounded theory, Sulik used a theoretical sampling strategy and comparison groups to verify, challenge, and refine the core concepts used to develop a substantive model of women's coping strategies. Since the women's health and breast cancer movements have increased the likelihood that women with breast cancer would be associated with support groups, advocacy groups, or other community organizations, she used a *comparative* analysis of three groups: members of a breast cancer advocacy organization ($n = 18$), participants in a breast cancer support group ($n = 22$), and women who were unaffiliated with formal breast cancer-related organizations ($n = 20$). Sulik recruited respondents for these groups from one education/advocacy organization, five support groups, two treatment centers, two breast cancer community events, public bulletin boards, and through snowball sampling. See Table 1 for sample characteristics.

Expanding the analysis, Sulik and Eich-Krohm collaboratively apply the model developed to a fourth group of women, those who participated in the infertility study.

The Infertility Study

The infertility study also used qualitative methods to explore women's experiences and decision-making when facing infertility (Eich-Krohm, 2000). Eich-Krohm conducted 18 in-depth interviews to explore how these women identify and evaluate their options, the role of emotional responses, and social support from the family, friends, and the medical profession (Lofland & Lofland, 1995; Kvale, 1996). She recruited respondents through an infertility support group in the greater New York City metropolitan area and snowball sampling. Because infertility treatment is usually located in cities and metropolitan areas, these women had greater access to infertility specialists compared to women in rural settings. Taped interviews were 1–3 hours, occurring in a location of the respondent's choice.

Eich-Krohm developed an interview guide covering topics such as: philosophies about families and parenthood; how infertility influenced the

Table 1. Sample Characteristics – Breast Cancer Study.

Marital Status		*Age*	
Married	76.7% ($n = 46$)	Mean age (in years)	53.6
Divorced	11.7% ($n = 7$)	Age range	31–79
Widowed	5.0% ($n = 3$)		
Never married	6.7% ($n = 4$)		
Race/Ethnicity		*Number of Children*	
White	90.0% ($n = 54$)	3 or more	15.0% ($n = 9$)
African American	5.0% ($n = 3$)	1–2	56.7% ($n = 34$)
Other	5.0% ($n = 3$)	0	35.0% ($n = 17$)
Educational Attainment		*Number of Years of Survivorship*	
High School Degree	16.6% ($n = 10$)	1 year	21.7% ($n = 13$)
Some college	15.0% ($n = 9$)	2–4 years	41.7% ($n = 25$)
Bachelor's degree	31.7% ($n = 19$)	5 years	3.3% ($n = 2$)
Beyond Bachelor's	36.7% ($n = 22$)	6–9 years	20.0% ($n = 12$)
		10 or more years	13.3% ($n = 8$)
Occupation			
Service	11.7% ($n = 7$)		
Administrative	35.0% ($n = 21$)		
Education	35.0% ($n = 17$)		
Professional	25.0% ($n = 15$)		

respondents' lives, relationships, and perspectives; knowledge and beliefs about reproductive technologies; and experiences of stigma. These topics were woven throughout the respondent's holistic "infertility story," which began with how one learned of the fertility "problem" and continuing through resolution. The classification and coding produced a framework for analyzing patterns of similarity and difference among women with infertility. See Table 2 for sample characteristics.

Re-analysis of qualitative data involves asking new questions and investigating and interpreting themes different from the original research (Wiseman, 1987; Corti & Thompson, 2004). Throughout this process, the authors traced the core theoretical concepts through each case, identified their properties, and then refined their definitions to accommodate both cases. The researchers could then verify, challenge, and/or refine the model of the medical consumer. The identity of the medical consumer is analogous across these women's health conditions despite their situational contexts. Themes pertaining to the balance of power between individuals and the medical system include: how women navigate the system, how they are transformed, and how strategies for gaining medical expertise impact their sense of empowerment as patients. The transition from patient to medical

Table 2. Sample Characteristics – Infertility Study.

Marital Status		*Age*	
Married	94.4% ($n = 17$)	Mean age (in years)	40.0
Divorced	0	Age range	21–64
Re-married	5.6% ($n = 1$)		
Race/Ethnicity		*Number of Children*	
White	88.9% ($n = 16$)	1–2 (adoption)	27.8% ($n = 5$)
Hispanic	11.1% ($n = 2$)	1–2 (treatment)	33.3% ($n = 6$)
		1–2 (treatment & adoption)	11.1% ($n = 2$)
		0	22.2% ($n = 5$)
Educational Attainment		*Number of Years Managing Infertility*	
High School Degree	11.1% ($n = 2$)	1	5.6% ($n = 1$)
Some college	27.8% ($n = 5$)	2–5	66.6% ($n = 12$)
Bachelor's degree	22.2% ($n = 4$)	6–9	5.6% ($n = 1$)
Beyond Bachelor's	38.9% ($n = 7$)	10 or more	5.6% ($n = 1$)
Occupation			
Full-time	33.3% ($n = 6$)		
Part-time	16.7% ($n = 3$)		
Self-employed	5.6% ($n = 1$)		
Stay-at-home	38.9% ($n = 7$)		
Retired	5.6% ($n = 1$)		

consumer requires understanding medical information provided by the medical establishment with the help of other sources to determine choices. Personal responsibility redefines the role of the patient from passive recipient of medical intervention to active contributor in a cooperative model of care.

BECOMING A MEDICAL CONSUMER

Modern medicine has permeated American culture, circulating messages that influence the identity and behavior of the medical consumer. Public representations of health and illness, political and social attention to particular illnesses and medical advancements, and social and economic stratification contribute to social investment in the medical consumer role. Often, before a person is even diagnosed with a medical condition or illness that person has been exposed to the characteristics associated with the medical consumer, and is primed to take on these characteristics. Following a diagnosis, the process of *becoming* a medical consumer requires personal investment. This begins with specific information about the condition and transforms into embodied knowledge with the development of a plausible illness narrative. As individuals integrate their embodied knowledge with lay and professional expertise, the potential for empowerment and informed decision-making increases.

There are important limitations to this potential. First, the proliferation of information sources (both reliable and fallacious) and the developments in research, medicine, and health care are continually changing. New treatments are constantly being developed, studied, and marketed to the general population, sometimes before there is clear evidence that they are effective (Loe, 2004; Moynihan & Cassels, 2005). Clinical trials test new drugs and therapies, and complementary and alternative therapies are increasingly being used as supplemental forms of treatment. Staying up-to-date on this information is a challenge to the level of expertise an individual can develop. Second, medical information is complex and specialized. Laypersons may not have the background to understand it enough to make truly informed decisions.

Third, information can only be helpful if it applies to one's specific condition. In this regard, individuals must rely on diagnostic information from doctors. However, doctors are not always aware of the latest research, do not necessarily have adequate information to make unequivocal recommendations, or withhold information they think is beyond the person's comprehension or need to know (Weitz, 1999; Love, 2005).

Fourth, Americans are accustomed to choice and autonomy in health care (Mechanic, 1996). The ability to pay (out-of-pocket or by way of health insurance) is a crucial structural factor that undermines the potential of the medical consumer to achieve it. With one-sixth of the population uninsured at any given time, there is no role to play when a person has no access to care (Mechanic, 2004; Quadagno, 2006).

Public Representations of Health

Messages circulating in mass media lay the foundation for medical consumerism. In addition to contributing to a more open discussion of health issues and increased political and social attention to particular illnesses and treatments, public representations stress the need for information and proactive behavior, which will presumably lead to greater choice and empowerment. Notable public figures such as Michael J. Fox, Katie Couric, Lance Armstrong, Christopher Reeves, and Ronald Reagan, made numerous public appeals for medical interventions. Media publicized the choices and experiences of singer Celine Dion with in-vitro fertilization (IVF), and recently, public figures discussed their breast cancer experiences, including Suzanne Sommers, Robin Roberts, Elizabeth Edwards, and Dorothy Hamill. While the full impact of this public attention is unclear, there is evidence that the stories affect recognition if not behavior. For example, in 2005 Australian singer Kylie Minogue announced her own breast cancer diagnosis and then urged women to be screened. In the two weeks following her public statement, scheduled mammograms rose 40 percent (Chapman, McLeod, Wakefield, & Holding, 2005).

Media and medical representatives convey messages that people should be optimistic about medical science and the expansion of medical jurisdiction. This assumption, which saturates the literature about breast cancer and infertility, underlies the role of the medical consumer. For example, each October public service announcements, news articles, and community events bring women's health to the forefront of the collective consciousness in observation of Breast Cancer Awareness Month. Focusing on advances in clinical and genetic research in treating breast cancer, *Valley Health & Fitness* magazine reports, "But we shouldn't sit around and wait while we progress in those areas. Early detection is the key. The good news is that we are now catching breast cancer in its earliest stages" (Cassese, 2006, p. 13). This statement idealizes the benefits of medical surveillance, urgent and aggressive treatment, and faith in medical science to ultimately find a cure. Such common representations construct the medical consumer as one who is *proactive* in seeking medical attention.

This sentiment prevails with infertility treatment. When discussing the desire to parent, many stress the importance of having a biological child instead of adopting. Stressing the biological imperative increases the pressure to conceive and heightens social concern about infertility, which the American Society for Reproductive Medicine (ASRM) and the American College of Obstetricians and Gynecologists (ACOG) define as a *disease*. RESOLVE: The National Infertility Association stresses this point throughout its website, stating "Our bodies are incredible machines that have the ability to tell us when something is wrong ... Your fertility is a key function of this machine ... Infertility is a medical problem that may be treated" (2007). Problematizing infertility in need of a medical solution is a clear example of medicalization. The message to be informed and proactive saturates the organization's information: "Part of the problem is that women don't know what they don't know. It is important to talk to your doctor, who you should be checking in with regularly" (RESOLVE, 2006).

Medical consumerism makes it increasingly more difficult for individuals to opt out of medical surveillance and intervention.

Until someone is diagnosed with a medical condition, available information is simply part of the cultural background. Faith in medical science and its developments blend in with the medical consumer messages about being informed, rational, proactive, responsible, and empowered. Within breast cancer and infertility support materials, the medical consumerism message is framed in terms of *quality care* and is defined in ways that encourage a specific definition of health that involves urgency and choice. Making rational and responsible decisions about medical interventions involves tailoring one's choices to the options available and deciding whether the proposed medical service is appropriate for the individual: "There are no right or wrong decisions here; there is only your need, and your right, to have the most accurate information possible, and to decide based on who you are, what choices make the most sense for you" (Love, 2000, p. 346). Variations on this statement abound in informational sources, personal narratives, medical resources, and public accounts.

Choice is central to medical consumerism. The NBCC identifies choice as one of the key dimensions of breast cancer quality care, which is tied to "choosing your doctors and care centers" as well as "making decisions about your care" (NBCCF, 2006). Here, however, there are right and wrong choices. The Coalition's Guide to Quality Breast Cancer Care (2002) states:

> In breast cancer care, what you don't know *can* hurt you. Your choices can affect your chances of surviving, other parts of your health, and your **quality of life**. Asking a question doesn't mean you don't respect your doctor's or nurse's opinion. It means that you respect them – and yourself – enough to get all the information you need." (p. 50, original emphases)

Encouraging women to "respect" themselves (not just their doctors and nurses) can be empowering to women. This excerpt promotes information as a basic right and the ultimate key to survivorship, a message that works within a cooperative model of care. By encouraging women to be proactive, informed, and rational, the NBCC's stated goal is to help women to judge the quality of their health care, understand medical evidence, and get the highest quality of care possible. Further reinforcing the characteristics of the medical consumer, the implication is that women who do not take on this role do not respect themselves.

The National Infertility Association reiterates medical consumerism in its individualized and problem-focused response to infertility, stating: "The most important thing you can do is to be an informed consumer"

(RESOLVE, 2007). Likewise, the organization has published *Understanding Infertility*, designed to be a roadmap to navigating the vast landscape of infertility options (Aronson & Levert, 2001). The book emphasizes the options available to people and encourages them to talk to other consumers as they make the choices that are right for them. This encourages medical consumers to view their medical experiences subjectively and seek reinforcement for their accounts. Cultural representations foster the notion that information and choice will lead to empowered decision-making and quality of care. The medical community, mass media, individuals, and organizations who advocate for women, strongly pressure women to take it upon themselves to become as informed as possible to make the *right* choices.

Embodied Knowledge

Medical conditions like breast cancer and infertility rely on technoscientific diagnostics, treatments, and the promise of new advances. These factors complicate the medical consumer role as individuals decipher medical information, make medical decisions, and take full responsibility for their choices. The ongoing process of becoming a medical consumer is influenced by education, socialization, and belief systems. Individuals familiar with health behaviors or celebrities who have dealt with particular illnesses incorporate this information into their understanding of illness when they are diagnosed. Former experience and knowledge about health and illness influence their sources of information (physician, Internet, books, self-help groups, family and friends), how much information they need, how they interpret it, and how it influences their decisions. While women rely on the advice and options presented by their doctors, many believe they must become experts to decipher medical information. To aid in the information-gathering process, breast cancer and infertility treatment centers frequently offer libraries or support groups as an accompaniment to medical care and treatment where people can learn about science, research, and even doctors from others.

Illness is also an embodied experience, so the interpretation of illness must take into account the social knowledge and situational context of a person's life. The pressure to become a medical consumer shapes *embodied knowledge* – how people view themselves and their bodies in relation to their medical experience, including treatment options, coping strategies, and relationships with those providing medical information and care.

The search for information contributes to the development of this subjectivity in the construction of an identity as a medical consumer. How much individuals become empowered as medical consumers varies as they become embedded within the medical system and try to make sense of its successes and failures. The following narratives reveal the tensions inherent to the medical consumer role.

Cassandra was 42 when she was diagnosed with breast cancer, but her awareness began a decade earlier when Olivia Newton-John was diagnosed. As a fan, Cassandra followed Newton-John's story with interest. Years later when her neighbor was diagnosed with breast cancer, she began to learn more. However, it was not until she received her own breast cancer diagnosis that Cassandra actively began the process of becoming a medical consumer. Beginning with a "stack of materials" she brought home from her doctor's office and the medical library, Cassandra tried to sort out what the information meant, how it applied to her situation, and what it would mean for her life and her health. In the following excerpt, she describes its usefulness, its impact on her emotional state, and her strategy for simply reading it.

> There was all of this stuff about types of breast cancers, biopsies, lumpectomies, mastectomies, radiation, chemotherapy, hormone treatment, prostheses, reconstruction, information for husbands, and information on how to talk to your children ... I was standing at my kitchen counter looking at this stack of books and papers and videos, just crying ... I didn't even know where to start ... so I read as much as I could tolerate. But, after awhile many of the booklets were just repeating ... it was so much information. It was very overwhelming and you just kind of go through it and you've got so many questions ... and they didn't answer my questions ... but also, I felt like I did not know enough to know what to ask ... I would put the books aside until I thought of one more question ... then I'd start digging through it again.

Cassandra draws attention to the task of reading medical information. She highlights the difficulty of prioritizing, evaluating, and trying to discern answers to questions that are not even addressed. Even with information, Cassandra still believed she did not know enough to ask the right questions or make the right choices. She wanted the authoritative opinions of her doctors, but she continued to evaluate information on her own. Samantha further illustrates the urgency of gathering information for medical decision-making: "I need more research. I need other books. I need research papers. I need to know what I'm going to be dealing with. I can't make a decision without it." The role of the medical consumer creates a default position in which individuals are required to take an active role in making informed choices.

After researching and interpreting a large quantity of medical information, medical consumers must develop a subjective, embodied understanding of what it means to them. The diagnosis and presumed "cause" are important factors in shaping how individuals view their embodied experiences and ultimately their role as medical consumers. As individuals interpret their diagnoses to make sense of them in relation to their health histories, lifestyle choices, feelings, and relationships, they more fully develop a subjective understanding of their bodies as both biological and social. At this point, the qualities of the medical consumer have serious implications for one's sense of control. The responsibility to be proactive, informed, and responsible for one's health establishes a sense of control that is undermined in the face of a medical diagnosis that requires consumers to become embedded within the medical system.

For example, following diagnosis the women we interviewed experienced feelings of inadequacy, regret, and guilt for past decisions especially if these involved "risky" behaviors or not taking "good enough" care of themselves. On the other hand, women also felt betrayed by their bodies, saying "you do everything right, and then." Roslyn was intent on identifying a cause for her breast cancer. She said, "After my diagnosis, my big study was, 'How did I get it? What did I do to cause this?'" Roslyn had done "so much research trying to find out why." She recounted her list of possible causes: "Was it taking birth control pills ... I was never on hormones. Was it environmental? I run every day ... Was it that pounding ... the cars?" Roslyn spent two years trying to discern a cause for her breast cancer. Because she had no family history of the disease, she ruled out the possible role of genetics. She eventually adjusted to the uncertainty of not knowing the cause but was disappointed that she could not rule out those potential causes she had identified. The possibility remained open that she was to blame.

Similarly, after being diagnosed with infertility Cindy began to doubt herself and her choices: "We [we]re going to buy a house, wait ... five years, and then try to get pregnant." In preparing for a child in advance of pregnancy, Cindy and her partner believed they were acting responsibly. When she did not conceive easily, she began to question the "good choices" she thought she had made. Cindy's anxiety encouraged her to rely on the expert advice of her doctor and she immediately took action and began artificial insemination. Cindy's husband was less confident with infertility treatment. When the insemination process did not work, they were in disagreement about the next steps. After researching options more fully the couple opted out of infertility treatment and decided to adopt. Like Cindy, the other women diagnosed with infertility had also assumed that the decision to have children was theirs to make. With the diagnosis of infertility, the first response was self-blame: a personal problem with a medical solution.

For women who had a prior history of chlamydia or abortion, self-blame was especially strong. Rose said: "The issue is with guilt. Many girls ... in the support group ... had abortions when we were young, and now that we are old enough to have children we are experiencing infertility. It makes you wonder. And you have to deal with that." There is no evidence that abortion procedures uncomplicated with scar tissue or infection will cause infertility or make it more difficult to carry a later pregnancy to term (NYSTF, 1998). However, the women in the support group were compelled to speculate guiltily about their potential role in causing their infertility. Although sexually transmitted diseases and abortion were the most guilt-inducing factors, others involved personal choices such as alcohol, tobacco, and drug use as adolescents.

Reaching a subjective conclusion about what caused their diagnoses allowed women to determine who or what was at fault. This further individualized the situation and enabled them to take on the medical consumer role. The quest for a cause was a reasonable approach for taking control of the situation, thereby enabling a construction of self that was responsible, proactive, prevention-conscious, and rational. This enabled women to face their anxiety, not only about their medical situations but the implications of their personal decisions and lifestyle choices. As medical consumers they could restore a sense of self that was respected in the broader society.

The Synthesis of Lay and Professional Knowledge

Throughout diagnosis, treatment, and aftercare both lay and professional knowledge become synthesized into an individual understanding of the medical condition. Whereas lay knowledge refers to a wider conception of health and illness in relation to society, professional knowledge originates from within the scientific and medical establishment (Gabe et al., 2004). Individuals use both types to evaluate their medical situation, make sense of what is happening, and make decisions about the role they will play. In addition to interactions with doctors and medical staff, this knowledge synthesis influences whether the medical consumer is constrained or empowered. The women we interviewed interpreted and used lay and professional information to evaluate their medical options and support their decisions. Medical consumers want to be *informed enough* to believe they are responsibly and proactively making the right choices. Amid complicated or inconclusive information, this requires people to place confidence in professional knowledge. Especially at the early stages of diagnosis, many prioritized the authority of doctors and medical staff. Throughout the illness experience, however, they synthesized professional knowledge with their own lay understandings of the condition.

At age 59 Alice was diagnosed with Stage 4 breast cancer, meaning that her tumor had metastasized. She had no symptoms. Prior to her diagnosis, she had followed medical protocols and had routine mammograms every other year from about age 45.[1] As she progressed through diagnostics and treatment Alice faced decisions that involved complex scientific information that fell outside of her expertise: "My pathology report was very scary, especially because I didn't know how to read it ... I asked what this ... and ... that meant? [The oncologist] wasn't cheerful about it. I think he was trying to tell me the truth without actually telling me." Alice did not trust this dialogue, but she felt responsible for making (or agreeing to) the right decisions. To do so, she translated medical evidence into something familiar. Alice said to the oncologist, "Put your wife's name instead of my name on that report. What would you do?" The oncologist replied, "If it was my wife, I'd want her to have a mastectomy because [the cancer] had already spread to the lymph nodes." After hearing this, Alice *decided* to have a mastectomy.

This dialogue may suggest a cooperative relationship between doctor and patient. Questions are asked and answered, and the doctor reveals a personal (as opposed to entirely medical) opinion. Yet, the medical consumer remains confounded and fearful. Alice still does not understand her pathology report, but she reaches a decision through the doctor's guidance. Specialized medical information enables physicians to retain a level of authority. Once this power dynamic is cultivated, medical authority permeates the relationship and limits the agency of the consumer. Nora spent two years and hundreds of thousands of dollars to pursue medical treatment for infertility. She said, "The doctor was this very charismatic person. He really presented it as if he could make [the pregnancy] happen. He is a big person in the field." In doctor–patient interactions, personal and social sources of knowledge work alongside professional knowledge as medical consumers try to understand complexity and take action.

How doctors convey medical information, options, and outcomes can lead to compliance rather than cooperation. Jenny's discussion of infertility illustrates this: "The doctors talk to you so mechanical[ly]. Everything was, 'Well, if you want this, then you have to do that, because there is no other way ... ' They don't talk to you about how you feel and what you want." Jenny's physician told her about the range of options but was not interested in her individual situation and provided no emotional support. After having surgery and several treatments that did not work, Jenny decided to adopt. Rose described the lack of control in reaching a medical solution to infertility as "sitting at a slot machine ... saying, this machine is going to pay out. I know it is." Trusting one's choices based on the advice of medical authorities or even a perceived wheel of fortune offers relief when dealing with a situation outside of one's control. The medical consumer (as responsible, proactive, and rational) seeks and evaluates information thought to enable empowered decision-making and increase the odds of a successful outcome.

In some cases, medical consumers do influence their medical experience. The following example represents the medical consumer who uses embodied knowledge and information to make an empowered decision to avoid continued medical treatment for infertility. When an earlier treatment for infertility failed, Debbie considered a more invasive strategy. She and her husband scheduled a consultation with a clinic that offered IVF. During an initial consultation physicians generally review the woman's medical history, ask questions, and offer a preliminary opinion contingent upon specific clinical and laboratory tests. The initial consultation is a sales pitch designed for the medical consumer who must decide if the treatment options are "right" for her. However, the logistics, time constraints, structure and processes involved in IVF are not discussed until the second consultation, usually several weeks later. Debbie's physician presented the general plan: They would "[implant] up to four embryos ... and hope one would take." When the couple asked what would happen if more than one embryo were to take, they were told that "someone of [Debbie's] body structure/size could handle twins, but it would be difficult ... With quadruplets, they would suggest a reduction, which loosely translates into an abortion." At the end of the consultation, the couple learned that "15 percent ... who go in for IVF actually go home with a baby."

Up to this point in the process Debbie had faith in the doctors and the medical science that promised her a biological child. However, after the consultation Debbie immediately sensed that she did not want IVF: "We don't want triplets, or quadruplets ... I wasn't going to go through all of this to have a baby and then kill a baby ... I was like, 'There are too many moral issues here, and I am not ready to handle any of them.'" Having become a medical consumer through a combination of knowledge and experience, Debbie was now willing to opt out of this particular medical service. The low success rates, unsure outcomes, and ethical implications were glossed over in the consultation. Rather than question the responsibility of the medical system to clarify these issues, Debbie put this on herself. The personal responsibility of the medical consumer individualizes medical experiences such that the consumer must tailor her choices to the available options, not question the options.

The next example represents the quintessential medical consumer who seeks and critically evaluates information and then uses this information to influence doctor–patient interactions. In her mid-thirties, Liz believed that her age had become a critical factor for conception. Although her gynecologist thought she only had a "light case" of infertility, Liz believed it was important to be proactive so she would be a candidate for infertility treatment. She was not confident in her gynecologist, so she started researching infertility treatment on her own: "I really had the feeling my OB/GYN wasn't up to date ... he put me on hormone drugs without doing a blood test and I didn't get pregnant for months. I wasn't able to because my hormone level was too high." Liz learned this from her research after the fact. She said, "I felt I had to do all the research on my own ... I was on the Internet and ... you get misinformation there too." Having learned to evaluate information on infertility, Liz eventually asked her gynecologist for a referral to a specialist. After questioning where she got her information, he agreed to give her one. Liz's assertiveness increased as she evaluated information and used it to test the knowledge of her doctors. She said, "When I was referred to the infertility center, they knew what I was talking about." Liz's research gave her the knowledge to decide whether or not her physician was doing the right thing, increasing her agency in doctor–patient interactions.

Although the compulsory development of lay expertise can be a stressor, many women believed that taking the time to learn about their options would lead to the right decisions. Once the characteristics of the medical consumer are integrated into one's sense of self, many maintain this status when they are no longer in treatment. Samantha is a breast cancer survivor who said, "I had time ... to ... understand what it was I was dealing with and make a good, logical decision about what was right for me ... I am constantly online now ... to stay up with the research on breast cancer." Samantha sees herself as the informed medical consumer: proactive, informed, and rational. As she stays apprised of scientific medical research and information, she strengthens these elements of her identity.

CONCLUSION

American society has created a health care market where people see themselves first as consumers, and then as patients. The qualities of the medical consumer now function as a common sense way of dealing with health and illness. Focusing on *personal responsibility*, *proactive and prevention-conscious behavior*, *rationality*, and *choice*, the medical consumer role suggests an active orientation to health decisions and services. There are barriers in transitioning to this role, including information gaps and limitations in a person's capacity to understand abstract scientific and medical information or know what applies to a particular diagnosis. As our data show being an informed medical consumer is not always something people want to do or feel capable of doing. The obligation to be informed pressures even these people to find a way to get enough information to feel that they have made the best choices for themselves. Half of our study participants represented the full expression of the medical consumer as an ideal, and the others represented a continuum of the medical consumer's characteristics. These women tried to make rational and responsible decisions through reliance on doctors and treatment centers they perceived to be *the best*. They relied on public representations, embodied knowledge, and other sources of lay and professional information to take ownership of their illness experience.

By examining the impact of the medical consumer model on women facing breast cancer and infertility, we uncover several factors that undermine its empowerment potential. First, the medical consumer is an individualized role. The medical consumer must gather and decipher medical information, make the right choices, and take full responsibility for these choices regardless of their outcomes. While ownership can be empowering to some, it can also be a burden. In addition, this model tends toward a person-blame paradigm that creates unrealistic views of prevention, risk, and cure/success. In the health contexts we researched, the message is that women can control their fertility or breast cancer if they locate the problems/causes within their lifestyles and decisions, and the solutions within the system of modern medicine. The medical consumer role enables women to collaborate in medicalization processes because of their own needs for information and a sense of control.

Second, while medical science continues to expand the sheer amount of information available to the media and the public on a range of health issues, people tend to be on their own to evaluate it, contextualize it, and use it. The women in this study represented a range of educational backgrounds and exposure to medical knowledge. Yet, even those who had backgrounds in science and medicine, or even experience in medical settings, were overwhelmed by information and the urgency with which they felt they needed to digest it. Because many did not have the tools to understand and evaluate complex medical details, they continued to rely on others (including doctors, support groups, friends, and others) for guidance and expertise, and on their own embodied knowledge. Although one of the major goals of the WHM was to encourage women to educate themselves and other women about health issues, the role of information and choice within the medical consumer role may limit communication as specialized information clearinghouses dictate its type and quality.

Third, the social construction of the medical consumer accommodates processes of medicalization and the expanding challenges to medical authority. This has the potential to absolve the system of medicine from culpability. When a person chooses (or agrees to) medical procedures and interventions, signing the informed consent document is a necessary condition for obtaining them. With this signature, the person agrees contractually to a wide range of procedures and acknowledges a variety of potential outcomes thereby limiting medical liability at least to the extent addressed in the document. More importantly, the person symbolically asserts her identity as a medical consumer. When this occurs, it is the *idea* of being informed, rational, and responsible rather than its manifestation that informs the social transaction. The medical consumer, who has become socialized into this role and practiced in its implementation, thereby assumes responsibility for the decision.

The shift from patienthood to medical consumerism benefits the medical system. When transferring responsibility for decision-making to the consumer, neutralizing these decisions as neither right nor wrong, and promoting consumer accountability through informed consent, the complexity and specialization of professional knowledge allows the medical system to influence strongly the decisions that medical consumers will make. The medical system still determines the options. Allowing a person to choose from a proscribed set of options allows people to feel like they have a choice, but does not alter existing protocols. The proactive medical consumer consumes a wide range of products and services aimed at prevention. While the medical consumer has the potential to use information to become self-determined, the medical consumer role serves the interests of a medical system that seeks to expand its client base, sell more products and services, and increase profits.

The individualization of the medical consumer role runs counter to the early aims of US consumerist movements that focused on systemic health issues and social change. The WHM specifically sought to illuminate the struggle for professional dominance in western medicine as a gender struggle that repositioned women from their former healing roles into the roles of worker, consumer, and even research subject (Ehrenreich & English 1989). The masculine dominance of the medical profession resulted in a nearly complete medicalization of women's lives and permeated doctor–patient interactions. To remedy the gender imbalance, the WHM prioritized greater decision-making roles for women and *choice* oriented toward the laywoman to increase women's agency with the medical system. Contrary to this, the twenty-first century model of the medical consumer is defined as a gender-neutral role. Regardless of gender, a person needs only information to develop agency in the medical system. This construction renders invisible the gendered aspects of the system that the WHM fought so strongly to bring to light. The medical consumer role disallows both attention to gender within the medical system and systematic inquiry into the extent to which women are getting the care they need in ways that effectively protect or restore their health.

NOTE

1. The American Cancer Society recommends beginning mammography at age 40. However, medical researchers are not in agreement about whether starting them before age 50 has any survival benefit (see IOM, 2001).

ACKNOWLEDGMENTS

An earlier version of this chapter was presented at the American Sociological Association 100th Annual Meeting in Philadelphia, PA in August, 2005. We would like to thank Denise Copelton, Stephanie Nawyn, Barbara Katz Rothman, Marybeth Stalp, Susan Chambré, and Melinda Goldner for their helpful comments on earlier versions of this chapter.

REFERENCES

Aronson, D., & Levert, S. (2001). *Resolving infertility* (1st Harper Resource Edition). New York, NY: Collins.

Borkman, T. & Munn-Giddings, C. (2008). Self-help groups challenge health care systems in the US and UK. In: S. M. Chambré & M. Goldner (Eds), *Advances in medical sociology: Patients, consumers and civil society* (pp. 127–150). Bingley, UK: Emerald Group Publishing Limited.

Boston Women's Health Book Collective (BWHBC). (1973, 1998). *Our bodies, ourselves*. New York, NY: Simon & Schuster.

Bourgeault, I., Declerq, E., Sandall, J., Wrede, S., Vanstone, M., van Teijlingen, E., DeVries, R., & Benoit, C. (2008). Too Posh To Push? Comparative perspectives on maternal request caesarean sections in Canada, the US, the UK and Finland. In: S. M. Chambré & M. Goldner (Eds), *Advances in medical sociology: Patients, consumers and civil society* (pp. 99–123). Bingley, UK: Emerald Group Publishing Limited.

Bryan, S., Gill, P., Greenfield, S., Gutridge, K., & Marshall, T. (2006). The myth of agency and patient choice in health care? The case of drug treatments to prevent coronary disease. *Social Science and Medicine*, *63*, 2698–2701.

Cassese, S. (2006). Q&A. Valley health & fitness. *Poughkeepsie Journal*, Pulse Lifestyle Publication, New York, October, pp. 13–14.

Centers for Disease Control and Prevention, US Department of Health and Human Services (CDC). (2005). *Assisted reproductive technology success rates: 2003 national summary and fertility clinic reports*. Atlanta: Centers for Disease Control and Prevention 2005.

Chapman, S., McLeod, K., Wakefield, M., & Holding, S. (2005). Impact of news of celebrity illness on breast cancer screening: Kylie Minogue's breast cancer diagnosis. *Medical Journal of Australia*, *183*(5), 247–250.

Clarke, A. E., Shim, J. K., Mamo, L., Fosket, J., & Fishman, J. R. (2003). Biomedicalisation: Technoscientific transformations of health, illness, and US biomedicine. *American Sociological Review*, *68*(2), 161–194.

Conrad, P., & Leiter, V. (2004). Medicalisation, markets and consumers. *Journal of Health and Social Behavior*, *45*(extra issue), 158–176.

Copelton, D. (2006). Popular pregnancy advice books and the medical encounter – A patient-centered perspective on the doctor–patient relationship. American Sociological Association 101st Annual Meeting, Montreal, Quebec, Canada.

Corti, L., & Thompson, P. (2004). Secondary analysis of archive data. In: C. Seale, G. Gobo, J. F. Gubrium & D. Silverman (Eds), *Qualitative research practice* (pp. 327–343). London: Sage.

Davison, C., Smith, G. D., & Frankel, S. (1991). Lay epidemiology and the prevention paradox: The implications of coronary candidacy for health education. *Sociology of Health and Illness*, *13*(1), 1–19.

Dill, A. & Coury, J. (2008). Forging a new commons: Self-help associations in Slovenia and Croatia. In: S. M. Chambré & M. Goldner (Eds), *Advances in medical sociology: Patients, consumers and civil society* (pp. 247–271). Bingley, UK: Emerald Group Publishing Limited.

Ebizmba.com. (2007). 20 most popular health websites: November 2007. Available at http://www.ebizmba.com/articles/health.html. Retrieved on January 18, 2008.

Ehrenreich, G., & English, D. (1989). *For her own good: 150 years of the experts' advice to women*. New York, NY: Anchor Books.

Eich-Krohm, A. (2000). *Infertility: Transition to non-parenthood?* Unpublished M.A. Thesis, University at Albany, State University of NY.

Eisenberg, J. M., & Power, E. J. (2000). Transforming insurance coverage into quality health care: Voltage drops from potential to delivered quality. *Journal of the American Medical Association*, *284*(16), 2100–2107.

Fisher, J. A. & Ronald, L. M. (2008). Direct to consumer responsibility: Medical neoliberalism in pharmaceutical advertising and drug development. In: S. M. Chambré & M. Goldner (Eds), *Advances in medical sociology: Patients, consumers and civil society* (pp. 29–51). Bingley, UK: Emerald Group Publishing Limited.

Fosket, J., Karran, A., & LaFia, C. (2000). Breast cancer in popular women's magazines from 1913 to 1996. In: A. Kasper & S. Furguson (Eds), *Breast cancer: Society shapes an epidemic*. New York, NY: St. Martin's Press.

Franklin, S. (1990). Deconstructing 'desperateness': The social construction of infertility in popular representations of new reproductive technologies. In: M. McNeil, I. Varcoe & S. Yearly (Eds), *The new reproductive technologies*. New York, NY: Macmillan.

Freidson, E. (1970). *Professional dominance*. Chicago, IL: Aldine.

Gabe, J., Bury, M., & Elston, M. A. (2004). *Key concepts in medical sociology*. Thousand Oaks, CA: Sage Publications.

Glaser, B. G., & Strauss, A. L. (1967). *The discovery of grounded theory: Strategies for qualitative research*. Hawthorne, NY: Aldine de Gruyter.

Glickman, L. (1999). *Consumer society in American history: A reader*. Ithaca, NY: Cornell University Press.

Greenspan, I., & Handy, F. (2008). From discovery to recovery and beyond: The role of voluntary health sector organizations in the lives of women with breast cancer. In: S. M. Chambré & M. Goldner (Eds), *Advances in medical sociology: Patients, consumers and civil society* (pp. 151–176). Bingley, UK: Emerald Group Publishing Limited.

Gubrium, J. F., & Holstein, J. A. (Eds). (2002). *Handbook of interview research*. Thousand Oaks, CA: Sage Publications.

Hardey, M. (2001). E-Health: The Internet and the transformation of patients into consumers and producers of health knowledge. *Information, Communication and Society*, *4*(3), 388–405.

Hardon, A. (2006). Contesting contraceptive innovation – Reinventing the script. *Social Science and Medicine*, *62*(3), 614–627.

Haug, M., & Lavin, B. (1983). *Consumerism in medicine*. Beverly Hills, CA: Sage Publications.

Henwood, F., Wyatt, S., Hart, A., & Smith, J. (2003). Ignorance is bliss sometimes: Constraints on the emergence of the 'Informed Patient' in the changing landscapes of health information. *Sociology of Health and Illness*, *25*(6), 589–607.

Hulka, B. S., & Stark, A. T. (1995). Breast cancer: Cause and prevention. *Lancet*, *346*(8979), 883–887.

Institute of Medicine Committee on the Quality of Health Care in America (IOM). (2001). *Crossing the quality chasm: A new health system for the 21st century*. Washington, DC: National Academy Press.

Jost, T. (2003). *Disentitlement? The threats facing our public health care programs and a rights-based response*. New York, NY: Oxford University Press.

Kapp, M. B. (1999). From medical patients to health care consumers: Decisional capacity and choices to purchase coverage and services. *Aging & Mental Health*, *3*(4), 294–300.

Kohn, L., Corrigan, J., & Donaldson, M. (Eds). (1999). *To err is human*. Washington, DC: National Academy of Sciences.

Kronenfeld, J. (2001). New trends in the doctor–patient relationship: Impacts of managed care on the growth of a consumer protections model. *Sociological Spectrum*, *21*(3), 293–317.

Kvale, S. (1996). *Interviews: An introduction to qualitative research interviewing*. Thousand Oaks, CA: Sage Publications.

Landzelius, K. (2006a). The incubation of a social movement? Preterm babies, parent activists, and neonatal productions in the US context. *Social Science and Medicine*, *62*(3), 668–682.

Landzelius, K. (2006b). Introduction: Patient organization movements and new metamorphoses in patienthood. *Social Science and Medicine*, *62*(3), 529–537.

Light, D. W. (1993). Countervailing power: The changing character of the medical profession in the United States. In: F. W. Hafferty & J. B. McKinlay (Eds), *The changing medical profession: An international perspective*. New York, NY: Oxford University Press.

Loe, M. (2004). *The rise of Viagra: How the little blue pill changed sex in America*. New York, NY: NYU Press.

Lofland, J., & Lofland, L. (1995). *Analyzing social settings: A guide to qualitative observation and analysis*. Belmont, CA: Wadsworth.

Love, S. (2000). *Dr. Susan Love's breast book*. New York, NY: Addison-Wesley.

Love, S. (2005). *Dr. Susan Love's breast book*. New York, NY: Addison-Wesley.

Lupton, D. (1997). Consumerism, reflexivity and the medical encounter. *Social Science and Medicine*, *45*(3), 373–381.

Lyman, K. (2000). Infantalization: The medical model of care. In: P. Brown (Ed.), *Perspectives in Medical Sociology*. Long Grove, IL: Waveland Press, Inc.

McGlynn, E. A., Asch, S. M., Adams, J., Keesey, J., Hicks, J., DeCristofaro, A., & Kerr, E. A. (2003). The quality of health care delivered to adults in the United States. *New England Journal of Medicine*, *348*(26), 2635–2645.

Mead, N., & Bower, P. (2000). Patient-centeredness: A conceptual framework and review of the empirical literature. *Social Science and Medicine*, *51*, 1087–1110.

Mechanic, D. (1996). Changing medical organization and the erosion of trust. *The Milbank Quarterly*, *74*(2), 171–189.

Mechanic, D. (2004). The rise and fall of managed care. *Journal of Health and Social Behavior*, *45*(extra issue), 76–86.

Morgen, S. (2002). *Into our own hands: The women's health movement in the United States, 1969–1990*. New Brunswick, NJ: Rutgers University Press.

Moynihan, R., & Cassels, A. (2005). *Selling sickness: How the world's biggest pharmaceutical companies are turning us all into patients*. New York, NY: Nation Books.

Mykytyn, C. E. (2006). Anti-aging medicine: A patient/practitioner movement to redefine aging. *Social Science and Medicine*, *62*(3), 643–653.

National Breast Cancer Coalition Fund (NBCCF). (2006). Guide to quality breast cancer care, 1101 17th Street, NW Suite 1300, Washington, DC 20036.

National Institutes of Health. (2007). Homepage. Available at http://www.nih.gov. Retrieved on January 15, 2008.

National Institute of Medicine/National Research Council (NIM/NRC). (1999). *Ensuring quality cancer care*. Washington, DC: The National Cancer Policy Board.

Quadagno, J. (2006). *One nation uninsured: Why the US has no national health insurance*. New York, NY: Oxford University Press.

Rabeharisoa, V. (2006). From representation to mediation: The shaping of collective mobilization on muscular dystrophy in France. *Social Science and Medicine*, *62*(3), 564–576.

Radin, P. (2006). To me, it's my life: Medical communication, trust, and activism in cyberspace. *Social Science and Medicine*, *62*(3), 591–601.

Reinharz, S. (1992). *Feminist methods in social research*. New York, NY: Oxford University.

RESOLVE. (2006). First Response® announces national education initiative spearheaded by newly formed conception council: Latest survey data reveals widespread misconceptions about conception, June 12, 2006. Available at http://www.resolve.org/site/PageServer?pagename = fmed_mcpr2006612. Retrieved on July 122007.

RESOLVE. (2007). Coping with infertility. Available at http://www.resolve.org/site/PageServer?pagename = cop_home. Retrieved on July 12, 2007.

Rutherford, M., & Gallo-Cruz, S. (2008). Selling the ideal birth: Rationalization and re-enchantment in the marketing of maternity care. In: S. M. Chambré & M. Goldner (Eds), *Advances in medical sociology: Patients, consumers and civil society* (pp. 75–98). Bingley, UK: Emerald Group Publishing Limited.

Schneider, C. E. (1997). *Patients, doctors, and decisions: Rethinking autonomy*. New York, NY: Oxford University Press.

Smith-Warner, S. A., Spiegelman, D., & Yaun, S. S. (1998). Alcohol and breast cancer in women: A pooled analysis of cohort studies. *Journal of the American Medical Association*, *279*(7), 535–540.

Sulik, G. (2005). *When women need care: How breast cancer 'survivors' cope with being care-receivers*. Unpublished doctoral dissertation, University at Albany, State University of NY.

The New York State Task Force on Life and the Law (NYSTF). (1998). *Assisted reproductive technologies: Analysis and recommendations for public policy*. New York, NY: The New York State Task Force on Life and the Law.

Thomas, J. (2000). Incorporating empowerment into models of care: Strategies from feminist women's health centers. *Research in the Sociology of Health Care*, *17*, 139–152.

WebMD. (2007). Yahoo! to power WebMD's sponsored search WebMD to extend its advertising reach across Yahoo's network. October 16, 2007. Sunnyvale, CA and New York. eMarketer Pharmaceutical Marketing online report. Available at http://investor.shareholder.com/wbmd/releasedetail.cfm?ReleaseID = 269568. Retrieved on January 18, 2008.

Weitz, R. (1999). Watching brian die: The rhetoric and reality of informed consent. *Health*, *3*(2), 209–227.

Wiseman, J. P. (1987). The development of generic concepts in qualitative research through cumulative application. *Qualitative Sociology*, *10*(4), 318–338.

Zetka, J. (2008). Radical logics and their carriers in medicine: The case of psychopathology and obstetricians and gynecologists. *Social Problems*, *55*(1), 95–116.

Zimmerman, M., & Hill, S. (2000). Reforming gendered health care: An assessment of change. *International Journal of Health Services*, *30*(4), 771–795.

DIRECT TO CONSUMER RESPONSIBILITY: MEDICAL NEOLIBERALISM IN PHARMACEUTICAL ADVERTISING AND DRUG DEVELOPMENT

Jill A. Fisher and Lorna M. Ronald

ABSTRACT

Purpose – *This chapter explores the pharmaceutical industry's strategic utilization of empowerment discourse in two realms: direct-to-consumer advertising (DTCA) and clinical drug development.*

Methodology – *It draws upon two research projects that examine the role of the pharmaceutical industry in the political economy of healthcare in the United States: Ronald's policy analysis and participant observation of DTCA policy hearings and Fisher's participant observation and interviewing of the clinical trials industry.*

Findings – *Empowerment rhetoric is mobilized by the pharmaceutical industry to create specific expectations about patient-consumer behavior, particularly the responsibilities associated with the consumption of drugs.*

Patients, Consumers and Civil Society
Advances in Medical Sociology, Volume 10, 29–51

ISSN: 1057-6290/doi:10.1016/S1057-6290(08)10003-1

Research implications – *The social and economic implications of DTCA and drug trials must be understood within their broader historical and contemporary contexts of health advocacy, consumerism, and medical neoliberalism.*

Practical implications – *The chapter offers alternative constructions of healthcare subjects and pharmaceutical practices that can mitigate the power of the pharmaceutical industry and bring about better pharmaceutical governance.*

Originality/value of chapter – *By analyzing findings from two empirical projects, this chapter is able to shed light on trends in the pharmaceutical industry's discourse about empowerment and consumption from the clinical testing to marketing of new drugs.*

The pharmaceutical industry has effectively appropriated empowerment discourse for its own ends. With origins in health-related social movements, empowerment focused on reclaiming patients' rights to make decisions about and for their bodies (Darvall, 1993; Morgen, 2002). Now, however, empowerment is increasingly redefined in terms of consumption (Grace, 1991; Thomas & Zimmerman, 2007). Although individuals may still feel empowered, the meaning has shifted from equalizing power relations between patients and providers to emphasizing choice of health-related products and services. A greater power imbalance results: between patients and physicians, on one hand, and the pharmaceutical industry, on the other.

This chapter explores the pharmaceutical industry's strategic utilization of empowerment discourse in two realms: direct-to-consumer advertising (DTCA) and clinical drug development. It aims to show how "empowerment" is mobilized to further a particular mode of consumption that creates specific demands on patient-consumers. Empowerment discourse pairs diagnosis, treatment, and compliance with responsibilities that "engaged" healthcare consumers must assume. In the United States Food and Drug Administration (FDA) policy process, narratives construct DTCA as responding to and enabling the transformation of patients into empowered consumers. In clinical trials practice, narratives construct participation in pharmaceutical studies as empowering in spite of the questionable benefits to subjects. This chapter argues that the dominant discourses in DTCA and drug development shape patients' subjectivities as consumers, and it offers alternative constructions of healthcare subjects and pharmaceutical practices that can mitigate the power of the pharmaceutical industry and bring about better pharmaceutical governance.

BACKGROUND

The rise of a movement contesting the traditional doctor–patient power structure coincided with profound national, political, and economic changes in the United States. Beginning in the 1960s and 1970s, activists and policymakers challenged the established sovereignty of the medical profession (Starr, 1982). The Women's Health Movement critiqued physicians' control of information and decision-making (Morgen, 2002). Likewise, in the 1980s, the HIV/AIDS movement further undermined medical authority, advocating for increased patient participation in treatment and research into HIV/AIDS drugs (Epstein, 1996; Chambré, 2006).

During the same time period, the US government – as well as other post-industrialized countries, such as the United Kingdom – attempted to alleviate perceived crises in multiple domains, including energy, healthcare, housing, employment, and the environment, by implementing neoliberal economic policies (Pierson, 1994; Biven, 2001). As a mode of governance, neoliberalism prioritizes free markets and free trade and deprioritizes state provision of social goods. In the 1970s and 1980s, the rhetorical frame of crisis allowed conservatives to usher in domestic and international economic reform by reducing federal funding of public programs and introducing free trade agreements (Harvey, 2005). Neoliberal domestic policies characterize the US systems of welfare (Gilliom, 2001; Schram, 2006), healthcare (Frank, 2002; Fisher, 2007), education (Giroux, 2004; Monahan, 2005), and social security (Niggle, 2003).

Activists and policymakers – both conservatives and liberals – in the 1970s agreed that healthcare was in crisis, even if they disagreed about how to define the problem and its solutions. Regardless of their differences, both groups effectively drew on the rhetoric of progressive social movements. Activists successfully employed the discourse of autonomy and individual rights to change the nature of the doctor–patient relationship, increasing patient information and control over decision-making. However, corporations strategically appropriated the discourse of autonomy and individual rights into their marketing strategies to encourage mass consumption of all types of consumer goods (Talbot, 2000; Cohen, 2003; Rutherford & Gallo, this volume).

Within healthcare, an empowerment discourse was used to underscore the kind of personal responsibility for health deemed necessary for broad policy reform in healthcare delivery (Morgen, 2002). However, empowerment rhetoric can also depoliticize social problems by focusing on individual behavior. For example, the therapeutic culture of "self-help" and related "empowerment" have led women to blame themselves for their own and their families' experiences of societal problems (Becker, 2005). To the extent that patients have become empowered, this empowerment is mediated by a consumerist, individualized approach to healthcare that reflects and augments the influence of the pharmaceutical industry.

Neoliberal economic policies are evident in the US model of healthcare delivery, where healthcare is not a right guaranteed to citizens but is instead composed of products and services to be purchased by those who can afford them (Shaffer & Brenner, 2004; Fisher, 2008). Even with government programs such as Medicare and Medicaid enabling access to healthcare for the elderly and the poor, uneven availability of diagnostic tests and treatments persists. Moreover, the federal government's orientation to healthcare highlights their belief that industry can and should profit from their customers' health and illnesses (Scott, Caronna, Ruef, & Mendel, 2000; Boehm, 2005).

The particular commodification at work casts the conditions of health and illness ever more in terms of products that can be purchased by health-engaged consumers (Elliott, 2003). Described by some scholars as the pharmaceuticalization of healthcare (Nichter & Nichter, 1996; van der Geest, Whyte, & Hardon, 1996; Petryna, Lakoff, & Kleinman, 2006), the US system commodifies not only healthcare delivery but also illness so that individuals' bodies are fragmented into discrete systems for which there are tailored products. The responsibility to consume those products is passed to patients, so that consumption becomes an obligation if one wants healthcare at all (Monahan & Wall, 2007).

These trends towards commodification are evident in recent shifts in drug marketing and development. Prior to the 1990s, prescription drugs were marketed almost solely to healthcare professionals. However, in the late 1990s, the US FDA changed its guidelines on consumer-directed advertisements to enable widespread broadcast advertising of prescription drugs (Ronald, 2006). In response to pressure from industry, interest groups, and think tanks – as well as a First Amendment challenge to the regulation of pharmaceutical promotion (Washington Legal Foundation v. Friedman, 1998) – the FDA reduced the quantity of risk information required in TV advertisements (Guidance for Industry on Consumer-Directed Broadcast

Advertisements, 1999). As a result, DTCA exploded, with spending escalating from $300 million in 1995 to $3 billion in 2003 (Pines, 1999; Arnold, 2005).

DTCA intensifies commodification by encouraging viewers to choose the newest brand name drugs and by skewing pharmaceutical research priorities to favor drugs with improved consumer characteristics that offer little, if any, clinical improvement over existing treatments (Angell, 2004). For example, the same drug can be rebranded into a drug for a slightly different condition – such as Prozac into Sarafem for premenstrual dysphoric disorder (Greenslit, 2005) – or combined with another drug to create a new brand and, hence, patent. One such combination, Vytorin (a combination of the cholesterol medications Zocor and Zetia) was heavily advertised until research showed that it was less effective than Zocor alone, a drug which is available as a generic at a third of the cost (Associated Press, 2008).

A less visible, but equally problematic, shift in the structure of US healthcare has been the privatization of pharmaceutical clinical development. Since the 1990s, the majority of clinical trials are conducted in the private sector on a contractual basis by private practice physicians who are paid by pharmaceutical companies to recruit their own patients or local community members into drug studies (Bodenheimer, 2000). By outsourcing clinical trials to the private sector, especially to private practices, pharmaceutical companies take their studies directly to existing patient populations around the United States and globally (Fisher, 2007). The majority of new products being developed target illnesses that already have effective treatments available on the market, so studies often attract patients without health insurance who know they need medical attention but may not be able to afford appropriate care (Kolata & Eichenwald, 1999). Most clinical trials provide a limited form of access to the medical establishment during the course of studies and are paid for by the pharmaceutical companies.

Although deploying the language of individual empowerment, the limited types of access that subjects have to medical care is dictated foremost by the needs of the pharmaceutical companies as they design studies to prove that their products are safe and efficacious (Timmermans & Berg, 2003). Patterns of drug development and subject recruitment indicate that pharmaceutical science is centered on identifying the next blockbuster medicine (and commodity) rather than addressing unmet healthcare needs.[1] Moreover, clinical trials provide pharmaceutical companies with a way to pre-market and generate interest in their products: after new drugs are approved for use, the community physicians and patient-subjects are already consumers of those products.

METHODS

This chapter draws upon two research projects that examine the role of the pharmaceutical industry in the political economy of healthcare in the United States. From 2003 to 2006, Ronald carried out qualitative research on DTCA policymaking, including content analysis and participant observation of FDA hearings and interviews with policy actors. She conducted focused content analysis of texts that had been produced to influence the framing of policy problems and solutions, including transcripts from FDA and congressional public hearings; court cases and law review papers; journal articles; media accounts; and policy actors' publications. Together, these materials gave a broad overview of the policy arena, particularly the way that participants shaped policy through arguments about the value of commodified health information. In addition, Ronald carried out participant observation (i.e., observing interactions between participants and attendees and posing questions) at two meetings – one public and one industry-sponsored. Finally, interviews were conducted with 17 participants involved in DTCA policymaking, including FDA officials and representatives of industry, consumer groups, and think tanks.

Fisher's research on the clinical trials industry consisted of 12 months of fieldwork in the southwestern US from 2003 to 2004. This qualitative research included 63 interviews and observation at over 20 for-profit research organizations in two major cities. Semi-structured interviews were clustered to get the perspective of multiple employees at individual investigative sites, including physicians, research staff, site administrators, and human subjects. Investigative sites were chosen to create a diverse sample of organizational forms: private practices, dedicated research sites, site management organizations, contract research organizations, and large (non-academic) hospitals. The sample also included interviews at two not-for-profit investigative sites. Additionally, Fisher attended industry conferences, joined industry professional organizations, and subscribed to industry publications. The purpose of the study was to investigate the relations, structures, and logics produced through the privatization of clinical trials.

MEDICAL NEOLIBERALISM IN DIRECT-TO-CONSUMER ADVERTISING (DTCA)

The pharmaceutical industry insists that DTCA can and should be thought of as a means to empower patients. It argues that advertisements educate the public about diseases and the novel therapies that are available to treat them. The industry claims that millions of Americans would benefit from being aware of the latest treatment for depression or insomnia, for example, not only because of the product itself but also because it would encourage them to visit their doctors to seek a diagnosis. In short, the pharmaceutical industry frames DTCA and the information it provides to consumers as a solution to major public health problems, including the underdiagnosis and undertreatment of illnesses (Hogle, 2002).

While it may be no particular surprise that the pharmaceutical industry has mobilized consumer empowerment rhetoric for its own benefit, what is remarkable is the extent to which the US FDA seemingly accepted the argument that DTCA is empowering, propagated it within hearings, and used it to justify looser regulatory guidelines. This section explores the way empowerment rhetoric has dominated DTCA policy discourse. It then shows how what is labeled as empowering can be better thought of as a neoliberal maneuver to make individuals increasingly responsible for their health and well-being through the consumption of pharmaceutical products.

The Empowered Consumer in DTCA Policy Discourse

> We saw that direct-to-consumer ads helped patients feel empowered so that they were better able to ask their doctor questions ... that they were better able to take charge of their own health care. (Hausman, 2003, p. 232)[2]

Within policy discourse, proponents of DTCA justified its introduction by describing the emergence of a new healthcare subject, the *empowered consumer*. At DTCA meetings and hearings held in 1995, 1996, 2003, and 2005, a majority of participants claimed that DTCA would act in two ways: to turn passive individuals into empowered consumers and to help already-empowered consumers better manage their health (Division of Drug Marketing, Advertising, and Communications, 2006). Specifically, empowered consumers, according to the discourse, would ensure drug consumption by watching advertising, visiting their doctors, requesting prescriptions, and adhering to treatment regimens. DTCA discourse frames empowered consumers as aware, informed, and enlightened, as well as healthcare advocates, partners with doctors, and managers of their own health. Policy actors in favor of DTCA also include compliance as a key aspect of consumer empowerment (Calfee, Winston, & Stempski, 2002). This reveals a possible contradiction: consumers should be active enough to visit doctors and request medications, but should not be so active that they decide not to consume those drugs.

Underlying these arguments about DTCA is the perspective that empowered consumers represent highly evolved patients. For example, an FDA official stated

> The phenomenon of DTC advertising must be seen within the larger picture of the evolution of the patient's and consumer's role in their own health ... It was not until the time of HIV and cancer activism in the late 1980s that the concept of patient empowerment really took hold. And I think it is no coincidence that around that time we began to see, again, reemergence in the interest ... in direct-to-consumer advertising. (Woodcock, 2003, pp. 18–19)

Statements like these illustrate that FDA officials such as Janet Woodcock, then the director of the branch of the FDA responsible for regulating drug promotion, subscribed to the empowered consumer discourse. This evolutionary rhetoric implies that there is something both inevitable and progressive about the new kinds of consumers and drug promotion, while it simultaneously frames criticisms of DTCA as obstructions to progress.

DTCA discourse stresses the importance of empowered consumers by constructing at least two oppositions. First, empowered consumers are no longer in paternalistic doctor–patient relationships. Woodcock (2003) explained, "In the middle of the last century ... [it] was viewed as proper that the patient might not know the name of their medication and that their prescriptions be written in a manner that they could not read. That was viewed as protective of the patient" (p. 18). Second, empowered consumers are not irrational mobs demanding prescriptions. Market researcher for *Prevention* magazine Ed Slaughter (2003) emphasized, "We don't have angry mobs of consumers with torches and pitchforks stampeding towards the doctor's office because they saw an ad on television or in a magazine" (p. 84). Setting up these two oppositions not only works to solidify the figure of the empowered consumer, but it also ridicules critiques that DTCA may lead to inappropriate prescribing. Patients as empowered consumers are reasoned, rational subjects who have access to the right information to get the medications they need.

The empowered consumer figure plays a strategic role within DTCA discourse, framing the policy problem as inadequate access to information that would enable drug use. Any risks associated with drug advertising and use are displaced by an emphasis on underdiagnosis, undertreatment, and noncompliance as more critical healthcare problems. For example, proponents of DTCA argue that advertising could help the 19 million

Americans with depression, most of whom are undiagnosed (American Advertising Federation, 2007). Furthermore, increased drug use will not only improve public health but also improve productivity by helping citizen-consumers to stay at work (Lichtenberg, 2003). In these various ways, policy actors consistently defined DTCA as information that empowers consumers and, in that context, opposition to DTCA came to sound like opposition to consumer empowerment.

Problems with the Empowered Consumer Discourse

The dominant actors in DTCA policy hearings strategically chose an appealing policy figure – the empowered consumer. Unlike HIV/AIDS activists who worked together to change medical and regulatory practices (Epstein, 1996; Chambré, 2006), these "empowered consumers" act as individuals who consume commodified information and healthcare, especially blockbuster drugs. The dominant policy actors expect consumers neither to question authority nor to change medical practice, but simply to request information and prescriptions from their doctors (which does happen, according to Iizuka & Jin, 2005). In other words, policy actors co-opted the rhetoric of patient activism whilst defining empowerment narrowly in terms of unquestioning individual consumption.

Although individuals have little power to enact change in healthcare governance overall (compared with collective action of social movements), truly informed patients may indeed be able to better manage their health. Unfortunately, prescription drug advertisements provide incomplete information for patients to make well-informed decisions about their own health. As a result of the 1997 FDA guidance, television and radio advertising need only state a handful of side effects and point viewers to print advertising elsewhere for fuller disclosure of risks. Studies have shown that risk information is "functionally absent" from advertisements, which are aimed at making the specific prescription drugs appeal to viewers (Day, 2005; Kalsher, 2006). In addition, a handful of prescription drugs dominate the mass media, while others go unadvertised. In 2005, the 20 most advertised prescription drugs accounted for more than 50% of all DTCA spending (General Accounting Office, 2006). Likewise, in the first half of 2007, only 15 drugs accounted for half of all spending (Mack, 2007). The high cost of advertising creates a bias towards new, expensive blockbuster medicines, rather than older drugs, generics, or even alternative treatments

(Avorn, 2003). Information from DTCA alone cannot therefore properly inform patients about the range of treatment options available to them.

Furthermore, describing healthcare subjects as "consumers" assumes that healthcare acts as a marketplace in which individuals make choices among products. Healthcare is far from an ideal marketplace, however, as patients are neither the sole decision-makers, nor usually the direct purchasers of the product. Moreover, autonomous decision-making is a role that many patients may be either unsuited to or unwilling to take on (Henwood, Wyatt, Hart, & Smith, 2003; Sulik and Eich-Krohm, this volume) and is further constrained by the vagaries of insurance plan reimbursement. By portraying patients as consumers in search of the best pill, "consumer choice" downplays the serious nature of illness as well as important safety concerns about pharmaceuticals.

DTCA policy discourse constructs the figure of an empowered consumer to define healthcare problems in terms of too little drug use and the solution as DTCA, which would catalyze individuals to consume medications. Empowerment is narrowly conceived in DTCA policy hearings in terms of advertisements prompting patient-consumers to visit doctors and request medications. By encouraging consumer advertising in 1997, the FDA did not so much empower consumers as turn patients, like doctors, into targets of pharmaceutical promotion. Patients are expected to govern their own health in this version of medical neoliberalism wherein proper governance means consumption of the latest blockbuster drug.

MEDICAL NEOLIBERALISM IN CLINICAL TRIALS

As with DTCA, pharmaceutical clinical trials are framed within a discourse of human subject empowerment. This section illustrates how research staff, such as physician investigators and study coordinators who conduct pharmaceutical industry studies, mobilize messages about empowerment during recruitment of subjects. It also shows a slippage between how research staff describe the empowerment of subjects and neoliberal discourses about responsibilization, wherein responsibility for the studies' success or failure is shifted to subjects. In other words, while the goal of empowering human subjects may be admirable, the subtext within the clinical trials industry is to benefit the broader economic goals of pharmaceutical product development.

Subjects participate in clinical trials for myriad reasons, but several factors are common motivations: source of income, access to healthcare, hope for a "magic bullet," and desire to please physicians. The pharmaceutical industry relies heavily on impoverished and uninsured populations in the United States to become human subjects (Kolata & Eichenwald, 1999; Fisher, 2008). For healthy subjects, clinical trials provide an unparalleled source of income because many studies pay well over $3,000 in exchange for participation. For others, especially patients without health insurance, pharmaceutical clinical trials offer "free" access to physicians and research staff, to diagnostic tests and services, and often to investigational drugs (others only receive placebos). The majority of pharmaceutical studies are double-blind placebo-control trials, meaning that subjects are randomized to treatment and placebo arms of the study but they – as well as the research staff – do not know who is receiving the investigational product. Placebos are widely used in pharmaceutical clinical trials because the majority of products being tested are for non-life-threatening diseases or illnesses. It is far easier for the pharmaceutical companies to show that their products are efficacious in trials comparing them to a placebo (that is, no treatment) than to a product already available on the market.

Although the practice of including disenfranchised groups could – and perhaps should – be perceived as ethically questionable or exploitative, the companies that are involved in clinical trials, particularly the sites conducting studies, instead frame their activities in terms of the service they provide to people who are in need of financial or healthcare resources. What is left unexamined is that patients in clinical trials do not receive individualized treatments for their illnesses, but they are the vehicles for testing the efficacy and safety of new drugs for the benefit of those who can afford them once they become available in the market. Because clinical trials seem like the only viable option for many people given the structural conditions motivating them to participate, they want to benefit personally from the studies (Fisher, 2008). Research staff use a discourse of empowerment to shift expectations regarding benefits that subjects can receive from studies, regardless of the effects of the investigational products or placebos on their bodies.

The Empowered Subject in Clinical Trials Industry Discourse

Research staff consider study participation empowering because human subjects are supposed to take on a more structured and active role in clinical trials than they do in standard medical care. For example, the process of informed consent to participate in drug studies is designed to engage potential subjects in formal decision-making during which they are supposed to consider the benefits and risks of enrolling (Appelbaum, 1996). A research coordinator explained her role in that process, "It falls down to educating and *empowering* someone to make a good informed decision." Yet, it is the responsibility of research staff to empower subjects, rather than subjects empowering themselves, because few subjects express interest in the content of informed consent forms (Zussman, 1997; Corrigan, 2003; Fisher, 2006). This is because many have already decided to participate in studies before they ever receive the forms (Siminoff, Caputo, & Burant, 2004).

Moreover, patients' involvement with their medical treatments is perceived as relatively passive compared to study participation. Patients must simply be compliant with the treatment regimen created by their providers. In this view, physicians, as well as the products they prescribe to patients, perform the work to ameliorate illness. According to research staff, clinical trial participation, conversely, requires a different orientation between subjects, providers, and the pharmaceuticals they take as part of studies. As a coordinator explained, "It's just important that people don't think that 'Okay, I'm going to volunteer for a clinical trial, and everything is out of my hands and I don't know anything.' I mean, that's kind of the way it is in private practice ... *Not* in clinical research." The difference is that subjects, unlike patients, produce data about the products they consume as part of studies.

In order to make those data as robust as possible for the pharmaceutical companies, subjects must be active participants. In part, this means being compliant with all formal data collection measures. For example, many clinical trials require that subjects agree to attend frequent study visits in the clinic and/or to complete daily diaries tracking their symptoms. It also means that subjects need to be much more reflective and aware of the effects of the investigational products on their bodies. As a coordinator explained, "They know their own bodies, so they need to know that if they're taking this drug and something strange feeling or strange thing happens, they need to write those things down."

Research staff emphasize that it is empowering for subjects to be active study participants through their compliance with protocols and engagement with the effects of the drugs on their bodies. One coordinator said

> I really impress upon them from the very beginning: "Your feedback, your documentation, your response is all that we have to give to the FDA for approval."

> This is again [part of] the education and the empowering [of subjects]. Okay, it's not just I'm going down there and letting them draw blood out of my arm and getting a swab with the pap smear. [I tell them,] "The information from you, *your* perception of all of this, whether it's pain level whatever, is *critically* important to whether or not a medication or device is approved."

While individual human subjects may indeed feel empowered by their experiences in clinical trials, this is not the only outcome gained by encouraging subjects to be active participants.

Problems with the Empowered Subject Discourse

Regardless of the extent to which subjects are actively engaged in studies, the benefits of such "empowerment" are rather specious for subjects themselves. Ultimately, their compliance and reporting of symptoms are less in their interest than in the interest of pharmaceutical companies, on one hand, and public safety, on the other. Thus, instead of understanding subjects' participation in clinical trials through the lens of empowerment, it can be seen as evidence of responsibilization that accompanies neoliberal trends in healthcare (Rose, 1999).

Part of the thrust of research staff's discourse about subjects' participation is the point that subjects have rights granted by federal regulation but they also have responsibilities to pharmaceutical companies. In other words, instrumental reasons for participating are acceptable for the *initial* decision to enroll in studies, but subjects cannot seek only personal benefit, given the nature of clinical research. For example, a coordinator said, "You have to enroll patients who can understand *their* commitment toward the clinical trial that they're participating in ... [I say,] 'Let me tell you what we need from you. This is *your* responsibility in this clinical trial: being there for these visits, documenting your diaries whether it's electronic or paper or whatever.'" Because the goal of studies is not to treat individual patients but to test the efficacy and safety of new products, subjects are told that they must commit to the data they help to produce rather than expect individual benefit. This is not to say that all subjects accept that the data must come before their own health, but the task for research staff, especially coordinators, is to impress upon subjects the importance of their participation in these terms.

As is the case in healthcare more generally, human subjects are cast as neoliberal consumers who make choices about their health for which they are responsible for the outcomes. The difference, however, between standard medical care and pharmaceutical research is that subjects have fewer options and less control within the context of a study than do patients within the context of treatment. Subjects are presented simply with the decision to participate in studies, not to shape the details of their involvement. Nonetheless, they are responsible for tolerating any side effects, taking placebos, and completing all study logistics, such as appointments and study diaries. The goal of the neoliberal framing of personal responsibility is for subjects to internalize a new (learned) subjectivity toward clinical trials and to accept the goals of the research in spite of instrumental motivations they have to improve their own health or make money. As good neoliberal subjects, they are told to *choose* to remain in these studies not for themselves, but for the "advancement of science" and the profit of the pharmaceutical industry.

CONCLUSION

This chapter has examined the figure of the empowered consumer in neoliberal discourse about two aspects of pharmaceutical governance: DTCA policy and clinical trials practice. We have shown how empowerment rhetoric appropriates activist discourse to further industry goals. Individuals are expected to actively consume medication either through self-diagnosis and requesting prescriptions (DTCA) or through self-surveillance as research subjects (clinical trials practice).

On one hand, DTCA treats pharmaceuticals as consumer products, glorifying convenience and novelty, creating brands and brand loyalty of blockbuster drugs, and commodifying the conditions they treat. DTCA aims to persuade viewers that they suffer from conditions that can be treated with convenient new pills. DTCA thus intensifies the commodification of health by encouraging drug consumption and also by incentivizing the development of expensive new products that offer little, if any, clinical advantage over older treatments. As part of a neoliberal mode of pharmaceutical governance, DTCA enables the development of "me-too" drugs (Angell, 2004); the construction of new brands from old drugs (e.g., Sarafem, the rebranded Prozac) (Greenslit, 2005); and the marketing of a plethora of "lifestyle" drugs when major diseases across the globe go untreated (Shaffer & Brenner, 2004).

On the other hand, most clinical trials investigate relatively banal drugs, leading research subjects to give their bodies for the sake of consumer characteristics, like dosage. Approximately two-thirds of all new drug applications made to the FDA are for products that are not significantly clinically different from drugs already on the market (Lee, 2006). In some cases, minor therapeutic advantages are coupled with major safety disadvantages (e.g., Vioxx and other cox-2 inhibitors) (Biddle, 2007). There is a disjunction, therefore, between the ideal of scientific research for the public good and the neoliberal governance of clinical trials wherein research facilities recruit impoverished, uninsured, or otherwise marginalized populations to investigate drugs that often represent little scientific and clinical advance. Moreover, these research agendas contribute to the further globalization of clinical trials as pharmaceutical companies seek disenfranchised populations around the world to test their products (Shah, 2006; Petryna, 2007).

Together, an examination of DTCA and clinical trials highlights the problematic nature of medical neoliberalism and the falsity of describing individuals within this system as "empowered." The use of empowered consumer rhetoric is *strategic*: pharmaceutical industry actors and their allies require subjects to be empowered solely when it furthers the industry goal of increasing the production and consumption of blockbuster drugs.[3] The notion that empowered consumers may choose *not* to consume is denied within the industry rhetoric of empowerment, especially when coupled with the language of compliance. Rather than making active decisions, compliant consumers must instead obey instructions and take medications in spite of any problems that arise.

Difficulties with medicine consumption – that neoliberal discourse largely ignores – include inherent hazards and inequitable access. Consumer empowerment rhetoric implies both that consumption is an overall good and that new pharmaceuticals represent scientific progress. In clinical trials practice, patients subject themselves to unknown hazards for the sake of relatively meaningless drugs. Once a drug is approved, DTCA broadens and hastens its use without adequate surveillance (Fontanarosa, Rennie, & DeAngelis, 2004).

Consumer empowerment rhetoric also obstructs questions of access. Framing healthcare as a marketplace wherein individuals are free to make consumer choices ignores the fact that US healthcare is a grossly inequitable system, with about 43 million Americans with no health insurance at all (Reuters, 2007). The neoliberal representation of the undertreatment of illness resulting from ignorant individuals is at best a distraction from these severe social and economic inequities. Pharmaceutical clinical trials take advantage of the current system by promising access to a version of healthcare. This limited access comes at an obvious price, with healthy or uninsured people subjecting themselves to unknown risks for the sake of new drugs with little therapeutic advantage over older, cheaper products.

What Would Meaningful Empowerment Look Like?

This chapter has thus far demonstrated (1) the presence of a neoliberal discourse of empowered consumers in DTCA policy and clinical trials practice and (2) the unlikelihood of meaningful consumer empowerment in the current mode of pharmaceutical governance. Depending on their position within US society, some patients have the "choice" between no healthcare at all or the limited healthcare afforded to research subjects, while others – fortunate to have health insurance – choose among new pharmaceutical brands, with relatively unknown safety profiles. In both cases, patients help pharmaceutical companies expand their profit margins by consuming the latest blockbuster drug (e.g., sleeping pills, statins for cholesterol control, or SSRIs for depression or anxiety). Instead of asking first how best to inform and empower consumers, industry uses the notion of consumer empowerment post hoc to justify its predetermined goals. This section suggests several changes in pharmaceutical governance that would more truly empower patients and consumers.

DTCA policy discourse claims that advertising provides useful information that empowers health consumers. However, DTC advertisements provide incomplete and biased information, existing only for a narrow range of treatments and communicating risks ineffectively. Consumer empowerment can only arise via *complete* information of a wide range of treatment options produced by an independent source. Examples include online information produced by governmental organizations (e.g., National Library of Medicine) and independent consumer organizations (e.g., Consumers Union and Public Citizen). This kind of balanced information, however, cannot compete with television or magazine advertising unless they run alongside product advertising with equal media presence and advertising force. Independent advertising could be produced by the government[4] – with input from a consortium of noncommercial consumer and professional groups – and could be both non-specific (about the unknown, substantial risks of new prescription drugs) and specific (outlining the variety of treatment options for particular conditions). The goal would be meaningful understanding of risks and benefits of all treatment options, and knowledge that the most practical option may be an older treatment with a well-understood safety profile.

In addition, while it is widely agreed that health movements have enabled patients to participate more fully in healthcare decisions, consumer empowerment may still require the safeguards built by strong doctor–patient relationships wherein patients use doctors' advice to weigh their clinical options. Particularly valuable professional advice would come from doctors who are themselves relatively neutral. Currently, this is not the case as doctors regularly rely on pharmaceutical promotion for drug information and accept pharmaceutical industry gifts (Kassirer, 2005). State medical boards should draft specific, stringent guidelines to limit these relationships between physicians and the pharmaceutical industry and to enable unsponsored continuing medical education for balanced treatment information.

Improved pharmaceutical governance for truly empowered consumers also requires thorough postmarketing reporting. For example, although Vioxx was responsible for an estimated 27,000 deaths or heart attacks, Merck delayed its withdrawal for four years, while heavily marketing the drug and receiving $2.5 billion per year in sales (Berenson, Harris, Meier, & Pollack, 2004). Prescription drugs are responsible for 180,000 deaths in the United States each year (Strand, 2006). If data were gathered methodically after drugs are released to the general public, regulators would be able to provide fuller warnings and, where needed, remove drugs from the market promptly. In 2008, Consumers Union began a campaign to persuade Congress to require that all DTCA include the toll-free number for reporting adverse effects. Another mechanism to improve postmarketing reporting would be to mandate that pharmacists collect this information – and compensate them for doing so. Reporting should become so routine that it is done for every prescription drug. To facilitate this information exchange, pharmacists could include a drug use questionnaire with every prescription they dispense and should be routinely notified of deaths.

The problem remains, however, that most new drugs are relatively meaningless contributions to our pharmacopoeia, in terms of clinical advantages over existing medications, and thereby needlessly expose consumers to risk – whether through prescription use or as part of clinical trials. For example, the prescription drug Lamisil, widely advertised – and prescribed – for treating toenail fungus, comes with serious risks, including liver failure. One solution to this dilemma would be to shift pharmaceutical priorities by mandating that clinical trials compare new drugs to *existing drugs*, using the standard of care and comparable dosages (Angell, 2004). The burden on pharmaceutical companies should not merely be to prove that new products are better than a sugar pill but that they add to treatment options in a clinically meaningful way.

These four changes to pharmaceutical governance – complete, unbiased information provision, limitations on financial arrangements between doctors and the pharmaceutical industry, adequate postmarketing reporting, and more meaningful clinical trials – would help safeguard patients against the problems generated by neoliberal pharmaceutical governance. Such changes might prompt the pharmaceutical industry to reprioritize drug development and to put into practice its own rhetoric about its mission of improving health and curing diseases. By modifying the ways in which pharmaceutical companies could gain profits from their products, power relations between the industry and consumers – patients as well as providers – could be made more equitable.

Nonetheless, useful and safe drugs are only one part of the necessary shift. For meaningful empowerment to occur, the current coercive structures of US healthcare would have to be altered, such that individuals could make a wider range of decisions about their health and well-being. The current model of consuming prescription medications, including participating in pharmaceutical clinical trials, is too limiting to allow for much patient empowerment. For example, subjects should not be in the position that the only way to access any healthcare is to "choose" to be research subjects. Without health insurance for all Americans, consumer empowerment will remain a powerful myth that perpetuates health inequalities.

NOTES

1. There is a well-documented history of the clinical development of AIDS drugs (Chambré, 2006; Epstein, 1996) and cancer therapies (Hess, 1997), but those cases do not generalize well to the development of other pharmaceutical products. There are several important differences. First, HIV/AIDS and cancer are life-threatening illnesses; the majority of products currently being developed by pharmaceutical companies are for illnesses that can already be managed by other products and therapies available on the market. Second, HIV/AIDS and cancer are unique illnesses in that there are well-organized patient advocacy and activist groups supporting research activities. Third, the bulk of research support for HIV/AIDS (76%) and cancer (67%) is generated by the public sector, particularly the National Institutes of Health, and these diseases represent only a fraction of the pharmaceutical industry's research and development (R&D) investment. Roughly only 12% and 22% of industry R&D each year is spent on developing products targeting treatments or cures for infectious disease (including HIV/AIDS) and cancer respectively (CenterWatch, 2006).

2. Angela Hausman, a marketing professor, has recently carried out research on the effects of attitude towards DTCA on prescription drug requests (Hausman, 2008). It is worth noting that most empirical research on DTCA examines consumer attitudes to DTCA in general rather than consumer behavior or health effects. A notable exception showed how advertisements for HIV/AIDS treatments downplayed the severity of the condition such that they prompted viewers to engage in risky sexual behavior (Klausner, Kim, & Kent, 2002).

3. See Bourgeault et al. (this volume) on the strategic use of consumer choice rhetoric by obstetricians to justify the high rate of cesarean births in the United States and United Kingdom.

4. In a recent case, the Supreme Court determined that federally mandated beef promotion did not violate the First Amendment because it was government speech (*Johanns v. Livestock Marketing Association*, 2005). This opens up the possibility for the government to create its own prescription drug campaigns.

REFERENCES

American Advertising Federation. (2007). Letter to Senate Committee on Health, Education, Labor and Pensions, January 30. Retrieved on 13 July 2007. Available at http://www.aaf.org/government/pdf/tac_kennedy012907.doc

Angell, M. (2004). *The truth about the drug companies: How they deceive us and what to do about it*. New York, NY: Random House.

Appelbaum, P. S. (1996). Commentary: Examining the ethics of human subjects research. *Kennedy Institute of Ethics Journal*, *6*(3), 283–287.

Arnold, M. (2005). Changing channels. *Medical Marketing and Media*, *40*(4), 34–39. Retrieved May 21, 2006, from http://offlinehbpl.hbpl.co.uk/Misc/MMM/Features/APR05%2034-42%20DTC%20OUTLOOK.pdf

Associated Press. (2008). Companies pull TV ads for Vytorin. King5.com, January 24. Available at http://hosted.ap.org/dynamic/stories/V/VYTORIN_ADS

Avorn, J. (2003). Advertising and prescription drugs: Promotion, education, and the public's health. *Health Affairs*, *W3*, 104–108.

Becker, D. (2005). *The myth of empowerment: Women and the therapeutic culture in America*. New York, NY: New York University Press.

Berenson, A., Harris, G., Meier, B., & Pollack, A. (2004). Dangerous data: Despite warnings, drug giant took long path to Vioxx recall. *New York Times* online, November 14. Available at http://www.nytimes.com/2004/11/14/business/14merck.html

Biddle, J. (2007). Lessons from the Vioxx debacle: What the privatization of science can teach us about social epistemology. *Social Epistemology*, *21*(1), 21–39.

Biven, W. C. (2001). *Jimmy Carter's economy: Policy in an age of limits*. Chapel Hill, NC: The University of North Carolina Press.

Bodenheimer, T. (2000). Uneasy alliance: Clinical investigators and the pharmaceutical industry. *New England Journal of Medicine*, *342*(20), 1539–1544.

Boehm, D. A. (2005). The safety net of the safety net: How federally qualified health centers 'subsidize' Medicaid managed care. *Medical Anthropology Quarterly*, *19*(1), 47–63.

Calfee, J. E., Winston, C., & Stempski, R. (2002). Direct-to-consumer advertising and the demand for cholesterol-reducing drugs. *The Journal of Law and Economics*, *45*, 673–690.

CenterWatch. (2006). *2006 state of the clinical trials industry*. Boston, MA: Thomson CenterWatch.

Chambré, S. M. (2006). *Fighting for our lives: New York's AIDS community and the politics of disease*. New Brunswick, NJ: Rutgers University Press.

Cohen, L. (2003). *A consumers' republic: The politics of mass consumption*. New York, NY: Alfred Knopf.

Corrigan, O. P. (2003). Empty ethics: The problem with informed consent. *Sociology of Health and Illness*, *25*, 768–792.

Darvall, L. (1993). *Medicine, law and social change: The impact of bioethics, feminism and rights movements on medical decision-making*. Brookfield: Dartmouth Publishing Group.

Day, R. (2005). Comprehension of benefits versus risks: Is there fair balance? *Public hearing on direct-to-consumer promotion of medical products*, November 1. Retrieved on July 13, 2007. Available at http://www.fda.gov/cder/ddmac/dtc2005/default.htm

Division of Drug Marketing, Advertising, and Communications. (2006). *Meetings*. Retrieved on 13 July 2007. Available at http://www.fda.gov/cder/ddmac/meetings.htm

Elliott, C. (2003). *Better than well: American medicine meets the American dream*. New York, NY: W.W. Norton.

Epstein, S. (1996). *Impure science: AIDS, activism, and the politics of knowledge*. Berkeley, CA: University of California Press.

Fisher, J. A. (2006). Procedural misconceptions and informed consent: Insights from empirical research on the clinical trials industry. *Kennedy Institute of Ethics Journal*, *16*(3), 251–268.

Fisher, J. A. (2007). 'Ready-to-Recruit' or 'Ready-to-Consent' populations? Informed consent and the limits of subject autonomy. *Qualitative Inquiry*, *13*(6), 875–894.

Fisher, J. A. (2008). *Medical research for hire: The political economy of pharmaceutical clinical trials*. New Brunswick, NJ: Rutgers University Press.

Fontanarosa, P. B., Rennie, D., & DeAngelis, C. D. (2004). Postmarketing surveillance: Lack of vigilance, lack of trust. *Journal of the American Medical Association*, *292*, 2647–2650.

Frank, A. W. (2002). What's wrong with medical consumerism?. In: S. Henderson & A. Petersen (Eds), *Consuming health: The commodification of health care* (pp. 13–30). New York, NY: Routledge.

General Accounting Office. (2006). Prescription drugs: Improvements needed in FDA's oversight of direct-to-consumer advertising [GAO-07-54]. Available at http://www.gao.gov/htext/d0754.html

Gilliom, J. (2001). *Overseers of the poor: Surveillance, resistance, and the limits of privacy*. Chicago, IL: University of Chicago Press.

Giroux, H. A. (2004). *The terror of neoliberalism: Authoritarianism and the eclipse of democracy*. Boulder, CO: Paradigm Publishers.

Grace, V. M. (1991). The marketing of empowerment and the construction of the health consumer: A critique of health promotion. *International Journal of Health Services*, *21*(2), 329–343.

Greenslit, N. (2005). Depression and consumption: Psychopharmaceuticals, branding, and new identity practices. *Culture, Medicine, and Psychiatry*, *29*, 477–501.

Guidance for Industry on Consumer-Directed Broadcast Advertisements, 64 Fed. Reg. 43197. (1999).

Harvey, D. (2005). *A brief history of neoliberalism*. New York, NY: Oxford University Press.

Hausman, A. (2008). Direct-to-consumer advertising and its effect on patient requests. *Journal of Advertising Research*, *2*, 42–56.

Hausman, A. V. (2003). DTC advertising and its impact on patient healthcare behaviors, in Food and Drug Administration, *Direct-to-consumer promotion: Public meeting*, September 22. Retrieved on 13 July 2007. Available at www.fda.gov/cder/ddmac/DTCmeetingTranscript.doc

Henwood, F., Wyatt, S., Hart, A., & Smith, J. (2003). 'Ignorance is bliss sometimes': Constraints on the emergence of the 'informed patient' in the changing landscapes of health information. *Sociology of Health and Illness*, *25*(6), 589–607.

Hess, D. J. (1997). *Can bacteria cause cancer? Alternative medicine confronts big science*. New York, NY: New York University Press.

Hogle, L. F. (2002). Claims and disclaimers: Whose expertise counts? *Medical Anthropology*, *21*, 275–306.

Iizuka, T., & Jin, T. Z. (2005). The effect of prescription drug advertising on doctor visits. *Journal of Economics and Management Strategy*, *14*(3), 701–727.

Johanns v. Livestock Marketing Association, 544 U. S. 550. (2005).

Kalsher, M. (2006). Influence of presentation modality on communication of pharmaceutical risk information in direct-to-consumer (DTC) television commercials. Paper presented at 16th World Congress in Ergonomics, Maastricht, The Netherlands.

Kassirer, J. P. (2005). *On the take: How America's complicity with big business can endanger your health*. New York, NY: Oxford University Press.

Klausner, J. D., Kim, A., & Kent, C. (2002). Are HIV drug advertisements contributing to increases in risk behavior among men in San Francisco, 2001? *AIDS*, *16*, 15–16.

Kolata, G., & Eichenwald, K. (1999). Stopgap medicine: For the uninsured, experiments may provide the only treatment. *New York Times*, June 22.

Lee, C. (2006). New drugs declining, research costs increasing, GAO says. *Washington Post*, December 20, p. A08.

Lichtenberg, F. R. (2003). DTC advertising and public health, in Food and Drug Administration, *Direct-to-consumer promotion: Public meeting*, September 23. Retrieved on July 13, 2007. Available at www.fda.gov/cder/ddmac/DTCmeetingTranscript2.doc

Mack, J. (2007). Lunesta's Ad spending spree and other DTC oddities. Pharma marketing blog, December 13. Retrieved on January 26, 2008. Available at http://pharmamkting.blogspot.com/2007/12/lunestas-ad-spending-spree-and-other.html

Monahan, T. (2005). *Globalization, technological change, and public education*. New York, NY: Routledge.

Monahan, T., & Wall, T. (2007). Somatic surveillance: Corporeal control through information networks. *Surveillance and Society*, *4*(3), 154–173.

Morgen, S. (2002). *Into our own hands: The women's health movement in the United States, 1969–1990*. New Brunswick, NJ: Rutgers University Press.

Nichter, M., & Nichter, M. (1996). *Anthropology and international health: Asian case studies*. Amsterdam, NL: Gordon and Breach.

Niggle, C. (2003). Globalization, neoliberalism and the attack on social security. *Review of Social Economy*, *61*(1), 51–71.

Petryna, A. (2007). Clinical trials offshored: On private sector science and public health. *BioSocieties*, *2*(1), 21–40.

Petryna, A., Lakoff, A., & Kleinman, A. (Eds). (2006). *Global pharmaceuticals: Ethics, markets, practices*. Durham, NC: Duke University Press.

Pierson, P. (1994). *Dismantling the welfare state? Reagan, Thatcher, and the politics of retrenchment*. Cambridge, UK: Cambridge University Press.

Pines, W. L. (1999). A history and perspective on direct-to-consumer promotion. *Food and Drug Law Journal*, *54*, 489–518.

Reuters. (2007). Survey finds 43.6 million uninsured in U.S. *New York Times*, June 26. Retrieved on 13 July 2007. Available at http://www.nytimes.com/2007/06/26/washington/26insure.html

Ronald, L. M. (2006). *Empowered to consume: Direct-to-consumer advertising and pharmaceutical governance*. Troy, NY: Rensselaer Polytechnic Institute.

Rose, N. (1999). *Powers of freedom: Reframing political thought*. New York, NY: Cambridge University Press.

Schram, S. F. (2006). *Welfare discipline: Discourse, governance and globalization*. Philadelphia, PA: Temple University Press.

Scott, W. R., Caronna, C. A., Ruef, M., & Mendel, P. J. (2000). *Institutional change and healthcare organizations: From professional dominance to managed care*. Chicago, IL: University of Chicago Press.

Shaffer, E., & Brenner, J. (2004). Trade and healthcare: Corporatizing vital human services. In: M. Fort, M. A. Mercer & O. Gish (Eds), *Sickness and wealth: The corporate assault on global health*. Cambridge, MA: South End Press.

Shah, S. (2006). *The body hunters: How the drug industry tests its products on the world's poorest patients*. New York, NY: The New Press.

Siminoff, L. A., Caputo, M., & Burant, C. (2004). The promise of empirical research in the study of informed consent theory and practice. *HEC Forum*, *16*(1), 53–71.

Slaughter, E. (2003). *Direct-to-consumer promotion: Public meeting*, September 22. Retrieved on 13 July 2007, from Food and Drug Administration www.fda.gov/cder/ddmac/DTCmeetingTranscript.doc

Starr, P. (1982). *The social transformation of American medicine: The rise of a sovereign profession and the making of a vast industry*. New York, NY: Basic Books.

Strand, R. D. (2006). *Death by prescription: The shocking truth behind an overmedicated nation*. Nashville, TN: Thomas Nelson.

Talbot, M. M. (2000). Strange bedfellows: Feminism in advertising. In: M. Andrews & M. M. Talbot (Eds), *All the world and her husband: Women in twentieth-century consumer culture* (pp. 177–191). London, UK: Cassell.

Thomas, J. E., & Zimmerman, M. K. (2007). Feminism and profit in American hospitals: The corporate construction of women's health centers. *Gender and Society*, *21*, 359–383.

Timmermans, S., & Berg, M. (2003). *The gold standard: The challenge of evidence-based medicine and standardization in health care*. Philadelphia, PA: Temple University Press.

van der Geest, S., Whyte, S. R., & Hardon, A. (1996). The anthropology of pharmaceuticals: A biographical approach. *Annual Review of Anthropology*, *25*, 153–178.

Washington Legal Foundation v. Friedman, 13 F. Supp. 2d 51. (1998).

Woodcock, J. (2003). *Direct-to-consumer promotion: Public meeting*, September 22. Retrieved on 13 July 2007, from Food and Drug Administration www.fda.gov/cder/ddmac/DTCmeetingTranscript.doc

Zussman, R. (1997). Sociological perspectives on medical ethics and decision-making. *Annual Review of Sociology*, *23*, 171–189.

MAKING CONNECTIONS: EGG DONATION, THE INTERNET, AND THE NEW REPRODUCTIVE TECHNOLOGY MARKETPLACE

Kristin Holster

ABSTRACT

Purpose – *This chapter addresses the transformation of patient into consumer, focusing on the specific population of human egg recipients. This work also analyzes medicine, and reproductive medicine and egg donation specifically, as marketplaces, particularly as they function in the Internet environment.*

Methodology – *This chapter utilizes a content analysis of egg donation related websites using both inductive and deductive coding schemes.*

Findings – *Egg donation related websites and their practices do indeed fit the model of a reproductive medicine marketplace, particularly those practices related to marketing strategies and cost.*

Originality/value – *This work focuses on the Internet as a primary location for a reproductive medicine marketplace, and develops a new understanding of the ways in which consumers are transformed by and operate in this market. It also demonstrates the emerging need for policy to govern this marketplace.*

Patients, Consumers and Civil Society
Advances in Medical Sociology, Volume 10, 53–73

ISSN: 1057-6290/doi:10.1016/S1057-6290(08)10001-8

INTRODUCTION

In 1999 an advertisement placed in Ivy League college newspapers throughout the United States incited a public debate. The ad in itself was not so unusual; instead it was the product at the center of it that caused controversy. The product in question was a human egg, not just any egg, but one that would ideally come from an athletic, blonde, tall, healthy, highly educated woman. The price offered for the egg was not typical either, as a woman with the right qualities would be paid $50,000 for her egg(s) (Frase-Blunt, 2001). Though the reproductive technologies associated with egg donation had existed since 1984, the appearance of this advertisement caused immediate media reaction, and forcefully thrust egg donation and reproductive technologies in general, into the public consciousness. This famous example, atypical as it was, forced the recognition that reproduction and reproductive medicine had been transformed into a business in which buyers, sellers, and brokers were carefully defining and negotiating distinctive products.

This chapter will address the integration of business and medicine that some have called the "medical–industrial complex" (Relman, 1980). Emerging from the integration of these two institutions are newly formed "medical markets," including a reproductive medical marketplace or what some call a "baby market." This work analyzes a specific segment of this emerging market, human eggs advertised and sold for reproductive use, to determine if the trade of human eggs appropriately fits within a market model. Furthermore, grounded in previous research on organ, blood, and semen donation, this work will address the policy implications of an egg donation market. Data gathered from Internet sites, a major location for promotion and exchange, reveal a complex structure that does indeed fit the market model. This newly emerging industry that is built around a multifaceted product serves to transform infertile women from patients into consumers.

THEORETICAL FRAMEWORK

Medicine as a "Market"

The medical market is an intricate one, particularly as it does not meet many of the requirements often put forth in traditional definitions of a competitive marketplace. In a free market, consumers are supposed to be informed, recognize differences in quality, and have negotiation power and free choice about buying. These assumptions are often violated in health care markets (Lown, 2000). Inconsistency of information can be a major concern, particularly in medicine, as there are many information sources of varying quality, and these sources attempt to present knowledge that is constantly changing (Sulik & Eich-Krohm, 2008). Information is further compromised in that there is a time lag between the data collection, evaluation, and publication, making it difficult for the consumer to determine if the available information is still valid or useful.

Additionally, defining health care as a market concerns those who worry that applying a business model to a health care structure will compromise patient care (Mariner, 1995). They believe that it is difficult to merge the patient-centered orientation of medicine with the profit-seeking orientation of business. However, this perspective rests on the notion that business and health care are, and long have been, inherently mutually exclusive domains, such that what is good for one can not possibly be good for the other. In addition, this point of view presumes medicine to be built on charity and altruism, thus bestowing upon medicine a level of moral righteousness, while depicting business as selfish and unethical, two portrayals that are exaggerated and inaccurate (Wong, 1998). In fact, the application of business ideals to medicine has a long history, as evidenced by the common historical transformation of hospitals from charity institutions to medical facilities where patients paid for services from professional physicians (Rosner, 1982).

Although the health care industry may not appear to fit a traditional paradigm of a market, sociologists such as Peter Conrad and Valerie Leiter offer strong evidence that despite the differences, medicine is indeed a market. As they state,

> When medical products, services, or treatments are promoted to consumers to improve their health, appearance, or well being, we see the development of medical markets ... With the development of managed care, corporatized medicine, and the rise of the biotechnology industry, medical markets are increasingly important in the analysis of health care. (Conrad & Leiter, 2004, p. 160)

This is not a unidirectional market, and both supply and demand elements must be considered. On the demand side, consumers have increasingly sought out medical solutions for physical problems. However, this consumer demand "Is not simply unfettered desire for medical solutions, but it is shaped by the availability and accessibility of medical interventions" (Conrad & Leiter, 2004, p. 171). On the supply side, as new technologies, treatments, and drugs are developed, particularly as relate to specialty services such as reproductive technologies, new medical markets emerge (Conrad & Leiter, 2004).

If medicine is recognized as a market, and medical care a product, it must have a location in which transactions take place, and the virtual world of the Internet has developed as a new consumer vehicle for this medical market. Pharmaceutical companies, hospitals, and advocacy and support groups have positioned themselves on the Internet, and many of these sites offer consumer-oriented information (Barker, 2008; Conrad, 2005; Rutherford & Gallo-Cruz, 2008).

As health care becomes increasingly commodified and medical care becomes more like other products, so are individuals transformed from *patients* into *consumers*. This transformation is a dialectical one, as not only do patients become consumers in order to gather information about and purchase health care, but individuals who have become familiar with the consumer role often find themselves in the position of patient, transferring the skill set of one status to the other. Lupton explains that this consumerist subject is connected to the assumption that "In late modern Western societies individuals constantly seek to reflect upon the practices constituting the self and the body and to maximize, in an entrepreneurial fashion, the benefits for the self" (Lupton, 1997, p. 374). In other words, instead of simply accepting the state of the body as it is, the consumerist subject is reflective, analyzing his/her own needs and not simply accepting that purveyors of health care are more expert. In this consumerist model, patients can act as rational decision makers, being conscious actors (Fox, Ward, & O'Rourke, 2005; see also Burrows, Nettleton, Pleace, Loader, & Muncer, 2000; Hardey, 1999; Henwood, Wyatt, Hart, & Smith, 2003). This model is in contrast to a more traditional paternalistic model in which patients are expected to be passive and dependent (Lupton, 1997).

It is imperative that we recognize this transformation from patient to consumer and the Internet's significant role in it. By providing both an information source as well as a global collective meeting place, the Internet has contributed to a change in the illness experience from one that is privatized and very individual to one that is far more public. Though there is always the possible danger of inaccuracy and inconsistency of information, this new forum for medical knowledge and support does serve to empower individuals as consumers of medical care (Conrad, 2005). Individuals acting as empowered consumers, rather than simply patients, have the potential to "Help shape the scope, and sometimes the demand for, medical treatments for human problems" (Conrad, 2005, p. 9).

Markets in Human Goods

It can be argued that there exists both a general medical market, and also specific sub-markets within the medical arena. These markets focus on particular elements of health care, and even include an exchange in human goods. Included in this category of human goods are "Body parts or products, from corneas to cadavers," that are included in any form of transfer, "From altruistic donation to for-profit sales" (Healy, 2006, p. 2).

Blood, Organ, and Semen Donation

Though there are many human goods that are available for exchange, the three whose nature and means of exchange come closest to eggs are blood, human organs, and semen. Organ donation has the least obvious connection, as the market for donor organs is not currently complicated by the element of sale.[1] However, although outright payment for organs is forbidden in the United States, there are circumstances in which money has entered the organ exchange.[2] Though on the surface this may sound like a dangerous practice leading toward commodification, Kieran Healy argues,

> The key to understanding the role of money in this area lies in its expressive rather than its instrumental qualities. Rewards are set up so they are commensurable to the organ being exchanged; the payment reimburses the donor in an appropriate way. (Healy, 2006, p. 36)

This discussion is directly related to egg donation, as it lays the foundation for a sociological justification for the payment structure in egg donation. In this construction, the monetary exchange from the egg recipient to the donor acts as a symbolic expression of the social relationship between the parties involved.

Blood products, and the market for them, have a more patent connection to egg donation, as blood donation is an area that has been both a paid marketplace and a donor system reliant on altruistic donors (Titmuss, 1971). Though today donation of whole blood is constructed as an altruistic process with no payment structure to donors, this has not always been the case. In fact, until a decommodification process in the 1970s, suppliers/donors of whole blood were offered financial compensation. However, there is still a legal market for plasma, as plasma donors are paid a monetary reward, both for the plasma itself, and also for the time needed to collect the plasma (Healy, 2006).

Sperm is of course the most similar product to eggs, not only because of a similar payment structure, but also because they both involve the provision of a substance that will contribute to the creation of a third party, the offspring, as a result of the transaction (Daniels & Lewis, 1996). Though analogous, the difference in the process necessary to acquire eggs creates an apparent distinction between the two products.

There are many ways to view the market structure and the concern that eventually almost everything, including organ donation, will be market-driven. The first is an economic perspective that states that "money is money" and that it is expedient and sensible to offer financial compensation to donors when a shortage of any human good exists (Healy, 2006). The second is that providing payment eliminates the feeling of obligation that one might feel when accepting something of such value as a "gift." By offering payment, the gift ceases to be a gift, and can become a product (Daniels & Lewis, 1996). A final argument, from an economic sociology perspective, argues that markets and monies certainly exist, but they rest on webs of shared understanding and facilitative social interaction (Zelizer, 1994). In other words, both the behavior and the compensation offered for it has meaning, and this meaning could be lost if "market rhetoric" determines our thoughts and actions (Radin, 1996).

The Reproductive Medicine Market

Just as I have described markets for human goods, it can also be asserted that there is a reproductive medicine market. Included in a general construction of this market is the way in which the result of reproduction, the child, is born, in other words a market in childbirth and maternity care (Bourgeault et al., 2008; Rutherford & Gallo-Cruz, 2008). My focus is on the process and requisite components necessary to create a child as they are an integral part of this emerging market.

Debora Spar analyzes this reproductive medicine market from a business perspective noting that while we certainly

> Don't like to think of children as economic objects, over the past thirty years, advances in reproductive medicine have indeed created a market for babies, a market in which parents choose traits, clinics woo clients, and specialized providers earn millions of dollars a year. (Spar, 2006, p. xi)

She recognizes that many have a strong distaste for the association of children with a market and an even more intense aversion to the notion that there is a baby business, since the mere mention of a marketplace for children is objectionable (Prichard, 1984; Radin, 1996; Sandel, 1997). However, Spar (2006) argues against this position, contending that it is necessary to make a more complete analysis before passing judgment. Though she identifies and explores the moral questions associated both with defining reproductive technology as a market, and with the market itself, she makes no attempt to resolve these moral issues. She asserts that if markets in themselves are considered good, and children in themselves are considered good, then it is not necessary that the intersection of the two would be inherently immoral.

Alternatively, Spar (2006) argues for an acceptance of the existence and continued success of this high-tech marketplace. Instead of ignoring its business elements which has led to limited regulation and inconsistency, acceptance of the market's existence would allow it to be embedded in a proper political and regulatory context, have a common set of definitions and guidelines, and avoid the potential risks associated with reproductive science.

While my work does address many of the moral issues surrounding reproductive technologies, and specifically egg donation, I agree with Spar that a true analysis of the phenomenon cannot take place without at least a provisional recognition of the field as a market, and I argue that such an analysis should not be avoided because of an aversion to "market rhetoric."

In accepting Spar's definition of reproductive medicine as a market, we must note that it is for now certainly a niche market, one that is irrelevant to 85–90 percent of the population. It is, however, likely to expand. Spar estimates that "About 75 percent of fertility's potential customers are not yet buying the product" (Spar, 2006, p. 64). The fertility industry has remained relatively constrained since many potential buyers do not have the financial capacity to become consumers (Neumann, 1997). This is a market that is driven by price. While the cost of a specific product may not decrease (and may actually increase), as states begin to require insurance coverage for assisted reproductive technologies, demand will likely increase dramatically, leading to rapid growth (Spar, 2006). In addition to policy changes that may increase demand, demographic and structural changes are predicted to contribute to these changes as well. The U.S. Census Bureau reports that age at first marriage is at its oldest ever. As of 2006, the median age at first marriage rose to 26 for women and 27 for men, up from 21 and 23 respectively in 1970 (U.S. Census Bureau, 2006). Furthermore, increasing numbers of women seeking higher education and prioritizing career ambitions has led to a larger portion of the population seeking pregnancy later in life, a time when they are more likely to need technological assistance in order to achieve their goal (Abma & Martinez, 2006; Martin, 2000). These trends have created the ideal consumer base for the assisted reproductive technology market, a group of women who are highly educated, and financially able to afford the technology.

Market Structure and Policy

Two types of organizations control the egg donation market: medical clinics that offer egg donation as one of their reproductive technology services, and egg broker agencies. Fertility clinics are staffed by fertility specialists and by definition have a bricks and mortar location in which they practice and perform medical procedures. While some clinics maintain their own pool of egg donors and provide a matchmaking service as well as the actual medical procedures, many contract with external brokering agencies. Egg broker agencies may be staffed by anyone from any background and are often located in an office environment, since they do not provide the actual medical procedures involved in the preparation and retrieval of the eggs. Instead, they act as what Spar (2006) refers to as "intimate intermediaries," mediators whose job is to make the process appealing enough to attract the right donors in order to procure the product desired by the consumer, or potential egg recipient.

The fertility industry basically governs itself. While clinics operate under the auspices of the American Society for Reproductive Medicine (ASRM), and must report success rates of their medical procedures to the Centers for Disease Control (CDC) based on the Fertility Clinic Success Rate and Certification Act of 1992 (1992), this act is far from comprehensive. Fertility clinics are allowed to define success as they wish. Some refer to pregnancy rates, others to live birth rates, and the CDC discourages their use as a basis for comparison, therefore making it difficult for the egg consumer to be a fully educated one. Though the CDC is responsible for centralizing and publishing the data from fertility clinics, they are not an authoritative body, and there is not a scheduled standardized accreditation process for all facilities practicing assisted reproductive technologies. There is even less oversight for egg broker agencies since they do not participate in any medical procedures and are not officially governed by the ASRM or CDC.

The insurance industry also strongly influences the egg donation market. It has a two-pronged effect. When insurers cover reproductive technology related treatments it helps to define infertility as a medical illness and potentially increases demand for fertility treatments. However, insurance coverage comes at a cost, such that treatment providers are only able to charge what insurers are willing to pay, thus capping prices and constraining the marketplace (Spar, 2006).

Additional policies related to egg donation include Food and Drug Administration (FDA) mandated "good tissue practices" involving comprehensive infectious disease testing of donors and tissue storage requirements, laws pertaining to parental rights and custody when donor gametes are involved,[3] as well as basic laws forbidding malpractice, fraud and misrepresentation (American Society for Reproductive Medicine, 2006; Spar, 2006). However, these guidelines are predominantly aimed at the fertility clinics actually controlling the medical procedures, not the broker agencies hiring the egg donors and matching them to recipients. Egg donation agencies can establish their own guidelines both for accepting and rejecting donors and recipients, and there are no licensure standards or a specific educational or professional background required to become an egg broker or to establish an egg donation agency.

Though egg broker agencies and fertility clinics recruit donors using a variety of methods including newspaper advertising and clinic-sponsored donor information sessions, the Internet, through the individual agency websites, provides an unprecedented opportunity for targeted marketing. The Internet allows organizations with a product to offer to track the interests and purchase preferences of consumers such that their requests can be addressed directly.[4] It is a logical location for such a market in that demographic research has shown that there is an overlap between the categories of people most likely to use the Internet and the categories of women seeking donor eggs, particularly as relates to the variables of age, education, and income (Centers for Disease Control, 2006; Martin & Robinson, 2007; Pew Research Center, 2007). Regulation of the Internet is a complex and unresolved issue however, and the Internet, like the egg donation marketplace operating within it, remains largely self-regulated (Eko, 2001).

The Consumer

In the egg donation market, the end users, the individuals or couples seeking out donor eggs, are the primary consumers. They are the group that is the focus of advertising, of media representations, of Internet marketing campaigns. However, to describe them as a unified group, with the same motivations and needs in the marketplace would be inaccurate. The consumers seeking out donor eggs are a widely disparate group. While they all seek eggs, they are not all looking for the same egg, but instead specific characteristics from an egg donor that they hope will be transferred to an egg and ultimately the child born of that egg.

Being a consumer in this marketplace is demanding. Although in general, patients are often described as not having the motivation to practice consumer behaviors such as seeking information, exercising independent judgment, and applying cost sensitivity (Montagne, 1992), this is not the case when discussing egg recipients. They practice all three consumer behaviors, seeking information on websites, independently selecting an agency and donor with which to work, and considering cost as a major factor in their decision-making process.

While fertility customers care about cost, price or more specifically value, is an abstract concept and is often characterized as what the consumer can *afford* to pay (Spar, 2006). The notion of financial constraint divides fertility customers into three distinct classes. The first is those individuals who are wealthy enough to pay for whatever treatment or technology is available. The second are those who have comprehensive insurance plans or who live in states that require coverage of infertility diagnosis and treatment, and are therefore also able to afford whatever treatment they seek, for as long as it takes. The third group is made up of those who have more limited resources, but who share with the first two an intense determination to procure a greatly desired product, and therefore often go beyond their means in order to do so (Spar, 2006). In short, the inconsistency of insurance coverage and the hierarchy of financial status among those seeking donor eggs has resulted in the creation of a private medical market. If consumers can afford it, they are likely to find a medical provider willing to supply the treatment.

The Product

Another key aspect of defining egg donation as a market lies in the construction of the product for sale. Attempting to do so often results in a debate between those who argue that in egg donation human eggs are being sold, and those who believe that the product is instead the time and effort of the donor. I take a more inclusive approach to defining the product in this marketplace as I feel that these two arguments are neither mutually exclusive, nor the only two possibilities. Instead I posit a product that has a three-part identity.

The first part of what is being sold in the egg donation transaction is the time and effort endured by the donor.[5] According to the ASRM, "Almost all professionals working with egg donors agree that compensation for the donors' time, effort, and discomfort is appropriate" (American Society for Reproductive Medicine, 2006, p. 2).

The second part of what is being sold in an egg donation transaction is the egg itself, though many find it controversial to describe eggs in this manner because it seems frighteningly close to the idea of selling human organs, a practice that as I have discussed is neither legal, nor generally socially acceptable. It is important to note, therefore, that the legal community (though not necessarily the bioethical or medical communities) has constructed eggs as "replenishable" tissue, thus avoiding the laws that prohibit monetary compensation for human organs. This makes it possible to define the egg as a product as it is legally comparable to both blood and sperm, two goods that have a long history of being defined as products and for which donors have long received monetary compensation (Daniels & Golden, 2004; Daniels & Lewis, 1996; Titmuss, 1971). Defining the egg as a part of the product requires also defining it as something that can be sold and for which there is a set price. Unlike the United Kingdom, which outlaws the sale of human eggs, the United States makes no restrictions on the sale or cost of eggs for reproductive use. This has become a topic of debate both in the popular media as well as among bioethicists who worry about the commodification of the egg and about the possibility that unless legislators step in there may be no limit on the amount of money that could be paid for human eggs (Frase-Blunt, 2001; Larkin, 2000; Resnik, 1998; Resnik, 2001). Complicating the debate about commodification is what some perceive as a blatant inconsistency between payment practices for eggs for reproductive use, and those for eggs donated for scientific research (Spar, 2007). While in the United States it is legal to pay women to provide eggs for the purpose of creating a child, scientists have vowed not to purchase eggs for research purposes and to only accept those that are altruistically donated (Spar, 2007).

Eggs cannot be considered in isolation, as they cannot be entirely disembodied from the donor who produced them, and this donor can be considered a third aspect of the product. Though the egg is ultimately the object that is transferred from the donor to the recipient, it is not possible to visually display the egg. Consequently, it is not a depiction of the egg that is offered on the websites, but instead, a description and at times photographs of the woman offering her eggs. Indeed, the donor profile may serve to embody the genetic material such that it is the personification of the egg and donor that the recipient is purchasing (Almeling, 2007). Though some clinics and broker agencies allow recipients to meet their donors, this process still does require a tremendous leap of faith, as there is no absolute guarantee that the eggs a recipient receives actually came from the woman she has met in person or seen pictured on the website.

Through a theoretical analysis of the structure of markets in human goods, especially eggs, it appears that the trade in eggs includes all of the traditional components of a market, including consumers, a multifaceted product, and a location in which the eggs are exchanged. However, it is unclear exactly how agencies and clinics use their websites to construct, promote, and sell their product. What I hope to reveal in my analysis of egg agency and clinic websites is the way in which the organization and presentation of the product for sale through text and photo databases, as well as specific discussions of financial costs and rationales for these costs, creates a structure that indeed fits a traditional consumer-oriented market model.

Methods

To demonstrate the use of the Internet by those involved in egg donation I conducted a content analysis of egg donation related websites. A total sample of 100 websites was selected, including 32 fertility clinics and 68 egg broker agencies. This sample was chosen from two sampling frames consulted in July of 2007: a list of 112 egg donor and surrogacy programs available on the IHR.com (Internet Health Resources) website and a list of 78 egg brokers and clinics obtained from the ASRM.[6,7,8] The final sample excluded 69 programs that either did not have websites or did not provide sufficient information for analysis at the time the data were collected.[9]

Data were organized using a combination of an inductive and deductive coding scheme. Though some variables resulted from the literature review, including type of business, location, and egg donor payment, other variables emerged from a preliminary analysis of the initial sites. In addition to location, and type of business, I also coded for variables including services offered, the egg donor payment, as well as the rationale for the payment, donor qualifications, text and photo database availability and description, qualifications of people managing the business, images on website, and statement of success rates.

FINDINGS

Appearance

When exploring egg donation related websites, one of the first things that strikes the observer is the similarity in the websites, both in name and appearance. More than half of the agencies and clinics in my sample included the words *reproductive*, *fertility*, or *egg/egg donation* in their titles. Similarly, of the 94 sites that display images, 75 of these pictures are of babies, children, or families, making it difficult to differentiate between the sites based on name or image. This level of similarity makes it difficult for the consumer to differentiate between the sites and to decide with which agency or clinic to work.

Broker Qualifications

If, as a consumer, it is a challenge to separate agencies/clinics by name or appearance one may able to distinguish between them based on the qualifications of those operating the organization. While medical professionals manage all of the clinics in this sample, egg broker agency owners/operators come from a variety of backgrounds including law, social work, and counseling. Additionally, 25 of the egg broker agency operators in this sample state on their websites that their primary qualification for being egg brokers is "personal experience." This includes experience as an egg donor or gestational surrogate, having become a parent through egg donation or surrogacy, or knowing family members or friends who have struggled with infertility.

Donor Qualifications

Though there are no definitive qualifications for egg brokers, this is not the case for donors. Ninety-one of the sites in this sample describe specific prerequisites for their donors. Included in these criteria are behavioral requirements such as no drug or cigarette use, as well as medical and psychological evaluations and criminal background checks.

Though there are no specific demands of physical appearance (such as hair or eye color) as this allows for a more varied product, almost half (44) of the clinics/agencies do request that donors be height/weight proportionate as measured by the Body Mass Index (BMI) scale. The expectation is that donors with a recommended BMI are more likely to successfully complete the egg donation process with little trouble and little impact on their health.

The final major qualification of egg donors is that they be within a specific age range. Though the age requirements vary by clinic/broker, there appears to be a minimum age of 18 and a maximum age limit of 35. The inconsistency of age requirements allows for donors to be ineligible at one clinic or broker and eligible at another. However, the age requirements are not completely arbitrary, but are instead based on legal and biological viability as donors must be at least 18 in order to legally contract with the broker or clinic, and the eggs from younger donors are more greatly demanded due to increased potential of biological viability.

For those exceeding the basic qualifications demanded by clinics/agencies, 11 organizations in this sample also have specific categories for exceptional or extraordinary donors, generally defined by having a high collegiate GPA, high SAT or ACT scores, an Ivy League education or a graduate or professional degree. Exceptional donors are often able to request additional compensation for their eggs, as much as $3,000 more than the average first time donor.

Databases and Profiles

To apply to be an egg donor, a woman must complete a donor profile in order to assure that she meets the above standards. If accepted, she is then added to a database where her characteristics are organized for display. The presentation of this information, as well as the level of access to it, varies. The most limited presentation form is a text only database, represented in this sample by six broker agencies and two clinics. Another more comprehensive option used by 38 agencies and three clinics in this sample is to provide both text descriptions and photos of the donors.

Agencies and clinics must find a public/private compromise between accessibility of information and maintenance of private control over their donor information. To achieve this many allow access to their databases only with an agency assigned password obtained by the potential recipient after providing some identifying information. Identifying oneself does not require that one contract with the organization, only that one has identified oneself as a potential participant in the marketplace. In this sample, of those agencies and clinics providing both text and photo databases, 28 allow only password access. Some agencies prefer to make their databases publicly accessible, meaning that anyone with an Internet connection can observe the list while remaining anonymous. In this sample 12 broker agencies and one clinic allow public access to their text and photo database. This method allows the consumer to comparison shop without having the website administrators know that he/she is interested.

Of the templates I was able to view, characteristics displayed range from the more customary such as age, ethnicity, height, weight, and eye and hair color, to the less common like religion, first name, hobbies, and even predominant hand. Though it is unclear which variants within these genetic and non-genetic qualities are more desirable than others, it does create a hierarchy of traits.

These databases provide evidence for my assertion that the consumer is not simply seeking any egg, but a specific one that she/they is able to locate by matching her/their desired criteria to the characteristics described in the databases.

Cost and Payment

When discussing payment, the ASRM's ethics committee advises, "Sums of $5,000 or more require justification and sums above $10,000 are not appropriate" (American Society for Reproductive Medicine, 2007, p. 308). Seventy-eight agencies have signed agreements stating that they will comply with these recommendations. However, even the ASRM admits that signing the agreement does not necessitate compliance. According to its own review of 51 agencies, the ASRM found an average egg donor compensation of $5,204, right at the compensation level requiring justification, and six of the agencies it surveyed had premium fees for donors with specific characteristics, with one listing compensation of more than $10,000 (American Society for Reproductive Medicine, 2006).

My data show that in general, egg broker agencies and clinics present themselves as supporting the recommendations of the ASRM in relation to donor compensation, rationale for compensation, and definition of product for sale. However, despite their claims, in reality many are not compliant with the ASRM recommendations. In my sample, of the 69 agencies/clinics reporting specific compensation rates on their websites, 16 offer donors less than $5,000, while 44 offer between $5,000 and $8,000. Higher levels of compensation are available however, as six sites offered maximum compensation levels of $10,000 and one a maximum of $15,000, though such high fee levels are generally reserved for exceptional donors or donors with "unique backgrounds." Six additional sites allow their donors to set their own price, though two do place a ceiling of $10,000 on donors' demands.

In discussing the payment available to donors, sites often include specific language ranging from contending that the money is not for personal characteristics to blatantly saying that the money is not for the eggs, to convince visitors that it is not the eggs that are for sale. Of the 48 organizations who offer an explanation on their website of the compensation they provide to donors, 45 repeat the words of the ASRM and emphasize that the money is for the risk, time and effort, inconvenience, commitment, and discomfort involved in the process.

However, their claims appear dubious since many of these agencies' payment schedules are unambiguously hierarchical. One particular example of this is an agency that offers an additional $250 to those with a GPA of 3.7 or higher, an additional $250 for those with high SAT scores, and an extra $350 to donors in graduate school. Additionally, four clinics and 17 broker agencies provide supplemental compensation for repeat donors. I argue that this money, which ranges from an additional $500 to $2000, is not *solely* for her time and effort, but instead acts as recognition that this donor is "proven," that is, that she has shown both the agency and the potential recipient that she can both be expected to complete the process, and that she can successfully produce eggs that can be retrieved. Future research could more fully explore these contradictions by addressing them directly with the agency administrators.

The cost of the eggs themselves, in the form of the payment to the egg donor is only part of the total cost involved in this process. Using a broker agency can cost between $10,000 and $15,000, a sum that includes the donor fee, the agency fee (which ranges from $4,000 to $6,000), insurance costs for the agency, legal fees associated with the donor contract, and donor psychological evaluation fees. This is only the cost of the matching process, and must be added to the cost of the in vitro fertilization process, which according to the ASRM averages $12,400 per cycle.

Conclusion

The merging of business and medicine into what has been labeled the "medical–industrial complex" (Relman, 1980) has created an opportunity for newly constructed medical markets to emerge. These are predominantly niche markets, aimed at offering specialty services to a targeted consumer base (Conrad & Leiter, 2004). Those involved with reproductive medicine have taken advantage of this opportunity, utilizing the development of technologies such as egg donation and in vitro fertilization to create a very specific marketplace. While some have elected to operate their market in traditional venues, the egg market has chosen to incorporate another technology, using the Internet as a primary location in which to advertise and trade its product.

While there are certainly ethical concerns related to the construction of medical markets, particularly as they are applied to the marketing and purchase of human eggs, these concerns are best addressed after first accepting the existence of the industry as a market. Succumbing to the discomfort associated with the idea of selling eggs, and the uneasiness at applying market-oriented terminology to human goods only allows such a market to flourish, unimpeded by regulation or governance. Acceptance of the market does not require that society provide moral approval, only that it have an awareness of the market and its newest incarnation today. Only with regulation and data reporting requirements, not only for fertility clinics but for all those affiliated with the industry, can a full analysis of the market, its complex product, and its participants be achieved.

Acknowledging that the exchange of human goods meets many of the standards of a market does not mean that market rhetoric must be wholeheartedly adopted, or that we must accept a totally market-driven approach, focused solely on profit with no attention to altruism or benevolence. Though the industry for human organs still struggles with the direction its market will take (Healy, 2006), it seems that egg and sperm donation have already established their form. The exchange of gametes merges the practice of a market-driven approach, through the organization of the transaction and the definition of both the product and the consumer, with the rhetoric of altruism. It appears that it is the agencies that control this construction, balancing the financial equations with the language of gifts and donations. My data show that this is a complex balance to maintain, as the lack of regulation, as well as the specific demands of the consumer, makes it difficult to avoid creating a financially compensated hierarchy of donors and their eggs.

Contending with this complex market in its Internet location is a new form of consumer. This consumer must be both patient and consumer, using her experience and skill set as a consumer to inform her status as an infertility patient, negotiating not only her medical treatment and the purchase of health care, but also participating in an exchange for human goods. This consumer is an active one, not accepting the role of the passive, dependent patient, but instead taking advantage of the information, support, and market environment that the Internet can provide. The transformation of the consumer has also transformed the illness experience, from one that is private and often unseen, to one that is public and visible. Through analyzing the clinic and broker agency websites that market their product to these consumers, we are able to learn about both the consumer and the supplier. As the consumers select egg donors, indicating which qualities they find most attractive in the product, clinics and agencies are able to use this information to modify their product and adjust their inventory through the addition and deletion of egg donors from their databases.

The market for human eggs is a constantly evolving one, transformed not only by the continuous development of its primary setting, the Internet, but also by the progress of similar markets for human goods and the regulations that govern all. As new avenues of opportunity develop for health care consumerism, particularly as related to the consumption of human goods, the necessity for control through policy creation will almost certainly emerge. Sociologists must follow the course of these regulations and their impact on the evolving industries, as they will likely create an extensive field for future research.

NOTES

1. The Uniform Anatomical Gift Act (UAGA) originally passed in 1968 and universally adopted across the United States by 1973 specifically prohibits the purchase or sale of parts for transplantation or therapy, though does allow for a person to charge a reasonable amount for the "Removal, processing, preservation, control, storage, transportation, implantation, or disposal of a part." This act has been amended most recently in 2006, though these amendments have not been universally adopted (Uniform Anatomical Gift Act, 2006).

2. One example of how money has entered the organ exchange is the practice created in Pennsylvania in 1999 in which state health officials offered a small stipend to help families of organ donors cover funeral expenses.

3. These laws include the Uniform Parentage Act and the Uniform Status of Children of Assisted Conception Act.

4. There is currently no data about which methods of locating egg donors are most popular or successful. I would argue however, that the expanding list of brokers who do business on the Internet provides some initial indication that this method is successful.

5. Though each agency or organization that participates in egg donation has its own rules, there is a consistent ordering and general time commitment with the procedures involved. Egg donation agencies recruit young women to produce eggs for paying recipients who are using reproductive technologies such as in vitro fertilization in order to conceive children. Once a donor/recipient match has been made by the agency, the donor takes hormone injections to both synchronize her reproductive cycle with that of the recipient, and then to stimulate egg production. Multiple doctor visits are required to check hormone levels and to determine both the number and level of maturity of the eggs. Once eggs are determined to be mature,

ovulation is triggered and within 36 hours the eggs are retrieved through outpatient surgery. Successfully retrieved eggs are then usually mixed with sperm and the resulting embryos implanted in the uterus of the recipient (American Society for Reproductive Medicine, 2003). This entire process usually takes between six and eight weeks.

6. These sampling frames and the data collected in this study are like all information on the Internet, constantly being updated. The data presented here reflect the lists and the websites at the time I conducted the content analysis.

7. This list includes those who signed an agreement with the Society for Assisted Reproductive Technology (SART) that states that they will abide by the American Society for Reproductive Medicine Ethics Committee Guidelines governing the payment of egg donors.

8. Additional agencies were added through a general Internet search.

9. Twenty-nine agencies/clinics were listed on both lists.

REFERENCES

Abma, J., & Martinez, G. (2006). Childlessness among older women in the United States: Trends and profiles. *Journal of Marriage and Family*, *68*(4), 1045–1056.

Almeling, R. (2007). Selling genes, selling gender. *American Sociological Review*, *72*(3), 319–340.

American Society for Reproductive Medicine. (2003). *Assisted reproductive technologies: A guide for patients*. Alabama: American Society for Reproductive Medicine.

American Society for Reproductive Medicine. (2006). Highlights from the 62nd Annual Meeting of the American Society for Reproductive Medicine, Policy. Part II: Egg Donation: Cost of Implementing FDA Regulations; Influence of Donor Compensation in Recruitment; Donor Agencies' Compliance with ASRM Guidelines, American Society for Reproductive Medicine, New Orleans. Available at http://www.asrm.org/Media/Press/policyeggdonation.html. Retrieved on August 12, 2007.

American Society for Reproductive Medicine. (2007). Financial compensation of oocyte donors. *Fertility and Sterility*, *88*(2), 305–309.

Barker, K. (2008). Electronic support groups, patient-consumers, and medicalization: The case of contested illness. *Journal of Health and Social Behavior*, *49*(1), 20–36.

Bourgeault, I. L., Declercq, E., Sandall, J., Wrede, S., Vanstone, M., Van Teijlingen, E., DeVries, R., & Benoit, C. (2008). Too Posh To Push? Comparative perspectives on maternal request caesarean sections in Canada, the US, the UK and Finland. In: S. M. Chambré & M. Goldner (Eds), *Advances in medical sociology: Patients, consumers and civil society* (pp. 99–123). Bingley, UK: Emerald Group Publishing Limited.

Burrows, R., Nettleton, S., Pleace, N., Loader, B., & Muncer, S. (2000). Virtual community care? Social policy and the emergence of computer mediated social support. *Information, Communication and Society*, *3*(1), 95–121.

Centers for Disease Control. (2006). *Assisted reproductive technology success rates: National summary and fertility clinic reports*. Atlanta: Centers for Disease Control.

Conrad, P. (2005). The shifting engines of medicalization. *Journal of Health and Social Behavior*, *46*(1), 3–14.

Conrad, P., & Leiter, V. (2004). Medicalization, markets, and consumers. *Journal of Health and Social Behavior*, *45*, 158–176.

Daniels, C. R., & Golden, J. (2004). Procreative compounds: Popular eugenics, artificial insemination and the rise of the American sperm banking industry. *Journal of Social History*, *38*(1), 5–27.

Daniels, K. R., & Lewis, G. (1996). Donor insemination: The gifting and selling of semen. *Social Science and Medicine*, *42*(11), 1521–1536.

Eko, L. (2001). Many spiders, one worldwide web: Towards a typology of Internet regulation. *Communication Law and Policy*, *6*(3), 445–484.

Fertility Clinic Success Rate and Certification Act of 1992. (1992). Pub. L. 102-493, 42 U.S.C. 263a-1 et seq.

Fox, N. J., Ward, J., & O'Rourke, A. J. (2005). The 'Expert Patient': Empowerment or medical dominance? The case of weight loss, pharmaceutical drugs and the Internet. *Social Science and Medicine*, *60*(6), 1299–1309.

Frase-Blunt, M. (2001). Ova-compensating? Women who donate eggs to infertile couples earn a reward-but pay a price. *Washington Post*, December 4.

Hardey, M. (1999). Doctor in the house: The Internet as a source of lay health knowledge and the challenge to expertise. *Sociology of Health and Illness*, *21*(6), 820–835.

Healy, K. (2006). *Last best gifts: Altruism and the market for human blood and organs*. Chicago: University of Chicago Press.

Henwood, F., Wyatt, S., Hart, A., & Smith, J. (2003). Ignorance is bliss sometimes: Constraints on the emergence of the 'Informed Patient' in the changing landscapes of health information. *Sociology of Health and Illness*, *25*(6), 589–607.

Larkin, M. (2000). Curb costs of egg donation, urge US specialists. *Lancet*, *356*(9229), 569.

Lown, B. (2000). Market health care: The commodification of health care. *Philosophy and Social Action*, *26*, 57–71.

Lupton, D. (1997). Consumerism, reflexivity and the medical encounter. *Social Science and Medicine*, *45*(3), 373–381.

Mariner, W. (1995). Business vs. medical ethics: Conflicting standards for managed care. *Journal of Law, Medicine, and Ethics*, *23*(3), 236–246.

Martin, S. (2000). Diverging fertility among women who delay childbearing. *Demography*, *37*(4), 523–533.

Martin, S. P., & Robinson, J. P. (2007). The income digital divide: Trends and prediction for levels of Internet use. *Social Problems*, *54*(1), 1–22.

Montagne, M. (1992). The promotion of medications for personal and social problems. *Journal of Drug Issues*, *22*(2), 389–405.

Neumann, P. (1997). Should health insurance cover IVF: Issues and opinions. *Journal of Health Politics, Policy, and Law*, *22*(5), 1215–1239.

Pew Research Center. (2007). Demographics of internet users. The Pew Internet and American Life Project, June 15, 2007. Available at http://www.pewinternet.org/trends/User_Demo_6.15.07.htm. Retrieved on July 6, 2007.

Prichard, J. R. S. (1984). A market for babies? *University of Toronto Law Review*, *34*(3), 341–357.

Radin, M. (1996). *Contested commodities: The trouble with trade in sex, children, body parts and other things*. Cambridge: Harvard University Press.

Relman, A. S. (1980). The medical industrial complex. *New England Journal of Medicine*, *303*(17), 963–970.

Resnik, D. B. (1998). The commodification of human reproductive materials. *Journal of Medical Ethics*, *24*(6), 388–393.

Resnik, D. B. (2001). Regulating the market for human eggs. *Bioethics*, *15*(1), 1–25.

Rosner, D. (1982). *A once charitable enterprise*. New York: Cambridge University Press.

Rutherford, M., & Gallo-Cruz, S. (2008). Selling the ideal birth: Rationalization and re-enchantment in the marketing of maternity care. In: S. M. Chambré & Goldner, M. (Eds), *Advances in medical sociology: Patients, consumers and civil society* (pp. 75–98). Bingley, UK: Emerald Group Publishing Limited.

Sandel, M. (1997). The baby bazaar. *New Republic*, October 20, p. 25.

Spar, D. L. (2006). *The baby business*. Boston: Harvard Business School Press.

Spar, D. L. (2007). The egg trade-making sense of the market for human oocytes. *New England Journal of Medicine*, *356*(13), 1289–1291.

Sulik, G. A., & Eich-Krohm, A. (2008). No longer a patient: The social construction of the medical consumer. In: S. M. Chambré & M. Goldner (Eds), *Advances in medical sociology: Patients, consumers and civil society* (pp. 3–28). Bingley, UK: Emerald Group Publishing Limited.

Titmuss, R. (1971). *The gift relationship: From human blood to social policy*. New York: Vintage.

Uniform Anatomical Gift Act. (2006). National conference of commissioners on uniform state laws.

U.S. Census Bureau. (2006). Households by type and size. *Current Population Survey*. Available at http://www.census.gov. Retrieved on March 2, 2007.

Wong, K. L. (1998). *Medicine and the marketplace: The moral dimensions of managed care*. Notre Dame, IN: University of Notre Dame Press.

Zelizer, V. (1994). *The social meaning of money*. New York: Basic Books.

SELLING THE IDEAL BIRTH: RATIONALIZATION AND RE-ENCHANTMENT IN THE MARKETING OF MATERNITY CARE

Markella Rutherford and Selina Gallo-Cruz

ABSTRACT

Purpose – *This chapter briefly outlines the history of childbirth in the United States and describes the influence of the natural birth movement and consumer demand in shaping the contemporary advertising of mainstream maternity services.*

Design/methodology/approach – *Qualitative content analysis of 59 hospital websites was undertaken in order to understand how hospitals depict childbirth in their online advertising.*

Findings – *Our findings illustrate how contemporary medical institutions idealize childbirth through their depictions of its physical and social dimensions. Although hospital advertising has adopted some of the rhetoric of the natural birth movement in describing the social and symbolic dimensions of the childbirth experience, this rhetoric is shown to stand in tension to the highly rationalized and bureaucratic institutional*

Patients, Consumers and Civil Society
Advances in Medical Sociology, Volume 10, 75–98

ISSN: 1057-6290/doi:10.1016/S1057-6290(08)10005-5

nature of hospitals. These tensions are most apparent in advertised descriptions of the physical environment of maternity centers and in the attempt to depict hospitalized birth as an opportunity for the individual empowerment of women.

Research limitations/implications – *This research is limited to an analysis of how providers advertise their services and does not provide data on whether practices actually reflect the rhetoric of the ideal birth. Future research should consider the fit between rhetoric and reality in hospital maternity practices in order to better understand the social structural constraints of delivering these services in a hospital maternity center.*

Originality/value – *This chapter highlights the importance of consumer demand for how maternity services are portrayed and identifies key tensions between an idealized image of birth and the rational, bureaucratic demands of modern medical institutions.*

INTRODUCTION

The process of giving birth in the United States has undergone as many drastic changes in understanding and practice as have the cultural roles of women and the normative expectations of sexual behavior in the past 200 years. In the 20th century, the hospital became the dominant institution for birth; since the 1950s, 99% of American women have given birth in hospitals (Rooks, 1997). However, the nature of that practice has been in some aspects radically transformed since then, in part due to the influence of the natural birth movement and in part due to the growing transformation of healthcare as a commodity marketed through profit-driven advertising. Pregnancy today initiates women as consumers into a process of becoming collaborative designers of the desired object of consumption, the ideal birth (Rutherford & Gallo-Cruz, 2008). As contemporary hospitals have been increasingly affected by profit motives, they have responded by tailoring maternity and birth services to appeal to consumer preferences for birth as an experiential commodity that can build a solid consumer base for hospital-based medical services. Therefore, in addition to broader cultural shifts regarding gender roles and sexuality, the consolidation of medical authority and expertise by physicians, and the expansion of medical technology, the pressures of commodification and consumer movements are also pivotal for understanding contemporary birthing practices.

In many ways, the contemporary scene of childbirth services can be characterized as one of cyclical rationalization, re-enchantment, and rationalization. In the first half of the 20th century, childbirth was subject to intense rationalization and birth was culturally transformed from a potentially risky event to a pathogen-like state to be medically managed and controlled. In the "technocratic" model of birth developed in hospitals, birth was understood according to an industrial paradigm, in which the mother's body, machine-like, produces a baby (Rothman, 1991; Davis-Floyd, 2003; Simonds, Rothman, & Norman, 2007). Hospital deliveries in this technocratic model reflect the modern impetus toward rationalization, with its drive toward efficiency, calculability, predictability, technology, and control (Ritzer, 1996). As is often the case, rationalization came with dehumanizing consequences – for example, the routine inclusion of pubic shaving, enemas, "sterile" draping, physical restraints, episiotomies, and sedation in hospital procedures, as well as the exclusion of familiar people from the delivery room and the separation of mother and baby following birth. The birth experience was stripped of many of its subjective qualities. Not only was a woman's sensual experience of birth diminished through the use of drugs and anesthesia promising to reduce pain, but so, too, was her sense that her own experience of giving birth was unique and singularly important. Moreover, a techno-scientific approach to birth often denied – and at the least downplayed – the sense of mystery, spirituality, and aesthetic beauty that have accompanied childbirth throughout most of human history. Scientific rationalization, in Weber's (1946) words, meant that the birth experience was "disenchanted."

This rationalization, or disenchantment, of birth is a feature of modernity. Along with other existential experiences that threaten to disturb the abstract systems by which modern life is organized, birth has become sequestered from the day-to-day experience of life (Giddens, 1991). However, the natural birth movement attempts to re-enchant birth by allowing nature – unpredictable and uncontrollable – to have free reign and by recapturing the subjective experience of birth with its sensuality and mystery. This is most clearly seen in the emphasis by homebirth advocates on the spiritual and/or symbolic meaning of birth (Klassen, 2001). But it is also seen in the emphasis on both the birthing mother's individual empowerment as well as the importance of birth being a shared family experience, as these themes reassert the power of human autonomy and interpersonal connection over the dehumanizing aspects of birth in the technocratic model.

In the final decades of the 20th century, the natural birth movement created overwhelming consumer demand that hospitals adapt their procedures to assist women in achieving an individualized ideal birth experience that included a renewed sense of enchantment. Hospitals responded to this demand with several significant adaptations resulting in maternity care that is packaged simultaneously as "humanized" and commodified. In this chapter, we briefly outline the history of childbirth in the United States and offer an analysis of how the natural birth movement as a consumer movement has influenced the marketing of hospital maternity care. Drawing on qualitative content analysis of 59 hospital websites, we illustrate the idealization of childbirth as an experience that involves both physical and social dimensions and analyze how Internet advertising has incorporated both of these dimensions into hospital promotions. Our analysis reveals that the natural birth movement has been successful in infusing rhetoric about the social and symbolic aspects of labor into the institutionalized approach to labor services. However, our examination also points to tensions inherent between a rationalized medical approach and the re-enchantment of birth that illustrate a cycle of rationalization, re-enchantment, and further rationalization.

MEDICALIZATION, CONSUMERISM, AND NATURAL BIRTH

In the colonial era, childbirth in America was an entirely female affair and offered an opportunity for building female solidarity among community members (Wertz & Wertz, 1989). However, birth was a potentially risky event and it was not uncommon for women or babies to die in childbirth. For primary assistance women turned to midwives, the community specialists in birth. Because birth was understood as an activity subject to nature and divine will, in which the birthing mother was the object of forces beyond her own control, the midwife was also typically seen as a guardian of the mysterious aspects of the unknown (Gillis, 1997). Gradually, during the 19th century, cultural beliefs shifted from the dominance of magic and providence toward an enthusiasm for reason, scientific training, and technology; during this time, doctors rose in social status and professional prestige from inexperienced, irregular, and risky caregivers to established, legitimized authorities on all things related to health, beginning with birth (Edwards & Waldorf, 1984; Sullivan & Weitz, 1988; Wertz & Wertz, 1989; Rothman, 1991; Davis-Floyd, 2003). This shift in cultural beliefs accompanied the professionalization of medicine as a sphere of male dominance.

Women, already deterred from doctoral training because of social norms of female behavior, were also excluded because of the sharply rising fees for medical school and blatant discrimination in admission (Ehrenreich & English, 2005).

The medicalization of birth relied as heavily on political and economic maneuvering as it did upon technical advances in medical practice. The formation of the American Medical Association (AMA) (in large part as an organized campaign against lay healers, midwives, and homeopaths) helped to eradicate midwifery in America and secure the position of male physicians as primary health care providers (Dye, 1986; Sullivan & Weitz, 1988). Beginning with a rhetorical campaign that characterized midwives as dirty, ignorant, incompetent, and un-American, medical spokesmen convinced the public that midwifery blocked the way of scientific progress and hampered the assimilation of immigrants (Ehrenreich & English, 2005). Enlisting the cooperation of states and the federal government, the AMA lobbied for strict regulation and licensing requirements for medical practice, the legal prohibition of midwifery practice, and the expansion of free public hospitals in which physicians and medical students would care for the urban poor. Urban hospitals ensured a steady stream of clinical research subjects for medical interns and obstetric surgeons, eventually leading to advances in the obstetric techniques and technologies of assisting birth (Dye, 1986; Leavitt, 1986). By the 1930s, the AMA had largely succeeded in its campaign to see midwifery outlawed, except in some rural areas and immigrant enclaves, and during the rest of the 20th century the medicalization of American birth proceeded full force.

By the early 20th century, the localization of patients in hospitals had allowed doctors to standardize their services, and the optimism that birth could be efficiently controlled in the hospital opened the door to the consumerism of birth. Maternity hospitals and obstetricians began to attract wealthy and middle-class women by advertising safety, convenience, comfort, and service in their newly designed maternity suites (Wertz & Wertz, 1989). The hospital eventually became the preferred locale for labor for all women: in 1900 more than 95% of women birthed at home, but by 1940, more than half of all births occurred in hospitals, a percentage which grew rapidly following World War II and then more gradually until 1970, when 99.4% of births occurred in hospitals (Wertz & Wertz, 1989; Mathews & Zakak, 1997; Rooks, 1997). The new hospital consumers were particularly interested in the possibility of giving birth without pain: after the introduction of scopolamine as an amnesiac relieving women from the pain and trauma of labor and delivery, consumer demand for pain-free birth won out over some physicians' reservations about its use (Mathews & Zakak, 1997). Later, "twilight sleep" became ubiquitous medical practice, but it liberated women not only from pain but also from the memory of labor and birth, a part of the experience women would soon deem valuable. No longer active birthing agents but passive patients to be delivered, women were vulnerable to the control of medical authority – typically represented by the male physician – over this important moment of life change and self-definition. Furthermore, freedom from pain in childbirth ushered in a collective scrutiny and reflection on the symbolic experience of birth and a consumer movement toward greater pleasure in the birth experience (Sandelowski, 1984).

The natural birth movement arose in the mid-20th century in response to this social vulnerability and collective reflection. Dissatisfaction with the technocratic model of childbirth began as early as the 1940s, coinciding with the rapid increase of hospital births following World War II (Mathews & Zakak, 1997). In 1947, the Maternity Center Association, a national not-for-profit organization to improve the quality of maternity care, organized a forum on prepared childbirth featuring a series of lectures by Dr Grantly Dick-Read (1944) throughout the United States, popularizing the natural childbirth relaxation techniques outlined in his book *Childbirth Without Fear*. In 1956 La Leche League formed, a traditionalist organization that embraced the "natural feminine" roles supported in Dick-Read's natural birth philosophy, and advocated a return to nature in childbirth, infant feeding, and in women's feminine role as the nurturing mother. A new technique to achieve relaxation through breathing and concentration exercises designed by Dr Ferdinand Lamaze of France was introduced by Marjorie Karmel (1959) in *Thank You, Dr. Lamaze* and women began to experiment (again) with drug-free conscious birthing. Also during this period new mothers began writing to women's journals, describing their traumatic birth experiences, such as one continuous op-ed discussion in the *Ladies Home Journal* that lasted nearly one year between 1955 and 1956 (Wertz & Wertz, 1989). This provoked a dialogue with nurses and doctors over the ethics of standard maternity ward protocol and patients' demands for improved labor care. The medical industry responded to the groundswell of discontents over the use of heavy sedatives during birth by making greater efforts to offer medically managed but conscious births which were also pain-free. By the late 1960s some hospitals began to offer a spinal epidural during first and second stages of labor (Rooks, 2000).

During the late 1960s and the 1970s the natural birth movement gained momentum from two larger movements that also focused on the issue of paternalistic control and decision-making – the feminist movement and the consumer movement in healthcare (Mathews & Zakak, 1997). The burgeoning consumer movement in healthcare was characterized by a broad social structural shift in the dynamics of the doctor–patient relationship in which patients were re-cast as consumers who shop around for doctors who are responsive to patients' demands for a more participatory role in healthcare decisions (Reeder, 1972). Feminist birth advocates such as Lester Hazell, co-founder of the International Childbirth Education Association (ICEA), promoted women's education about birth in order that they could become active and responsible participants in the process. More radical feminists supported a new movement of midwifery and homebirth, arguing that the reclamation of birth from the control of male doctors could be achieved through the wisdom of women, and woman-initiated childbirth education spread across the country. Women not only informed themselves about their health and bodies in these classes but were exposed to new ideas about what they should be entitled to in their childbirth experience (Kushner, 2005). They began to request changes in hospital procedures, most notably demanding that fathers be allowed to be present during labor and delivery (Apple, 2006).

By the late 1970s, natural birth had become a catchphrase of the pregnant female consumer, signifying the optimal, feminine, healthy, and sometimes spiritual experience that she hoped to achieve during her labor and delivery. The movement drew from not one, but three overlapping ideologies of birth: a traditionalist ideology that emphasizes a woman's femininity and role within the family, a feminist ideology that emphasizes a woman's autonomy and personal fulfillment, and a more mainstream medical ideology that incorporates consumer demand for a more humane and less interventionist style of birth. The consumerist thrust of this movement emphasizes women's autonomy in the decision-making process and throughout her labor and delivery, moving women to shop around for the services that meet their demands and to hold providers accountable to their desires for the ideal birth. Although some traditionalists and feminists have revived the practice of midwifery, out-of-hospital births remain marginal, constituting less than 2% of US births (Rooks, 1997). Therefore, the transformation of in-hospital birth remains the primary target for natural birth movement leaders, consumer advocacy groups, and the majority of childbearing women who seek to influence maternity policy and practice. Organizations like Citizens for Midwifery work to expand the legal mandate of midwives, most of whom practice within the hospital setting, while also educating birthing consumers about birth alternatives and the "midwifery model of care."

More than 50 smaller local organizations banded together to form the Coalition for the Improvement of Maternity Services which works to promote the "mother friendly childbirth initiative," a 10-point certification providers and institutions can attain through espousing the ideals of natural birth, informed choice, and availability of alternatives and resources. Additionally, self-help books and consumer websites abound that educate women about the many options available for childbirth and guide them to identify their personal preferences for giving birth.

In response to the growing demands of expectant parents for new accommodations, hospitals have incorporated some of the ideals of natural birth in their procedures and repackaged their services to appeal more to consumer desires. Maternity care is currently the greatest footing that most hospitals hold in the community healthcare market. Childbirth is the most common reason for hospitalization, bringing in four times more patients than any other procedure. Charges related to labor, delivery, and postpartum care of mothers and infants constitute a significant revenue stream for hospitals: four of the top 10 most expensive charges are for delivery and newborn complications, which average $90,000 per stay, and one out of every four discharges for privately insured patients relates to pregnancy, delivery, or postpartum complications (Merril & Elixhauser, 2002, 2003). Effective marketing has therefore become essential in the increased market orientation of hospital care (Scott, Ruef, Mendel, & Caronna, 2000), evident in renovations of new luxury family maternity centers (the term "wards" having been shed long ago) and aesthetically pleasing and user-friendly web catalogs of those services, now a significant representation of the hospital's public image and policies. Of course, such marketing assumes that women have the ability to freely exercise consumer choice, an accurate assumption only when targeting middle class or wealthy women and those with adequate health insurance.

SELLING BIRTH: A THEMATIC ANALYSIS OF CHILDBIRTH MARKETING

In *The Language of Advertising*, Vestergaard and Schrøder (1985) argue that through advertising, objects of consumption are semanticized into a language that carries signifiers of imagined identity, symbolic codes of what kind of people marketers perceive consumers to be or what kind of experiences they desire. Through a content analysis of maternity center advertisements, we assess the language providers utilize in marketing their services. Our analysis reveals how hospitals as institutions have responded to consumer demands in birthing. While we cannot empirically account for how services are actually delivered through ad analysis, advertisements illustrate the socially idealized experience of birth – what providers collectively identify as the standard criteria that should define a good birth experience. Because the data we analyze are a public discourse about the ideal birth providers claim to offer, our analysis aims to reveal the normative social conceptions of what should occur as other sociological studies of discourse have done (Wuthnow, 1989; Swidler, 2003; Zavisca, 2005). We postulate the relationship between the natural birth movement and contemporary mainstream providers, and therefore compare hospitals' treatment of the scientifically framed physical aspects of birth with the symbolically imbued social aspects of the birth experience (Miles & Huberman, 1984). In our comparison, we reveal how these themes are idealized and articulated, which aspects hospitals emphasize most, and which they neglect or struggle to articulate.

As evidenced by other chapters in this volume, the Internet has become an important site for constructing the role of medical consumers: as a source of health information (Sulik & Eich-Krohm, 2008), as a marketplace for commodities (Holster, 2008), as a site for networking and mutual support among patients (Greenspan & Handy, 2008), and as a vehicle for health policy activism (Ganchoff, 2008). Many hospital websites incorporate several of these purposes, combining online resources for existing patients, consumer-targeted advertising, and links to community services and health information. Our study constructs a discursive sample of maternity care advertising across the United States including hospital websites from every geographic region of the nation, based on a theoretically driven selection of qualitative data (Lofland, Snow, Anderson, & Lofland, 2005). We first targeted several geographic regions covering a diverse range of major urban and rural, private and community hospitals across the United States, allowing us to compare advertisements regionally and economically (Best & Krueger, 2004). Web pages were accessed online as consumers would access them through the most widely used search engine, Google (Sullivan, 2006; Nielsen Online, 2008), using the search term "maternity care" with the selected city or region name. Then, the most frequently accessed sites listed in order of access frequency were selected. We intentionally included more hospitals in highly populated urban centers as well as hospitals that catered to middle and upper-middle class patients, based on the assumption that women who have more consumer choices will be more inclined to shop around (Lupton, 1997). This method of selection yielded 59 sites as cases for analysis. Although our analysis does not claim to track actual consumer use of the Internet for selecting maternity care, it does recognize that consumers' options are both geographically and economically constrained and highlights the significance that hospitals place on the presentation of their services when communicating with potential consumers.

We combined deductive and inductive approaches to coding all text and images from the websites. We began with open and axial coding and progressed to selective coding to allow for themes to emerge from the data while systematically linking them with the principal variables we hypothesized (Miles & Huberman, 1984). From the literature describing the transformations of mainstream maternity care in response to the natural birth movement, we expected to find that hospitals advertised social as well as physical attributes of the birth experience. We also expected some particular themes to be present in maternity center ads, those that addressed the option to birth naturally and new amenities attractive to the modern birthing consumer. We began coding with two initial categories, physical and social labor, and thoroughly coded the data by openly assigning descriptive codes. From open coding we moved into axial coding sorting emergent themes as they related to our original concepts. We then refined our coding scheme by selectively linking significant themes under the two main variables, physical and social labor, and under three sub-variables in each major category. Through an iterative and collaborative process of code analysis we worked toward inter-coder reliability and used the constant comparative method to comprehensively and systematically analyze the data, with the assistance of qualitative analysis software, MAXqda.

Our results show that the advertised image of the ideal birth experience consists of both physical and social aspects of labor and delivery. Fifty-seven percent of the content coded dealt with physical aspects, while 43% dealt with social aspects. On the physical side, the ideal birth experience is represented through claims of safety, a pleasing environment, and the effective management of pain and anxiety. On the social side, the ideal birth experience entails attention to relational bonds, a sense of individual empowerment, and acknowledgement of the symbolic meaning of birth. A brief description of how each of these themes is manifested in web-based advertising follows.

Physical Labor

Safety

Safety is a key selling point in marketing birth services to consumers, and hospitals devote more space to this theme than any other. Over one-third of all coded content (36%) addressed ideas relating to safety. For hospitals, safety is most often emphasized through touting the "state-of the art" technologies available, the specialized medical training and expertise of providers, the hospital's affiliations and accreditation, and the availability of neonatal intensive care units. Safety as a selling point always keeps one eye on the risks of childbirth and the possibility of complications, with prominent use of phrases such as "unfortunately, emergent situations can occur during the birthing process" (St. Peter's Hospital, 2007), "we are prepared to handle any complication that may arise"(Allina Hospitals and Clinics, 2007), and "it's comforting to know we have a Level II perinatal nursery just in case special treatment is needed" (Middletown Regional Hospital, 2007).

Extending their reach beyond delivery, hospitals also adopt safety as an advertising point in their prenatal education classes, when discussing newborn health screenings, and in describing the role of education in postpartum nursing care. Most hospitals offer some form of prenatal education classes in infant care and/or infant safety. Typical topics covered in such classes range from "picking up, holding and carrying your baby; dressing and swaddling; diapering; feeding and burping; taking temperatures; bathing" (North Austin Medical Center, 2007) to "CPR and choke-saving skills" as well as "childproofing your home; product, fire and water safety; home safety supplies; poison prevention; how to choose and use a car seat; and toy safety" (Newton-Wellesley Hospital, 2007). The message is clear – trained hospital personnel are the experts in safe baby care, and parents who want to properly care for their newborn infants must listen to their guidance and instruction.

Environment

Sixteen percent of coded content describes or depicts the hospital's physical environment, advertising the physical setting and ambiance in which birth is to take place. Hospitals often market their birthing suites and postpartum rooms as spacious, luxurious, attractive, warm, private, comfortable, or home-like. Care is taken to point out the convenient design of Labor-Delivery-Recover Suites (LDRs), the convenient location of waiting rooms for family and friends, as well as the convenient location of the hospital. Hospital websites advertising maternity services often resemble hotel or retreat center advertisements, with advertised amenities offered to maternity patients including Jacuzzi bathtubs, valet parking, entertainment systems, and wireless Internet access. Online tours allow women to virtually explore their potential birth environment including the stylishly decorated rooms, as well as the bathrooms, hallways, waiting rooms, and registration stations.

Pain and Anxiety Management

The third component of physical labor discussed on hospital websites is pain and anxiety management, making up 5% of the coded content. While hospitals often mention their 24-hour on-call anesthesiologists and the availability of other pain-relieving medications, they also devote a great deal of attention to discussing alternative pain-relieving therapies and comfort measures, addressing both the need for relaxation and freedom from anxiety. Services such as massage or water immersion are mentioned, and some hospitals offer aromatherapy, soft-lighting in the birthing room, and relaxation CDs, as well as stressing the helpfulness of walking, changing positions and using a birthing ball to tolerate contractions. They discuss the experience they offer as one that will be "relaxing" and "worry-free" and emphasize that under their care, mom can have "peace of mind." Many hospitals offer natural birth classes that prepare women and partners with relaxation and massage techniques and some are now offering "hypnobirthing" classes, a method of relaxation enhanced through hypnosis techniques. Frequently giving equal attention on their websites to both medical and non-medical approaches, hospitals take care to assure potential consumers that a range of pain-relief measures is available for their choice.

Social Labor

Relational Connection

Twenty percent of the coded hospital website content addresses the relational connections formed and strengthened in the birth experience. Much of this content portrays hospital birth as a "family-centered" experience. Hospitals describe the importance of the inclusion of family members and loved ones at the birth experience and the benefits to be gained from having a support person throughout the labor. They also draw attention to relational bonds beyond the family by discussing health professionals' own vocations of care, offering links to a new community of families, and employing the rhetoric of community wellness. Through their ads, hospitals convey the message that the ideal birth experience they offer is one which can facilitate the establishment of new social connections or the expansion and deepening of preexisting ties.

Some of the most notable changes that hospitals have made in response to the natural birth movement's demands for a more humanized birth experience have been in the area of their increased attention to the relational importance of birth. By including fathers, partners, or other support persons in delivery rooms and by redesigning postpartum care to keep babies with mothers and to allow fathers to stay overnight, hospitals at least partially recognize birth as a familial event. (At most hospitals extended family members and children are still only welcome after delivery and during visiting hours.) Hospitals also go beyond the physical location to recognize relational connections through their online virtual nurseries that allow extended family members secure but nearly immediate access to photographs of the newborn. They also emphasize that visitors and friends are welcome within the timeframes indicated by hospital policy and point to the convenient accommodations of waiting rooms and coffee shops available for visitors.

Individual Empowerment

A second social aspect of birth is the attention given to the theme of individual empowerment, making up 18% of the coded content. The hallmark of consumerism in childbirth is the freedom of the modern woman to shop around for providers, settings, and protocol that she "chooses" in the creation of her ideal childbirth experience.[1] Attention to individual empowerment appears in the rhetoric of individualized birth plans and personalized experiences. For example,

> Central Baptist Hospital's obstetrical staff will work closely with you to personalize your childbirth experience. We want your delivery to be as unique as the package. Options may be discussed with your individual practitioner. We are very receptive to new ideas and innovations in labor and delivery concepts. (Central Baptist Hospital, 2007)

Often, though, these statements are followed by gentle reminders of the parameters of freedom, as in, "We believe in the patient's right to make decisions and will strive to make every attempt to meet the needs and expectations of patients *provided they do not compromise patient safety*" (St. Vincent Health Center, 2007, emphasis added).

Because the patient's autonomy is tightly constrained by institutional procedures and guidelines, offering transparency of process and knowledge and information is often the biggest claim that hospitals make for individual empowerment. On their maternity websites, hospitals reveal the steps of the process a woman will go through upon registration, examination, who will be present in her room during labor and after the birth, what interventions she may be asked to agree to, what procedures may ensue in the case if an emergency, and who may come in to conduct newborn screenings and examinations. They remind mother/patients that they "have the right to ask questions" throughout the process as well as to inquire what procedures nurses assigned to care for their babies will perform. In this way, women can be informed, even if not in control.

Symbolic Meaning

The symbolic meaning of birth has been a cornerstone of the natural birth movement from the first wave of discontents against unconscious birth that collectively asked: "What is the meaning and the significance of giving birth?" The answers to this question have varied greatly as indicated by the fragmentation of different strains of the movement and varieties of response within each of those strains. Descriptions of birth on hospital websites are interlaced with references to the "miracle of birth," the sacredness of the rite of passage into parenthood, or even more generally that birth is a "special," "momentous," or "profound" occasion. These descriptions make up 5% of coded content, meaning that hospital websites devote roughly equal space to describing the symbolic meaning of birth as they do to discussing pain management during labor and delivery.

In responding to the popularity of birth practices infused with symbolism and aesthetic commemoration, hospitals have begun to offer (in a highly consumerist fashion) celebratory flourishes for the birth experience. Some bring "celebration of life meals" or "stork club meals" and birthday cake and balloons to the new baby and mother (for an additional fee, of course), and others play Brahms' lullaby over the hospital loudspeakers each time a baby is born. Parents may also commemorate by donating to one of the hospital's foundations and having their baby's name forever etched in a brick or on a wall somewhere on hospital grounds. Commemorative items, like first photo albums and framed footprints, are also available for purchase.

TENSIONS IN THE RATIONALIZATION AND RE-ENCHANTMENT OF BIRTH IN THE HOSPITAL

Hospital maternity ads reveal that, at least rhetorically, hospitals have taken great strides since the days of the isolated maternity wards where women were ushered into delivery alone, unconscious, and sanitized. However, inherent in the quest for more humane maternity care and the promises of an ideal birth experience that hospitals make today, several tensions between the rational organization of the hospital and the re-enchantment of childbirth arise. First, in responding to consumer desire for an environment that was less hospital-like, many hospitals completely redesigned entire floors or added semi-detached birth centers, in which an attractive and inviting environment was a key selling point. In some cases, hospital birth centers have become what George Ritzer calls "cathedrals of consumption": "they have an enchanted, sometimes even sacred, religious character for some people. In order to attract ever-larger numbers of consumers, such cathedrals of consumption need to offer or at least appear to offer, increasingly magical, fantastic, and enchanted settings in which to consume" (Ritzer, 1999, p. 8). Through manipulation of space and introduction of a sense of spectacle, cathedrals of consumption offer a sense of transcendence and a façade of personalization to rationalized, homogenizing institutions. An example of the transformation of the hospital to a cathedral of consumption is DeKalb Medical Center's new freestanding birth center, connected to the main hospital by two aboveground, glassed-in walkways called "skybridges." In a promotional video on its website, DeKalb advertises the enchantment of its new space:

> Featuring classical architecture and a dramatic two-story lobby, this stunning facility offers the most clinically advanced maternity facilities along with special amenities to pamper new mothers and their babies ... The grand lobby features natural light, a garden, soothing colors, stacked stone accents, cozy fireplaces, and upscale, comfortable furnishings. Our inviting bistro will serve delicious fare in a relaxing, sidewalk café atmosphere ... With its state of the art facilities, beautiful surroundings, and highly qualified and compassionate staff, the new women's center ... offers the next generation of mothers a truly special place to experience the miracle of birth.

In describing their physical space in terms like these, hospitals are not only describing an appealing environment, but one that is designed to help parents achieve the ideal of an enchanted birth experience, reminding parents that they offer "a wonderful setting for this important time in your life" (DeKalb Medical Center, 2007). Thus, the hospital not only offers a setting in which parents can purchase the ideal birth experience; the hospital setting gives shape to that ideal: "The new means of consumption attract consumers not only because they are centralized locations where commodities can be purchased, but because they embody, give concrete form to, and even help to create the ideals and images that circulate within consumer culture" (Ritzer, Ryan, & Stepinsky, 2005, p. 294).

Despite all of the attention given to creating a setting for an enchanting experience, birth in the hospital setting is still highly rationalized. While an appealing setting is both a consumer good in itself and a space that allows for the birth experience to be commodified, the hospital environment clearly remains in service to the goal of safety, as measured with a scientific and technological calculus. Even while they are being sold an enchanted and enchanting setting, parents are reassured that rational science is in control – just behind those attractive panels are hidden away all of the technology that may be necessary in case of emergency: "Unfortunately, emergent situations can occur during the birthing process. Whether the emergency pertains to the mother or the baby, all immediately needed supportive equipment and supplies are available in the LDRPN suite, hidden behind whitewashed oak walls, easily accessible on all occasions" (St. Peter's Hospital). This is a tension inherent in all of the contemporary cathedrals of consumption, from malls to cruise ships to engineered town centers: even as they create spaces in which consumers can find or construct personal and symbolic meaning or emphasize the communal and non-monetary value of an experience, the activities that occur in such spaces are always dependent upon the modern logic of rationalization, a logic that is tied to the larger project of global capitalism (Ritzer et al., 2005, p. 294). In the case of hospital birth centers as spaces of consumption, the logic of rationalization is also tied to the larger project of modern science and medical technology, and the advertised birth experience is always subject to the quality control measure of safety.

A second notable tension apparent in the response of hospitals to consumer demand for a less thoroughly rationalized birth experience is in the arena of individual empowerment. Two key aspects of the individual empowerment theme – prenatal education and birth plans – reveal the tensions that hospitals face in balancing the standardized rationality of a complex, bureaucratic organization with the demands of its consumers for greater individuality and personalized control.

Most hospitals offer prenatal classes focused on prepared or natural childbirth, and many offer hypnobirthing, prenatal yoga, and exercise classes, in addition to an array of workshops on family preparation and infant care. However, in-depth empirical analysis of these classes reveals that there is more to them than the empowering rhetoric that meets the consumer's eye. In her ethnographic study of prenatal preparation, Elizabeth Armstrong (2000) concludes that hospital-provided prenatal education often serves institutional needs for patient compliance rather than empowering women to be active participants in decision-making.

Her empirical observations reveal that childbirth education serves primarily to prepare women to expect and comply with hospital regulations and procedures without complaining. Rothman also argues that through the adoption of numerous prenatal classes by hospitals, "the goal of a 'natural' childbirth has been replaced by the goal of a 'prepared' childbirth" (1991, p. 31).

Although the practice of writing a birth plan began as a way for women to assert their own autonomy and exercise control over their birthing, as hospitals adapted to consumer demands for including birth plans, the plans have become increasingly rationalized, until they, too, primarily serve the bureaucratic interests of the institution. Printed, menu-like birth plans offered by many hospitals, in which women simply mark what options they want, serve as symbols of consumerism that give the appearance of choice within a very narrow frame. An example is Maine Medical Center's Birthplan Guide, a two-page questionnaire with room at the top of each page for a bar code and patient name label: "Listed below are some options that you may utilize at The Family Birth Center. Please check those that you would like to try during your birth experience." On the first page, birth care plan options are listed under the headings "relaxation techniques," "movement," "family/support in labor," "touch," "warmth/cool," and "medication/anesthesia pain management" with a space for checking those that are desired. The second page contains a baby care plan with similar menu-style items regarding newborn care and feeding and a space for indicating which childbirth preparation classes the patient has attended. The question, "Do you have any disabilities or special needs for which we will need to make accommodations?" is followed by a single line in which to write an answer (Maine Medical Center, 2007). There is very little room provided for writing in anything that is not already listed on the form, and there is effectively no space for open-ended instructions or comments regarding the birth plan.

Kitzinger's (2005) analysis describes how printed birth plans use several strategies to minimize women's input on these forms. These include framing choices as very limited and trivial, providing very little space in which to record independent wishes, marginalizing certain preferences as abnormal, using birth plans primarily as a means of "reassuring" the patient, presenting options in such a way that the response is a foregone conclusion, and using emotional blackmail by implying that alternative choices may endanger the baby. When hospitals do encourage women to be active in making decisions, they frequently include strategic reminders that these decisions must be made in cooperation with hospital personnel and policies.

For example, Emory's Crawford-Long Hospital advises that "Visitation in the labor and delivery suite is decided by you – the laboring woman, your physician or midwife and your primary nurse during labor"(Emory Health Care, 2007).

The actual nature of the choices being offered to and made by patient-consumers is a recurrent theme in several chapters of this volume. Echoing the concerns raised by Sulik and Eich-Krohm (2008) and Fisher and Ronald (2008), our analysis of maternity advertising reveals that although hospitals employ the rhetoric of empowerment, choice, and informed consent, this rhetoric does not alter existing protocols and may even promote the more strategic goal of patient compliance. Bourgeault et al. (2008) raise the serious question of whether Maternal Request Caesarean Sections – procedures that are popularly framed in North American medical discourse as resulting primarily from consumer choice – are in reality a result of patient compliance with current obstetric protocols and the power of physician suggestion, rather than true "choices" on the part of expectant mothers. Although it may be tempting to attribute this control and standardization of birth to obstetric practice and point toward the patriarchal control of women by (male) physicians, Kitzinger (2005) finds that even midwives practicing in hospitals are skilled in using the rhetoric of choice to convince mothers to conform to the midwives' wishes. The rationalization of birth is not just a feature of the medical approach to birth; rather it is a feature of hospitalized birth. Even when hospitals respond to consumer pressures for a more idealized birth experience, these preferences are met within the context of a bureaucratic organization that requires a highly standardized and rationalized approach.

A third area of tension lies in the simultaneous pressures to make health care profitable and to make it responsive to community health needs, which Shortell, Gillies, & Devers (1995) argue has become vital to the hospital's survival as a dominant health care institution. In the early 1990s, US hospitals experienced a general trend in cost-shifting as for-profit hospitals' profit margins began to soar above non-profits' margins. The pressure to preserve the bottom line is nevertheless felt by all hospitals, and in response to the reduction of investment by public agencies, hospitals have raised the prices of services to privately insured patients at whom online ads are aimed (Weisbrod, 1998). However, shifts in the institutional logics of marketing maternity care also reflect a transformation in the cultural norms governing the health care industry. In an environment of increasing public attention to rising health care costs and awareness of holistic alternatives to mainstream healthcare, the community needs model of health care management represents a paradigm shift toward recognizing the relational connections between health care providers and patients as well as constructing the hospital as an institutional foundation for civil society. Emphasis on the hospital as the locus of family health services, beginning with maternity services, aids in the management of the hospital's image as a community-needs driven institution which caters to the demands of the new consumer model that emphasizes patient empowerment and family integration. With childbirth services representing a critical source of revenue for meeting the rationalized demands of an economic bottom line, hospitals are ever more eager to appeal to consumers with a birth experience that constitutes part of a re-enchantment of the hospital's role as a community-building institution.

CONCLUSION

Ultimately, both providers and consumers have responded to the natural birth movement by expanding the concept of natural birth to be defined in a variety of ways, ranging from an entirely drug-free birth, to birth without epidural anesthesia, to simply meaning any vaginal birth.

As a consumer movement, natural birth has transformed the idealized birth experience itself into a commodity for both patient-consumers and attendant-providers. The natural birth movement is suffused with the notion that birth can become the medium for achieving one's feminine ideal if it is experienced in a way and environment that optimize a woman's autonomy and allow her to express her feminine nature (Rutherford & Gallo-Cruz, 2008). As an idea that has permeated medical institutions for nearly half a century, natural birth has been contested and redefined; yet "natural birth" continues to stand as a value against which other forms of childbirth are judged. In this social context hospitals must market their services by appealing to the consumer's image of an idealized birth experience.

Lupton (1997) suggests a nuanced approach to understanding consumerism in healthcare, one that will account for both the individual agency possible through "shopping around" for providers and services and the need for care and the vulnerability this entails. Similar to illness, the physical state a woman passes through in labor and birth and her need for care in that state means that childbirth is a commodity which places the consumer in a position of vulnerability and greater physical need than the provider. In contrast to many states of disease, pregnancy is a temporary condition and is often assumed to be a "choice"; it is also a critical transformational experience that marks a significant life transition. In addition to its temporary and chosen nature, pregnancy is becoming less frequent: consumers who have, on average, only two births may have little reason to actively invest in social change in birthing practices after their birth experience ends. Therefore, providers – not consumers – may be most likely to contribute the time and resources necessary to effect changes in practice. Nonetheless, it is clear that consumers remain significant to changes in birth practices as providers attempt to appeal to consumers' idealizations of the health care experience.

Even as birth has become less frequent, it has become all the more invested with emotional weight. Current practices reflect the consumerist ethos by describing birth as an idealized experience of epic proportions. Our study reveals that on one hand, this ethos of consumption reflects the idealization of the individual, in which birth becomes one more celebration of "having it your way," where the birthing mother is the star of the show. On the other hand, hospitals must increasingly compete in a highly rationalized market economy while maintaining their promise to "re-humanize" the birth experience with a sense of social bonding. As in all forms of healthcare, this personalization of care ultimately increases the value of the birth experience, both in terms of its use value for the individual and its exchange value in the market (Zelizer, 2005). With this increased value comes greater pressure for hospitals to compete in attracting patients.

Our analysis of advertisements is strictly limited to the rhetoric of idealized services hospitals claim to offer. Further study could elucidate how far beyond the marketing department the ideals of natural birth travel. An ethnographic account of nurse and physician attitudes that takes into account their interaction with patients might articulate the boundaries and limits of the natural birth ideal and the social structural constraints of delivering these services in a hospital maternity center. Nonetheless, the current analysis reveals how the ideals of the natural birth movement have been influential in the repackaging of hospital services to satisfy expectant consumer desires. As a consumer movement, the natural birth movement has also been effective in transforming protocol and policy to a certain degree in its introduction of alternatives that are economically viable, widely available, rationally organized, and increasingly culturally legitimate. These changes are evident in the presence of nurse-midwives on staff, the availability of alternative pain-relief remedies, the inclusion of fathers and family members of friends in celebration of the birth, the option of rooming-in with the baby, and the growing presence of lactation consultants and natural birth educators. Just as hospitals lured patient/consumers in through advertisements of plush, luxurious birthing suites over 100 years ago, online maternity sites continue to try to dazzle potential consumers with florid descriptions of the ideal birth experience they claim to offer. The experience of childbirth has become an object of technological innovation and scientific calculation on one hand, and on the other has been the object of processes of re-enchantment that infuse it with symbolic meaning and moral import.

NOTE

1. Again, in constructing this model consumer, both hospitals and natural birth advocates have frequently ignored poor women, as well as recent immigrants and women of color. It is likely that our analysis of online advertising further increases the appearance of marketing primarily to those with means to choose, since this form of promotion is intended for those with access to computers and the Internet.

ACKNOWLEDGMENTS

We wish to thank Susan Chambré, Melinda Goldner, and Phillip Fuerst for their helpful advice and comments, as well as Sanja Jagesic for her capable assistance.

REFERENCES

Allina Hospitals and Clinics. (2007). Available at http://www.abbottnorthwestern.com/ahs/anw.nsf/page/bc_home

Apple, R. D. (2006). *Perfect motherhood: Science and childrearing in America.* New Brunswick, NJ: Rutgers University Press.

Armstrong, E. M. (2000). Lessons in control: Prenatal education in the hospital. *Social Problems, 47*, 583–605.

Best, S. J., & Krueger, B. S. (2004). *Internet data collection.* Thousand Oaks: Sage Publications.

Bourgeault, I. L., Declercq, E., Sandall, J., Wrede, S., Vanstone, M., van Teijlingen, E., DeVries, R., & Benoit, C. (2008). Too Posh To Push? Comparative perspectives on maternal request caesarean sections in Canada, the US, the UK and Finland. In: S. Chambré & M. Goldner (Eds), *Advances in medical sociology: Patients, consumers and civil society* (pp. 99–123). Bingley, UK: Emerald Group Publishing Limited.

Central Baptist Hospital. (2007). Available at http://www.centralbap.com/hospitalservices/women-children/ob/care.cfm

Davis-Floyd, R. (2003). *Birth as an American rite of passage.* Berkeley: University of California Press.

DeKalb Medical Center. (2007). Available at http://www.dekalbmedicalcenter.org/maps.asp?location = central

Dick-Read, G. (1944). *Childbirth without fear*. New York: Harper and Brothers.

Dye, N. S. (1986). Medicalization of birth. In: P. S. Eakins (Ed.), *The American way of birth* (pp. 21–46). Philadelphia: Temple University Press.

Edwards, M., & Waldorf, M. (1984). *Reclaiming birth: History and heroines of America's childbirth reform*. New York: The Crossing Press.

Ehrenreich, B., & English, D. (2005). *For her own good: Two centuries of the experts' advice to women*. Garden City, NY: Anchor.

Emory Health Care. (2007). Available at http://www.emoryhealthcare.org/departments/maternity_center/patient_info/Maternity_Center_Tour.html

Fisher, J. A., & Ronald, L. M. (2008). Direct to consumer responsibility: Medical neoliberalism in pharmaceutical advertising and drug development. In: S. Chambré & M. Goldner (Eds), *Advances in medical sociology: Patients, consumers and civil society* (pp. 29–51). Bingley, UK: Emerald Group Publishing Limited.

Ganchoff, C. (2008). Speaking for stem cells: Biomedical activism and emerging forms of patienthood. In: S. Chambré & M. Goldner (Eds), *Advances in medical sociology: Patients, consumers and civil society* (pp. 225–245). Bingley, UK: Emerald Group Publishing Limited.

Giddens, A. (1991). *Modernity and self-identity*. Stanford, CA: Stanford University Press.

Gillis, J. R. (1997). *A world of their own making: Myth, ritual, and the quest for family values*. Cambridge, MA: Harvard University Press.

Greenspan, I., & Handy, F. (2008). From discovery to recovery and beyond: The role of voluntary health sector organizations in the lives of women with breast cancer. In: S. Chambré & M. Goldner (Eds), *Advances in medical sociology: Patients, consumers and civil society* (pp. 151–176). Bingley, UK: Emerald Group Publishing Limited.

Holster, K. (2008). Making connections: Egg donation, the Internet, and the new reproductive technology marketplace. In: S. Chambré & M. Goldner (Eds), *Advances in medical sociology: Patients, consumers and civil society* (pp. 53–73). Bingley, UK: Emerald Group Publishing Limited.

Karmel, M. (1959). *Thank you, Dr. Lamaze, J. B.* Philadelphia: Lippincott.

Kitzinger, S. (2005). *The politics of birth*. Philadelphia: Elsevier.

Klassen, P. (2001). *Blessed events: Religion and home birth in America*. Princeton: Princeton University Press.

Kushner, L. (2005). The journey of an early Lamaze childbirth educator. *The Journal of Perinatal Education*, *14*(10), 22–29.

Leavitt, J. W. (1986). *Brought to bed: Childbearing in America, 1750–1950*. New York: Oxford University Press.

Lofland, J., Snow, D., Anderson, L., & Lofland, L. (2005). *Analyzing social settings: A guide to qualitative observation and analysis*. Belmont: Wadsworth.

Lupton, D. (1997). Consumerism, reflexivity, and the medical encounter. *Social Science Medicine*, *45*, 373–381.

Maine Medical Center. (2007). Available at http://www.mmc.org/mmc_body.cfm?id = 724

Mathews, J. J., & Zakak, K. (1997). The alternative birth movement in the United States: History and current status. In: R. D. Apple & J. Golden (Eds), *Mothers and motherhood: Readings in American history* (pp. 278–292). Columbus, OH: Ohio State University Press.

Merril, C. T., & Elixhauser, A. (2002). *Healthcare cost and utilization project: Hospitalization in the United States* (Vol. 6). Washington, DC: Agency for Healthcare Research and Quality.

Merril, C. T., & Elixhauser, A. (2003). *Healthcare cost and utilization project: Hospitalization in the United States* (Vol. 7). Washington, DC: Agency for Healthcare Research and Quality.

Middletown Regional Hospital. (2007). Available at http://www.middletownhospital.org/birth.htm

Miles, M. D., & Huberman, A. M. (1984). *Qualitative data analysis: A sourcebook of new methods*. Beverly Hills: Sage Publications.

Newton-Wellesley Hospital. (2007). Available at http://www.nwh.org/itemDetail.asp?categoryID = 410&itemID = 16490

Nielsen Online. (2008). Nielsen online reports topline us data for may 2008. Nielsen Online news release. Available at http://www.nielsen-netratings.com/pr/pr_080610.pdf

North Austin Medical Center. (2007). Available at http://northaustin.com/CustomPage.asp?guidCustomContentID = 56966CD8-1FDE-11D4-81D7-00508B1249D5

Reeder, L. G. (1972). The patient-client as consumer: Some observations in the changing professional client relationship. *Journal of Health and Social Behavior*, *13*(4), 406–412.

Ritzer, G. (1996). *The McDonaldization of society: An investigation into the changing character of contemporary social life*. Thousand Oaks, CA: Pine Forge.

Ritzer, G. (1999). *Enchanting a disenchanted world: Revolutionizing the means of consumption*. Thousand Oaks, CA: Pine Forge.

Ritzer, G., Ryan, M., & Stepinsky, J. (2005). Transformations in consumer settings: Landscapes and beyond. In: S. Ratneshwan & D. G. Mick (Eds), *Inside consumption: Perspectives on consumer motives, goals, and desires* (pp. 292–308). New York: Routledge.

Rooks, J. P. (1997). *Midwifery and childbirth in America*. Philadelphia: Temple University Press.

Rooks, J. P. (2000). Epidural analgesia as used during childbirth in the United States. *The Japanese Journal for Midwives*, *54*, 9–14.

Rothman, B. K. (1991). *In labor: Women and power in the birthplace*. New York: W. W. Norton.

Rutherford, M., & Gallo-Cruz, S. (2008). *Great expectations: Emotion as central to the experiential consumption of birth*. Boston, MA: American Sociological Association.

Sandelowski, M. (1984). *Pain, pleasure, and American childbirth: From twilight sleep to the read method, 1914–1960*. Westport, CN: Greenwood Press.

Scott, W., Ruef, M., Mendel, P. J., & Caronna, C. A. (2000). *Institutional change and healthcare organizations*. Chicago: University of Chicago Press.

Shortell, S. M., Gillies, R. R., & Devers, K. J. (1995). Reinventing the American hospital. *The Milbank Quarterly*, *73*(2), 131–160.

Simonds, W., Rothman, B. K., & Norman, B. M. (2007). *Laboring on: Birth in transition in the United States*. New York: Routledge.

St. Peter's Hospital. (2007). Available at http://www.stpetes.org/html/Services/familyobstetrics.php

St. Vincent Health Center. (2007). Available at https://www.stvincenthealth.com/women-children/index.html

Sulik, G. A., & Eich-Krohm, A. (2008). No longer a patient: The social construction of the medical consumer. In: S. Chambré & M. Goldner (Eds), *Advances in medical sociology: Patients, consumers and civil society* (pp. 1–28). Bingley, UK: Emerald Group Publishing Limited.

Sullivan, D. (2006). Nielsen netratings search engine ratings. Search Engine Watch. Available at http://searchenginewatch.com/showPage.html?page = 2156451

Sullivan, D. A., & Weitz, R. (1988). *Labor pains: Modern midwives and home birth*. New Haven: Yale University Press.

Swidler, A. (2003). *Talk of love: How culture matters*. Chicago: University of Chicago Press.

Vestergaard, T., & Schrøder, K. (1985). *The language of advertising*. New York: Basil Blackwell.

Weber, M. (1946). Science as a Vocation. In: H. H. Gerth & C. W. Mills (Eds), *From Max Weber: Essays in sociology* (pp. 129–156). New York: Oxford University Press.

Weisbrod, B. A. (1998). *To profit or not to profit*. Cambridge: Cambridge University Press.

Wertz, R. W., & Wertz, D. C. (1989). *Lying in: A history of childbirth in America*. New Haven: Yale University Press.

Wuthnow, R. (1989). *Meaning and moral order: Explorations in cultural analysis*. Berkeley: University of California Press.

Zavisca, J. (2005). The status of cultural omnivorism: A case study of reading in Russia. *Social Forces*, *84*(2), 1233–1255.

Zelizer, V. A. (2005). *The purchase of intimacy*. Princeton: Princeton University Press.

TOO POSH TO PUSH? COMPARATIVE PERSPECTIVES ON MATERNAL REQUEST CAESAREAN SECTIONS IN CANADA, THE US, THE UK AND FINLAND

Ivy Lynn Bourgeault, Eugene Declercq, Jane Sandall, Sirpa Wrede, Meredith Vanstone, Edwin van Teijlingen, Raymond DeVries and Cecilia Benoit

ABSTRACT

Purpose – *This chapter critically examines the purportedly growing phenomenon of Maternal Request Caesarean Sections (MRCS) and its relative contribution to the rising caesarean section (CS) rates.*

Methodology – *We apply a decentred comparative methodological approach to this problem by drawing upon and comparatively examining empirical data from Canada, the US, the UK and Finland.*

Patients, Consumers and Civil Society
Advances in Medical Sociology, Volume 10, 99–123

ISSN: 1057-6290/doi:10.1016/S1057-6290(08)10006-7

Findings – *We find that the general argument that has emerged within the obstetric community, evidenced in particular by a recent "State of the Science" conference, is that the reduced risks and benefits of MRCS are evenly balanced, thus ethically it could be seen as a valid choice for women. This approach, taken in particular in the North American context, negates the problematic nature of accurately measuring, and therefore assessing the importance of maternal request in addressing rising CS rates. Moreover, although some of the blame for rising CS rates has focused on MRCS, we argue that it has a relatively minor influence on rising rates. We show instead how rising CS rates can more appropriately be attributed to obstetrical policies and practices.*

Originality – *In presenting this argument, we challenge some of the prevailing notions of consumerism in maternity care and its influence on the practice patterns of maternity care professionals.*

Practical implications – *Our argument also calls into question how successful efforts to address MRCS will be in reducing CS rates given its relatively minor influence.*

Rising caesarean section (CS) rates in many nations have become a cause for concern. In Canada, for example, except for a slight dip in the early 1990s, the CS rate has increased in the past two decades reaching an all-time high of 26% of in-hospital deliveries in 2005/2006 (CIHI, 2007). Similarly, in the United Kingdom (UK), CS rates increased from 12% in 1990–1991 reaching 23% in 2005/2006 (ONS, 2007). CS rates have followed a similar trend in the United States (US), reaching 30% in 2005 (Hamilton, Martin, & Ventura, 2007). In contrast, Finland has seen no increase in its CS rates of 16–17% since 1994; indeed, the Finnish rate has declined slightly since 2005/2006. Increasingly, some of the blame for these rising rates with the exception of the rates in Finland – particularly in the North American context – has focused on the phenomena of Maternal Request Caesarean Sections (MRCS) or, as it has been coined by the popular media: women being "too posh to push" (Alves & Sheikh, 2005; CBC News, 2004). It has been estimated that 18% of all CSs in the US are requested by the mother without clinical indications (Young, 2006). Indeed, MRCSs have garnered much attention in the North American scientific and maternity care policy communities, culminating in a National Institutes of Health (NIH) "State of the Science" conference in March 2006.[1]

The comparative perspective we undertake in this chapter offers some important insights on the role maternal request plays in the rising CS rates.

By examining empirical data from Canada, the US, the UK and Finland, we argue that MRCS have a relatively minor influence on rising CS rates. Similar to the previous decline in rates in the mid-1990s, we show how rising CS rates are more appropriately attributed to obstetrical policies and practices.[2] These include, among others, the increased fear of litigation,[3] economic incentives in terms of higher fees for physicians,[4] how CSs allow obstetricians to see more patients and thus accommodate a more normal work week and reduce staff costs, and the increased induction of labour and continued practice of repeat CSs (*cf.* Brown, 1996; Denk, Kruse, & Jain, 2006; Francome & Savage, 1993). We explore why some obstetrical opinion leaders are seemingly diverting attention away from the influence of obstetrical policies and practices and in doing so question why the rhetoric of maternal "choice" is being propagated as the cause of rising CS rates. Hence, we challenge some of the prevailing notions of consumerism in maternity care and its influence on the practice patterns of maternity care professionals.

SHIFTING PERSPECTIVES ON MEDICAL AND MATERNITY CONSUMERISM

In many high-income countries, women's request for CS births has been linked to the growing consumerism that has been widely reported in both lay and academic literature. Haug (1973) and colleagues (Haug & Sussman, 1969; Haug & Lavin, 1984) were among the first medical sociologists to not only describe, but also provide a heuristic theoretical model on the rising consumer movement challenging academic medicine's traditional authority. These scholars argued that consumerism as a social movement arose as a countervailing force to medical power and physicians' ability to make unilateral decisions on the part of their patients. A vocal consumer movement, it was argued (Haug & Lavin, 1984), was indicative of declining medical dominance, with patients (renamed "clients" or "consumers") demanding an equal say in the decision-making process about their health care.

These elements of participation and control in care decisions became critical elements of what is now known as the *alternative birth movement*. "Awake and Aware" (Chabon, 1966), "Immaculate Deception" (Arms, 1974) and "Reclaiming Birth" (Edwards & Waldorf, 1984) were just a few of the calls for greater consumer choice in childbirth. The major direction of this greater control and choice was to demedicalize birth. Previously, we mapped out how maternity consumer groups have effectively lobbied for changes in childbirth practice, particularly around the choice of woman-centred midwifery care (Bourgeault, Declercq, & Sandall, 2001). It seems ironic that decades later similar rhetoric around choice is used – and primarily by members of the obstetrical community – to support the desire for more *interventive* birth practices, and surgical birth, in particular (Young, 2006).

It is easy to point to examples of the rise of consumerism through consumer groups and literature they produce which makes patients more active and aware (*cf.* Boston Women's Health Book Collective, 1998). Consumerism *in practice*, however, is seen by some as a more malleable phenomenon. Lupton's (1997) interactional analysis of doctor–patient encounters revealed that lay persons adopt both consumerist and passivist roles, often interchangeably, depending on the context of the health encounter. She argued gender, class, sexual orientation, disability and social/cultural capital influence the way that patients and providers interact. Specifically, wealthier, more educated people are the ones who tend to take a more consumerist approach to health care. One problem with the consumerism literature is that it largely assumes a non-differentiated subject and does not take these considerations into account. Moreover, Lupton notes that the public does not exclusively seek medical knowledge from health care professionals, but also "emotional comfort, concern and empathy" (p. 380), as well as an assurance that everything will be fine. Similarly, Zadoroznyj (2001) produces considerable evidence of child-bearing women as both "consumers" and "patients" in their birth narratives. The participants in her study, the majority highly educated and generally well-off enough to afford private health insurance (in Australia), demonstrated strong consumerist behaviour by making deliberate efforts to identify and select maternity and obstetrical services that suited them. One of the important factors for many participants was congruence between the obstetrician's view on medical interventions during birth and the mother's own views (both pros and cons). Zadoroznyj found a pattern of women who were unhappy with their first experience of birth because their views differed from those of their more interventionist attendants and became more active consumers in their subsequent pregnancy.

Beyond these social movement and interactional analyses debating whether power relations in the professional/patient encounter has shifted or not, medical sociologists and others have pointed out the ideological dimensions of medical consumerism reflecting a broader shift from welfarist to neo-liberalist health care policies (Henderson & Petersen, 2002). Typically labelled "health system partnership" or "patient-centred care," these broader policy initiatives highlight how this shift is away from community and collective approaches to participation to individual choice and freedom Hogg (1999). Consumption becomes shaped not simply in terms of necessity or perceived health benefits but also by association with cultural tastes, preferences and lifestyles (Henderson & Petersen, 2002). Maternity consumerism is particularly interesting to examine in this regard, because as Zadoroznyj (2001) highlights: "having to make choices is almost structured into the experience of giving birth for many women" (p. 120). Even in this context of consumer choice, the reality may not be consistent with the rhetoric. Henderson and Petersen (2002) argue that neo-liberal ideas about consumerism often clash with other crucial health care issues, including economic constraints, medical dominance in hospital settings and the omnipresence of advanced technology. Rutherford and Gallo-Cruz (2008) provide a fascinating example in this volume of how US hospitals have adopted the language of consumerism into the marketing of their maternity care while carefully maintaining control over all processes of birth by emphasizing the primacy of "safety."

Reflecting upon this broader ideological frame, Frank (2002) argues that what we need to do as sociologists is not just critique the individual choices made by consumers, but rather problematize the society that promotes these consumerist tendencies

> The critique of medical consumerism is not about the triviality or authenticity of the individual lives of people who seek and purchase these services. The object of critique is the society in which these services are offered as they are … [of which] the effects … may ultimately be as great, and possibly greater, on those who do not themselves receive these services. (p. 16)

In doing so we can see how society mediates "needs" for medical attention and particular medical procedures.

Clearly, medical and maternity consumerism are complex and multi-layered phenomena. It seems that at each level of analysis – from micro to macro – we have had to recast our thinking about the status and autonomy of the health care consumer, not just in the face of medicine's challenge but also from the broader health system and societal imperatives (Henderson & Petersen, 2002). The comparative research we report on below makes a critical contribution to this literature by asking the specific question that Frank (2002) encourages: What is it in particular about American and to a lesser extent Canadian society that makes maternal request CSs a valid maternity care choice? Equally perplexing, why is the validity of that choice not recognized in Finland, where the rate of surgical birth has declined somewhat in recent years? Why in the UK where there are also rising CS rates, has there been less of a focus on maternal requests? What we hope to reveal in our analysis is how the social context of maternity care really does matter in whether a particular phenomenon – i.e., escalating CS rates – is recognized as a societal concern in the first instance and, secondly, what is considered to be the driving force behind the change in rates and what should be done about it.

METHODS

Our comparative critical analysis employs a particular method coined the *decentred method* (Wrede et al., 2006). Unlike typical methods of comparative research where one or two researchers situated in one country collect and interpret comparative data, this method brings together a team of researchers from strategic geographical locations that are chosen because they represent significant variability in the issue being addressed. Each of these "local experts," with in-depth knowledge of the health and in this case maternity care systems, draw upon and present data on their case country in a way that challenges some commonly held assumptions when non-comparative research is undertaken (Benoit et al., 2005). This is a complex and time-consuming approach but one which we feel yields much richer and *context-sensitive* findings.

Canada, the US and the UK seemed natural choices to include in this analysis because of their relatively high (and rising) CS rates, and of the importance that has been placed on the maternal request phenomenon. The inclusion of the Finnish case is illuminating in this particular instance because of the very different CS rate trends than in these other three countries and the lack of salience of MRCS. From each of the countries, we draw upon a variety of sources of data – primarily documentary. Across all four cases, the focus of our data has been post-2000 – which corresponds to the rise in attention to MRCS.

- For the *Canadian* case, we draw upon three main sources of data. The first includes media reports gathered through online searches and the searching of the Canadian Business and Current Affairs (CBCA) database. The second source includes editorials and position papers from the Society of Obstetricians and Gynecologists of Canada (SOGC). Finally, research articles, commentaries and letters from the *Canadian Medical Association Journal* (CMAJ) were searched online.

- In the case of the *US*, vital statistics, administrative databases and a national survey of the experiences of 1,573 mothers who gave birth to a singleton infant in a hospital in 2005 (i.e., *Listening to Mothers II*,[5] Declercq, Sakala, Corry, & Applebaum, 2006) were drawn upon, in addition to documents, journal articles and reports and commentaries from the NIH "State of the Science" conference.
- For the *UK*, we draw upon reports from professional organizations and government agencies and public and professional responses to these reported in the public and professional press. We also draw upon the UK-based survey "Recorded Delivery" (Redshaw, Rowe, Hockley, & Brocklehurst, 2007).
- In addition to documentary data and statistics from the Finnish birth register, the Finnish section draws on a review of medical journals *Duodecim* and *Suomen lääkärilehti* (Finnish Medical Journal). The selection of materials for the current analysis was aided by a recent study on the obstetric research on the "fear of childbirth" in Finland and Sweden (Liljeroth, 2009).

Our data analysis involved deconstructing the rhetoric of MRCS by first teasing apart obstetrical from maternal influences on the so-called "choice" of CS. We began with the evolving obstetrical perspective, highlighting the impetus for the argued rise in MRCS in terms of the negative consequences of vaginal birth (i.e., pelvic floor dysfunction). We asked why doctors agreed with women who chose CSs and consider how professional behaviours and practices contribute to MRCS. We then focused on to what extent and why women chose to have CSs and how this is an extension of the principles of consumerism. In the following sections, we unpack the perspectives of professionals and consumers drawing upon data from Canada, the US, the UK and the contrasting case study of Finland. We first, however, identify some of the problems with accurately measuring MRCS.

DEFINING MATERNAL REQUEST CAESAREAN SECTIONS

There remains considerable imprecision in the defining of both medically elective and maternal-request CSs. The key difference between MRCS and elective CS rates is the issue of the procedure being at the request of the mother. It is near impossible, however, to accurately measure *maternal intentions* from the sources of data available: hospital discharge and birth certificate data. These data do not include any accurate estimation of maternal intention. Rather, they simply identify CSs where no medical indication was noted and there is no evidence of labor having occurred (Anonymous, 2006). As argued emphatically by Peralta, "to infer from patient charts and birth certificates of CSs performed for no medical indication that it was mothers themselves who ask for the surgical procedure is unadulterated fraud" (as cited in Young, 2006, p. 171).

Moreover, most of the public debate over MRCSs has focused on mothers who might be requesting them in their first birth (primary CSs), but current methods of measuring MRCS often fail to distinguish primary and repeat CSs. This is exemplified in the NIH State of the Science conference definition of MRCS as "a caesarean delivery for a singleton pregnancy, on maternal request, at term, in the absence of any medical or obstetric indications" (Young, 2006, p. 171). Mothers are far more likely to request a repeat CS than a primary CS (Declercq et al., 2006), in part because of limited availability of vaginal births after CS (VBACs), and studies that fail to distinguish between them can suggest higher rates of maternal request, which the media then apply to primary CSs.

In spite of these problems distinguishing between elective and medically indicated caesarean births and that there are no credible data on the extent of MRCS,[6] the NIH conference announcement asserted that MRCS comprise 2.5% of all surgical births.[7] To support this assertion, those convinced of an attention-worthy rise in the MRCS rate used a statistical sleight of hand: they showed the number of primary CSs rising, even though maternal risk profiles remained unchanged. They concluded, with little regard to other important factors such as changed professional practice patterns, that the "unexplained" rise in the rate of primary CSs must be the result of maternal request.

Bracketing these definitional concerns for the moment, let us examine what factors have given rise to the issue of MRCS. In the following sections, we "unpack" some of the obstetrical influences on MRCS by looking at the framing of MRCS as an acceptable (indeed, preferred) model of delivery, and related to this how the issue of the need to recognize maternal "choice" arose.

IMPETUS FOR THE RISING CONCERN WITH MRCS

The impetus for the rise in MRCS or the increasing responsiveness of the obstetrical community to MRCS is based on concerns over the relationship between vaginal birth and pelvic floor injuries. In the late 1990s studies investigating a link between vaginal delivery and pelvic floor damage began to populate the medical literature, expanding along with the rise of urogynaecology, a medical specialty that focuses on the pelvic floor of women. Obstetric and urogynaecological specialists cautiously surmized that harm to the pelvic floor might be averted with surgical delivery. It followed (in a self-fulfilling fashion) that "preserving the pelvic floor" could then be a medically indicated rationale for choosing a surgical instead of a vaginal birth (De Lancey, 2000; Devine, Ostegard, & Noblett, 1999; O'Boyle, Davis, & Calhoun, 2002).

This argument has been reflected in the Canadian literature. Farrell (2002), a Halifax-based obstetrician argued that pelvic injury should be included in the risk–benefit equation of vaginal vs. CS delivery:

> There is a growing body of evidence that implicates childbirth in general, and specific peripartum risk factors in particular, in postpartum pelvic dysfunction. This pelvic dysfunction results from a combination of structural damage and neurologic injury that occurs during labour and, most certainly, during vaginal birth. This evidence has sparked a debate among health care professionals and the public regarding the use of elective caesarean delivery for the reason of avoiding the discomfort of vaginal birth and the accompanying postpartum pelvic dysfunction ... Women have a right to consider the evidence and weigh the potential risks and benefits, and thereby participate more equally in the decisions concerning their pregnancy and mode of delivery. (p. 337)

One could also find proponents of this argument in other obstetrical communities. In the UK, for example, the question of MRCS was raised over two decades ago by obstetrician Marion Hall (1987). Debate within professional journals, including in the *British Medical Journal*, peaked in the late 1990s (e.g., Amu, Rajendram, & Bojali, 1998; Paterson-Brown, 1998) and early years of 2000 (e.g., Bewley & Cockburn, 2002; Feinmann, 2002; Johanson, El-Timini, Rigby, Young, & Jones, 2001; Penna & Arulkumaran, 2003). These published debates also discussed the importance of women's autonomy in light of the emerging evidence of pelvic floor dysfunction but note the lack of available research evidence.

Contrary to the approach taken in the US NIH Conference, the SOGC took a more conservative perspective. In its statement on planned CS, it argued that,

> lacking a genuine medical reason, doctors typically advise against caesarean delivery, as it can produce side-effects such as future pregnancy complications, injury to adjacent organs, or even hysterectomy. Still, despite these risks, many women and physicians are citing this research and using pelvic floor damage and incontinence as a medical reason for a caesarean ... Incontinence is certainly an embarrassing and inconvenient condition, but women who use it to justify a caesarean section are putting themselves

> at risk of serious complications in future pregnancies or even sterility – it's a very high price to pay, particularly when science isn't there to back them up. (Federokow, no date or page number)

There was concurrence at the NIH conference mentioned above with the lack of research, but this was framed to be a lack of research around maternal request, for which virtually no outcomes research exists. Following the conference, NIH conveners issued a press release with the headline "Panel Finds Insufficient Evidence to Recommend For or Against Maternal Request Caesarean Delivery." A tagline recommended that those women requesting a caesarean delivery should be thoroughly counselled on potential risks and benefits. Not mentioned in the media was that the evidence supporting the claims that vaginal birth damages the pelvic floor was very weak; yet, concern with pelvic floor damage is a primary rationale for choosing elective surgery. Thus, the conference concluded that there is no ethical objection when the desire of an "informed" woman for a surgical birth meets the desire of a physician to apply the "best" of medical technology to the natural process of birthing. Disregard for other sources of the rise in surgical births allowed conference organizers to frame the debate in terms of women's choices.

FRAMING MRCS AS AN ISSUE OF A WOMAN'S RIGHT TO CHOOSE

Encouraged by some proponents, the NIH State of the Science conference opened up the ethical issue that a woman has the right to make decisions regarding her body and that requesting a CS is a legitimate choice of childbirth method (*cf.* Minkoff, 2004). Such research suggests that "maternal preference" is a factor driving increasing rates of CSs because women fear the pain of vaginal birth, have concerns about postpartum sexual functioning and the safety of the baby. This begs the question as to whether women are indeed asking for CSs and if so, why? We found very little information about maternal influences on CSs generally and on elective more specifically, and even less on maternal preferences for this surgical procedure.

Maternal "Choice" of Caesarean Sections

Hoping to shed light on the suggested growing increase in MRCS, Alves and Sheikh (2005), using NHS hospital data, found that affluent women were more likely to have elective CSs. They explained that "[w]hile much of this variation is likely to be explained by biological factors including increased maternal age and infant birthweight in the more affluent ... , the association persists even after adjustment for these factors suggesting that social factors may also play an important role" (p. 995). McCourt et al. (2007) found further that women who do want elective CSs request it because of psychological reasons (e.g., bad experiences, fears about births, poor prenatal care) and safety issues (believe it is safer for baby and mother, less trauma for mother), rather than weight/convenience/sexual reasons, as popular press promotes with stories of celebrity CS.

In the case of women's decision-making experiences following a previous CS, Emmett, Shaw, Montgomery, & Murphy (2006) results revealed considerable variability. The women, of which more than half chose to give birth vaginally (VBAC), described having to actively seek out relevant information and eventually made their own decision without much professional guidance. The women felt that the information commonly provided by the obstetrician more often related to the procedure than long-term health risks and benefits. Declercq et al. (2006) similarly found that women are more likely to request a repeat CS than a primary CS, in part because of limited availability of VBAC.

We also know little about whether women freely make an informed choice when they choose to have a CS. Studies of maternal preference for caesarean fail to assess whether women were told of the potential harms of caesarean surgery, whether alternatives were discussed, the accuracy of the information provided, and what opinion their maternity care professional held (Gamble & Creedy, 2000). The studies that do exist on this topic are also inconsistent in the timeframe studied, with some researchers using a prospective model asking mothers about their attitudes while pregnant, and others using retrospective designs, based on postpartum interviews.

The National Sentinel Caesarean Section Audit conducted in the UK (RCOG, 2001) found a small number of women (5.3%) who would prefer to be delivered by CS. These women also were more likely to express a preference for a pain-free labour. The study is limited as only 31% of eligible women responded to the questionnaire. These women were older, more likely to say they were white, and more likely to be having their first baby. Women's key concerns were to have a birth that was the safest and least stressful option for the baby, and for themselves. This audit showed that some of the theories put forward in the popular and professional press as reasons for the increase in CS rates in the UK (i.e., maternal request) proved to be red herring.

Following the NIH State of the Science conference, Pakenham and colleagues (2006) undertook a study of maternal request for a CS among Canadian women. The authors provided women with a brief and reasonably balanced listing of the risks and benefits of vaginal births and CSs and then asked them to indicate their preferred mode of delivery if, in a hypothetical scenario, they were to have a choice. They reported that 13% women who had not yet given birth, and 5% of those who had, would elect to have a CS. Klein (2007), however, pointed out the problematic nature of that particular research design: the survey was conducted of a convenience sample at a specialty facility and the authors did not disclose why women were being seen at the clinic (i.e., whether they were "low risk" or not). This he felt leads to an unavoidable bias and overestimation of the proportion of women who would truly elect to have a CS.

Recent data from a comprehensive national study in the US, *Listening to Mothers*, showed that less than 1% of mothers (1 out of 1,300 surveyed) requested their CS (Young, 2006). By way of contrast, about 10% felt pressured towards accepting an elective caesarean by their obstetrician.[8] This issue of pressure begs the question as to whether and to what extent physicians are responsive to a woman's choice of CS or whether women are directed towards these choices by their maternity provider.

Physician-Responsive or Physician-Directed Maternal "Choice"?

The American College of Obstetricians and Gynecologists (ACOG) has issued a series of position statements regarding elective CSs for normal pregnancies. In its initial statement, published in 2003 it supported the right of physicians to choose what they thought best, concluding, "If the physician believes that caesarean delivery promotes the overall health and welfare of the woman and her fetus more than vaginal birth, he or she is ethically justified in performing a caesarean delivery" (ACOG, 2003). This has more recently been replaced by a 2008 document on Surgery and Patient Choice (ACOG, 2008) which, while more temperate in language, repeated verbatim the conclusion above. The Christilaw (2004) released a statement that does not support caesareans on demand, but leaves this decision up to the woman and her physician

> The Society of Obstetricians and Gynaecologists of Canada does **not** promote Caesarean sections on demand ... At this time, there is no indication that a Caesarean section carries less risk than a vaginal delivery for mother and baby. The Society is concerned that a natural process would be transformed into a surgical process and that elective

> procedures would create added pressure on health care resources that are already overextended in Canada ... The SOGC believes that each individual woman should receive the best information available on her options for labour and birth. The final decision rests between the woman and her health care provider as to the safest route for the birth of the baby. (emphasis in original)

Mary Hannah (2004) – a well known Canadian obstetrical scientist – wrote a commentary on the issue of maternal choice where she argues, paralleling these arguments that, "if a woman without an accepted medical indication requests delivery by elective caesarean section and, after a thorough discussion about the risks and benefits, continues to perceive that the benefits to her and her child of a planned elective caesarean outweigh the risks, then most likely the overall health and welfare of the woman will be promoted by supporting her request" (p. 814).

The National Institute for Clinical Effectiveness (NICE) guidelines in the UK are somewhat stronger stating that "Maternal request is not on its own an indication for CS and specific reasons for the request should be explored, discussed and recorded" (NICE, 2004, p. 11). According to the guidelines, a doctor can refuse to do a "CS in the absence of an identifiable reason. However the woman's decision should be respected and she should be offered referral for a second opinion" (NICE, 2004, p. 12). The strictest guideline came earlier from the International Federation of Gynecology and Obstetrics (FIGO). In 1998, FIGO's Committee for the Ethical Aspects of Reproduction and Women's Health published its position on MRCS: "Ethical Aspects of Caesarean Delivery for Non-Medical Reasons." The committee starts with two observations: (1) "Caesarean section is a surgical intervention with potential hazards for both mother and child"; and (2) [Caesarean section] "uses more resources than normal vaginal delivery." Given that FIGO members "have a professional duty to do nothing that may harm their patients" and "an ethical duty to society to allocate health care resources wisely," the committee concludes: "At present, because hard evidence of net benefit does not exist, performing caesarean section for non-medical reasons is not justified." (FIGO, 1999, p. 74)

It is not clear what impact these statements and commentaries have had. In an ACOG sponsored survey of female obstetricians in 2003, it was found that while 36% said that they would not perform an elective CS if asked, and almost equal proportion – 32% – said that they would (ACOG Press Release 12/9/2003). In this case, younger obstetricians were also more likely to say no. Similarly, Farrell, Baskett, and Farrell (2005) found that 23% of Canadian obstetricians approve of elective CSs in first time mothers without any medical indications. Significantly, more male than female obstetricians approved of this procedure. The principle of informed choice was noted as a more important factor influencing their decision than concerns with the pelvic floor. In the UK, nearly 70% of obstetrical consultants said that they would agree to maternal request CSs even without medical indications (Cotzias, Sara, & Fisk, 2001). These results were confirmed in a more recent study that also compared obstetrician attitudes toward MRCS in eight European countries (Habiba et al., 2006). It was found that 79% of physicians in UK would comply with MRCS believing it is the woman's *choice* vs. 22% in the Netherlands. In contrast, 79% of Swedish physicians would comply with MREC because of maternal *fear* vs. 10% in Spain. Habiba et al. (2006) also found a sizeable proportion of physicians would prefer CS for themselves or their partners.[9]

There are dissenting voices to be sure. Michael Klein (2004), a Canadian family physician and strong supporter of low-tech birth, responded to Mary Hannah's commentary by stating that it "arrives at a time when women are losing confidence in their ability to give birth vaginally. To suggest, as Hannah does, the equivalence of maternal and newborn outcomes for caesarean and vaginal birth in the face of confusing science is to contribute to fear and an increase in caesarean procedures." Similarly, Abby Lippman, a sage women's health commentator, argued in the 2004 Canadian Women's Health Network newsletter that CS on demand is not just a matter of choice: "All this talk of informed choice is curious. For starters, research on medically unnecessary elective C sections for first pregnancies is sparse, and there is general agreement that we lack the full information needed to assess the risks of CSs for women and their babies when these are not medically needed. How can physicians view CSs as a possible option when critical data about the effects of this unnecessary surgery are missing or incomplete?" (p. 2)

Beyond these critiques, it is important to point out that what women hear from obstetricians has a powerful influence on them. Green and Baston (2007), for example, examined changes between 1987 and 2000 in women's willingness to accept obstetric interventions in the antenatal period in the UK. The authors found that an increased willingness of women to accept obstetrical interventions directly correlated to a higher chance of caesarean; indeed, they were more likely to have elective CS *as prompted by their obstetrician*. Younger women and first time mothers were more likely to accept obstetrical interventions, and therefore more likely to have CS (and by extension often a repeat CS). Moffatt, Bell, and Porter (2007) similarly found that when questioned about their decision-making following a CS delivery, many women said that despite wanting to be actively involved, they did not feel they participated actively and were uncomfortable with the responsibility of decision-making. Wax, Cartin, Pinette, and Blackstone (2005) have also argued that some obstetricians think so little of the risks, pain and recovery of caesarean surgery that they feel that "convenience," "certainty of delivering practitioner" and "[labour] pain" justify performing this major operation on healthy women. The Listening to Mothers II survey also asked mothers if they felt pressured by their providers to have a caesarean; 25% of mothers who had experienced a primary or repeat caesarean indicated that they had been pressured to have a caesarean, while 35% of mothers who had a VBAC reported being so (Declercq et al., 2006). Together these findings raise the question whether maternal "choice" is often physician directed.

Kalish, McCullough, Gupta, Thaler, and Chervenak (2004) argued similarly that elective CSs should not necessarily be equated with "patient" or "maternal choice" because they could equally well represent "physician choice" caesareans. More emphatically, Demott (2000), argues that

> 'Offering' caesarean delivery or consenting to perform it electively at term is irresponsible, dangerous, and ultimately unfair to many women ... [T]he advice of physicians is seriously heeded by many under our care ... The less informed woman is merely agreeing to our recommendation without true knowledge of the [potentially life threatening] consequences. This is inherently unfair and a blatant misuse of power. (pp. 264–265)

In sum, the available evidence indicates that the link between maternal request and elective CS is precarious at best. Kingdon, Baker, and Lavender (2006), in their systematic review of women's views of planned caesarean birth, reported that the literature has severe methodological, conceptual and cultural weaknesses. In the following section, we briefly highlight other approaches undertaken to address rising CS rates or the factors that have been identified as fostering women's choice of this surgical intervention. We focus in particular on obstetrical practices and policies that focus on women's fear, on the one hand, and the opposition to surgical interventions, on the other, drawing in large part on the Finnish and British cases.

RE-ORIENTING OBSTETRICAL POLICY AND PRACTICE

Resisting Surgical Birth by Addressing the Issue of Fear

We have already alluded to the finding that fear of birth can contributes to the MRCS phenomenon. Recent research evidence indicates that when maternal fear is taken into account and addressed the proportion of women opting for CS can be diminished. Nerum, Havorsen, Sorlie, and Oian (2006) found that 86% of their study group changed from elective CS to vaginal birth after between 1 and 15 h of psychological counselling. These researchers argued in light of these findings that CS rates could be lowered if obstetricians took more time to explain carefully birthing risks/benefits and listened to fears/wishes of women. Paralleling this argument, the NICE (2004, p. 12) guidelines in the UK state: When a woman requests a CS because she has a fear of childbirth, she should be offered counselling (such as cognitive behavioural therapy) to help her to address her fears in a supportive manner, because this results in reduced fear of pain in labor and shorter labor. The publication of the NICE guideline on CS became a key focal points for both professionals and consumers groups. The prevailing attitude among all maternity care professionals has been that the CS rate was too high and that the culture and the organization of care may hold the key to reducing the rate (Sandall, 2002). A great deal of effort has thus been put into reducing variations in provider behaviour through guidelines, standards, policies and toolkits.

Even without the impetus of rising CS rates, Finnish research reflecting a psychological perspective on birth began to emphasize the importance of fear of childbirth (Toivanen, Saisto, Salmela-Aro, & Halmesmäki, 2002). In 1997, soon after the first Finnish study on the topic had been published, an obstetric diagnosis for fear of childbirth was included in the Finnish version of the ICD-10, International Classification of Diseases (Liljeroth, 2009). In 1999, a section on fear of childbirth was included into the guide on recommendations to maternity care, compiled by the expert group on maternity care at the National Centre for Welfare and Health (STAKES). Rather than focus only on physiological factors, the new discourse takes into account the psychological challenge and the strain that pregnancy and birth pose not only to the woman but to her partner (Saisto, 2000). Training women in the use of relaxation is promoted as one of the central elements of this new approach.

The new style of practice was developed through a multidisciplinary approach involving collaboration between obstetricians and psychologists. With the publication of an authoritative article outlining recommendations for care, as well as instructions on how to relate to women's and their partner's request for surgical birth in the Finnish medical journal *Duodecim*, the recognition of fear as a central childbirth complication that requires professional attention became recognized as mainstream obstetric practice (Saisto, 2000). The article argues that it is relevant to take the psychological perspective on birth into account for all pregnant women. It is further recognized that in order to meet these needs, the obstetric workforce needs to develop new skills and the contribution of psychologists should be recognized, not only for the clients but for guiding maternity care professionals who work with women fearing childbirth. The article also forcefully recognizes women's legitimate demand to be heard in the planning of their care (Saisto, 2000, p. 1487).

Contrasting the obstetric discourse that is currently gaining prominence in Finland with that in place in the other countries considered in this chapter suggests that attention to the fear of childbirth helps to keep the surgical birth rate lower than in countries where obstetrics remains less attentive to women's needs, even when they say they are accommodating women's wishes such as MRCS. Currently, throughout Finland, maternity hospitals offer women counselling aimed at relieving their fears and helping them encounter a vaginal birth. At the same time, the possibility of surgical birth is available for those whose fears are so severe that they still opt for that solution. In 2005, maternity hospitals reported to the Birth Register deliveries with 520 women with the diagnosis when the total number of deliveries was 56,963, thus corresponding to less than 1% of all deliveries. Even though nearly 80% of the women with the diagnosis underwent surgical birth, their proportion of all caesareans was low. In 2005, the percentage of surgical births for the indication fear of childbirth was 4.3% (Lappi-Khabbal, 2007).

The fact that the official discourse of the Finnish ob-gyn profession continues to reject surgical birth as a valid choice and currently recognizes fear of childbirth does not change the fact that birth care continues to be primarily defined through the technocratic medical discourse. Indeed, the profession's resistance to surgical birth may be interpreted as insensitivity to women's wishes and fears. Rather, if the providers of birth care actually want to listen to women's wishes and are actively reshaping care policies so that they better take into account what women want, the demand for surgical birth will remain limited without fuelling a sense of discontent among women. Achieving such a goal would mean a maternity care that more than the current system recognizes women as true partners in their care.

DISCUSSION

As noted at the outset, one of the intentions of our chapter is to de-emphasize the role that MRCS have on rising CS rates by re-emphasizing the importance of obstetrical policies and practices. Our analysis reveals how obstetrical opinion that the reduced risks and benefits of MRCS are evenly balanced and thus ethically seen as a valid choice for women (e.g., Knight, Kurinczuk, Spark, & Brocklehurst, 2008; Villar et al., 2007) was developed. We are collectively concerned with this approach taken in particular in the North American context (explicit as it is in the US and more implicit in Canada) because it negates the problematic nature of accurately measuring, and therefore assessing the importance of maternal request in addressing rising CS rates. This interventionist approach also negates the increasing evidence of long-term risk to women from CSs. Our overall argument also calls into question how successful these efforts will be in reducing CS rates given the relatively minor influence of MRCS.

It is interesting to contrast the North American approaches with more upstream policies in Finland, and to a lesser extent in the UK, that have focused on the factors leading some women to request CSs, specifically fear. The focus of debate does seem to reflect the values of health systems and health care delivery. In the US, choice is reified, and thus MRCS debates seem to have a much higher profile in both the professional and lay press. In the UK, the MRCS debate is raised in the popular press, but seems to be less of a focus in the professional press where concerns regarding safety, management of pain, are concerns for professionals, and cost implications are cause for concern for policy makers. Canadian dialogue exists somewhere in-between these two approaches. The Finnish case is particularly interesting because of its focus on the fear of childbirth rather than maternal request, even in light of relatively stable CS rates. In this volume, Borkman and Munn-Giddings (forthcoming) similarly emphasize the importance of national context when considering trends in patient consumerism. We hope that our analysis can begin to address the universalistic tendencies of this literature that they note as being a key limitation.

What should also become clear from our analysis is that MRCS is a procedure that begs for ethical advice. The use of an expensive, highly technological and risky procedure to assist at a birth that everyone agrees could occur without intervention pushes all the buttons of contemporary clinical ethics. When asked to give advice or to help develop policy, bioethicists generally use the "principalist" approach (Beauchamp & Childress, 2001) that seeks to balance the principles of autonomy, beneficence, non-maleficence and justice. With regard to MRCS, ethicists and ethics committees must weigh the right of a woman to determine her own care (autonomy), promotion of the welfare of the mother and her baby (beneficence), the need to avoid unnecessary harm to either the mother or her baby (non-maleficence) and the fair use of health care resources (justice). Not surprisingly, bioethical advice about MRCS reflects the social location of the bioethicists providing the advice and the physicians being advised. This can be clearly seen in looking at the responses to MRCS offered by two professional associations of obstetricians, one based in the US (ACOG) and the other an international organization (FIGO). Both organizations base their advice on the principles of bioethics, but their different social locations result in different advice (De Vries, Kane Low, & Bogdan-Lovis, 2008).

Beyond these important practical and ethical issues, we are impressed with how this case study can help us to advance current conceptualizations of maternity and more broadly medical consumerism. In a recently published commentary on the debate over rising CS rates, Wendland (2007) argues that in this milieu of obstetrics supposed ascription to evidence-based practice, "The mother's body disappears from analytical view; images of fetal safety are marketing tools; technology magically wards off the unpredictability and danger of birth" (p. 218). What we have found in the case of policy addressing MRCS somewhat to the contrary is that the woman's body – including all of its rights, needs and desires – is conjured up to provide justification for obstetrical preferences. As such, our case reveals how maternity consumerism can interface with the health care establishment (Landzelius, 2006).

It has been long held that consumers are an important element of the medicalization process (*cf.* Conrad, 1992). Indeed, in some cases, patients have had to fight to get medical recognition for their "illnesses," from alcoholism to chronic fatigue and multiple chemical sensitivity syndromes (Dumit, 2006). What we cannot say equivocally is whether those (few) women who do choose CS without medical indications are doing so as active, involved participants in the obstetrical decision-making process. This is not necessarily because we hold an essentialist view that maternity consumerism can only be truly real when it contradicts medical prerogatives. We agree with Beckett's (2005) argument that the alternative childbirth movement can be just as moralistic in its idea that women's preference for high-tech obstetrics is the result of a passive "socialization" into "dominant values' is theoretically inadequate. The author questions the "empowerment" of the alternative birth movement participants, instead finding them equally controlling as those promoting the medicalization of birth. In both cases, women's right to choose is invoked. At the same time, Beckett argues that critiques of the alternative birth movement often obscure the connection between women's choices and the very real consequences.

In the UK, the formalized approach to best evidence through NICE means that women's choice to have a CS when she wants is clearly seen as less important than evidence-based guidelines. In other words, women cannot have what they want if the evidence does not justify the intervention. In Finland, it seems that maternity care staff are increasingly inclined to take women's views into consideration, but they also seem to be facing strong pressure to ration costs (Kurunmäki, 2004).

Finally, following Frank's (2002) encouragement, we would like to problematize a single minded obstetrical focus on maternal request by highlighting some of the potential implications for those who do not choose to undergo surgical birth. The potential is real for the debate to shift from the current question, "why would you choose to have a CS?" to a future question, "why *wouldn't* you choose to have a CS?" In this volume, Fisher and Ronald (2008) also show how "empowerment" is mobilized – in their case, the pharmaceutical industry through direct to consumer advertising (DTCA) – to further a particular mode of consumption and demands on patient-consumers. Empowerment discourse pairs diagnosis, treatment and compliance with responsibilities that "engaged" health care consumers must assume. In the US Food and Drug Administration (FDA) policy process, narratives construct DTCA as responding to and enabling the transformation of patients into empowered consumers. The present cost-conscious context may discourage CS consumerism as a more costly practice. It may be very likely in the future, however, that because of dwindling maternity care human resources globally (obstetricians, midwives and nurses) and the predictability that scheduled CS entails, there may be a shift in the discourse and accepted practices towards its greater use, even when not indicated medically. Thus the directive may become, "you *should* have a CS."

NOTES

1. A State of the Science conference reviews currently available research on a topic to identify critical gaps in knowledge about a health problem or medical issue. A conference is convened when an issue reaches a critical point where NIH funding may (or may not) be warranted to fund further research. The proceedings of the conference can be watched in the NIH videocast website (http://videocast.nih.gov/).
2. We also acknowledge the importance of changing demographic factors such as increasing age of first-time mothers, increasing obesity among pregnant women (which often leads to CS delivery) and increased multiple pregnancies as a result of IVF.

3. Obstetricians have a very real fear of being sued. This fear drives beliefs, actions and advice to mothers. In their study of "caesarean on request" in eight European countries, Habiba et al. (2006, p. 651) discovered: "A consistent, statistically significant trend emerged between obstetricians' self-reported feeling that their clinical practice was influenced, occasionally or often, by fear of litigation and the willingness to perform a caesarean delivery at the patient's request.

4. Brown (1996), for example, noted that the costs for CSs in the mid-1990s in the US were approximately $2,850 more than vaginal births; physician's fees are in the range of $500 or higher.

5. The study results, drawn from both Internet and telephone respondents, were weighted and the final sample was comparable to US birthing mothers (Declercq et al., 2006).

6. The significance of the "problem" of MRCS was repeatedly challenged by skeptical members of the audience during the program.

7. See http://consensus.nih.gov/2006/2006CaesareanSOS027main.htm

8. Mothers Opinions from Listening to Mothers 2. Women should have the right to choose elective primary caesarean: Agreed 46%, Disagreed 31%; Women should have the right to choose VBAC: Agreed 85%, Disagreed 5%.

9. Similarly, a London survey found 17% choosing elective CS (Al-Mufti, McCarthy, & Fisk, 1997) and 16% more broadly across the UK (Wright, Wright, Simpson, & Byce, 2001). An informal survey of 117 obstetrician at an ACOG regional meeting found 46% would choose ECD: 57% male vs. 33% female (Gabbe & Holzman, 2001). The respondents would opt for elective CSs over forceps delivery for themselves more than they would offer it to their patients (Farrell et al., 2005).

REFERENCES

ACOG Committee on Ethics Opinion # 289. (2003). Surgery and patient choice: The ethics of decision making. *Obstetrics and Gynecology*, *102*, 1105.

ACOG Committee on Ethics Opinion # 395. (2008). Surgery and patient choice. *Obstetrics and Gynecology*, *111*, 243–247.

Al-Mufti, R., McCarthy, A., & Fisk, N. (1997). Survey of obstetricians person preference and discretionary practice. *European Journal of Obstetrics, Gynecology, and Reproductive Biology*, *73*(1), 1–4.

Alves, B., & Sheikh, A. (2005). Investigating the relationship between affluence and elective caesarean section. *British Journal of Obstetrics and Gynaecology*, *112*(7), 994.

Amu, O., Rajendram, S., & Bojali, I. I. (1998). Should doctors perform an elective caesarean section on request? Maternal choice alone should not determine method of delivery. *British Medical Journal*, *317*, 463–465.

Anonymous. (2006). National Institutes of Health State-of-the-Science Conference Statement Cesarean Delivery on maternal request. *Obstetrics and Gynecology*, *107*, 1386–1397.

Arms, S. (1974). *Immaculate deception: A new look at women and childbirth in America*. San Francisco: San Francisco Book Company.

Beauchamp, T. L., & Childress, J. F. (2001). *Principles of biomedical ethics* (5th ed.). New York: Oxford University Press.

Beckett, K. (2005). Choosing cesearean: Feminism and the politics of childbirth in the USA. *Feminist Theory*, *6*(3), 251–275.

Benoit, C., Wrede, S., Bourgeault, I., Sandall, J. Van Teijlingen, E., DeVries, R. (2005). Understanding the social organisation of maternity care systems: Midwifery as a touchstone. *Sociology of Health and Illness*, *27*(6), 722–737.

Bewley, S., & Cockburn, J. (2002). I. The unfacts of 'request' caesarean section. *British Journal of Obstetrics and Gynaecology*, *109*, 597–605.

Borkman, T., & Munn-Giddings, C. (2008). Self-help groups challenge health care systems in the US and UK. In: S. Chambré & M. Gouldner (Eds), *Advances in medical sociology: Patients, consumers and civil society* (Vol. 10, pp. 127–150). Bingley, UK: Emerald Group Publishing Limited.

Boston Women's Health Book Collective. (1998). *Our bodies ourselves: For the new century* (Rev. ed). New York: Touchstone.

Bourgeault, I. L., Declercq, E., & Sandall, J. (2001). Changing birth: Consumers, politics and policy. In: R. DeVries, C. Benoit, E. van Teijlingen & S. Wrede (Eds), *Birth by design: The social and cultural aspects of maternity care in Europe and North America*. New York: Routledge.

Brown, S. (1996). Physician demand for leisure: Implications for caesarean section rates. *Journal of Health Economics*, *15*, 233–242.

CBC News. (2004). Mothers, doctors debate 'too posh to push' C-sections. Available at http://www.cbc.ca/health/story/2004/02/27/c_sections040227.html

Chabon, I. (1966). *Awake and aware: Participation in childbirth through psychoprophylaxis*. Philadelphia: Saunders.

Christilaw, J. (2004). SOGC's position on elective caesarean sections. Press Release. March 2, 2004.

CIHI (Canadian Institute of Health Information). (2007). *Giving birth in Canada: Regional trends from 2001-2 to 2005-6. Analysis in Brief*. Ottawa: CIHI.

Conrad, P. (1992). Medicalization and social control. *Annual Review of Sociology*, *18*, 209–232.

Cotzias, C. S., Sara, P.-B., & Fisk, N. M. (2001). Obstetricians say yes to maternal request for elective caesarean section: A survey of current opinion. *European Journal of Obstetrics, Gynecology, and Reproductive Biology*, *97*(1), 15–16.

Declercq, E. R., Sakala, C., Corry, M. P., & Applebaum, S. (2006). *Listening to mothers II: Report of the second national U.S. survey of women's childbearing experiences*. New York: Childbirth Connection.

De Lancey, J. O. L. (2000). Identifying and managing anal sphincter injury. *Obstetric and Gynecology Management*, *2000*, 18–29.

Demott, R. K. (2000). A blatant misuse of power? *Birth*, *27*(4), 264–265.

Denk, C., Kruse, L., & Jain, N. (2006). Surveillance of caesarean deliveries, New Jersey 1999–2004. *Birth*, *33*(3), 203–209.

Devine, J. B., Ostegard, D. R., & Noblett, K. L. (1999). Long term complications of second stage labor. *Contemporary Obstetrics and Gynecology*, *1999*, 119–126.

De Vries, R., Kane Low, L., & Bogdan-Lovis, E. (2008). Choosing surgical birth: Desire and the nature of bioethical advice. In: H. Lindemann, M. Verkerk & M. Urban Walker (Eds), *Naturalized bioethics*. Cambridge: Cambridge University Press, 2008.

Dumit, J. (2006). Illnesses you have to fight to get: Facts as forces in uncertain, emergent illnesses. *Social Science and Medicine*, *62*(3), 577–590.

Edwards, M., & Waldorf, M. (1984). *Reclaiming birth*. Trumansburg, NY: The Crossing Press.

Emmett, C. L., Shaw, A. R. C., Montgomery, A. A., & Murphy, D. J. (2006). Women's experience of decision making about mode of delivery after previous cesearean sections. *British Journal of Obstetrics and Gynaecology*, *113*(12), 1438–1445.

Farrell, S., Baskett, T., & Farrell, K. (2005). Choice of elective caesarean delivery in obstetrics. *International Urogynecology Journal*, *16*, 378–383.

Farrell, S. A. (2002). Caesarean section versus forceps assisted vaginal birth: It's time to include pelvic floor injuries in the risk benefit equation. *Canadian Medical Association Journal*, *166*(3), 337–338.

Feinmann, J. (2002). How to limit cesareans on demand-too NICE to push? *Lancet*, *359*, 774.

FIGO. (1999). FIGO committee for the ethical aspects of human reproduction and women's health. *Gynecologic and Obstetric Investigation*, *48*, 73–77.

Fisher, J. A., & Ronald, L. M. (2008). Direct to consumer responsibility: Medical neoliberalism in pharmaceutical advertising and drug development. In: S. Chambré & M. Gouldner (Eds), *Advances in medical sociology: Patients, consumers and civil society* (Vol. 10, pp. 29–51). Bingley, UK: Emerald Group Publishing Limited.

Francome, C., & Savage, W. (1993). Caesarean sections in Britain and the USA: 12 or 24% is either the right rate? *Social Science and Medicine*, *37*(10), 1199.

Frank, A. (2002). What's wrong with medical consumerism? In: S. H. Petersen (Ed.), *Consuming health* (pp. 13–30). New York: Routledge.

Gabbe, S., & Holzman, G. (2001). Obstetricians choice of delivery. *Lancet*, *357*(9357), 722.

Gamble, J. A., & Creedy, D. K. (2000). Women's request for a caesarean section: A critique of the literature. *Birth*, *27*(4), 256–263.

Green, J., & Baston, H. (2007). Have women become more willing to accept obstetric interventions and does this relate to mode of birth? *Birth*, *34*(1), 6–13.

Habiba, K. M., Da Fre, M., Marsal, K., Bleker, O., Librero, J., Grandjean, H., Gratia, P., Guaschino, S., Heyl, W., Taylor, D., & Cuttini, M. (2006). Caesarean section on request: A comparison of obstetric attitudes in eight European countries. *British Journal of Obstetrics and Gynaecology*, *113*(6), 647–656.

Hall, M. (1987). When a woman asks for a caesarean section. *British Medical Journal*, *294*, 201–202.

Hamilton, B. E., Martin, J. A., & Ventura, S. J. (2007). Births: Preliminary data for 2006. *National Vital Statistics Reports*, *56*(7). Available at http://origin.cdc.gov/nchs/data/nvsr/nvsr56/nvsr56_07.pdf

Hannah, M. (2004). Planned elective caesarean section: A reasonable choice for some women? *Canadian Medical Association Journal*, *170*(5), 813–817.

Haug, M. (1973). Deprofessionalization: An alternate hypothesis for the future. *Sociological Review Monographs*, *20*, 195–211.

Haug, M., & Lavin, B. (1984). *Consumerism in medicine: Challenging physician authority*. Beverly Hills: Sage Publications.

Haug, M., & Sussman, M. (1969). Professional autonomy and the revolt of the client. *Social Problems*, *17*(2), 153–161.

Henderson, S., & Petersen, A. (2002). Introduction: Consumerism in health care. In: S. Henderson & P. Petersen (Eds), *Consuming health* (pp. 1–10). New York: Routledge.

Hogg, C. (1999). *Patients, power and politics*. London: Sage.

Johanson, R. B., El-Timini, S., Rigby, C., Young, P., & Jones, P. (2001). Caesarean section by choice could fulfill the inverse care law. *European Journal of Obstetrics and Gynecology and Reproductive Biology*, *97*, 20–22.

Kalish, R. B., McCullough, L., Gupta, M., Thaler, H. T., & Chervenak, F. A. (2004). Intrapartum elective caesarean delivery: A previously unrecognized clinical entity. *Obstetrics and Gynecology*, *103*(6), 1137–1141.

Kingdon, C., Baker, L., & Lavender, T. (2006). Systematic review of nulliparous women's views of planned caesarean birth. *Birth*, *33*(3), 229–237.

Klein, M. (2004). Elective caesarean section. *Canadian Medical Association Journal*, *171*(1),14.

Klein, M. (2007). Women's views of elective primary caesarean section. *Journal of Obstetrics and Gynaecology of Canada*, *29*(3), 214–218.

Knight, M., Kurinczuk, J. J., Spark, P., & Brocklehurst, P. (2008). Caesarean delivery and peripartum hysterectomy. *The American College of Obstetricians and Gynecologists*, *111*(1), 97–105.

Kurunmäki, L. (2004). A hybrid profession – The acquisition of management accounting expertise by medical professionals. *Accounting, Organizations and Society*, *29*(3-4), 327–347.

Landzelius, K. (2006). Introduction: Patient organization movements and new metamorphoses in patienthood. *Social Science and Medicine*, *62*(3), 529–537.

Lappi-Khabbal, R. (2007). *Synnytyspelon hoidon kustannusvaikuttavuus*. Master's Thesis in Health Economics, University of Kuopio. Available at http://www.uku.fi/tht/opinnaytteet/graduLappi-Khabbal.pdf. Retrieved on January 7, 2008.

Liljeroth, P. (2009). *Rädsla inför förlossningen – ett uppenbart kliniskt problem? Konstruktionen av förlossningsrädsla som medicinsk kategori*. Åbo, Finland: Åbo Akademi University Press. [In press].

Lippman, A. (2004). C-Section on demand: Not just a matter of choice. *Canadian Women's Health Network Magazine*, *7*(2/3), 2–3.

Lupton, D. (1997). Consumerism, reflexivity and the medical encounter. *Social Science and Medicine*, *45*, 373–381.

McCourt, C., Weaver, J., Statham, H., Beake, S., Gamble, J., & Greedy, D. (2007). Elective caesarean section and decision making: A critical review of the literature. *Birth*, *34*(1), 65–80.

Minkoff, H. (2004). Ethical dimensions of elective primary caesarean delivery. *Obstetrics and Gynecology*, *103*, 387–392.

Moffatt, M. A., Bell, J. S., & Porter, M. A. (2007). Decision making about mode of delivery amongst pregnant women who have previously had a caesarean section. *British Journal of Obstetrics and Gynaecology*, *114*(1), 86–93.

Nerum, H., Havorsen, L., Sorlie, T., & Oian, P. (2006). Maternal request for caesarean section due to fear of childbirth. *Birth*, *33*(3), 221–228.

NICE (National Institute for Clinical Excellence). (2004). *Caesarean section: Clinical guideline*. London, UK: National Collaborating Centre for Women's and Children's Health.

O'Boyle, A. L., Davis, G. D., & Calhoun, B. C. (2002). Informed consent and birth: Protecting the pelvic floor and ourselves. *American Journal of Obstetrics and Gynecology*, *187*, 981–983.

ONS. (2007). NHS Maternity Statistics, England: 2005–06, Bulletin: IC 2007 10, Information Centre, Government Statistical Service.

Paterson-Brown, S. (1998). Should doctors perform an elective caesarian on request? Yes, as long as the woman is fully informed. *British Medical Journal, 317*, 462–463.

Penna, L., & Arulkumaran, S. (2003). Caesarean section for non-medical reasons. *International Journal of Gynecology and Obstetrics, 82*, 399–409.

RCOG (Royal College of Obstetricians and Gynaecologists) Clinical Effectiveness Support Unit. (2001). *The National Caesarean Section audit report*. London: RCOG.

Redshaw, M., Rowe, R., Hockley, C., & Brocklehurst, P. (2007). *Recorded delivery: A national survey of women's experience of maternity care*. Oxford: National Perinatal Epidemiology Unit, University of Oxford.

Rutherford, M., & Gallo-Cruz, S. (2008) Selling the ideal birth: Rationalization and re-enchantment in the marketing of maternity care. In : S. Chambré & M. Gouldner (Eds), *Advances in Medical Sociology: Patients, consumers and civil society* (Vol. 10, pp. 75–98). Bingley, UK: Emerald Group Publishing Limited.

Saisto, T. (2000). Synnytyspelot ja niiden hoitaminen. *Duodecim, 116*, 1483–1488.

Sandall, J. (2002). The national sentinel caesarean section audit report: What have we learnt and what do we still need to find out? Implications for further research. *MIDIRS Midwifery Digest, 12*(1), 78–81.

Toivanen, R., Saisto, T., Salmela-Aro, K., & Halmesmäki, E. (2002). Synnytyspelon hoito terapeuttisen ryhmän ja rentoutumisharjoituksen avulla. *Suomen lääkärilehti, 57*(45), 4567–4572.

Villar, J., Carroli, G., Zavaleta, N., Donner, A., Wojdyla, D., Faundes, A., Velazco, A., Bataglia, V., Langer, A., Narváez, A., Valladares, E., Shah, A., Campodónico, L., Romero, M., Reynoso, S., Simônia de Pádua, K., Giordano, D., Kublickas, M., & Acosta, A. (2007). Maternal and neonatal individual risks and benefits associated with caesarean delivery: Multicentre prospective study. *British Medical Journal, 335*(7628), 1025.

Wax, J. R., Cartin, A., Pinette, M. G., & Blackstone, J. (2005). Patient choice caesarean the Maine experience. *Birth, 32*(3), 203–206.

Wendland, C. (2007). The vanishing mother. *Medical Anthropology Quarterly, 21*(2), 218–233.

Wrede, S., Benoit, C., Bourgeault, I., van Teijlingen, E., Sandall, J., & De Vries, R. (2006). Decentred comparative research: Context sensitive analysis of maternal health care. *Social Science and Medicine, 63*(11), 2986.

Wright, J. B., Wright, A. L., Simpson, N. A. B., & Byce, F. C. (2001). A survey of trainee obstetrician preferences for childbirth. *European Journal of Obstetrics, Gynecology, and Reproductive Biology, 97*, 23–25.

Young, D. (2006). Caesarean delivery on maternal request: Was the NIH conference based on a faulty premise? *Birth, 33*(3), 171–176.

Zadoroznyj, M. (2001). Birth and the 'reflexive consumer': Trust, risk and medical dominance in obstetric encounters. *Journal of Sociology, 37*(2), 117–139.

PART II
ORGANIZATIONS, CULTURE AND POLITICAL CONTEXT

SELF-HELP GROUPS CHALLENGE HEALTH CARE SYSTEMS IN THE US AND UK

Thomasina Borkman and Carol Munn-Giddings

ABSTRACT

Purpose – *This research considers how self-help groups (SHGs) and self-help organizations (SHOs) contribute to consumerist trends in two different societies: United States and United Kingdom. How do the health care systems and the voluntary sectors affect the kinds of social changes that SHGs/SHOs make?*

Methodology/approach – *A review of research on the role of SHGs/SHOs in contributing to national health social movements in the UK and US was made. Case studies of the UK and the US compare the characteristics of their health care systems and their voluntary sector. Research reviews of two community level self-help groups in each country describe the kinds of social changes they made.*

Findings – *The research review verified that SHGs/SHOs contribute to* national *level health social movements for patient consumerism. The case studies showed that* community level *SHGs/SHOs successfully made the same social changes but on a smaller scale as the national movements, and the health care system affects the kinds of* community *changes made.*

Patients, Consumers and Civil Society
Advances in Medical Sociology, Volume 10, 127–150

ISSN: 1057-6290/doi:10.1016/S1057-6290(08)10007-9

Research limitations – *A limited number of SHGs/SHOs within only two societies were studied. Additional SHGs/SHOs within a variety of societies need to be studied.*

Originality/value of chapter – *Community SHGs/SHOs are often trivialized by social scientists as just inward-oriented support groups, but this chapter shows that local groups contribute to patient consumerism and social changes but in ways that depend on the kind of health care system and societal context.*

INTRODUCTION

Health consumerism as an explanatory framework in relation to the development of various health related organizations in an international context is the focus of this volume. Within this general approach, our chapter considers more narrowly how self-help groups (SHGs) and self-help organizations (SHOs) contribute to some consumerist trends in two very different health care systems: US and UK.

First, we consider the relevant consumer theory to set the stage conceptually. Second, the health care systems and the voluntary sectors including self-help/mutual aid of UK and US are described and compared to set the context. Important policy differences that shape patient and consumer opportunities in the two health care systems are highlighted. Third, a two-part thesis is advanced. The first part which has been described in the literature and is fairly well known is that SHGs/SHOs have contributed to successful *national social movements in health in the US and UK* including the women's health, AIDS, disability, and mental illness movements. The second but untold story is that on a *community level* hundreds and thousands of SHGs/SHOs have successfully changed patients into self-determining consumers, have challenged medical diagnoses and claims of effective treatment, and have created de-medicalized and non-stigmatized identities; the research evidence documenting these changes is limited. Due to space limitations, we can only present four brief case studies of SHGs, two from each country. They were selected to represent a range of social changes from the modest to the dramatic. Dramatic changes such as patient/consumers challenging a psychiatric diagnosis (UK) or mental patients creating a non-stigmatized alternative identity for themselves (US); moderate changes learned by people who stutter to challenge professional claims of treatment and cure and use their experiential knowledge to fashion workable solutions

(US); modest changes of carers' groups whose sharing of experiences leads them to reject popular notions of caretaking and to become empowered to advocate for changes with their local health authorities (UK). The chapter concludes by examining what our two-part thesis contributes to theory on consumerism in health care and what can be learned from the cases that shows the different characteristics of the two health care systems.

CONCEPTUALIZATIONS OF CONSUMERISM IN HEALTH

The Consumer Society, an iconic label to characterize modern industrialized Western societies and the title of Baudrillard's (1998) book, argues that: consumption has become institutionalized not only as a right but as the duty of citizens; we consume not just goods but also services, and human relationships become commodified. While the consumerist approach has generated extensive interest and research in many areas of sociological and cultural analysis, medical sociology has lagged behind in its attention and application of theories of consumerism to health, illness, the body, and health care (Henderson & Petersen, 2002).

One reason for the lag in the application of consumerist theory to health and illness is the nature of the economic relationship between the provider and recipient of services. Unlike the general economy, in health care there is a third party or parties who sets policies and pays the bills of the provider – either government (UK) or government and free market economy (US). Given the inevitability of third party involvement contextualizing consumerism in health care, comparative sociology studying how consumerism behavior is expressed is invaluable. In researching mental health SHOs in England, USA, and Sweden (Borkman, Karlsson, Munn-Giddings, & Smith, 2005) we became aware that the very different health care systems provide a context that shapes and responds to the contours of self-help/mutual aid; but, exactly how to decipher the interrelationships is not clear. In this chapter we characterize the health care systems and the voluntary sector of USA and UK viewing them as possibilities and potentialities within which self-help/mutual aid groups and organizations innovate and respond.

The 1960s and 1970s were the decades of social movements in the US. They began with the civil rights movement for blacks and other minority groups: the activism then spreading to anti-Vietnam War, women's (Morgen, 2002), gay and lesbian rights (Minton, 2002), and disabilities including mental illness (Barnartt & Scotch, 2001). The Vietnam War, Watergate over which President Nixon resigned, and other social movements resulted in an increasing distrust of government, politicians, and traditional institutions. People questioned authority. The women's movement, disabilities and mental illness movements became transnational, showing up in UK, Europe, Canada, and Australia, among other places.

In medical sociology in the late 1970s and early 1980s Marie Haug and colleagues (Haug & Lavin, 1983) investigated the public's and patient's attitudes toward challenging their physician's authority in a medical encounter. People thought that they had a right to know the information in their medical records and some would disregard their physician's treatment orders under some conditions. In retrospect these findings seem like minor challenges, especially since they have now been incorporated into patient's Bill of Rights (Weitz, 2004).

Much more dramatic were the successes of the women's health movement in the 1960s and 1970s, and later the AIDS and breast cancer movements. Women created "C-R groups" (consciousness-raising groups) which became the symbol and tactic of women's liberation (Morgen, 2002, p. 4) – small C-R groups sprang up that were self-help/mutual aid groups although not identified as such (Borkman, 1975). Radicalized women demanded more knowledge about their bodies, invented collectives – democratically run health clinics, to have control over their health care – and protested patronizing and humiliating gynecological procedures, among other things (Morgen, 2002).

In the early 1980s when HIV/AIDS was evolving as a major killer of gays, the uncertainty and urgency of people who were fighting for their lives (Chambré, 2006) underlay much of the early invention and creativity in developing services such as buddy services, hotlines, and hybrid organizations that provided services and advocacy.

The epitome of medical sovereignty and control is in the area of knowledge production or medical research and clinical treatment decisions (Starr, 1982). Lerner (2001) chronicles the conflict in the 1960s among women patients and physicians treating breast cancer. Pressured by female patients in conjunction with evidence from new randomized controlled clinical trials finally convinced physicians to change their treatments. AIDS activists (Epstein, 1996) directly challenged scientific knowledge and the research process and were successful in modifying the rules, timing, and conduct of drug trials and obtaining representation on scientific decision-making boards.

Recently, several publications have brought together the knowledge of these individual movements in health with the theory and knowledge of social movements resulting in *Social Movements in Health*, edited by

Phil Brown and Stephen Zavestoski which points out that "Previous research has focused on individual cases of health social movements: we consider them as a collective group that when taken together have been an important force for social change" (Brown & Zavestoski, 2005, p. 2).

In the UK parallel movements have taken place. The recently emerging health social movements (HSMs) are distinguished by the focus on people with diseases or health conditions and their understanding and personal experiences of illness (Brown & Zavestoski, 2005, p. 3). Often the movements are motivated in part by the incongruity between the individual's experience of illness and the official system of diagnosis and treatment of that disease. (Hess, 2005, p. 18). The embodied health movements are challenging scientific knowledge and authority in extensive and fundamental ways; these include:

1. Questioning disease causation;
2. Confronting inadequate treatment options;
3. Criticizing strategies of prevention;
4. Challenging research funding priorities;
5. Advocating participation in policy making; and
6. Creating non-stigmatizing and constructive identities

A volume titled *Consuming Health: The Commodification of Health Care* (Henderson & Petersen, 2002) focuses on theoretical perspectives and research on empirical manifestations of consumerism and its limits (e.g., in [Australian] hospitals – (Henderson, 2002) or living with chronic heart failure [in Scotland] – (Reid & Clark, 2002)).

In the recent volumes on consumerism in health (Brown & Zavestoski, 2005; Henderson & Petersen, 2002), the writing is usually generalized and without a country context as if Australia, Britain, Canada, Norway, the United States, or other western democracies were alike (or their differences not worth noting). Titles give no country location; literature reviews and theory sections are couched in universalistic language – the reader being implicitly invited to infer that country location is irrelevant. Our research experience studying SHOs in health care systems of Sweden, UK, and USA convince us of the opposite – country is very relevant.

This chapter is distinctive in two ways:

1. We assume that theoretical perspectives on consumerism in health are not universally applicable to all Western democratic countries but their usefulness in various contexts needs to be determined. We speculate or hypothesize that British and US differences in health care systems and

voluntary sectors, among other factors shape or influence the nature of contributions that SHGs/SHOs make to health consumerism.
2. Instead of research on the *macro or national level* embodied health movements, we consider unrecognized research on *meso or community level* SHGs and SHOs. We show that similar challenges to scientific and professional knowledge, advocacy for participation in policy-making, and other innovations are occurring on the community or meso level.

While there are many unaddressed issues in consumerism in health, a major dividing line seems to be between the relatively modest meaning of "freedom of choice," "right to know," and "entitled to participate" (usually referring to patients selecting from among options provided by the health care system) and the more extensive structural changes involved when patients or consumers challenge the knowledge, authority, diagnoses, or treatment options (see also Rutherford & Gallo-Cruz, 2008, in this book). It is with these latter, more extensive changes upon which this chapter is focused.

CHARACTERISTICS OF HEALTH CARE SYSTEMS AND THE VOLUNTARY SECTORS OF SOCIETY

The US and UK, both western industrialized democracies, have been characterized as individualistic (US) and a post-welfare state (UK). UK refers to the United Kingdom which is comprised of England, Scotland, Northern Ireland and Wales.

These two Western democracies have very different health care systems and similarly strong but varying voluntary sectors. The major structural dimensions of the health care system are described in Table 1. A national health care system has been in existence in the UK since 1948 which is based on the concept of positive rights: governments and others incur obligations "to provide those goods and services necessary for each individual to exercise her/his rights" (Blank & Burau, 2004, p. 19). In contrast, the individualistic US is characterized by negative rights. With negative rights obligations are imposed on government and others not to interfere with the rights bearer. "They relate to the freedom to be left alone to use one's resources as one sees fit. Under negative rights, each person has a sphere of autonomy that others cannot violate ... The only claim on others is a freedom from intrusion" (Blank & Burau, 2004, pp. 18–19).

The UK's national health care system is based on the government providing care for all citizens. In contrast, the US has a mixed system with

Table 1. Dimensions of the Health Care Systems of US and UK.

Dimension	United States	United Kingdom
Citizen rights to health care?	Negative rights	Positive rights
Individual relates to society?	Individualistic	Egalitarian
Nature of system	Mixed and fragmented: Free market with governmental insurance for special vulnerable populations	Centralized with a national health system
Role of free market	Very high	Low but rising
Payment for care	Mixed: Government through taxes, private insurance, out-of-pocket	Government through general taxes
Extent health system publicly funded (2004)	44.7%	86.3%
Universal coverage	No	Yes
Ownership of facilities (hospitals, nursing homes, etc.)	Mixed: private for-profit, nonprofit, government	Predominately government
National policy on consumers involvement in health care system	No; variable policies for different diseases, government jurisdictions, & myriad of health insurance companies	Yes – consumers involvement mandated

Sources: Weitz (2004), Blank and Burau (2004), and World Health Organization (2007).

the market economy a central player along with governmental insurance for special populations (Medicaid, Medicare, Veteran's care, and public health facilities on state and county levels). The mixture includes many for-profit health insurance companies, self-insured health insurance of large corporations or labor unions, and non-profit health care insurance plans and providers. In the UK, the government pays health care costs through general taxes while in the US health care is funded by a mixture of private for-profit health insurance paid by employees and the organizations which employs them, government through general taxes, and consumers out-of-pocket. All citizens have health care coverage in the UK but access is limited in the US – more than 40 million Americans reported they did not receive needed health care services because of lack of health insurance (Weitz, 2004). Similarly with regard to ownership of facilities, the UK's facilities are owned predominately by the government and the US has a mixed system with some government facilities as well as extensive involvement of the non-profit and for-profit health insurance companies, hospitals, and nursing homes.

The UK's national health system has adopted a national policy requiring that consumers be involved in various aspects of the planning, development, delivery, and evaluation of services (DH, 1990, 2003). Although this policy has not yet been uniformly adopted across all conditions and diseases, the exemplars of consumers involvement in many aspects of service are in the field of mental health (Halliday & Sherwood, 2003).

The UK has adopted a national policy requiring that consumers be involved in all aspects of the nation's centralized national health system (DH, 1990, 2003); although this is not yet uniform across all diseases or conditions, there are examples from the mental health field of consumers being involved in all aspects of service delivery and development. (Halliday & Sherwood, 2003). The US has no national policy; instead, each disease area or silo has its own answer to the extent and ways in which it engages consumers. Some state-level policies are found where there are funded programs in mental illness, the developmentally delayed, and other disabilities.

The United States spends much more on health care per individual and as a percentage of GDP than the UK and generally has more high technology equipment, but health outcomes based on globally accepted indicators of life expectancy and infant mortality rates are lower (Table 2). Analysts attribute some of the extensive costs of the US system to the negative rights

Table 2. Expenditures, Health Outcomes, and Consumer Choice in the Health Care Systems of US and UK.

Dimension	United States	United Kingdom
$ spent on health care per capita (Intl dollars 2004)[a]	$6,096	$2,560
Health care: Percent of GDP (2004)[a]	15.4%	8.1%
Life expectancy at birth (2005)[a]	Male 75, Female 80	Male 77, Female 81
Infant mortality (per 1,000 live births 2005)[a]	7	5
MRI units per million population (1995)[b]	7.3	3.4
Patient choice of doctors[b]	Extensive, except some HMO's	Restricted: Sign up with GP in area
Primary care physician is gate-keeper to specialists[b]	Mixed: Some insurance yes; MDs averse to being gate-keepers	Yes: GP gate-keeper to specialist MD

[a]World Health Organization (2007).
[b]Blank and Burau (2004).

approach and the fact that adequately insured consumers expect extensive high technology equipment and expensive end-of-life care. Meanwhile, the uninsured lack even rudimentary prenatal care (Blank & Burau, 2004). In contrast, UK is known among European health systems for having the most efficient use of financial resources (Blank & Burau, 2004).

When policy analysts examine health care systems from the broadest perspective, very little about patient/consumer choice is mentioned. The major variables they discuss are governments (their policies and funding); health care professions, especially physicians; the free market economy of corporations, hospitals, health insurance companies, and pharmaceutical companies; the non-profit sector; and, issues of control, costs, and policies (Tuohy, 1999; Blank & Burau, 2004; Light, 2000). When changes in medical authority are analyzed by sociologists, the erosion in medical authority is not regarded as being due to patient/consumer choices or increasing consumer authority, but to shifts in financing and other policies by governments or strategies of the free market economy (Tuohy, 1999; Light, 2000). In these broad system-wide analyses of health care systems, consumer choice is viewed as important in whether or not health care systems allow consumers to choose their physician at initial point of contact and whether or not the initial point of contact is a gatekeeper to consumer's access to specialist physicians. US consumers are more likely to have a choice in their physician; UK consumers choices are very restricted – they have to sign up within the limited choices of GPs (general practitioner) available within their geographical area. Further, in the UK the GPs act as gatekeepers by referring consumers to specialists whereas in the US physicians are averse to this gatekeeping role although they are required to do it in some health insurance plans.

THE VOLUNTARY HEALTH SECTOR

An international study of the non-profit sector in a number of industrialized countries, known as the Johns Hopkins Comparative Nonprofit Sector project, was conducted in the late 1990s. US and UK were included among the 12 countries studied so direct comparisons can be made since standardized methodologies were used in all 12 countries. Researchers concluded that the differences in size among the voluntary sectors in US and UK were minor (Salamon & Anheier, 1996) but the composition of the sectors varied considerably. Education, health care, and social services sectors' share of the non-profit sector operating expenditure was 57% in Britain but 85% in US (Salamon & Anheier, 1996). Looking solely at health care, the voluntary sector operating expenditure was 52.67% in US and 3.5% in UK. Instead, UK's voluntary sector spends extensively on education and research (42%) and culture and recreation (20.2%).

An important and often forgotten part of the informal voluntary sector are SHGs and SHOs. We define SHGs as "autonomous, voluntary assemblies of people in similar situations or predicaments, or with the same disease or condition, who join together to cope with and resolve their troublesome issue through sharing knowledge and providing mutual social and emotional support" (Borkman, 2004, p. 428). Important to the definition is that SHGs are governed by and for the people with the shared experience, not by professionals or outsiders. SHOs are more formal than SHGs and often are "paid staff nonprofits" (Smith, 2000) – they are usually registered 501(C)3s (in the US) or charities (in UK) with budgets and goals to provide services to their peers but they use self-help/mutual aid approaches (Borkman et al., 2005). SHGs are usually too informal to be counted in tallies of voluntary organizations since they are not on tax rolls.

Service-user groups (UK) are like SHGs/SHOs in that they are voluntary assemblies of people with the same condition or disease but differ in that they tend to be advocacy or lobbying groups or formed specifically to comment on a specific service (e.g., in a locality) and do not necessarily provide emotional support, information, or develop collective experiential knowledge (Table 3).

Table 3. Characteristics of Self-Help and Advocacy Groups in US and UK.

Dimension	United States	United Kingdom
Percent population attend SHG per year[a,b]	4%–7%	4%
Number of 12th step SHGs[a]	1/3 of groups	Minor[c]
12-step SHGs impact on society	Major part of popular culture	Minor
University research on SHGs	Moderate	Minimal
Proportion of SHGs to official treatment units[d]	More SHGs in alcoholism & in mental illness	Fewer
Service-user advocacy groups	Few	Many
University research on service-users	Little	Extensive

[a]Wuthnow (1994) and Kessler, Mickelson, and Zhao (1997).
[b]Elsdon, Reynolds, and Stewart (2000) estimates that one in 25 of the population belong to a SHG in United Kingdom.
[c]Numbers of 12-step groups are not collated in United Kingdom.
[d]Goldstrom et al. (2006), SAMSHA (2006), and Room and Greenfield (1993).

NATIONAL AND COMMUNITY LEVELS OF SOCIAL CHANGE AND CONSUMER TRANSFORMATION

The contribution of SHGs and organizations to consumerism in health is found on two levels. First, SHGs contribute to *national* social movements: Relatively well documented is the importance of SHGs/SHOs to *national level health movements*. The typical process is that SHGs of concerned patients with disease X meet together to share their experiences of living with the disease; soon collective knowledge is created about what they need in daily living, deficiencies in their medical treatment or issues with unresponsive and inadequate health care system that leads to their empowerment as advocates for changes in the system. Often advocacy groups are created or the SHG becomes an advocacy group. Often elements of self-help/mutual aid are retained or reinstituted in the advocacy organizations to provide moral and emotional support and bolster new identities (the complexities of this process are theorized in Borkman, 1999). As a case in point, *Into Our Own Hands* (Morgen, 2002) chronicles the SHGs of women who learned about their bodies and appropriated the knowledge for women which culminated in the now-classic volume *Our Bodies, Ourselves: A Book by and for Women* (The Boston Women's Health Book Collective, 1971) which has become an icon of the women's health movement. Also see Chambré's (2006) discussion of SHGs and support groups for AIDS patients and Lerner's (2001) discussion of the SHG Recovery, Inc. for breast cancer (see Sulik & Eich-Krohm, 2008; Bourgeault et al., 2008 in this volume for a critique of how national level social movements run the danger of incorporation and individualization by neo-liberal policy making and the established medical systems).

Second, the *community* level of social change and consumer transformation made by SHGs/SHOs in the US and UK has not been recognized. We present four brief case studies based on published research to illustrate the kinds of changes SHGs/SHOs make at the meso level to both individual and collective change as well as their potential to impact the wider communities and services in which they are located (Table 4).

CASE 1: PERSONALITY DISORDER

The context for this 1999 study was that people labeled with personality disorder (PD) were not able to gain services for the diagnosis although they might receive services for other concurrent diagnoses, such as depression.

Table 4. Challenges to Medical Authority Made by Self-Help Groups.

Name of Group	Type Illness or Condition	Challenges to Medical or Popular Authority
1. Personality disorder	Mental illness: UK	Service-user research challenged (untreatable) psychiatric diagnoses & identified (treatable) condition to obtain medical care; advocacy
2. Carers	Caring for family member: UK	Reject popular idealistic views of caring; more realistic expectations; local advocacy to improve services
3. People who stutter	Speech disorder: US	Self-blaming "victims" evolve to empowered critics of professional therapies; change of meaning perspective and identity; advocacy to prevent stuttering and change research priorities
4. GROW adapted 12 step group	Mental illness: US	Role of ex-mental patient shed; normalized identity as member of "caring and sharing" community

The PD diagnosis was a "catch all" label with little scientific credibility, widely believed to be untreatable, and appeared to be a pejorative judgment rather than a clinical diagnosis (Lewis & Appleby, 1988). During the 1990s a number of people with PD diagnosis sought advocacy from a local branch of MIND, a national voluntary organization in the UK. Their experiences spanned the gamut from losing their children, being sent to psychiatric hospitals (hospitals for people with mental illness) to being denied mental health services. The UK Home Office had also developed policy proposals for managing people with a severe PD if they were deemed to be dangerous to the public – regardless of whether this was related to a deterioration in their clinical state – which included potential removal to special units.

A group of people with PD diagnosis formed a research partnership managed by Castillo, an advocate at the local MIND branch, and supervised by academic social scientists and funded by the local University. Castillo and the group developed a model of participatory research putting experiential knowledge at its center (Castillo, Allen, & Coxhead, 2001). Five of the original service-user group were trained as researchers and interviewed 50 people with PD diagnosis in the local area.

The results were groundbreaking. Common threads of childhood abuse and trauma were uncovered that were unknown to the medical model. The research was published extensively in national journals and the team presented at 18 professional conferences. Their questions and resulting findings provided credible empirical evidence of their collectively experientially based interpretations and contributed directly to national developments in the UK which now has developed services for people with this diagnosis.

CASE 2: CARERS

The official definition of a carer in UK is someone who cares, unpaid, for a relative, partner, or friend or for a child because of disability, illness, or frailty (DH, 1998). At the time of the study there were 5.7 million informal carers in the UK – one in eight adults, nearly as many men as women (42% and 58% respectively). In the UK there has been a national carers movement (Barnes, 1997) which has raised awareness about the personal and health consequences of providing long-term care and this lobby has contributed health and social policy initiatives such as the Carers (Recognition and Services) Act (DH, 1995) and The National Carers Strategy (DH, 1999). While health care is free in UK and welfare benefits are available for both the carer and the person they care for, the carers lobby has drawn attention to the inadequacy of existing benefits and social care services.

In the study (Munn-Giddings, 2003) of two SHGs, data were drawn from two taped sessions with each group as well as semi-structured interviews with 15 active members (who regularly attended meetings) and five inactive members who only received the newsletters. A significant finding was that inactive members' views on caring varied little from the dominant understandings and established literature (e.g., Finch, 1989). In contrast active members appeared to have undergone a subtle, but powerful, reinterpretation of their situations. Over time, they appeared to adjust their expectations in the light of empathetic and experiential exchanges with others. Their measure of being a (good enough) carer was in comparison with others in the group rather than to an abstract ideal.

Analysis revealed that it was the process of sharing and exchanging stories that made it possible for active members to share their coping strategies and to expose their difficulties (Munn-Giddings & McVicar, 2007). They found it difficult to expose their vulnerabilities even to sympathetic professionals and supportive family members were thought either not to fully understand the situation or had to be shielded from reality.

The carers groups implicitly challenged the conventional wisdom and through sharing their experiences confronted the realistic boundaries of their energy. They also realized the lack of governmental support to sustain them and became quiet advocates with local health and social care authorities to improve the support they received.

CASE 3: PEOPLE WHO STUTTER – FROM SELF-BLAMING "VICTIM" TO CRITIC OF STUTTERING THERAPY

This case study is based on Borkman's (1999, Chapters 5 & 6) longitudinal study of a SHG, the Caring Group for Stutters (pseudonym), which evolved over 10 years. The group began as a fragile collection of unselfconfident self-named "stutterers" and evolved into a mature organization of "people who stutter" who had reframed their stuttering and the results of therapies based on hundreds of attendees' testimonies.

The research relied on a variety of methods to collect and analyze data: participant observation of the group was done intensively for two years and less intensively for the following six years; periodic in-depth interviews were conducted with officers and leaders over the period; analysis of newsletters and other organizational documents were made; and two mail questionnaire surveys of attendees and of organizational functioning were done (see Borkman, 1999, p. 218).

The group began with the implicit goal of finding a cure for stuttering. A core of highly motivated members led the group while others attended, left, and/or returned. Attendees recounted their narrative of the types of therapies they had had (frequently, two or more) and the results: many stuttering therapies produced short term fluency of three or more months, but the individual then returned to his/her pre-therapy level of stuttering. They consistently attributed the therapy's failure to themselves. Over a period of several years, through the sharing of hundreds of experiences, a common understanding emerged of the serious limitations of stuttering therapies and that most commercialized "cures" were quacks. Reviewing the scientific research on stuttering from their experiential perspective, they realized no cure had been found. Note that it was only after developing confidence that their personal experiences with stuttering therapy constituted valid knowledge could they accept the reframing from stuttering being a personal deficiency to viewing it as a deficiency in the therapy per se.

With their reframed knowledge and research review of stuttering in children, they held public education sessions for parents advising them against therapy in order to prevent adult stuttering. From their experiential perspective, they reviewed and found major gaps in stuttering research funded by the National Institutes of Health (NIH) and became advocates challenging NIH to redress them. Finally, with their experiential expertise combined with a new consciousness from the rising disability movement (Charlton, 1998) they rejected the label of stutterer and referred to themselves as people who stutter: their speech handicap was but a part of the person.

CASE 4: GROW – FROM EX-MENTAL PATIENT TO RESPECTED MEMBER OF "A CARING AND SHARING" COMMUNITY

Community psychologists Julian Rappaport and Edward Seidman and their students (Rappaport et al., 1985) developed a collaborative research relationship with GROW, a self-help/mutual aid group for the mentally ill. Founded in Australia by previous mental patients, it was imported to Illinois in 1978; a decade later there were about 100 groups in Illinois. Using an adapted 12 step program, GROW holds weekly meetings, has official literature and creates "a caring and sharing community" with social gatherings, contact assignments, and friendships (Salem, Seidman, & Rappaport, 1988).

Professors Rappaport, Seidman, and their various students used a longitudinal study design to identify changes in individual member's psychological and social functioning over a 27 month period and a repeated cross-sectional design to periodically study meetings and the organization. Participant observation of over 500 meetings was in 15 locations in Illinois and over 300 individuals were interviewed from 2 to 8 hours and various measures of organizational climate, cohesion, and growth were taken. By the early 1990s GROW research was the subject of multiple graduate student dissertations and of publications in professional journals (e.g., Roberts et al., 1999; Salem et al., 1988; Kennedy & Humphreys, 1994).

GROW has a community narrative about its members, their identity, and potential. The "caring and sharing community" of givers as well as receivers provides hope and a sense of their own capacity for positive change (Rappaport, 1993, p. 245). Members' personal stories were often consistent with the community narrative. Members were less likely than their equivalents with similar histories of mental hospitalization to be rehospitalized (Rappaport, 1993). Rappaport who had studied chronic mental patients for decades did not find the typical emphasis on defining oneself as sick, being dependent on medications to control behavior, or longing to live an independent but lonely life. Instead, GROW members had many examples from their peers who had recovered and defined themselves differently. GROW members continued to use medication but did not see it as central to their self-definition. GROW members who were well into recovery had shed their internalized-societal view of the stigma of mental illness, no longer defined themselves as mentally ill and had self-images of being valuable and worthwhile. (Kennedy & Humphreys, 1994, p. 190). Rappaport concluded that the mutual help organization

> is a normative structure in social experience – not unlike families, religious organizations, political parties, labor unions, professional organizations, or other voluntary associations. Members are not clients receiving services and therefore somehow different from the rest of us; rather, they are people living lives. Professional treatment is not necessarily the appropriate comparison group if one wants to understand such experiences. (Rappaport, 1993, p. 246)

The group transformed persons labeled as mentally ill who were primarily consumers of health care to persons with positive and non-stigmatized identities who were members of a "caring and sharing community."

CONCLUSIONS

The US and UK share the phenomena of SHGs/SHOs; the peer led and owned nature of both is common in each country. In both countries SHGs/SHOs have contributed to social change and a broadened consumer "voice." SHGs/SHOs are embodied (Brown & Zavestoski, 2005, p. 3) change agents in which the participants base their problem solving on their personal experiences of illness or conditions. In the Introduction we listed six issues identified in the *national* embodied social movements (see p. 131) of greater consumer empowerment.

Examining the case studies, we identify which of the issues are illustrated in each case; this is presented in Table 5.

Thus, as is evident in Table 5, our cases illustrate all of the six issues of consumer challenges to medical authority indicating that local SHGs are confronting issues similar to the national level social movements, albeit on a smaller scale.

How do the health care systems shape the SHGs and SHOs? The major characteristics of the US health care system in this context are its mixed and decentralized nature, the lack of national policy on consumer decision-making in the health care system, and the extensive involvement of the

Table 5. Self-Help Groups Challenge of Medical Authority.

Consumer Challenges to Medical Authority	SHGs That Illustrate the Issue
1. Questioning disease causation	Case 1: Personality disorder – UK
2. Confronting inadequate treatment options	Case 1: Personality disorder – UK Case 3: People who stutter – US
3. Criticizing strategies of prevention	Case 3: People who stutter – US
4. Challenging research funding priorities	Case 3: People who stutter – US
5. Advocacy to participate in policy making	Case 1: Personality disorder – UK Case 2: Carers – UK
6. Creating non-stigmatizing and constructive identities	Case 1: Personality disorder – UK Case 3: People who stutter – US Case 4: Grow – US

voluntary sector in health care. How do these characteristics influence the reactions of SHGs in our case studies?

In the UK's centralized system with a national mandate for service user/consumer involvement, our cases illustrate that:

Case 1 – Personality disorder illustrates that the policy on consumer involvement encourages self-advocacy even in areas (disease causation) which had previously been regarded as the sole province of professional physicians.

Case 2 – Carers revolved more on popular notions of carers than to professionalized views within the health care system but showed that local SHGs can evolve into lobbying groups especially since and when there are local level units of the national health system available to hear their complaints. (In the US, such local groups might not have any local health authorities with jurisdiction to do anything about their grievances).

In the US's mixed, decentralized, and fragmented system that has no national policy on consumer involvement but an extensive participation of the voluntary sector in health care has arisen in various silos, our cases illustrate that:

Case 3 – People who stutter – local SHGs can raise the consciousness and transform individuals from being "victims" to experientially knowledgeable non-stigmatized persons and the local SHGs can evolve into organizations with advocacy goals such as educating peripheral groups (parents of children who stutter) and criticizing research priorities of federal agencies.

Case 4 – GROW, the 12-step based group that attracts people with mental illness diagnoses, illustrates that SHGs/SHOs can develop alternative and de-stigmatized meaning perspectives and identities to serious mental illness.

GROW also illustrates the high prevalence of 12-step SHGs in the US. Even though Australia is culturally and politically closer to the UK than it is to the US, GROW was successfully imported into US probably because of the fertile and extensive environment of 12-step based SHGs here.

Recovery identities that are non-stigmatized, de-medicalized (Conrad & Schneider, 1992), and anonymous are an integral part of US culture due to the long and strong influence of AA and other 12-step recovery (Room, 1992); GROW could build on this tradition.

The UK's national policy of consumer involvement in decision-making in health is exhibited in ways other than have been shown in our cases. Thus:

1. There is a policy of "expert patients" (DH, 2006) modeled on the Stanford Chronic Disease course (Lorig, 1982) which provides group based support for people in the management of their long term condition led by peers with the same condition and which now includes carers. The program is for all age groups; over 1,400 volunteer peer tutors are currently involved.
2. Involving service users in planning, providing, and evaluating education and training has been advocated in national health and social care policies since the late 1990s. For example, in 2003 UK universities were required to change the programmes they were delivering for the training of social workers by involving experiences consumers/expert patients and carers in all aspects of the course including the selection, teaching, and assessment of students, design and review of the degree, and preparation for and provision of placement (DH, 2002, p. 9).
3. A distinctive language of "service-users" has developed that is widely used in policy, practice, and academic writing that specifically replaces the term "consumer."
4. On a national level, United Kingdom appears to be developing a health consumer movement (Allsop, Jones, & Baggott, 2005; Allsop, Baggott, & Jones, 2002) of which SHGs are a part.

We propose that the national health policy mandating the engagement of service users or consumers in the policy process is both responding to and facilitating this social movement in the UK. There are concerns that incorporating consumers into mainstream services can both inhibit dissent and lead to "professionalized consumers" who do not necessarily represent the views of the wider consumer group. The key question is whether these measures lead to genuine power sharing in decision-making or to tokenism.

In contrast, in the US, there is no coherent health consumer movement. SHGs/SHOs appear to occupy both a role and space outside the main health care system. While forming links with local sympathetic health professionals (see GROW), meso level groups and organizations have limited opportunities to impact mainstream health policy and practice. Only the larger national social movements have been successful in this way. In this sense SHGs/SHOs remain an alternative form of health resource for consumers to "choose." Interestingly, in two major areas, treatment for alcoholism and for mental illness, more services are provided by SHGs/SHOs than by mainstream professionals (Goldstrom et al., 2006; Room & Greenfield, 1993; SAMSHA, 2006). These figures appear to be well kept secrets as mainstream services seem oblivious to the high prevalence of SHGs/SHOs providing services along side them; this is an indirect indicator that SHGs/SHOs are outside and separate from the mainstream system.

What is important to note is that while similarities and distinctions can be discerned in the global health movements, the distinctive nature of national health systems and policies enable and constrain the forms that SHGs/SHOs are likely to take. Dill and Coury (2008) in "Forging a new Commons: Self Help Associations in Slovenia and Croatia" in this volume found that SHGs/SHOs in post-Communist Yugoslavia (now Slovenia and Croatia) were not only less independent from the state but they also cultivated this dependence, among other differences, from their equivalents in US and Europe which were attributed to the societal context of transition to capitalism with an emerging voluntary sector.

How Do These Findings Contribute to Consumerism Theory in Health?

Two strands of theoretically based material seem relevant to our findings: First, the "consumerist model" with its implied limitation and baggage of "patient choice" seems inadequate conceptually to support the extensive and systemic changes in patient/service-user involvement in decision-making occurring in the British health care system. Croft and Beresford (1993) propose an expanded model – the consumerist versus the democratic approaches to involvement. The consumerist model focuses on the patient as a consumer gaining information and obtaining better managed services within the status quo context of professional dominance. In contrast, the democratic model views the "patient" as a citizen or service-user with rights to participate in decision-making and to be an advocate for changes in the system. These distinctions seem more applicable to the UK health care system than to that of the US.

Second, the activism of patients and citizens in SHGs and SHOs that challenge the frameworks, diagnoses, and treatments of medical professionals is on a community or meso level rather than the national macro-level. People that share a common health condition find through their participation in SHGs/SHOs a voice to challenge the prevailing medical or popular view of their condition when their lived experience does not match the model presented by medicine or the culture. Retaining the emphasis on collective community activities (the wellspring of many national movements) reminds us of the importance of grassroots peer led collective action that gives participants the opportunity to be both providers as well as consumers of services (see Greenspan & Handy, 2008; Staples & Stein, 2008, in this book). The SHGs/SHOs are advocating *or living* social change, but we have lacked conceptualizations of community-level social changes. A new book begins to fill in this gap: *From the Bottom Up: Grassroots Organizations Making Social Change* by Carol Chetkovich and Frances Kunreuther (2006) which describes 16 small locally-based grassroots organizations that are making systemic and structural changes in their communities.

In summary, we have preliminary evidence from this chapter and from Dill and Coury's (2008) chapter in this volume that the health care system and the voluntary sector of a country constitute a context that impacts the activities and outcomes of SHGs/SHOs and of consumer participation in policy making. Despite many similarities in SHGs in the UK and US, there are major differences in consumer participation in health care policy and we suggest that analysts who write in universalistic terms as if the country and its health care system were irrelevant are on shaky ground.

ACKNOWLEDGMENTS

We appreciate the constructive suggestions that improved the chapter made by the editors Susan M. Chambré and Melinda Goldner. Aina Stunz's incisive editing helped focus and sharpen our arguments in a concise and beneficial manner.

REFERENCES

Allsop, J., Baggott, R., & Jones, K. (2002). Health consumer groups and the national policy process. In: S. Henderson & A. Petersen (Eds), *Consuming health: The commodification of health care* (pp. 48–65). London: Routledge.

Allsop, J., Jones, K., & Baggott, R. (2005). Health consumer groups in the UK: A new social movement? In: P. Brown & S. Zavestoski (Eds), *Social movements in health* (pp. 57–76). Malden, MA: Blackwell Publishing Ltd.

Barnartt, S., & Scotch, R. (2001). *Disability protests: Contentious politics 1970–1999*. Washington, DC: Gallaudet University Press.

Barnes, M. (1997). *Private lives and public policy: The self-organisation of carers in care, communities & citizens*. Harlow: Longman.

Baudrillard, J. (1998). *The consumer society: Myths & structures*. Thousand Oaks, CA: Sage.

Blank, R. H., & Burau, V. (2004). *Comparative health policy*. England: Palgrave Macmillan.

Borkman, T. (1975). Changing sex roles: Consciousness-raising groups as a vehicle of adult resocialization. In: J. Williams, A. Schwartzbaum & R. Caney (Eds), *Sociological research symposium V* (pp. 296–300). Richmond, VA: Virginia Commonwealth University.

Borkman, T. (1999). *Understanding self-help/mutual aid: Experiential learning in the commons*. New Brunswick, NJ: Rutgers University Press.

Borkman, T. (2004). Self-help groups. In: D. F. Burlingame (Ed.), *Philanthropy in America: A comprehensive historical encyclopedia* (Vol. 2, pp. 428–432). Santa Barbara, CA: ABC-Clio.

Borkman, T., Karlsson, M., Munn-Giddings, C., & Smith, L. (2005). *Self-help organizations and mental health: Case studies of mental health self help organizations in US, England and Sweden*. Stockholm, Sweden: Skondal Institute and University.

Boston Women's Health Book Collective. (1971). *Our bodies, ourselves: A book by and for women*. Boston, MA: New England Free Press.

Bourgeault, I. L., Declercq, E., Sandall, J., Wrede, S., Vanstone, M., van Teijlingen, E., DeVries, R., & Benoit, C. (2008). Too Posh To Push? Comparative perspectives on maternal request caesarean sections in Canada, the US, the UK and Finland. In: S. Chambré & M. Goldner (Eds), *Advances in medical sociology: Patients, consumers and civil society* (Vol. 10, pp. 99–123). Bingley, UK: Emerald Group Publishing Limited.

Brown, P., & Zavestoski, S. (Eds). (2005). *Social movements in health*. Oxford: Blackwell Ltd.

Castillo, H., Allen, L., & Coxhead, N. (2001). The hurtfulness of a diagnosis: User research about personality disorder. *Mental Health Practice*, *4*(9), 16–19.

Chambré, S. M. (2006). *Fighting for our lives: New York's AIDS community and the politics of disease*. New Brunswick, NJ: Rutgers University Press.

Charlton, J. (1998). *Nothing about us without us: Disability oppression and empowerment*. Berkeley, CA: University of California Press.

Chetkovich, C., & Kunreuther, F. (2006). *From the bottom up: Grassroots organizations making social change*. Ithaca, NY: ILR press, an imprint of Cornell University Press.

Conrad, P., & Schneider, J. W. (1992). *Deviance and medicalization: From badness to sickness*. Philadelphia: Temple University Press.

Croft, S., & Beresford, P. (1993). *Getting involved: A practical manual*. London: Open Services Project.

DH – Department of Health. (1990). *National Health Service and Community Care Act*. London: HMSO.

DH – Department of Health. (1995). *Carers (Recognition and Services) Act*. London: The Stationery Office.

DH – Department of Health. (1998). *Living in Britain: Results from the 1998 General Household Survey*. London: The Stationery Office.

DH – Department of Health. (1999). *National strategy for carers*. London: The Stationery Office.

DH – Department of Health. (2002). *Requirements for social work training*. London: The Stationery Office.

DH – Department of Health. (2003). *Patient and public involvement*. London: The Stationery Office.

DH – Department of Health. (2006). *The expert patients programme*. London: The Stationery Office.

Dill, A., & Coury, J. (2008). Forging a new commons: Self-help associations in Slovenia and Croatia. In: S. Chambré & M. Goldner (Eds), *Advances in medical sociology: Patients, consumers and civil society* (Vol. 10, pp. 247–271). Bingley, UK: Emerald Group Publishing Limited.

Elsdon, K., Reynolds, J., & Stewart, S. (2000). *Sharing experience, living and learning: A study of self-help groups*. London: Community Matters.

Epstein, S. (1996). *Impure science: AIDS, activism and the politics of knowledge*. Berkeley: University of California Press.

Finch, J. (1989). *Family obligations and social change*. Cambridge: Polity Press.

Goldstrom, I. D., Campbell, J., Rogers, J. A., Lambert, D. B., Blacklow, B., Henderson, M. J., & Manderscheid, R. W. (2006). National estimates for mental health mutual support groups, self-help organizations, and consumer-operated services. *Administration and Policy in Mental Health and Mental Health Services Research*, *33*(1), 92–103.

Greenspan, I., & Handy, F. (2008). From discovery to recovery and beyond: The role of voluntary health sector organizations in the lives of women with breast cancer. In: S. Chambré & M. Goldner (Eds), *Advances in medical sociology: Patients, consumers and civil society* (Vol. 10, pp. 151–176). Bingley, UK: Emerald Group Publishing Limited.

Halliday, M., & Sherwood, L. (2003). *Mental health user/survivor research in UK. A policy briefing*. London: Mental Health Foundation.

Haug, M., & Lavin, B. (1983). *Consumerism in medicine: Challenging physician authority*. Beverly Hills, CA: Sage.

Henderson, S. (2002). Consumerism in the hospital context. In: S. Henderson & A. Petersen (Eds), *Consuming health* (pp. 105–120). London: Routledge.

Henderson, S., & Petersen, A. (Eds). (2002). *Consuming health: The commodification of health care*. London: Routledge.

Hess, D. J. (2005). Medical modernization, scientific research fields and the epistemic politics of health social movements. In: P. Brown & S. Zavestoski (Eds), *Social movements in health* (pp. 27–30). Oxford: Blackwell Publishing Ltd.

Kennedy, M., & Humphreys, K. (1994). Understanding worldview transformation in members of mutual help groups. In: F. Lavoie, T. Borkman & B. Gidron (Eds), *Self-help and mutual aid groups* (pp. 181–198). New York: Haworth.

Kessler, R. C., Mickelson, K. D., & Zhao, S. (1997). Patterns and correlates of self-help group membership in the United States. *Social Policy*, *27*, 27–46.

Lerner, B. H. (2001). *The breast cancer wars*. New York, NY: Oxford University Press.

Lewis, G., & Appleby, L. (1988). Personality disorder: The patients psychiatrists dislike. *British Journal of Psychiatry*, *153*, 44–49.

Light, D. W. (2000). The medical profession and organizational change: From professional dominance to countervailing power. In: C. E. Bird, P. Conrad & A. M. Fremont (Eds), *Handbook of medical sociology* (5th ed., pp. 201–216). Upper Saddle River, NJ: Prentice Hall.

Lorig, K. (1982). Anatormy of a patient education program: Arthritis self-management. *Rehabilitation Nursing*, *7*(4), 16–20.

Minton, H. L. (2002). *Departing from deviance: A history of homosexual rights and emancipatory science in America*. Chicago: University of Chicago Press.

Morgen, S. (2002). *Into our own hands: The women's health movement in the United States, 1969–1990*. New Brunswick, NJ: Rutgers University Press.

Munn-Giddings, C. (2003). *Mutuality and movement: An exploration of the relationship between self-help/mutual aid and social policy*. Unpublished doctoral thesis, Loughborough University, UK.

Munn-Giddings, C., & McVicar, A. (2007). Self-help groups as mutual support: What do carers value? *Health and Social Care in the Community*, *15*(1), 26–34.

Rappaport, J. (1993). Narrative studies, personal stories, and identity transformation in the mutual help context. *Journal of Applied Behavioral Science*, *29*(2), 239–256.

Rappaport, J., Seidman, E., Toro, P. A., McFadden, L. S., Reischl, T. M., Roberts, L. J., Salem, D. A., Stein, C. H., & Zimmerman, M. A. (1985). Collaborative research with a mutual help organization. *Social Policy*, *Winter*, *15*, 13–24.

Reid, M., & Clark, A. (2002). The active citizen works hard: Living with chronic heart failure. In: S. Henderson & A. Petersen (Eds), *Consuming health: The commodification of health care* (pp. 121–139). London: Routledge.

Roberts, L. J., Salem, D., Rappaport, J., Toro, P., Luke, A., Douglas, A., & Seidman, E. (1999). Giving and receiving help: Interpersonal transactions in mutual-help meetings and psychosocial adjustment of members. *American Journal of Community Psychology*, *27*(6), 841–868.

Room, R. (1992). Healing ourselves and our planet: The emergence and nature of a generalized twelve-step consciousness. *Contemporary Drug Problems*, *19*(Winter), 717–740.

Room, R., & Greenfield, T. (1993). Alcoholics Anonymous, other 12-step movements and psychotherapy in the US population, 1990. *Addiction*, *88*(4), 555–562.

Rutherford, M., & Gallo-Cruz, S. (2008). Selling the ideal birth: Rationalization and re-enchantment in the marketing of maternity care. In: S. Chambré & M. Goldner (Eds), *Advances in medical sociology: Patients, consumers and civil society* (Vol. 10, pp. 75–98). Bingley, UK: Emerald Group Publishing Limited.

Salamon, L. M., & Anheier, H. K. (1996). *The emerging nonprofit sector: An overview*. Manchester: Manchester University Press.

Salem, D. A., Seidman, E., & Rappaport, J. (1988). Community treatment of the mentally ill: The promise of mutual-help organizations. *Social Work*, *33*(5), 403–408.

SAMSHA – Substance Abuse and Mental Health Services Administration. (2006). *Results from the 2005 National Survey on Drug Use and Health: National Findings*. Office of Applied Studies, NSDUH Series H-30, DHHS Publication No. SMA 06-4194. Rockville, MD.

Smith, D. H. (2000). *Grassroots associations*. Thousand Oaks, CA: Sage.

Staples, L., & Stein, R. (2008). The clubhouse model: Mental health consumer–provider partnerships for recovery. In: S. Chambré & M. Goldner (Eds), *Advances in medical sociology: Patients, consumers and civil society* (Vol. 10, pp. 177–196). Bingley, UK: Emerald Group Publishing Limited.

Starr, P. (1982). *The social transformation of American medicine*. New York: Basic Books.

Sulik, G. A., & Eich-Krohm, A. (2008). No longer a patient: The social construction of the medical consumer. In: S. Chambré & M. Goldner (Eds), *Advances in medical sociology: Patients, consumers and civil society* (Vol. 10, pp. 3–28). Bingley, UK: Emerald Group Publishing Limited.

Tuohy, C. H. (1999). *Accidental logics: The dynamics of change in the health care arena in the United States, Britain, and Canada*. New York, NY: Oxford University Press.

Weitz, R. (2004). *The sociology of health, illness, and health care: A crticial approach* (3rd ed.). Belmont, CA: Wadsworth/Thompson Learning.

World Health Organization. (2007). Countries data and statistics. Accessed on February 24, 2008. Available at www.who.int/countries

Wuthnow, R. (1994). *Sharing the journey: Support groups and America's new quest for community*. New York: Free Press.

FROM DISCOVERY TO RECOVERY AND BEYOND: THE ROLE OF VOLUNTARY HEALTH SECTOR ORGANIZATIONS IN THE LIVES OF WOMEN WITH BREAST CANCER

Itay Greenspan and Femida Handy

ABSTRACT

Purpose – *The goal of this chapter is to understand the role of nonprofit voluntary health organizations (VHOs) in the lives of Canadian women coping with breast cancer.*

Methodology – *Through qualitative interviews with breast cancer survivors and records of VHOs active in this field, we assess the level and nature of their interactions and impact on women's quality of life.*

Findings – *Our findings suggest that at the micro-level, VHOs are venues for women to receive auxiliary services such as information, counseling, and support that complement the mainstream health care provision. While VHO services empower women as health care consumers, we show that they also serve as venues for women to reciprocate by volunteering. This process of reciprocity helps women cope with their own healing and*

Patients, Consumers and Civil Society
Advances in Medical Sociology, Volume 10, 151–176

ISSN: 1057-6290/doi:10.1016/S1057-6290(08)10008-0

allows them to be not only consumers but also producers of health services.

Research limitations – *The non-random nature and the small sample size make our findings not easily generalizable to the larger population of breast cancer survivors; rather they are indicative of the experiences of Canadian women in one large urban metropolitan area.*

Value of the chapter – *We demonstrate the role of VHOs as venues of health consumerism as well as places for consumers to become involved in the production of services by volunteering.*

INTRODUCTION

Breast cancer is not a new disease; cases of breast cancer have been described as early as ancient Egypt (Donegan, 2006). For centuries, the medical profession has made efforts to find ways of alleviating the pain and suffering caused by breast cancer and to increase survival rates (de Moulin, 1983; Donegan, 2006; Leopold, 1999). The range of medical options was limited, but over the years, various treatments have been developed (Sakorafas, 2001); none of them, however, could prevent or cure the disease.

In the past, a woman ultimately had to conform to treatments decided unilaterally by "the heroes in white coats" (Lupton, 1997, p. 379); little or no "consumerism" or choice was involved in her behavior.[1] However, today, due to the increasing range of medical options available, women diagnosed with breast cancer face difficult choices in deciding which treatment (if at all) to receive. Since many alternative and complementary treatments *are* available by government, private or nonprofit providers, both within and outside the mainstream health care system, and since physicians are no longer viewed as "doctor-as-God" personas (Lupton, 1997, p. 373), most women patients – willingly or not, consciously or not – are becoming health consumers (Henderson & Peterson, 2002; Sulik & Eich-Krohm, this volume).

While some scholars have argued for such consumerism to correct the "troubling imbalance of power between providers and consumers" (Kreps, 1996, p. 41), it is not at all clear whether the availability of multiple choices that have allowed women to get involved in treatment decisions have unequivocally reduced this imbalance. Treatment choices for women with breast cancer are constrained by systemic barriers such as accessibility to medical treatments or health insurance coverage, as well as personal work or family circumstances. Choices that give a sense of consumerism may be empowering for women with the wherewithal and resources, but can be stressful for those who lack them. And, many women overwhelmed with choices turn back to the opinion of an "expert" physician to be a single dominant voice. Yet, for the savvy consumer, this single opinion, even under stressful circumstances, may be inadequate, or insufficiently "reflexive" (Lupton, 1997), and she may seek alternatives to understand the disease and her available options.

Outside of the medical profession, nonprofit voluntary health organizations (VHOs) have a significant role to play. While there exists vast literature documenting the response of the medical establishment in the treatment and search for the cure of breast cancer, there is a relative dearth of research documenting the response of the voluntary health sector to breast cancer (Aronowitz, 2007; King, 2006), especially of VHOs involved in direct service provision rather than political advocacy. This chapter is an attempt to examine the response of VHOs to breast cancer in Canada. We document how women with breast cancer interact with VHOs – from discovery to recovery and beyond. We assess the nature, and level of interaction, and the impact of these interactions on women's quality of life, through qualitative interviews with breast cancer survivors.

We note that VHOs' impact occurs on two levels: (1) on the macro-level, it includes interactions with social, political, and medical institutions, and involves activities such as research, fundraising, lobbying, and advocacy; (2) on the micro-level, it includes direct interactions of non-medical service providers with women and their families, including activities such as networking, education, counseling, and self-help or peer-to-peer support.

In this chapter, we focus primarily on the micro-level impact. We argue that, at this level, VHOs promote health consumerism by expanding the diversity of services offered, and by empowering women to take part in their own healing through reciprocal relationships with the VHOs. We find that VHOs are venues where women may have a dual role, both as consumers and producers of health services. Our findings also shed light on the impact of these relationships on the quality of life of women recovering from breast cancer.

The chapter is structured as follows: the next section reviews the literature pertinent to our topic. This is followed by a description of the study's methodology and findings. Here we identify the types of breast-cancer-related VHOs in the City of Toronto (the study location) and provide a micro-level analysis of the interactions of these organizations with women with breast cancer during various stages of the disease. Subsequently, we introduce the story of Mary, a fictional character representing a composite of our interviewees, in order to portray how a typical breast cancer patient coped with the disease and interacted with VHOs. This leads us to the discussion and concluding sections.

REVIEW OF THE LITERATURE

Millions of women around the world are either living with breast cancer or have a close friend or relative who is affected by the disease. In Canada, one in nine women is diagnosed with breast cancer, and one in 27 women will die from it during their lifetimes (CCS, 2007, p. 55). Hence, it is no surprise that breast cancer has become a serious health concern facing Canadian women of all age groups (Pollard, 2005). Furthermore, despite the fact that breast cancer mortality rates have declined since the 1990s, as many as 22,000 Canadian women are still diagnosed with breast cancer every year (CCS, 2007, p. 2).

VHOs are nonprofit voluntary organizations "that engage in health-related activities, provide and administer both general and specialized health care services, as well as health support services, excluding hospitals" (Statistics Canada, 2005, p. 14). The non-medical services provided by VHOs often complement the medical services women receive through the mainstream health care system. In this study, we pay particular attention to the subset of VHOs that deal with breast cancer. Breast-cancer-related VHOs are actively advocating for patient rights, promoting early detection and prevention of the disease, engaging in fundraising for research to find a cure for the disease, and raising awareness among women, doctors, and the public. In addition, VHOs work to provide direct services to women with breast cancer. These services include, among others, distributing information on coping with breast cancer and choices of treatment, counseling, self-help support groups, visitations by volunteer breast cancer survivors, and provision of items through which women can regain their confidence (such as wigs, prostheses, or makeup) at low or no cost. Breast-cancer-related VHOs range from large, well-funded organizations to small grassroots organizations that function primarily as self-help or support groups.

Breast-cancer-related VHOs vary on several dimensions. The American Cancer Society (ACS) and the Canadian Cancer Society (CCS), for example, are considerably different in terms of their goals, structure, leadership, governance, politics, and funding from small, grassroots, volunteer-based self-help groups. The ACS and the CCS are national, policy-, advocacy-, and research-oriented, and are more likely to be controlled by physicians and other paid professionals, with funding coming from all levels of government (Leopold, 1999). The smaller organizations, on the other hand, are often run by and comprised of non-medical professionals and volunteers, many of whom are breast cancer survivors. They often rely on private donations and their services are either free or have a nominal charge.

Several accounts can be made in explaining the emergence of non-medical VHOs dealing with breast cancer. In the nonprofit literature, scholars have argued that VHOs' service provision is the result of the public and for-profit sector's failure to meet societal demands (Weisbrod, 1988). In Canada, for example, even a government-sponsored universal health care system does not provide sufficient services for women with breast cancer; hence, VHOs arise to supply the unmet demands for psychological and social support (Hart, 2007; Turner, Kelly, Swanson, Allison, & Wetzig, 2004).

In other social science literatures, VHOs concerned with breast cancer are part of the broader women's health movement which developed in the 1970s. This movement criticized the chauvinistic and paternalistic practices of male doctors (Lerner, 2001), sought equality and self-determination for women, and primarily promoted women's "right to choose" their medical treatments (Boehmer, 2000; King, 2006; Leopold, 1999). Although reproductive issues were central in the first wave of the women's movement, over time, public awareness and the fight against breast cancer moved to the forefront of the movement's agenda (King, 2006).

However, the rising visibility and the growth in funding of prominent breast cancer organizations distorted the original goals of breast cancer activists who lead the women's health movement. Much of the current literature on breast cancer politics, especially from the United States, critiques the large macro-level VHOs such as the ACS (Boehmer, 2000; Davis, 2007; King, 2006; Leopold, 1999; Lerner, 2001). These VHOs, the critics argue, cooperate with the established medical system and with big corporations in promoting agendas that do not focus on breast cancer prevention, but rather on early diagnosis and treatment that are revenue-generating for their for-profit partners or sponsors (Leopold, 1999). Recent works by Samantha King (2004, 2006) document thoroughly how breast cancer has been commodified in the past two decades, and how breast cancer organizations (such as Susan G. Komen for the Cure or the ACS) became central in this commodification process by facilitating consumer-oriented philanthropy. Events organized by these organizations enjoyed the sponsorship of private corporations, and encouraged private and corporate giving, which ultimately depoliticized the field and created a "corporatized public sphere" (King, 2004). This literature, while focusing on the politics of large national advocacy and fundraising organizations, ignores the myriad of micro-level VHOs that provide direct services to women with breast cancer; these VHOs are the focus of our chapter.

The two most prominent types of VHOs at the micro-level are support organizations and community self-help groups (Borkman & Munn-Giddings, this volume). As support organizations, VHOs provide many auxiliary services (transportation, day care, wellness clinics, prostheses and wigs, etc.) as well as one-on-one peer support delivered by breast cancer survivors. Research has shown that recipients of such services generally express satisfaction with the support they receive and report incremental benefits to their quality of life (Ashbury, Cameron, Mercer, Fitch, & Nielsen, 1998). Interestingly, the impact of these support programs was also found to be invaluable to those who deliver them, usually survivors-volunteers themselves (Lee, 1997; Matthew, Danette, Hann, Denniston, & Smith, 2002). In assessing the motivations of survivors to voluntarily lead such programs, Lee (1997) found that they chose to volunteer not only for helping others with emotional support and with knowledge sharing, but also for personal gains: volunteering played a role in promoting the survivors' overall recovery process and quality of life.

Community self-help groups are a second type of VHO helpful in navigating the short- and long-term impact of breast cancer (Borkman & Munn-Giddings, this volume; Edgar, Remmer, Rosberger, & Rapkin, 2003; Gray, Fitch, Davis, & Phillips, 1997). Emotional, informational, and practical support in these groups includes connecting with other breast cancer survivors, feeling understood, sharing experiences, and providing hope; interventions to remediate high levels of anxiety are also needed at all stages (Hodgkinson et al., 2007). Challenges that such intimate self-help groups pose are how to deal with deaths of a group member and how to balance the group's primary purpose of providing mutual support with secondary goals of dealing with group business and engaging in meaningful advocacy (Gray et al., 1997). The use of, and participation in, self-help organizations appears to represent an intentional approach to dealing with the distress of cancer (Edgar, Remmer, Rosberger, & Fournier, 2000). These groups transform patients into consumers who challenge medical knowledge and advocate for wider participation (Borkman & Munn-Giddings, this volume). Women in these groups had greater improvement in psychological symptoms and reported less pain than women in a control group. The result from this study and other literature (e.g., Davison,

Pennebaker, & Dickerson, 2000; Spiegel, Bloom, Kraemer, & Gottheil, 1989) suggest that such impact was significant. However, in assessing the impact of support groups on women's quality of life, Goodwin et al. (2001) found that, contrary to popular opinion, support groups do not extend the lives of women with advanced breast cancer.

Increased access to information is an added value that both self-help and support groups can provide to women with breast cancer. Several studies noted the importance of information for women with breast cancer (Degner et al., 1997; Gray et al., 1998; Vivar & McQueen, 2005). A study conducted in Canada on informational needs and decisional preferences among women with breast cancer concluded that 66 percent of women wanted to either make their treatment decisions on their own or in collaboration with their physicians (Degner et al., 1997). Another study reported that patients receiving appropriate information show greater involvement in treatment decision-making, better preparation for medical procedures, increased satisfaction with treatment choices and interactions with health professionals, and greater ability to cope during and after treatment (Gray et al., 1998).

THE CONTEXT: VHOs IN CANADA

Current trends suggest a growing number of VHOs in Canada. In 2003, over 5,300 Canadian VHOs existed, representing 3.3 percent of the total registered nonprofits in Canada and accounting for 8.2 percent of total revenues of the nonprofit sector (Statistics Canada, 2005). In 2004, VHOs attracted over $1.2 billion in donations and almost 400,000 hours of volunteering contributed by 57 percent of Canadians (Hall, Lasby, Gumulka, & Tryon, 2006). Statistics on VHOs are only available in aggregate form; breast-cancer-related VHOs are not reported separately. However, below we provide an estimated number of these organizations in the City of Toronto, where the study was conducted.

The choice of the study location is strategic: Toronto – the capital of the Province of Ontario and the largest city in Canada with a population of over 5.4 million within its metropolitan area (Statistics Canada, 2007) – houses the headquarters of many national, provincial, and local nonprofit organizations, including those dealing with breast cancer.[2]

Recognizing the capacity of VHOs to deliver services, conduct research, advocate, and represent the voice of health consumers, the Canadian federal government, through two separate initiatives launched between 1993 and

2003, funded VHOs to help them meet their goals (Health Canada, 1999). As a result, VHOs received increased funding from the government, which, in turn, generated greater organizational capacity-building at the national and local levels. In addition, in order to ensure levels of services across the country, the government encouraged networking among VHOs, and helped in establishing VHOs where services were deficient.

The health care system in Ontario, although funded and regulated by the federal government, is administered by the provincial government and is universally available to every resident. It covers all medical services, including doctor examinations, medical testing, emergency care, treatment, and hospital care. This implies that for women with breast cancer all essential medical services are presumably available at no cost, relegating the VHOs to a role of providing auxiliary and complementary non-medical services. Despite the universality of the Canadian health care system, very limited psychological and emotional supports are offered to patients as part of the system (Myhr & Payne, 2006; Romanow & Marchildon, 2003). This support is important and remains a focal point of unmet needs of breast cancer survivors (Hart, 2007; Turner et al., 2004). However, over the past two decades, Ontario has been undergoing fundamental structural reform in the health care system, in which publicly funded health services were amalgamated into regional governance structures, and some free services were curtailed. Although not formally part of this reform, VHOs became "part of the solution" by taking responsibility for some of the deficit (Birdsell, 2003).

METHODS

Qualitative methods – in particular in-depth interviews and organizational inventory – were used in this study for data collection. The need for such methods in the research of self-help and support groups has already been acknowledged in previous studies (Edgar et al., 2003; Harris & Templeton, 2001).

Voluntary Health Organizations (VHOs)

An inventory of Toronto-based organizations dealing with breast cancer was carried out. For this purpose, a list of organizations was obtained from the Internet, telephone directories, and local libraries where information on grassroots smaller organizations was posted. This list was augmented by information obtained from key personnel in two large and well-known breast cancer VHOs and from our interviewees (on the latter, see below). We reviewed the organizations' websites, annual reports (where possible), and their mission statements or equivalent to determine their geographic scope, size, and types of services offered. This was used to elicit the roles of VHOs in the lives of women with breast cancer.[3]

Interviews with Breast Cancer Survivors

In-depth, open-ended interviews, ranging from one to three hours, were conducted with a sample of 15 women survivors in order "to understand the world from the subjects' point of view, ... [and] to unfold the meaning of peoples' experiences" (Kvale, 1996, p. 1). Our aim was to estimate the level and nature of interaction that women with breast cancer had with nonprofit VHOs. Introductory questions were asked on issues such as socioeconomic status, and length of time since first diagnosis. Then, each interviewee was asked to tell her story since she discovered breast cancer, keeping in mind all her interactions and experiences with VHOs. Such interviews allow for narrative description of how women perceive their experiences with, communication about, and help from service providers (whether doctors or VHOs) in dealing with breast cancer (Harris & Templeton, 2001).

Interviewees were female breast cancer survivors who were treated medically in Toronto hospitals, and who, at the time of the interview, were at different stages on the road from "discovery to recovery." In recruiting our sample, we relied on a snowball sampling technique (Goodman, 1961). Despite criticism for being a non-probability sampling technique (Erickson, 1979), this method suffices for the nature of our research because we did not try to generalize to the entire population of breast cancer survivors, as our intention is to uncover the nature of contacts made with VHOs by a "typical" breast cancer survivor.

The initial contacts for our interviewees were made through the Canadian Breast Cancer Foundation (CBCF), which provided us a list of 30 women breast cancer survivors. These included, at our request, women from differing socioeconomic and ethnic backgrounds to ensure coverage of VHOs that cater to different types of survivors. Telephone calls were made to each woman, explaining her the nature of our research and asking permission to conduct face-to-face interviews while guaranteeing confidentiality. Twenty-three agreed to be interviewed. The sample size of 15 women was determined based on saturation of information in the interviews. As the interviews progressed, we noted an increasing overlap of names of VHOs in our list and those being mentioned by the interviewees. We continued our interviews, 17 in all, until we reached saturation; the last two interviews provided no new information on VHOs, hence we use a sample of 15 women.

All contacted women agreed to participate and signed a consent form at the time of the interview. Many of the women eschewed the caveat of guaranteed confidentiality, wishing to be identified with their stories. However, we had to decline their offer because no one story gave us the full extent of the reach of VHOs. Their stories, nevertheless, confirmed the significance of VHOs in their lives and provided rich information that allowed us to construct a fictional character representing a composite of the interviewed women in describing our findings.

The interviewees, ranging in age from 46 to 63, with an average age of 54, were women from all levels of income, and from four ethnic backgrounds: European, Chinese, South Asian, and Middle Eastern. Nearly 90 percent of them were college educated; 11 of the 15 were married at the time of the interview, three were either divorced or separated, and one was single. Of these women, seven discovered their breast cancer through routine mammograms, six through self-examinations, and only two women discovered their breast cancers at routine physical examinations. All but one interviewee underwent either radiation or chemotherapy. At the time of the interview, all women were in the recovery stage; the time from discovery to recovery (and beyond) ranged from 1 to 19 years.

The non-random nature and the small sample size make our findings not easily generalizable to the larger population of breast cancer survivors. Rather they are indicative of the experiences of Canadian women in one metropolitan area with VHOs that are easily accessible. In addition, being the first study of its kind, it provides insights for new directions for further study.

FINDINGS

In this section, we first report on an inventory of VHOs in the City of Toronto, and then focus the impact of VHOs on women who interact with these organizations and the potential contribution of VHOs to their recovery and improved quality of life of women with breast cancer.

Voluntary Health Organizations (VHOs)

Our inventory yielded a list of 55 VHOs in the metropolitan Toronto area with a complete or partial focus on breast cancer. These VHOs range in size, geographic scope, and type of activity. In terms of geographic scope, 10 organizations worked at the national level, 15 were organized provincially, and 25 were local organizations serving women and their families. The remaining five were independent cancer research centers affiliated with large hospitals offering medically oriented services (such as screening and oncology), as well as quality of life workshops and psychosocial and educational counseling such as stress reduction.[4]

VHO activities fall into three main categories: (1) research, education, and advocacy; (2) medical and non-medical service provision; and (3) self-help and supports for patients and families. The national organizations were more likely to be involved in education, research, and advocacy, often receiving funding from the federal government, whereas provincial organizations were more likely to focus on service provision. Local community-based organizations were largely those facilitating self-help groups and support for patients and families that were sometimes differentiated by language and ethnicity. Not all organizations had a direct interaction with women with breast cancer; some organizations are involved indirectly as portals for women to get further information on services that VHOs provide.

More specifically, the *research and advocacy* category includes activities such as funding and dissemination of research at Canadian universities, hospitals and other research institutions, program evaluation, policy advocacy, patient rights, and compilation of statistical information. For example, the CCS is a large VHO involved in cancer policy (and politics), focusing, among other things, on advocacy, research, knowledge dissemination, and fundraising, as well as some direct service provision such as transportation. The *medical and non-medical service provision* includes screening and oncology services, laboratory investigations, nursing assistance, education for prevention and early diagnosis, rehabilitation and recreational exercise (e.g., yoga, reflexology, and art therapy), referrals, hospice care, and stress reduction. These organizations also provide psychosocial support services such as drop-in centers, help lines, and family counseling. For example, the organization *Willow Breast Cancer Support & Resource Services* helps women navigate the health care system by offering a range of direct services, including help lines, and assists survivors in starting and sustaining support groups (*the Support Network Program*). *Willow* also has a *Corporate Education Program* working with companies on how to support employees impacted by breast cancer.

Finally, the self-help and support category includes organizations whose mission is to provide quality of life workshops, financial assistance for drugs, wigs and prostheses, community capacity-building (through facilitated workshops and support groups), networking partners, mentoring and matching patients to survivors, toll-free help lines, and multilingual services and home visiting. The *Breast Cancer Survivor Self-Help Group*, for example, is a local survivor-led group open for women with breast cancer on a drop-in basis. Group members help each other to deal with the crisis and shock of breast cancer diagnosis, treatment, and recovery.

This categorization is not mutually exclusive; for example, dissemination of information and education are often linked with all three categories. In addition, many of the larger organizations have multiple goals; a few of them even tend to fund and support smaller local affiliates.

Women's Interactions with VHOs

Thirteen out of 15 interviewees reported interactions with VHOs. Among them, there was a consensus about having positive outcomes from these interactions. Over half of the interviewees credited VHOs for contributing to their recovery and improved quality of life. Respondents felt that involvement of these organizations helped them deal with their fears, provided information regarding the long-term impact of the disease, and offered support and counseling. As a result, women felt they were better-informed consumers of medical and auxiliary services. However, we find significant differences in the level and nature of interaction in various stages of the disease. We differentiate between four stages: diagnosis or discovery, treatment, recovery, and beyond. The *discovery stage* is fairly short, starting with a suspected lump until a positive diagnosis is confirmed. The *treatment stage* is relatively short as well and covers surgical and post-surgical interventions, including but not limited to radiation and chemotherapy. The *recovery stage* is the one-year period of recuperation since treatment, with the "*beyond*" *stage* including all the years thereafter.

Although breast cancer survivors appear to attain maximum physical recovery from the trauma of cancer treatments by one year after surgery (Ganz et al., 1996), mental rehabilitation and psychosocial recovery usually takes longer. During this period, which varies from woman to woman, they continue to "live" with the disease and with the knowledge that it may return any time. Thus, even if physically recovered from the immediacy by the removal of the cancer, breast cancer is thought of as a chronic condition requiring a long-term healing process. Women's past diagnoses are likely to have ongoing physical and psychosocial implications on their lives and well-being (Vivar & McQueen, 2005; Wyatt & Friedman, 1996). Therefore, we separate the post-treatment period into two stages: recovery (the first year) and post-recovery, which we denote as the "beyond" stage.

The interactions of women with VHOs can occur at any of these stages and our findings are reported accordingly. On average, the number of contacts a woman with breast cancer made with VHOs was four, including no contacts during diagnosis (with the exception of online information seeking), an average of just over two during treatment, and two contacts during the recovery stage and beyond.

Discovery Stage

It would be reasonable to expect that during the intense and stressful times of the discovery phase, women would reach out to VHOs for support and information – especially information that would help them to make their choices regarding the nature of intervention. Our findings point to significant difference in that stage between direct contact with VHOs and online, indirect contact. Ten women in our sample accessed information on websites of VHOs. Two women explicitly mentioned that they relied heavily on these Internet sources. One woman noted that the "impersonal use of the Internet made it safer" for her to reach out. Given that the Internet is now an important tool for accessing information, one could argue that searching online for information is tantamount to being consumers of information made available by VHOs. With one exception, none of the interviewees had made any other direct contact with VHOs in this stage. The one exception involved a woman who reached out to a VHO to receive help with transportation to her medical appointments; and even this was undertaken at the advice of her doctor rather than her own initiative.

We also did not identify any noteworthy outreach effort from breast cancer VHOs during the discovery stage. At these times, the times between discovery and treatment, when each woman and her family are making important decisions on choice of treatment, the only advice seems to come from the physician and the surgeon.

The women's narratives can provide some explanation for this lack of interaction. One woman said, "I preferred not to think about it, hoping the diagnosis would be wrong." Another mentioned knowing of VHOs only after treatment (or as she labeled it, during their "fundraising drives"); she also attested that she did not know how VHOs might be of use to her. When going through the typical process of shock, denial, and acceptance, in these early stages, it is not obvious whether, and how, VHOs can assist.

The sentiment reflected by many women is summarized well by another respondent who remarked that the information available "was too much and too scary" at that early stage, so after a while she stopped going to the Internet. Perhaps in this technological age, accessing information on a website is sufficient at the discovery stage for most women.

Treatment Stage

Interaction with VHOs grows during the treatment stage. Six out of 15 interviewees had significant and protracted interactions with voluntary organizations during treatment. The nature of the interaction revolved around issues of direct service provision such as psychological counseling, transportation, and financial assistance. For example, one woman commented on how useful it was to have transportation arranged to take her to her treatments: "I cannot imagine how I would have done the treatments without this," she said. In two cases, interviewed survivors shunned almost all interaction with VHOs, dealing with these organizations only minimally at the medical centers where they underwent treatment. One woman explains this by saying, "I had all the information I needed and could handle; my family and friends were most supportive and I did not want to deal with strangers."

Recovery Stage

In this stage, all but one woman approached VHOs, or were approached by them. VHOs approached women as part of their outreach programs at hospitals, and disseminated materials that provided information on services available to women with breast cancer. One respondent describes a VHO that sent volunteer breast cancer survivors to speak to her in the days following her treatments. As she commented, the only meaningful conversation she had was not with her surgeon, oncologist, or nurse, but with the volunteer breast cancer survivor because "Only she could truly relate to how I felt." Referring to the volunteer, she added that, "Seeing her there gave me hope that I, too, might regain my life back." These volunteer-survivors are trained to listen to patients, and provide support and information regarding prostheses, wigs, and various other matters that help the woman recuperate and get back to her "normal" life.

Another woman commented on joining a support group facilitated by a VHO. She reports, "It was the antidote to my depression. I had felt quite alone up to this point. I now had a new group of people I could relate to, and it was not all grim and woe. I remember laughing there for the first time as we shared stories." Similar sentiments were echoed by six women in our sample who joined some form of support group.

And Beyond
A significant shift in the nature of interaction that women survivors had with VHOs occurs after recovery. We learned that in the post-recovery stage, nine of the 15 interviewees (60 percent) chose to join breast cancer VHOs as volunteers at an average of two organizations each. As one woman explained, "I was so pleased with the help I received, and I wanted to show my appreciation so after I felt better, I decided to volunteer. Now, I do it because it is enjoyable and I have made new friends in my volunteer job who understand better what I am going through [in coping] with my breast cancer ... it has given more meaning to my life." Women took on various roles in these organizations: walking or running at fundraising events like Run for the Cure, volunteering to talk about their experience with current breast cancer patients, organizing or participating in support groups, and accepting leadership roles in large breast cancer organizations (although in one case, this had happened prior to the onset of the disease). The most frequently mentioned volunteering venues were sporting fundraising events and peer-counseling organizations that provide one-on-one support for women with newly diagnosed breast cancer.

Another popular undertaking in this stage was the search for recuperation and healing in self-help groups. For example, one woman spoke of her experience in joining a group of survivors in the annual dragon boat-racing event in Toronto. This self-help group, facilitated by a VHO, trained together to compete at the annual dragon boat race.[5] That they could build strength together, focus on the race, and support each other, helped this woman. As she attested, it was "the psychological and social support that made an enormous difference" to her. It lifted her spirits to see others who had gained muscle and strength and who could focus on a physical activity that was also fun. They had laughed and cried together and when one team member's cancer returned, the whole team provided her with ongoing support until her death. Through that activity, our respondent claimed, she learned to face life again with "courage and compassion." Her involvement in physical activity organized through a VHO also improved her family life as her children and spouse saw her becoming physically healthier, and getting control of her life. "I am not sure how many more years I have," she said, "but I do know now that they will be good ones."

Among the six women who did not have direct interactions with VHOs at this stage, three had donated money, for the first time, to VHOs related to breast cancer; they did not, however, frame it as interaction with VHOs. The same issue of framing might explain the lack of interaction of the other three women with VHOs. As our interview protocol allowed women to tell their own stories, we did not follow up with leading questions on whether or not they purposely did not mention interactions with VHOs.

Finally, to illustrate findings about the nature of interaction between VHOs and women with breast cancer as reflected in the narratives of our interviewees, we offer Mary's story. Mary is a fictional character representing a composite of the 15 women interviewed for this research. Yet, the organizations that Mary interacts with do exist. Her narrative is made from various parts of stories told by our interviewees (Box 1). Mary's story identifies various points of interaction with VHOs along the road from discovery to recovery and beyond. It demonstrates that VHOs were instrumental at two levels: at providing information, and later on in supporting her physical and psychological recovery and improved well-being. Like most women in our sample, Mary's reliance on VHOs comes only after surgery, with the exception of an initial Internet search. Mary, however, is unusual in the number of contacts she made with VHOs; the average number of contacts made by our sample is four, whereas in Mary's story, at least 10 organizations are mentioned. We do this to illustrate the various possible interactions made by breast cancer survivors.

DISCUSSION

How can this shift – of survivors' growing volunteer involvement in breast-cancer-related VHOs – be explained? We argue that the notions of reciprocity and improvement of quality of life are central to such explanations. The narratives of all the interviewed women who decided to volunteer indicated their willingness to give back for the help they received and the benefits they enjoyed in doing so; several noted that their volunteering gave them some control over their lives. Motivations for volunteering ranged from "the opportunity to give back" or "doing something positive about the fight to end breast cancer," to "focusing on

Box 1. Mary's Story

I am a 54-year-old woman. I read about self-examinations in a local newspaper and had been doing these examinations monthly for almost a year. In January, I discovered a lump in my breast; I tried to ignore it, but a nagging voice told me to do something. Later in that week, I phoned my family doctor and received an appointment for the following week. Although the thought of breast cancer did not leave me, I decided not to distress my husband or children, as I had no idea what the lump was. Several of my friends had benign lumps, and I hoped that mine would also be benign.

I lived with this discovery on my own during the week until the appointment with my family doctor. I only checked out the website of the CBCF that was listed in a magazine article I had read that month. I found information on various aspects of breast cancer, although some of it was too scary and it felt premature, as I fully hoped and expected my lump to be benign. I have to admit that, later on, I did return to that website frequently for information and support.

At the first appointment, my physician advised me that there was some cause for concern. However, I was told not to worry until we had definitive results. She reminded me that often breast lumps are benign, but I would need a mammogram and ultrasound to determine my situation. After going for a mammogram and ultrasound, I had to wait a week or so for the results. It seemed like a long wait ... and during this time I frequently thought about the possibility of having cancer, and how this might change or even end my life. This distressed me and I found it was better if I did not talk about it, as it helped me not to think about it.

The test results showed that my lump was indeed suspicious. The physician informed me that there was a very high likelihood it was malignant and arranged for me to undergo investigative surgery leading to the removal of the lump or breast – and my glands, if needed. I was unprepared and in shock. Only later, when I recovered from the shock of knowing I had breast cancer, was I able to discuss the various options with my physician and surgeon. It was difficult to discuss it with my family, especially my children. At this time, my husband did some research on the Internet and shared with me what he found. I was not ready for this and felt that my doctor and oncologist could make the best decisions for me.

I underwent a lumpectomy and node removal in March. At that time, the Canadian Cancer Society (CCS) came to help by providing a caregiver for my young daughter. As some of my nodes were involved, I needed chemotherapy and radiation treatment. Suddenly I wanted more information and although I got some information from my doctor, it was not enough; I felt vulnerable and very depressed. Shortly after, a breast cancer survivor came and talked with me about what she had been through and what I should expect. I found her visits very useful and supportive. Despite the family and friends who supported me through this illness, the support of a survivor was essential to me. She had been there and lived to tell the tale: that gave me hope.

During the early days after my surgery and release from the hospital, I was contacted by a volunteer from the Reach to Recovery program and attended two support group sessions organized by them. Volunteers from CCS helped with transportation when I needed to go for my chemotherapy treatments. At this point, I started to actively research the disease through a variety of websites, such as the Breast Cancer Research Initiative and the Canadian Health Network. On these websites, I learned about the different treatments, and what breast cancer could mean in terms of life changes. This browsing of websites helped me stay focused on my illness without getting depressed.

I underwent chemotherapy for six months and I was offered support groups and information videos by the medical staff but I declined it at that time. During my radiation treatment, I was referred by a staff member to the Look Good, Feel Better program. This was a wonderful program. I attended a workshop and learned how to look better, including new ways of putting on makeup and how to choose wigs. In addition to receiving cosmetics, I left with a renewed sense of self-confidence, control, and hope. I also started to attend a local breast cancer support group. At these sessions, I shared my worries and fears with other women and listened to theirs. A level of camaraderie developed that nurtured and helped me deal with feelings of anger and helplessness.

After several months, when I felt better, I was determined to do something in support of breast cancer research so I decided to volunteer as a way of giving back for the support I received from many individuals and organizations along the way. The first opportunity came at the CIBC Run for the Cure- an annual event for raise money for breast cancer research. I volunteered at the event to register entrants on the day of the run, as well as taking part in it myself. I also raised $200 for the event by getting sponsors for my walk. I found it extremely rewarding. Many of my friends and family took part, too. Later that month, I approached the Willow Breast Cancer Support organization and offered to visit women diagnosed with breast cancer.

Two years later, I joined the Canadian Breast Cancer Foundation (CBCF) and served on their education committee. At that time, I also heard of the dragon boat race "Dragons Abreast," organized for breast cancer survivors. I joined other survivors and took part in this race. This was one of the activities I enjoyed most as it helped me to build physical strength and gave me a goal to work toward – a great emotional healing process!

My primary interest in volunteering with other organizations was to raise the profile of breast cancer and help fundraise. This helped me as a survivor to overcome the feelings of being alone in my fight with breast cancer. My work with other women through breast cancer support groups is very valuable to me. It reminds me of my time of great distress; it is rewarding to be able to help other women during their times of distress. By volunteering with these organizations, I felt I had really confronted my disease head-on and taken positive steps in my journey to recovery.

helping others," "having been in their shoes, I can empathize with them," and "this makes me feel that I am helping someone, as I was helped." Furthermore from our respondents' perspective, as recipients of peer support services, the voluntary caring that came from "the kindness of others" was therapeutic.

Five of our respondents, who chose to volunteer for a peer-to-peer breast cancer support VHOs, said that working with new breast cancer patients gave meaning to their lives. It was restorative, immensely helpful in regaining their own sense of well-being, and enhanced their quality of life both as health consumers and as producers. As one woman put it, "Seeing other breast cancer survivors doing positive stuff makes me feel I can be of use. I have a much more positive approach now. I do not see myself as a victim of the disease but a survivor." In other words, volunteering allowed women to feel that they were productively involved in a fight against the disease. Women also evoked the feeling of improved well-being from their interaction with other volunteers. These findings attest to the positive impact that VHO volunteer outreach had in helping women in our sample and explain their motivations to volunteer.

The literature lends further support to such findings that show the beneficial outcomes of volunteering for an improved quality of life of the volunteer (Davis, Leveille, Favaro, & LoGerfo, 1998; Matthew et al., 2002; Midlarsky, 1991; Van Willigen, 2000). For example, Midlarsky (1991) states that helping others serves as "a pathway to successful coping, which may have long-lasting positive consequences both for others and for oneself [...] Helping restores or maintains well-being by distracting oneself from one's current troubles, increasing or maintaining social integration, and/or lending a sense of meaning to one's life" (p. 259).

The decision of breast cancer survivors to join VHOs as volunteers is consequential in the context of health consumerism. As health consumers, these women received health services that not only helped them to overcome the acute threats of the disease but also to cope with it psychologically. Many of these services were made possible by volunteer efforts of other women with whom our breast cancer survivors could identify. In an effort to reciprocate and to form a social network with other survivors, many women chose to change their roles from consumers to producers of health services. While none of our interviewees saw this shift as intentional, such voluntary move from "consumption" to "production" suggests that women see these roles as interchangeable; and assume whichever role best fits their needs. VHOs are instrumental in this case since they provide a venue for women to exercise both these options – as consumers, as producers, or as both. The relatively high rate of volunteering among breast cancer survivors suggests that it is not unusual that a consumer of services can become involved in the production of these services, if given the opportunity. Improvement of quality of life by means of *mutuality* and *sharing* is also reflected among breast cancer survivors who decided to join a support group. As depicted in the story about the dragon boat racing, interacting with other breast cancer survivors was therapeutic to many of our respondents in the recovery stage. Such interactions gave group participants a proof of life after cancer (Ashbury et al., 1998). The ability of breast cancer survivors to share stories, to communicate, whether in formal organizational settings or in a more virtual environment over Internet spaces, as Orgad (2005) portrays, has been an important backdrop in women's recovery process.

While the focus of the study is formal VHOs, the interviews reveal that the majority of our sample relied also on informal networks of friends and family for support and information. Many informal ties through, for example, places of worship, book clubs, neighborhoods, or car pools, offered invaluable assistance. These informal networks – while important and not to be underestimated – complement rather than substitute for the kind of support available through VHOs. Although such networks are a significant phenomenon, the scope of this chapter does not allow us to elaborate further on them.

There are several limitations to this study. First, given our method of eliciting the sample, results are non-representative. By relying on VHOs for the initial contacts, findings about high levels of interaction in general and of volunteering in particular may not reflect an accurate picture of the entire survivor population. However, it does provide a sense of the extent of the phenomenon, and suggests that volunteering, for many of the women, enhanced their sense of well-being in the fight against breast cancer, and helped them reciprocate for services received. This requires further research with larger samples to determine the relationship between consumers and producers of VHO health services.

Second, by focusing on micro-level narratives using qualitative interviews, we consciously omit reference to a large body of work on the politics of breast cancer, especially in the United States (e.g., Blackstone, 2004; Boehmer, 2000; Davis, 2007; King, 2006; Leopold, 1999; Weisman, 2000). In this body of literature, breast cancer VHOs are criticized for their cooperation with large (multinational) corporations and biotechnology companies which leads to the advancement of diagnosis and treatment agendas in breast cancer research rather than agenda of breast cancer prevention.

CONCLUSION

In this research, we examine the interactions of VHOs with women diagnosed with breast cancer. Our analysis reveals that VHOs are an important venue of service provision for breast cancer survivors, and that despite the universality of the Canadian health care system, many complementary services are available through VHOs. This is in line with Bekkers' findings (in this volume) that show VHOs fill important gaps even in societies with universal health care. Our research also shows that VHOs have a significant role in improving women's quality of life through the services they provide. These organizations are not only venues for health consumption but also places where consumers can become involved in the production of services by volunteering. The shift in women's identity from a service consumer to a service producer is empowering for most women, and VHOs provide a unique venue for accomplishing this. Even VHOs, whose goals do not include direct service provision but are instead involved in raising funds, research, or lobbying, are important venues for volunteering (Blackstone, 2004). In this respect, VHOs support women on their way to recovery and well beyond. There is indeed a cycle of relationships: from the discovery and treatment stages – as consumers of services from VHOs; to the recovery stage and beyond – as volunteers, the producers of services to VHOs.

The question of VHO involvement (or lack thereof) in the early stages of discovery, diagnosis, and treatment is also crucial. In order to empower a woman to increase control over her life and her choice of treatment, alternative sources of counsel in addition to her physician are essential. Although one might argue that VHOs can provide such an alternative source, it is debatable whether or not VHOs should or could get involved in treatment advice. If VHOs rely on volunteer cancer survivors or other untrained non-medical personnel, it would be unadvisable for them to give medical advice; this undeniably should remain between the patient and her trained oncologist. Also, for reasons of confidentiality, it may not be possible for VHOs to reach out to women at the early stages of diagnosis with breast cancer. However, the role of the VHO at this early stage as a provider of generic information on treatment options and general coping support can be invaluable and should be promoted. Perhaps, in this early stage, family doctors could take the initiative in putting women recently diagnosed with breast cancer in contact with VHOs, and inform women about auxiliary services such as transportation or childcare that the VHOs can provide.

In a period of fear and other strong emotions, the anonymity of the Internet may indeed be very useful for women seeking information (Harbeck & Haidinger, 2007) or support (Orgad, 2005; Radin, 2006). If this is the case, more attention should be paid to developing online interactive tools that help women looking for information, with front-line service providers encouraging women to seek such information at trusted websites.

Finally, since this research has been an initial foray into the impact of VHOs on breast cancer, we point to a few areas of further research. One pertinent question is whether regions or countries where health care is not universal will experience greater (or lesser) involvement of VHOs to meet the increased needs of women with breast cancer. Another question can address issues of access and use: are services offered by VHOs accessible to all women with breast cancer or only to those in specific regions or from particular social groups. A spatial analysis could provide insights as to where VHOs are located and where the need for their services exists.

The findings on the dual role of women as consumers and producers warrants further research to document the prevalence of these roles in other domains of the health care system, such as alcohol and drug use, mental health, and among people with disabilities. In addition, it would be important to document what proportion of consumers play such a dual role and become producers of services. This chapter has examined the impact of VHOs on breast cancer at the micro-level; further research regarding their macro-level economic impact is required to understand the full force and role of VHOs in society. One such study is proposed in this volume (see Borkman & Munn-Giddings). Finally, VHOs often complement health care activities borne by government; the financial impacts of their contribution need to be understood in the context of the overall spending for breast cancer. New social accounting tools, such as those developed by Mook, Richmond, & Quarter (2003), which report the value added by volunteer labor for nonprofit organizations, can be useful in understanding such economic impacts.

NOTES

1. This is especially troubling considering the likelihood of gender imbalance of male doctors and female patients (Leopold, 1999).
2. The nonprofit and voluntary sector in Ontario commands a substantial economic presence. In 2003, it had reported $47.7 billion in annual revenues, which is 43 percent of nearly $112 billion in revenues generated by nonprofits across Canada (Scott, Tsoukalas, Roberts, & Lasby, 2006). Within Canada, Ontario has a relatively large share of organizations with a national and international reach.
3. A full list of organizations can be obtained from the second author.
4. Although hospitals are excluded from our analysis, we did include in our inventory these breast cancer facilities because they are primarily run by volunteers and are privately funded.
5. About the effects of dragon boat racing in the struggle to cope with breast cancer, see Tocher (2002).

ACKNOWLEDGMENTS

We acknowledge a grant received by the second author from Health Canada. We are also grateful to Christine Smith who organized and helped carry out many of the interviews, to Ida Berger for her helpful comments, and to the editors Susan Chambré and Melinda Goldner for their valuable comments on earlier versions of this chapter. Finally, to the many breast cancer survivors who courageously battle their own health problems while helping others, we salute them.

REFERENCES

Aronowitz, R. A. (2007). *Unnatural history: Breast cancer and American society*. New York, NY: Cambridge University Press.

Ashbury, F. D., Cameron, C., Mercer, S. L., Fitch, M., & Nielsen, E. (1998). One-on-one peer support and quality of life for breast cancer patients. *Patient Education and Counseling*, *35*(2), 89–100.

Birdsell, J. (2003). Voluntary organizations within the health sector: Towards a research agenda. In: *The voluntary health sector: Looking to the future of Canadian Health Policy and Research, Part II*. Health Policy Research Working Paper Series 02-10, Health Canada, Ottawa, pp. 40–51. Available at: http://www.hc-sc.gc.ca/sr-sr/pubs/hpr-rpms/wp-dt/2003-0210-vol-bene2/method-eng.php. Accessed on 12 October 2008.

Blackstone, A. (2004). It's just about being fair: Activism and the politics of volunteering in the breast cancer movement. *Gender and Society*, *18*(3), 350–368.

Boehmer, U. (2000). *The personal and the political: Women's activism in response to the breast cancer and AIDS epidemics*. New York, NY: SUNY Press.

CCS. (2007). *Canadian Cancer Statistics 2007* (Available at www.cancer.ca. Accessed on 12 October 2008). Toronto, ON: Canadian Cancer Society/National Cancer Institute of Canada.

Davis, C., Leveille, S., Favaro, S., & LoGerfo, M. (1998). Benefits to volunteers in a community-based health promotion and chronic illness self-management program for the elderly. *Journal of Gerontological Nursing*, *24*(10), 16–23.

Davis, D. (2007). *The secret history of the war on cancer*. New York: Basic Books.

Davison, K. P., Pennebaker, J. W., & Dickerson, S. S. (2000). Who talks? The social psychology of illness support groups. *American Psychologist*, *55*(2), 205–217.

Degner, L. F., Kristjanson, L. J., Bowman, D., Sloan, J. A., Carriere, K. C., O'Neil, J., Bilodeau, B., Watson, P., & Mueller, B. (1997). Information needs and decisional preferences in women with breast cancer. *Journal of the American Medical Association*, *277*(18), 1485–1492.

de Moulin, D. (1983). *A short history of breast cancer*. Boston, MA: M. Nijhoff.

Donegan, W. L. (2006). History of breast cancer. In: D. J. Winchester, D. P. Winchester, C. Hudis & L. Norton (Eds), *Breast cancer* (2nd ed., pp. 1–14). Toronto, ON: BC Decker.

Edgar, L., Remmer, J., Rosberger, Z., & Fournier, M. A. (2000). Resource use in women completing treatment for breast cancer. *Psycho-Oncology*, *9*(5), 428–438.

Edgar, L., Remmer, J., Rosberger, Z., & Rapkin, B. (2003). Evaluating a volunteer cancer support service. *Journal of Psychosocial Oncology*, *21*(1), 53–72.

Erickson, B. H. (1979). Some problems of inference from chain data. *Sociological Methodology*, *10*, 276–302.

Ganz, P. A., Coscarelli, A., Fred, C., Kahn, B., Polinsky, M. L., & Petersen, L. (1996). Breast cancer survivors: Psychosocial concerns and quality of life. *Breast Cancer Research and Treatment*, *38*(2), 183–199.

Goodman, L. A. (1961). Snowball sampling. *Annals of Mathematical Statistics*, *32*(1), 148–170.

Goodwin, P. J., Leszcz, M., Ennis, M., Koopmans, J., Vincent, L., Guther, H., Drysdale, E., Hundleby, M., Chochinov, H. M., Navarro, M., Speca, M., Masterson, J., Dohan, L., Sela, R., Warren, B., Paterson, A., Pritchard, K. I., Arnold, A., Doll, R., O'Reilly, S. E., Quirt, G., Hood, N., & Hunter, J. (2001). The effect of group psychosocial support on survival in metastatic breast cancer. *The New England Journal of Medicine*, *345*(24), 1719–1726.

Gray, R. E., Fitch, M., Davis, C., & Phillips, C. (1997). A qualitative study of breast cancer self-help groups. *Psycho-Oncology*, *6*(4), 279–289.

Gray, R. E., Greenberg, M., Fitch, M., Sawka, C., Hampson, A., Labrecque, M., & Moore, B. (1998). Information needs of women with metastatic breast cancer. *Cancer Prevention and Control*, *2*(2), 57–62.

Hall, M., Lasby, D., Gumulka, G., & Tryon, C. (2006). *Caring Canadians, involved Canadians: Highlights from the 2004 national survey of giving, volunteering and participating* (Catalogue no. 71-542-XIE. Available at http://www.statcan.ca/bsolc/english/bsolc?catno=71-542-X. Accessed on 12 October 2008). Ottawa: Statistics Canada.

Harbeck, N., & Haidinger, R. (2007). The patient experience. *Breast Cancer Research and Treatment*, *105*(Suppl. 1), 91–103.

Harris, S. R., & Templeton, E. (2001). Who's listening? Experiences of women with breast cancer in communicating with physicians. *Breast Journal*, *7*(6), 444–449.

Hart, J. (2007). Addressing the psychosocial needs of cancer survivors. *Alternative and Complementary Therapies*, *13*(4), 183–186.

Health Canada. (1999). *Building the relationship between national voluntary organizations working in health and health Canada: A framework for action* (Available at www.phac-aspc.gc.ca/vs-sb/pdf/jointframeworkforaction.pdf. Accessed on 14 July 2007). Ottawa: The Joint Working Group on the Voluntary Sector, Health Canada.

Henderson, S., & Peterson, A. (Eds). (2002). *Consuming health: The commodification of health care*. London: Routledge.

Hodgkinson, K., Butow, P., Hunt, G. E., Pendlebury, S., Hobbs, K. M., & Wain, G. (2007). Breast cancer survivors' supportive care needs 2–10 years after diagnosis. *Supportive Care in Cancer*, *15*(5), 515–523.

King, S. (2004). Pink Ribbons Inc: Breast cancer activism and the politics of philanthropy. *International Journal of Qualitative Studies in Education*, *17*(4), 473–492.

King, S. (2006). *Pink Ribbons, Inc: Breast cancer and the politics of philanthropy*. Minneapolis, MN: University of Minnesota Press.

Kreps, G. L. (1996). Promoting a consumer orientation to health care and health promotion. *Journal of Health Psychology*, *1*(1), 41–48.

Kvale, S. (1996). *Interviews: An introduction to qualitative research interviewing*. Thousand Oaks, CA: Sage Publications.

Lee, C. O. (1997). Quality of life and breast cancer survivors: Psychosocial and treatment issues. *Cancer Practice*, *5*(5), 309–316.

Leopold, E. (1999). *A darker ribbon*. Boston, MA: Beacon Press.

Lerner, B. (2001). *The breast cancer wars: Hope, fear, and the pursuit of a cure in twentieth-century America*. New York, NY: Oxford University Press.

Lupton, D. (1997). Consumerism, reflexivity, and the medical encounter. *Social Science and Medicine*, *45*(3), 373–381.

Matthew, B. A., Danette, F. B., Hann, M., Denniston, M., & Smith, T. G. (2002). Health status and life satisfaction among breast cancer survivor peer support volunteers. *Psycho-Oncology*, *11*(3), 199–211.

Midlarsky, E. (1991). Helping as coping. In: M. S. Clark (Ed.), *Prosocial behavior, review of personality and social psychology* (Vol. 12, pp. 238–264). Newbury Park, CA: Sage Publications.

Mook, L., Richmond, B. J., & Quarter, J. (2003). Integrated social accounting for nonprofits: A case from Canada. *Voluntas*, *14*(3), 283–297.

Myhr, G., & Payne, K. (2006). Cost-effectiveness of cognitive-behavioural therapy for mental disorders: Implications for public health care funding policy in Canada. *Canadian Journal of Psychiatry*, *51*(10), 662–670.

Orgad, S. (2005). *Storytelling online: Talking breast cancer on the Internet*. New York, NY: Peter Lang.

Pollard, J. (2005). *Ontario women and breast health: A report on public knowledge and understanding*. Toronto, ON: Institute for Social Research.

Radin, P. (2006). To me, it's my life: Medical communication, trust, and activism in cyberspace. *Social Science and Medicine*, *62*, 591–601.

Romanow, R. J., & Marchildon, G. P. (2003). Psychological services and the future of healthcare in Canada. *Canadian Psychology*, *44*(4), 283–295.

Sakorafas, G. H. (2001). Breast cancer surgery: Historical evolution, current status and future perspectives. *Acta Oncologica*, *40*(1), 5–18.

Scott, K., Tsoukalas, S., Roberts, P., & Lasby, D. (2006). *The nonprofit and voluntary sector in Ontario: Regional highlights from the national survey of nonprofit and voluntary organizations* (Available at www.imaginecanada.ca/files/en/nsnvo/d_ontario_sector_report.pdf. Accessed on 9 November 2007). Toronto, ON: Imagine Canada.

Spiegel, D., Bloom, H. C., Kraemer, J. R., & Gottheil, E. (1989). Effect of psychosocial treatment on survival of patients with metastatic breast cancer. *Lancet*, *8668*, 888–891.

Statistics Canada. (2005). *Cornerstones of community: Highlights of the national survey of nonprofit and voluntary organizations, 2003 revised* (Catalogue no. 61-533-XIE. Available at www.statcan.ca/bsolc/english/bsolc?catno=61-533-XIE#formatdisp. Accessed on 15 November 2007). Ottawa: Statistics Canada.

Statistics Canada. (2007). *Canada at a glance* (Table 2, Catalogue no. 12-581-XIE2006001. Available at www.statcan.ca/english/freepub/12-581-XIE/12-581-XIE2006001.pdf. Accessed on 15 July 2007). Ottawa: Statistics Canada.

Tocher, M. (2002). *How to ride a dragon: Women with breast cancer tell their stories*. Toronto, ON: Key Porter Books.

Turner, J., Kelly, B., Swanson, C., Allison, R., & Wetzig, N. (2004). Psychosocial impact of newly diagnosed advanced breast cancer. *Psycho-Oncology*, *14*(5), 396–407.

Van Willigen, M. (2000). Differential benefits of volunteering across the life course. *The Journals of Gerontology Series B: Psychological Sciences and Social Sciences*, *55*(5), S308–S318.

Vivar, C. G., & McQueen, A. (2005). Informational and emotional needs of long-term survivors of breast cancer. *Journal of Advanced Nursing*, *51*(5), 520–528.

Weisbrod, B. A. (1988). *The nonprofit economy*. Cambridge, MA: Harvard University Press.

Weisman, C. S. (2000). Breast cancer policymaking. In: A. S. Kasper & S. J. Ferguson (Eds), *Breast cancer: Society shapes an epidemic* (pp. 213–244). New York, NY: St. Martin's Press.

Wyatt, G. K., & Friedman, L. L. (1996). Long-term female cancer survivors: Quality of life issues and clinical implications. *Cancer Nursing*, *19*(1), 1–7.

THE CLUBHOUSE MODEL: MENTAL HEALTH CONSUMER–PROVIDER PARTNERSHIPS FOR RECOVERY

Lee Staples and Reva Stein

ABSTRACT

Purpose – *This chapter examines the international Clubhouse movement, which features a unique "partnership model" that enables individuals who have serious and persistent mental illness to take an active role in their recovery. Consumer–provider and consumer–consumer supportive relationships are deepened through engagement in a range of cooperative activities both in the Clubhouse and in the local community.*

Methodology – *Data for this study have been gathered via case materials, semi-structured interviews, review of official publications, direct experience, participant observation, primary and secondary sources.*

Findings – *This study is consistent with other research demonstrating the efficacy of the Clubhouse model in providing mental health consumer assistance and support to gain paid employment, an education, and adequate housing.*

Patients, Consumers and Civil Society
Advances in Medical Sociology, Volume 10, 177–196

ISSN: 1057-6290/doi:10.1016/S1057-6290(08)10009-2

Research limitations – *While data have been gathered from a variety of sources encompassing a large number of Clubhouses, this is a single case study that includes limited comparative analysis with other modalities.*

Practical implications – *The Clubhouse model is an option that shows great promise for assisting mental health consumers to obtain employment, education, housing, and supportive relationships including peer support. It also promotes leadership development and participation in collective action for policy reform.*

Originality/value – *The Clubhouse approach is grounded in an empowerment paradigm of helping that emphasizes a strengths-based perspective, resiliency, activated consumers, collaborative partnerships with professionals, high expectations, self-help, mutual assistance, self-advocacy, and collective action for social change.*

INTRODUCTION

This chapter explores the growth of the international Clubhouse movement, the philosophy that animates it, the culture that sustains it, and the distinctive methodology that sets it apart from other programs that serve people who have serious mental illness. Consumer–provider and consumer–consumer partnerships are a central feature of the Clubhouse model. Mental health clients – who are regarded as "members" – take an *active role* in their own recovery through work, decision-making, advocacy, social activities, and the formation of supportive, collaborative relationships with both professionals and other members.

This unique hybrid approach incorporates a number of elements that connect to themes in this volume, including self-help, mutual aid, and altered relations between consumers and providers of mental health services. Clubhouses are grounded in a resiliency and strengths-based perspective that embraces an empowerment oriented methodology consistent with the stance of moving "from patient to consumer." Unlike many mental health programs and services, there are ambitious expectations for Clubhouse members to participate in their own recovery by taking on responsibilities, engaging in productive work, and becoming involved with the larger community. There also are ample opportunities for paid employment, leadership development, and collective action for mental health reform and broader social change. Clubhouses are community-based recovery centers that offer vocational rehabilitation opportunities, supports, and services designed to enable individuals with persistent mental illness to rebuild their self-confidence and to take on the tasks of every day living in the community. The term "chronic" no longer is used by Clubhouse and other recovery activists since they associate this term with the medical model of mental illness and consider it to be a disparaging designation that connotes hopelessness. The term "persistent" is viewed as more consistent with the "recovery" approach which animates the Clubhouse movement.

These recovery-rehabilitation centers also are part of a human rights movement that seeks to elevate the role of former and current psychiatric patients to that of neighbor, employee, member, friend, leader, peer, voter, and colleague, thereby reducing isolation, stigma, and discrimination. The Clubhouse philosophy avows that those who have a mental illness need the same things that all people require in order to live a high quality life. That includes a place to live, adequate food and clothing, a job, supportive relationships, appropriate physical and mental health care, and a place to go where they are appreciated, wanted, and expected (Evarts, 2002). The Clubhouse is designed to help members achieve all these things. Currently, 315 clubhouses in 28 countries are part of the International Center for Clubhouse Development (ICCD) with over 65,000 members.

Data for this study have been gathered via case materials, semi-structured interviews, review of official publications, direct experience, participant observation, primary and secondary sources. Primary data were collected through the Massachusetts Clubhouse Coalition (MCC). Over 8,000 residents of the state who have a serious mental illness participate annually in the 32 comprehensive, recovery-oriented centers that comprise this coalition. Reva Stein has served as the Executive Director of the MCC since its inception in 1989. Lee Staples has been a part-time consultant and trainer for the MCC since 1998. The authors previously conducted a study that analyzed the MCC along 11 dimensions of organizational development: participation, leadership, staffing, structure, goals and objectives, target systems, strategies and tactics, resources, allies, communication systems, and policy outcomes. A semi-structured format was utilized to interview 12 coalition participants – six members and six staff, including three Clubhouse directors.

This chapter also includes data from the MCC's "Annual Employment Survey" which documents the hours, wages, length of stay on jobs, and categories of employment support (Independent, Supported, or Transitional Employment) that members achieve each year in Massachusetts. Secondary data have been collected through systematic review of the *Clubhouse Community Journal* and the *Clubhouse Papers* dating back to 2000, as well as examination of publications and official materials of the International Center for Clubhouse Development. Stein's tenure and standing within the Clubhouse movement has enabled her to be a participant observer in numerous meetings, workshops, training sessions, seminars, conferences, and advocacy campaigns over the past two decades.

DEINSTITUTIONALIZATION, EMPOWERMENT, AND THE CLUBHOUSE MOVEMENT

In 1944, a small group of former psychiatric patients in New York City, who were looking for a place to go during the day, formed a group called "We Are Not Alone" (WANA) (Anderson, 1999). The group continued to meet and founded the first Clubhouse-Fountain House on West 47th Street in Manhattan in 1948 (Flannery & Glickman, 1996). The program operated without professional staff until John Beard was hired as the Executive Director in 1955. Beard applied his innovative ideas based on his work in a psychiatric hospital in Michigan to help former psychiatric patients live successfully in the community (Flannery & Glickman, 1996). He rejected the "medical model," promulgating an approach that was rehabilitative and consistent with what later would become known as a "recovery model" (Davidson, Harding, & Spaniol, 2005).

Over time, a methodology developed that took people out of the "patient" role, as participants were regarded as Clubhouse "*members*" rather than "clients." The focus was on what these individuals *could do* instead of on their diagnoses, disabilities, and deficits, thereby anticipating the "strengths-based approach" that would rise to prominence more than thirty years later (Saleeby, 1992). Beard certainly did not come to Fountain House with a blueprint, and the approach that developed was the product of a collaborative, organic process that continues to animate the Clubhouse model to this day.

The Clubhouse approach in the United States began to expand rapidly in the 1970s, spurred by three separate phenomena – deinstitutionalization (Scull, 1984), the emergence of a consumer empowerment movement (Sulik & Eich-Krohm, 2008), and advances in psycho-pharmacology which enabled former patients to live more successfully in the community (Anesshensel & Phelan, 1999). The Fountain House model was replicated in other cities in response to the failure of the federal government and the individual states to designate sufficient funds for community supports such as housing, education, employment training, and mental health services following "deinstitutionalization," a response to the inhumane practice of warehousing people in psychiatric hospitals. Torrey (1988) reported a 79% decrease of in-patients nationwide from 552,150 in 1955 to 118,647 in 1984.

Scull (1989) saw the emptying of hospital beds as part of a larger social process of closing asylums and reformatories that he termed "decarceration," a policy driven by the goal of cutting costs but cloaked in the myths of humanitarianism and effective treatment. He contended that the deinstitutionalization of mental patients was rationalized by both the advent of psychoactive drugs and the recognition that psychiatric hospitals were "fundamentally anti-therapeutic institutions" which were actually detrimental to the interests of their inmate populations.

Regardless of the driving forces behind deinstitutionalization, huge numbers of mental patients were returned to the community and support programs to ease the transition back into society were slow to develop (Hatfield & Lefley, 1987). This failure to adequately assess and address mental health consumer needs in the community was compounded by the challenges and barriers faced by these individuals upon re-entry, since patients in total institutions lose self-determination, autonomy, and basic control over their own lives, undergoing "untraining" or "disculturation" which leaves them "temporarily incapable of managing certain features of daily life on the outside" (Goffman, 1961, p. 13). Seligman (1975) characterized this phenomenon as "learned helplessness," a state marked by lowered self-esteem, depression, apathy, feelings of incompetence, self-blame, submissiveness, frustration, withdrawal, and hopelessness. These symptoms of learned helplessness posed formidable impediments to a successful transition to independent living in the community.

Many individuals were unprepared for life outside the institution walls. Learned helplessness had stripped them of skills and capacities for mastery over their own lives. Stigma (Goffman, 1963) and discrimination also made the re-entry process difficult. Consequently, discharged mental patients often languished and died on the streets or wound up in jails where the treatment they received was worse than that originally experienced in psychiatric institutions. Hatfield and Lefley (1987) estimated that about 58–65% were taken in by relatives, who often lacked the resources, skills, or supports to provide adequate care. Many were stuck in a virtual revolving door, moving between these living situations, and in and out of mental hospitals or homeless shelters.

Since the 1980s, "managed care systems" (Kongstvedt, 2001) have been an additional force for the reduction of hospital in-patients, providing financial incentives for fewer admissions and more rapid discharges. As increased numbers of individuals with severe and persistent mental illness struggled to live successfully in the community, new Clubhouses were established alongside other models of psychiatric recovery and rehabilitation to meet the needs of this growing population.

But the expansion and achievements of the Clubhouse model cannot be understood fully simply by examining *what* types of programs and services are offered; it also is imperative to consider *how* these supports are delivered. For it is clear that the Clubhouse philosophy and principles are consistent with the "empowerment paradigm of helping" that has challenged traditional approaches over the past several decades.

> during the last twenty-five years of the twentieth century, users and consumers of a broad array of services began to assert their rights to question the judgment and performance of professionals who previously had operated as uncontested experts ... The expertise of professionals of every type and stripe was challenged, including that of doctors, psychiatrists, psychologists, nurses, social workers, lawyers, professors, and teachers. (Delgado & Staples, 2008, pp. 102–103)

This phenomenon has reduced the distance between professionals and their clients, a central dynamic in the Clubhouse model, empowering patients by having them take an active role in the helping process (Gutierrez, 1990), developing new knowledge, skills, and self-confidence in the process (Hirayama & Hirayama, 1985). Empowering relations between service users and providers are based on collaboration, trust, and the sharing of power, with interactions characterized by genuineness, mutual respect, open communication, and greater informality (Gutierrez, 1990).

Clubhouse methodology also is very much in alignment with the concept of *resiliency*, which is a key element within the empowerment paradigm. Resiliency denotes competency for a variety of adaptive behaviors in the face of adversity as a "process of, capacity for, or outcome of successful adaptation despite challenging or threatening circumstances" (Masten, Best, & Garmezy, 1990, p. 426). Finally, empowerment in the Clubhouse is not confined to the individual level; it also is a collective phenomenon that can entail action to change social conditions that perpetuate personal problems and pose barriers due to stigma (Staples, 1990; Itzhaky & York, 2002).

The empowering aspects of the Clubhouse approach clearly have resonated with many individuals among the growing numbers of consumers of mental health services who are attempting to live successfully in the community. As the number of Clubhouses has grown, both in the United States and internationally, the model has evolved to meet new societal conditions and challenges faced by people with long-term mental illness (see Borkman & Munn-Giddings, 2008; Dill & Coury, 2008, in this book for further discussion about the impact of the larger political and social context on relationships between consumers and professional providers).

CLUBHOUSE PHILOSOPHY, PRINCIPLES, AND METHODOLOGY

Participation in a Clubhouse is completely voluntary; members choose the extent and duration of their own involvement (Parsons, 2000). This is based on the idea that those who are *forced* to participate in a mental health program probably will be resentful and such an experience will not be useful in their recovery (Webb, 2002). The model is based on the assumption that mental illness is a long-term process and that many individuals will relapse periodically. Therefore, membership is offered for a lifetime with no re-entry barriers.

Members do not live at a Clubhouse, nor are medical or clinical services provided on site. Instead, these centers are set up like places of business which members use as a base of support that offers a welcoming environment that is work focused and provides assistance securing and sustaining employment, housing, health care, education, and social services. Over 90% of members in the United States are recipients of SSI (Social Security Insurance) and or SSDI (Social Security Disability Insurance) when they join, and most are low income. The majority secure housing in the community; some reside in group-homes or supported housing programs designed for people who have mental illness; others live in their own apartments or with family members; some dwell in affordable units managed by the Clubhouse off-site. Still others are homeless.

Clubhouses are not organized like most traditional direct service organizations with a sharp distinction between professional staff and clients. Instead, they feature a peer-led organizing approach to create systems of cooperative management. Staff and members use a model called the "work-ordered day" to operate the center, while giving members the opportunity to exercise vocational, management, and other leadership skills (Flannery & Glickman, 1996). Members and staff are responsible for the day-to-day operations of each of these community centers, from managing the physical plant to overseeing income generating activities (e.g., internal coffee shops) and public relations. *Work* is seen as the heart of recovery, along with the development of member *relationships* with both staff and other members that are deepened through engagement in a range of cooperative activities both in the Clubhouse and in the local community.

The Clubhouse staff typically is composed of lay people who may or may not have academic degrees. Many directors of these facilities have master degrees in some field of human services or business management. Staff manage caseloads, provide transitional employment coverage (see later), partner with members to run the Clubhouse, and act as "coaches," building a team spirit and helping members develop the confidence and skills to take on jobs and complete them. Relationships developed through the Clubhouse often serve as the foundation from which members are able to move forward in their process of recovery and in their efforts to gain employment, an education, and stable housing.

Paid employment is seen as a goal for all members who are not retired and many individuals move on to more demanding employment positions in local businesses at competitive wages. This is based on the belief that financial self-sufficiency is an important part of life and a very positive step in the recovery process. Since Clubhouses are funded primarily through tax dollars, helping members move towards a greater degree of independence from public funds also is a desired end. These centers often are effective in helping members find employment, even when they initially did not have a specific employment goal (Macias, 2001; Schoenbaum, Boyd, & Dudek, 2006). Clubhouse support is provided both on and off such paid job sites, since the work setting is considered to be an important locus of recovery. There is a central focus on maintaining strong member–staff and member–member relationships as critical elements for employment success.

The lines between Clubhouse members and staff are blurred intentionally, with a focus on developing "real" relationships of mutual support. Members are treated as though they are part of the Clubhouse staff, a "horizontal" approach that frequently is referred to as the "*Partnership Model*" of rehabilitation. Member-staff teams facilitate weekly or monthly meetings where Clubhouse policy is debated and decisions are made through consensus (Arnold, 1993). *Expectations of members are high*; there is a belief that they will rise to meet these challenges. Individuals who may have been treated as passive "patients" for much of their lives or during periods of hospitalization are regarded as active participants and are provided opportunities to rebuild their self-confidence and to learn (or re-learn) skills of leadership and independent living.

Certainly, the role of Clubhouse staff has been developed in a manner that should be conducive to *facilitating* member empowerment by employing nondirective practice principles and techniques that stimulate decision-making, initiative, and action (Gutierrez, 1990; Staples, 1999). Clubhouse staff is expected to engage members and encourage them to take on more responsibility, while simultaneously recognizing and respecting their right to choose to take on jobs or roles in the clubhouse or to decide not to so engage. The fact that by design there is an insufficient number of staff to do all the work in a Clubhouse (Beard, Propst, & Malamud, 1982) helps insure that members will need to play a central role in the decision-making and day-to-day operations of these recovery-rehabilitative centers, *providing* services for others as well as consuming them (also see Greenspan & Handy, 2008).

There are elements of "self-help" (Riessman & Carroll, 1995) within the Clubhouse model. The self-help literature holds that people should be active participants who redress their own problems "... taking responsibility for their behavior and becoming empowered" (Borkman, 1999, p. 4). When individuals interact face-to-face to work with others who share the same circumstances and challenges, the activity can be termed "mutual aid" (Borkman, 1999). Both self-help and mutual assistance are components of the Clubhouse methodology.

However, Clubhouses employ a "hybrid model" that differs from classic self-help/mutual aid principles in several important ways, including a unique *combination* of staff support and client participation. Paid staff plays an essential role alongside members in the policy-making, management, and operations of these recovery centers. The "Partnership Model" incorporates *shared* work responsibilities and decision-making between members and staff that is atypical of most mental health consumer–professional provider relationships. Nevertheless, the "helper" and "helped" roles are not interchangeable for staff – as they are for members (Vorspan, 2004) – thereby departing from a pure self-help approach (Riessman, 1990).

The governance of most "free-standing" Clubhouses also involves a *collaboration* between members, staff, relatives of members, and community representatives that differs from an archetypal self-help profile in which members would have complete control. However, the role of free standing Clubhouse boards usually is confined to hiring the executive director, fundraising, and general oversight. Consistent with ICCD standards which are created by Clubhouse members and staff, these are *not policy setting boards*, nor do they participate directly in most managerial decisions, which instead are made with heavy membership involvement through a process of consensus. The nature of these boards further exemplifies the "hybrid model." Board members from the private sector and academia provide linkages to potential employers and community resources, reach out to public officials/institutional decision-makers, and obtain funding. However, these benefits are not secured at the expense of limiting the role of members in either the operational or policy-making arenas of their Clubhouses.

Additionally, two-thirds of the Clubhouses in the United States are not free standing, and nearly 40% are part of mental health centers which receive state funds – two features that radically depart from central self-help principles. Nevertheless, any and all certified Clubhouses must be operated in a manner consistent with the fundamental principles and practices of the model, including a high degree of autonomy and a non-medical orientation (International Center for Clubhouse Development, 2002).

OPERATIONAL MODEL

As new programs were established in cities across the United States and later around the world, the ICCD developed international standards to guide these recovery-oriented centers and to help them stay true to the movement's core values (Propst, 1992). These standards have another purpose; they "also serve as a 'bill of rights' for members and a code of ethics for staff, board and administrators." They articulate four fundamental "Rights" for members (Forkowitz, 2000): the *Right to a place to come*, the *Right to meaningful relationships*, the *Right to meaningful work*, and the *Right to return*. Each "right" was developed in response to gaps that existed in the lives of many former patients and to barriers in many other mental health systems and models of rehabilitation and recovery.

Right to a Place to Come

> Having a place to come is so important. People want me to be at Fountain House. I feel needed and expected every day. If I don't come in one day when I'm expected, I get a reach out call saying I am needed on my Unit. That makes me feel really good. Staff and members make me feel that I belong to something; and belonging makes me feel well. (Forkowitz, 2000, p. 49)

The Clubhouse model is based on a belief that "recovery" from mental illness is facilitated by participation in a welcoming environment where members feel accepted, wanted, and respected. The "Right" to a place to come guarantees that members can spend time, during the day, in the evenings, and on weekends. One of the standards that guide certification requires that the facility's space be "... attractive, adequate in size and convey a sense of respect and dignity" (ICCD Clubhouse Directory, 2006, p. 61).

Centers almost universally exhibit a friendly, inviting, and inclusive atmosphere; the ethos is non-judgmental and supportive. It is common to hear members comment that, "The Clubhouse believed in me when no one else did," or words to that effect. The strong sense of community, becoming almost like a second family, promotes self-esteem, increased self-efficacy, and a sense of hope. In the words of one member, "A clubhouse is first and foremost a community of people. Much more than simply a program, or a social service, a Clubhouse is most importantly, a community of people who are working together toward a common goal" (Clubhouse Employment Manual, 2004, p. 5). These centers are both physical spaces to come to and social homes where members are favorably received and supported.

Right to Meaningful Relationships

> We all agreed that relationships that existed between clubhouse members and staff were quite different from what we had formerly experienced in traditional mental health settings, whether as patients or as staff workers. (Vorspan, 2000, p. 33)

While working side-by-side in a collegial manner, members and staff support fellow members and one another, offering positive feedback, encouragement, and mutual support for taking on difficult tasks, as well as praise for jobs well done (Halberg, 2000). These collaborative work experiences are "a vehicle for developing reciprocal relationships, building self-worth" (Wilson, 2002), and decision-making by consensus fosters a team building approach. Decisions about policies such as: whether or where people can smoke in the facility; what colors the walls will be painted; whether to offer salads and desserts with meals, or if money should be raised to purchase and rehabilitate a building for affordable housing are discussed, debated, and decided.

Clubhouses also feature a social component including evening and weekend programs where members and staff gather to have fun and play. Donations for discounted tickets to sports events, concerts, plays, or movies also may be sought. Social programs are organized to address the fact that people with mental illness often are socially isolated, which can be a significant barrier to recovery. These activities provide opportunities for relationships to be established and deepened.

Right to Meaningful Work

> The 'voluntary nature' of the Clubhouse means that a member's participation in the work necessary to running the Clubhouse is entirely at that member's discretion. Members decide when they want to participate in work, and if they choose to participate, what work they would like to do and for what length of time. Though often the work of a unit must be scheduled, nobody (except that member) sets a schedule for each individual member. (Parsons, 2000, p. 28)

Members are invited to participate in "Work Units" involved in all of the aspects of running the center, including managing the switch board; planning and cooking meals; shopping for food; giving tours to potential members and guests; and writing a daily or weekly newsletter. *The work is seen as rehabilitative; its voluntary nature is considered to be a necessary part of the recovery opportunity*. Members work an average of 144 h per month, including approximately 70% of the administrative and accounting work at certified Clubhouses (Stein, 2005).

Participation in the work-ordered day provides an opportunity to develop self-confidence, skills, and relationships that are seen as the foundation for moving into outside employment through the cornerstone of Clubhouse programming: Transitional Employment (TE), Supported Employment (SE), and Independent Employment (IE) (Flannery and Glickman, 1996). Approximately 25% of active members are engaged in TE, SE, or IE in a given year.

TE provides part-time, mostly entry-level jobs at local companies which are designed to last for 6–9 months. Examples would include pricing shoes at a retail store, serving food at a local elementary school, shelving books at a public library, bagging groceries at a supermarket, sorting mail at an art museum, or staffing a switchboard at a university. Members are paid the prevailing wage, receive a check directly from the employer, and perform the same tasks as any other employee. All work takes place at the company's place of business. Clubhouse staff or other members substitute at no cost to the employer if a member is unable to work. Once an individual completes the job and either finds work or moves to another TE job, the slot is used for another member. Thus, one TE position can help many members return to work.

The Clubhouse helps members prepare for and acquire IE, where the center does not build a relationship with the employer, who may not even know that the person has a mental illness. The Clubhouse helps members develop a resume, conduct a job search, and prepare for an interview. The Clubhouse approach treats un-completed attempts to perform a job as a learning experience that may help prepare the member for further employment in the future. Any time on that job is viewed as a success: "It's great that you had that job for two months. That's three weeks longer than last time. Come back into the work unit and you can try again another time."

Right to Return

> In my experience with the Clubhouse, I've always felt welcomed back after brief periods of illness or holiday time. No matter how long I might be away from the Clubhouse, I know that when I walk through the doors, I will be welcomed with open arms and open hearts. Indeed, the members and staff give me the sense that we are an extended family. (Thompson, 2002, p. 54)

Clubhouse philosophy and practice intentionally is designed to provide easy access for members at any point in their recovery when they may experience a setback or feel the need for additional assistance. The amount of support someone requires during their life may vary. The Clubhouse provides the assistance needed and trusts the member to be the best judge about the amount and type of help that is most useful at that stage of their recovery. With the increasing use of Medicaid dollars to pay for mental health services and the program's managed care approach, Clubhouses face a major challenge since services might not be reimbursed or their duration may be limited.

The current annual cost of Clubhouse participation nationally is quite low, approximately $3,532 per year per member with a mean cost of $28.98 per visit (McKay, Yates, & Johnsen, 2007). Unfortunately, the "paradox of prevention" often may blind policy makers to the financial savings of the Clubhouse model. Namely, those allocating the funding do not compare the *actual* costs of funding a rehabilitation center with the *potential* expenditures of increased homelessness, more extensive psychiatric interventions, greater involvement by the police and court system, and more frequent hospitalizations that are *avoided* when Clubhouses put adequately funded preventive community supports in place.

Leadership Development

The very nature of the Clubhouse facilitates the development of leadership skills. Some members become so effective at the work of engaging other members and helping to formulate Clubhouse policy that they develop an interest in being hired as staff. One in 10 Clubhouse staff members are self-identified consumers (International Center for Clubhouse Development, 2002). Members are encouraged to maintain *external* employment before moving into a staff position to become confident that they can be employed outside of the Clubhouse environment or to work at nearby Clubhouses so that they continue to receive support at their own recovery center.

Leadership development and citizenship skills are fostered in several other ways beyond involvement in Clubhouse governance. There are many opportunities within the Clubhouse to facilitate a variety of meetings, to give tours to newcomers, and to take part in the planning and evaluations of practices at the center. Members attend educational, social, and leadership building conferences. They also are encouraged to register to vote and to exercise their political franchise; centers may host events where members can meet candidates for elected office and ask questions about their own concerns.

In some locales, members participate in Clubhouse Coalitions involving advocacy on health care, mental health, disability, education, or housing policy. Typical initiatives include anti-stigma campaigns, efforts to expand access to dental care, attempts to increase the availability of affordable housing, or endeavors to explain the Clubhouse model to potential funding sources. Such coalitions may plan or participate in conferences, public hearings, rallies, demonstrations, training sessions, and other forms of collective action.

A Clubhouse may act to overcome community opposition to its efforts to expand affordable housing for its members, work with planners to improve public transportation to the center, or join with the Department of Mental Health to gain funding for a van to provide transportation for members to job sites or their homes. Members and staff may join with family members active in the National Alliance for the Mentally Ill (NAMI), consumer only organizations, mental health associations, and affiliations of mental health provider organizations in efforts to increase funding for the entire mental health system. Clubhouses also may work with local reporters in an effort to attract positive media coverage about people who have mental illness. This effort includes meeting with editorial boards and writing letters to the editor.

Another example of policy advocacy is the Massachusetts Clubhouse Coalition's (MCC) grant to conduct a National Clubhouse Employment Expansion Project to combat barriers related to the stigma of mental illness and to develop a list of prospective employers. The results of an annual survey are released at public events where legislators are invited to present awards to participating employers and to celebrate the success of members in obtaining employment. Such "employment celebrations" help to generate positive publicity for local residents who have mental illness, diminishing negative stereotypes while also demonstrating the efficacy of the Clubhouse model.

There also are international leadership roles within the ICCD. Members and staff may be interested in becoming part of the faculty that certifies Clubhouses. Working on a certification team affords wider possibilities for travel. Faculty members have gone to China, Russia, throughout Europe, and across the United States. When individuals take leadership by joining the "Clubhouse Faculty," it would be unusual for them not to move towards independent living apartments and paid employment, unless they already had achieved these goals. These roles help members develop and flower, while also contributing to the growth of the Clubhouse movement.

Challenges

The practice of under-funding Clubhouses is a major challenge for this model. When Clubhouses have all their necessary components adequately funded, employment and housing supports for members are more possible. One key is to raise salary levels in order to attract and retain quality staff and prevent constant turnover. When staff members do not remain in their positions for significant periods of time, they are unable to establish the quality and depth of relationships that are foundational to members' success. The lack of sufficient and consistent funding streams continues to be a barrier to the stability and growth of the Clubhouse movement. Additional problems are raised by funding sources that seek to re-introduce a medical model that defines members according to their illness and deficits rather than by their strengths and assets. This increases the risk that, staff workers will focus on diagnoses, thereby interfering with the goal of helping members step out of the patient role.

While a handful of critics claim that Clubhouses are an "old model," members and staff nationally and internationally are constantly seeking better ways to help members live successfully in the community, incorporating the latest thinking into their day-to-day operations. SE has proven to be very effective at helping members achieve success, as demonstrated by the Massachusetts Clubhouse Coalition employment study released in April 2007, documenting that SE jobs terminated by members lasted 36 months on average. The total combined earnings of the

1,899 employed Massachusetts Clubhouse members in 2006 was $11 million dollars. Two-thirds of these jobs were in SE or IE (Massachusetts Clubhouse Coalition Employment Survey, FY 2007. www.maclub.org).

The movement continues to wrestle with problems presented by those entities that utilize the name "clubhouse" but do not live by the ICCD Standards. Such programs typically are simply "social clubs" or "drop in centers," and this practice has caused widespread confusion about the true nature of the model. Many in the movement believe that such facilities tarnish the image of Clubhouses. Indeed, it is not uncommon for mental health professionals, elected officials, government bureaucrats, academics, and members of the general public to "lump together" actual certified facilities with other types of programs that do not adhere to the rigorous ICCD standards. This phenomenon has led to a lack of analytical precision when Clubhouses are examined, and could have negative consequences when the model is studied as an Evidence Based Practice.

The answer to this dilemma lies with ICCD certification which differentiates those centers that meet the quality standards from those that are merely drop-in centers and/or incorporate less of a work, employment, and leadership focus. Leaders of the movement hope that over time, funders will begin to understand the difference between certified Clubhouses and those that are not. The efficacy of the model has been demonstrated via an NIMH randomized, clinical study (Johnsen, McKay, Henry, & Manning, 2004), and studies conducted by the Program for Clubhouse Research at the University of Massachusetts Medical School which demonstrate a qualitative difference between ICCD certified Clubhouses and those that have not achieved this status. More research dollars are being sought to draw this distinction even more clearly.

CONCLUSION

The Clubhouse movement is a constantly evolving set of principles and practices designed to facilitate community re-integration for people who have a serious and persistent mental illness. Much of the success can be attributed to the philosophy, principles, and methodology that challenge the traditional "medical model" in the field of mental health. The "partnership" between members and staff also is a major departure from typical mental health provider–consumer relationships, and it is consistent with the empowerment paradigm of helping that has gained credibility and currency over the past several decades. This approach increasingly is attractive to individuals with long-term mental illness who are attempting to rebuild their lives.

The lack of re-entry barriers, supportive collaborative relationships, employment opportunities, peer support, and an empowerment orientation all contribute to a model that presents a strong preventive alternative to traditional approaches to mental health programming. The Clubhouse movement can be expected to grow in popularity as its achievements and cost effectiveness are demonstrated more broadly in the near future. Currently, it is on one Evidence Based Practice registry and pending review on a second. The model currently is supported by a variety of research, including randomized clinical trials. Ultimately these centers can save taxpayer dollars while providing the necessary resources for communities to better attend to the needs of an underserved population of individuals who can be quite costly to state and federal budgets. The multiple preventive aspects of the Clubhouse model decrease public expenditures, while those consumers who gain and maintain paid employment contribute to tax revenue streams.

This hybrid model offers the strengths of peer and professional support within an environment that also capitalizes on the talents of allies and partners, thereby mirroring productive relationships in the larger community. The relational concept of "membership" in a Clubhouse moves a step beyond "consumerism." Certainly, consumers take a more active role vis-a-vis professionals than relatively passive "patients." Indeed, consumers often may become *impatient* with substandard goods and services. Nevertheless, the essence of consuming is using, buying, taking, and being ministered to by providers of some type of commodity in a marketplace.

On the other hand, *members* are expected to join, participate, contribute, and *produce in their own right*. And that production can transcend the market, often entailing individual or collective action to engage in the arts, altruistic endeavors, social activities, community development, political processes, social change, or the spiritual realm. Members act; consumers react. According to most dictionaries, members are "a distinct part of a whole," they "belong," and thereby "have a proper or suitable place." What better concept to address the needs of individuals who often have been removed against their own will from the mainstream society due to their mental illness? Holding this status so often entails the loss of employment, financial independence, housing, skills, confidence, and self-esteem, as well as support from family and friends. Stigma, discrimination, marginalization, rejection, isolation – all are the antithesis of *"belonging" as a member of a Clubhouse community*, which "... can develop alternative and de-stigmatized meaning perspectives and identities to serious mental illness" in much the same manner as self-help groups (see Borkman & Munn-Giddings, 2008).

The Clubhouse provides a consistent membership base which can serve as a temporary or more permanent community of identity for participants. Certainly, it provides a *transitional as well as a transformational* function for many members, enabling them to develop pivotal relationships and skills necessary to successfully negotiate life in the external community *at their own pace* without pressure to meet benchmarks and deadlines prescribed by provider professionals or funding sources. It also remains as a home base which can be revisited and re-joined whenever deemed necessary by the member, so that s/he literally can *re-group* in order to move forward on the path to recovery. The importance of membership and group processes sets the Clubhouse model apart from other mental health programs and also makes it appropriate for further sociological analysis.

REFERENCES

Anderson, S. (1999). *We are not alone: Fountain house & the development of clubhouse culture*. New York: Fountain House, Inc.

Anesshensel, C., & Phelan, J. (1999). *Handbook of the sociology of mental health*. New York: Kluwer Academic.

Arnold, M. (1993). Decision-making in the clubhouse. *Selected Papers from the International Seminar on the Clubhouse Model*, Worcester, MA.

Beard, J. H., Propst, R. N., & Malamud, T. J. (1982). *Psychosocial Rehabilitation Journal*, *5*, 47–53.

Borkman, T. J. (1999). *Understanding self-help/mutual aid*. New Brunswick, NJ: Rutgers University Press.

Borkman, T., & Munn-Giddings, C. (2008). Self-help groups challenge health care systems in the US and UK. In: S. Chambré & M. Goldner (Eds), *Advances in medical sociology: Patients, consumers and civil society* (Vol. 10, pp. 127–150). Bingley, UK: Emerald Group Publishing Limited.

Clubhouse Directory. (2006). International Center for Clubhouse Development: New York.

Clubhouse Employment Manual. (2004). International Center for Clubhouse Development. Available at www.coalitionny.org/ccrr/projects/clubhouse-manual.pdf

Davidson, L., Harding, C., & Spaniol, L. (2005). *Recovery from severe mental illness: Research evidence and implications for practice*. Boston: Center for Psychiatric Rehabilitation, Boston University.

Delgado, M., & Staples, L. (2008). *Youth-led community organizing*. New York: Oxford University Press.

Dill, A., & Coury, J. (2008). Forging a new commons: Self-help associations in Slovenia and Croatia. In: S. Chambré & M. Goldner (Eds), *Advances in medical sociology: Patients, consumers and civil society* (Vol. 10, pp. 247–271). Bingley, UK: Emerald Group Publishing Limited.

Evarts, K. (2002). Venture house and my journey toward recovery. *The Clubhouse Community Journal*, *4*(August), 40–41.

Flannery, M., & Glickman, M. (1996). *Fountain house*. Center City, MN: Hazelden.

Forkowitz, R. (2000). The four 'Rights of Membership'. *The Clubhouse Community Journal*, *2*(December), 49–51.

Goffman, E. (1961). *Asylums*. Garden City, NY: Doubleday.

Goffman, E. (1963). *Stigma*. New York: Simon and Schuster.

Greenspan, I., & Handy, F. (2008). From discovery to recovery and beyond: The role of voluntary health sector organizations in the lives of women with breast cancer. In: S. Chambré & M. Goldner (Eds), *Advances in medical sociology: Patients, consumers and civil society* (Vol. 10, pp. 151–176). Bingley, UK: Emerald Group Publishing Limited.

Gutierrez, L. M. (1990). Working with women of color: An empowerment perspective. *Social Work*, *35*(2), 149–153.

Halberg, P. (2000). The right to meaningful relationships: The essence of the clubhouse. *The Clubhouse Community Journal*, *2*(December), 44–46.

Hatfield, A., & Lefley, H. (1987). Families and the mentally ill: Coping and adaptation. Chapter 1. In: A. Hatfield & H. P. Lefley (Eds), *Families as caregivers: A historical perspective* (pp. 4–9). New York: The Guilford Press.

Hirayama, H., & Hirayama, K. (1985). Empowerment through group participation: Process and goal. In: M. Parenes (Ed.), *Innovations in social group work: Feedback from practice to theory* (pp. 119–131). New York: The Haworth Press.

International Center for Clubhouse Development. (2002). Standards for clubhouse programs. Available at http://www.iccd.org/ClubhouseStandards.asp

Itzhaky, H., & York, A. S. (2002). Showing results in community organization. *Social Work*, *47*, 125–131.

Johnsen, M., McKay, C. E., Henry, A., & Manning, T. D. (2004). What does competitive employment mean? A secondary analysis of employment practices in the Massachusetts employment intervention demonstration project. In: W. Fisher (Ed.), *Employment for persons with severe mental illness, Research in community and mental health* (Vol. 13). Oxford, UK: Elsevier.

Kongstvedt, P. R. (2001). *The managed care handbook* (4th ed.). Maryland: Aspen Publiations, Inc.

Macias, C. (2001). Final report: Massachusetts Employment Intervention Demonstration Project. An experimental comparison of PACT and clubhouse. Cooperative Agreement No. SM 51831, 1–36.

Massachusetts Clubhouse Coalition Employment Survey, FY. (2007). Available at www.maclub.org

Masten, A. S., Best, K. M., & Garmezy, N. (1990). Resilience and development: Contributions from the study of children who overcome adversity. *Development and Psychopathology*, *2*, 425–444.

McKay, C. E., Yates, B. T., & Johnsen, M. (2007). Costs of clubhouses: An international perspective. *Administration and Policy in Mental Health and Mental Health Services Research*, *34*(1), 62–72.

Parsons, R. (2000). The voluntary nature of the clubhouse. *The Clubhouse Community Journal*, *2*(December), 28–32.

Propst, R. N. (1992). Standards for clubhouse programs: Why and how they were developed. *Psychosocial Rehabilitation Journal*, *11*, 25–30.

Riessman, F. (1990). Restructuring help: A human services paradigm for the 1990s. *American Journal of Community Psychology*, *18*(2), 221–223.

Riessman, F., & Carroll, D. (1995). *Redefining self-help: Policy and practice*. San Francisco: Jossey-Bass.

Saleeby, D. (Ed.) (1992). *The strengths perspective in social work practice: Power in the people*. White Plains, NY: Longman.

Schoenbaum, A. D., Boyd, J. K., & Dudek, K. J. (2006). *Psychiatric Services*, *57*(10), 1416–1420.

Scull, A. (1984). *Decarceration*. New Brunswick, NJ: Rutgers University Press.

Scull, A. (1989). *Social order/mental disorder*. Berkeley: University of California.

Seligman, M. E. P. (1975). *Helplessness: On depression, development and death*. San Francisco: Freeman.

Staples, L. (1990). Powerful ideas about empowerment. *Administration in Social Work*, *14*(2), 29–42.

Staples, L. (1999). Consumer empowerment in a mental health system: Stakeholder roles and responsibilities. In: W. Shera & L. M. Wells (Eds), *Empowerment practice in social work* (pp. 119–141). Toronto, Ontario: Canadian Scholars' Press.

Stein, R. (2005). Clubhouse work unit survey. Unpublished.

Sulik, G. A., & Eich-Krohm, A. (2008). No longer a patient: The social construction of the medical consumer. In: S. Chambré & M. Goldner (Eds), *Advances in medical sociology: Patients, consumers and civil society* (Vol. 10, pp. 3–28). Bingley, UK: Emerald Group Publishing Limited.

Thompson, S. J. (2002). The four rights of membership. Presentation at the Eleventh International Clubhouse Seminar, October 2001. Chattanooga, Tennessee. *The Clubhouse Community Journal*, *4*(August), 53–54.

Torrey, E. F. (1988). *Nowhere to go*. New York: Harper and Row.

Vorspan, R. (2000). Clubhouse relationships need work. *The Clubhouse Community Journal*, *2*(December), 33–36.

Vorspan, R. (2004). Member role/staff role: Another look. *The Clubhouse Community Journal*, *5*, 25–29.

Webb, B. (2002). The voluntary nature of the clubhouse. *The Clubhouse Community Journal*, *4*(August), 31.

Wilson, A. (2002). Clubhouse staff as unicyclist: Finding the balance. *The Clubhouse Community Journal*, *4*(August), 76–77.

STRAIGHT FROM THE HEART

René Bekkers

ABSTRACT

Purpose – *This study seeks to answer the question of whether donations to the Dutch Heart Association are a form of solidarity of the healthy with the sick. In doing so, I test hypotheses on the origins of charitable donations in awareness of need in conjunction with dispositional empathic concern, social networks and own health.*

Methodology – *I report probit, tobit and multinomial regression analyses on data from the Giving in the Netherlands Panel Survey (2002–2004;* n = *1,246) on donations to the Dutch Heart Association and other health charities.*

Findings – *I find that experience with cardiovascular diseases is associated with a higher likelihood of donating to the Dutch Heart Association, especially among those with higher levels of empathic concern and social responsibility, and among those who are not in excellent health themselves. Support for the Dutch Heart Association comes from those who are aware of the need for contributions and more easily imagine themselves in a situation similar to those of heart patients.*

Research limitations/implications – *The results confirm the role of empathic concern, explore the role of own health and seem to reject the role of ties to family members. The study is limited to the Dutch Heart Association. Future research should test whether these results can be generalized to donations to other charitable causes.*

Patients, Consumers and Civil Society
Advances in Medical Sociology, Volume 10, 197–221

ISSN: 1057-6290/doi:10.1016/S1057-6290(08)10010-9

Originality/value of chapter – *This study contributes to our knowledge on charitable donations, revealing new insights on the influence of awareness of need.*

GIVING TO HEALTH IN THE NETHERLANDS

Citizens in the Netherlands have access to extensive, publicly funded health care arrangements. In addition, numerous charities raise funds from the public for medical research, prevention of illnesses and provision of care for patients suffering from specific diseases. In 2005, the 130 major health charities in the Netherlands raised a total of €277 million in private contributions (CBF, 2006, p. 47). In that year, the total amount received by health charities from households, corporations, foundations and charitable lotteries was about €477 million, which constitutes 11% of total estimated donations by households (Schuyt, Gouwenberg, Bekkers, Meijer, & Wiepking, 2007, p. 17). Health charities are very popular among the Dutch public: about 70% of all households donate to at least one health charity (Schuyt et al., 2007, p. 118). In the United States, about 23% contribute to health charities, and donations to health represent about 7% of total estimated donations (Giving USA, 2007, pp. 141, 146).

The Dutch Heart Association

In several respects, the Dutch Heart Association is comparable to the American Heart Association. Like the American Heart Association, the Dutch Heart Association is supported by a large number of relatively small contributions. The Dutch Heart Association directs a somewhat higher proportion of yearly expenses to funding for research on causes and treatments of cardiovascular diseases than the American Heart Association: 35% vs. 22% (American Heart Association and American Stroke Association, 2007).

About a quarter of all expenses by the Dutch Heart Association is used for patient care such as the maintenance of Automatic External Defibrillator (AED) sites that enable on-the-spot treatment of arrhythmia by electric shocks and development of training materials for reanimation. Twenty percent is used for prevention and public education. This part of the work of the Dutch Heart Association is most visible to citizens. The Dutch

Heart Association has conducted national media campaigns educating the public to recognize symptoms of stroke and to improve knowledge about the optimal treatment of patients suffering a stroke. As a result of the campaign, the proportion of the public knowing that speech problems are a symptom of a stroke increased from 35% to 55% (Nederlandse Hartstichting, 2005, p. 23). In a collaborative action with a large food production company, a cholesterol awareness campaign was held in supermarkets. In 2005, about 200,000 consumers were tested for cholesterol levels in a quick blood test inside the supermarkets. In another campaign, pedometers were distributed to 932,000 consumers to stimulate walking habits. In addition, citizens have been warned about risk factors for cardiovascular diseases such as obesity and smoking through public education programs.

How does the role of the Dutch Heart Association relate to health consumerism? Theoretically, consumerism in health has been conceptualized as a more egalitarian relationship between patients and doctors (Haug & Lavin, 1981; Haug & Lavin, 1979). Questioning the authority of medical professionals, patients are redefining their role, away from the sick role (see also the chapters by Sulik & Eich-Krohm and Fisher & Ronald in this volume). Unlike the organizations studied by Borkman and Munn-Giddings in this volume, the Dutch Heart Association is not at all a ‘bottom up’ movement of patients who demand more say in medical issues. The Dutch Heart Association was founded in 1964 by cardiologists who believed that better treatment of cardiovascular diseases was possible by improving knowledge through research (Nederlandse Hartstichting, 2005). Thus, the organization can be seen as a professional response to the occurrence of a disease, and not so much as a patient movement. To some extent, however, the Association’s public education and prevention programs do contribute to an increased sense of agency among patients. The programs direct the public’s attention to their ability to prevent cardiovascular diseases by changing their life style. Consumers are made aware of their own ability and responsibility for their health. This change implies another role change, also away from the passive sick role, but in a less revolutionary direction. Patients are no longer viewed as victims of a disease that doctors may cure, but become active agents who have some power to prevent and recover from cardiovascular diseases.

From another perspective, the Dutch Heart Association is a clear example of a voluntary association in civil society. Private contributions to the Association fund programs that otherwise would probably not have been funded by the government. Despite the fact that the Netherlands still has a quite extensive welfare state, government funding of medical research is relatively low. The Dutch Heart Association (as well as many other charities raising money for health research) may be viewed as a response to low government funding in an area that is socially valued.[1]

In the literature on social capital (Putnam, 2000) philanthropy is viewed as an expression of 'social capital', a cluster of phenomena including trust, norms of reciprocity, social networks and contributions of time and money to voluntary associations. Donations to the Dutch Heart Association belong to this cluster. A common critique of the concept of social capital is that it is not clear how the different ingredients affect each other (Durlauf, 2002). In this chapter, I show how social networks have an impact on contributions to the Heart Association.

Research Questions

In this chapter, I study the donor base of the Dutch Heart Association. My general research question is to what extent donations to the Dutch Heart Association are a form of solidarity of the healthy with the sick. Are donors to the Dutch Heart Association primarily healthy persons who feel obliged to improve the situation of those suffering from cardiovascular diseases? Or are persons who have suffered from cardiovascular diseases themselves and are grateful for services provided by the Dutch Heart Association more likely to donate? Or perhaps both groups are more likely to contribute to maintaining cardiovascular health?

Awareness of Need and Donations

Cardiovascular diseases are the most common reason for hospitalization in the Netherlands: in 2005, 141,700 persons were hospitalized for cardiovascular diseases. This is 14.7% of all hospitalizations. Cardiovascular diseases are also the most common cause of death in the Netherlands. In 2005, 43,350 persons died because of cardiovascular diseases. This is 31.8% of all deaths. Stroke ranked fifth in an assessment of illnesses with the most negative consequences for quality of life (Hoeymans & Poos, 2006), after dementia, esophagus cancer, Parkinson's disease and schizophrenia.

Given the prevalence of cardiovascular diseases and the negative consequences for quality of life, it is not surprising that the Dutch Heart Association is one of the largest fundraising organizations of the country in

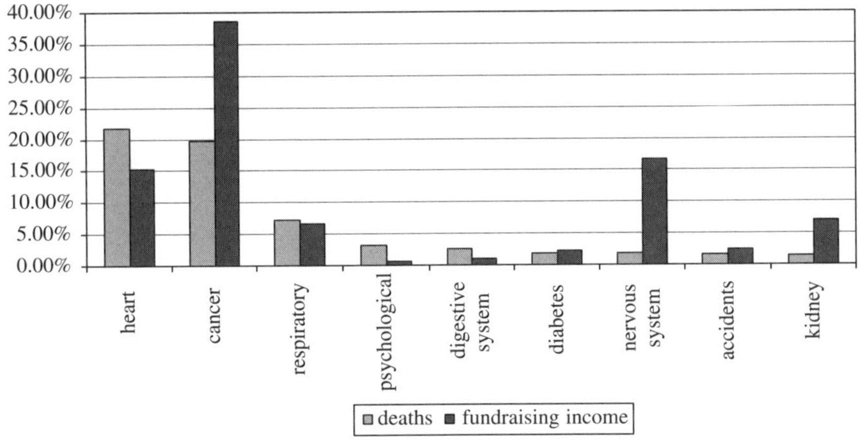

Fig. 1. Percentage of Deaths of the Nine Most Common Causes of Death and Percentage of Fundraising Income Raised by Charities Fighting These Causes of Death Among the 130 Major Health Charities in the Netherlands. (Author's compilation; *Sources:* CBF, 2006; CBS, 2007.)

the health sector.[2] In 2005, the Association raised private contributions worth €30.4 million. This is 15% of all private contributions to the 130 major health charities in the country. One would expect that the public is more willing to donate money to prevent more common causes of death. Fig. 1, plotting the percentage of deaths and the percentage of total fundraising income to the 130 major health charities for specific illnesses, reveals that this is not always the case.

Interestingly, cancer charities raised more than two times the amount raised for cardiovascular diseases (€77 million, 38.5% of total contributions to 130 major health causes), while cancer caused a lower proportion of all deaths (28.9%; second most common cause of death). Positive discrepancies between mortality risk and donations also occur for kidney diseases (7.1% of all private contributions to health charities; 2.1% of all deaths) and illnesses of the nervous system (16.7% of all donations; 1.8% of all deaths); a negative discrepancy occurs for psychological illnesses (0.6% of all donations; 3.2% of all deaths).

Why the public is sometimes more likely to support charities fighting less common causes of death is an interesting question. It is certainly not a peculiar finding for the Netherlands. Milofsky and Blades (1991) have noted similar discrepancies in the United States. Clearly there is more to giving than just the 'objective need' in terms of the number of deaths per year.[3]

In the present chapter, I focus not so much on differences in aggregate levels of giving for specific illnesses, but on contributions at the household level. I argue that there is a link between awareness of need among patients with cardiovascular diseases and giving to the Dutch Heart Association, and study three factors that may modify/break or support this link.

Experience with Cardiovascular Diseases and Support for the Dutch Heart Association

It is likely that the incidence of cardiovascular diseases in the population and the resulting awareness of the negative consequences of such diseases contributes to the level of support for the Dutch Heart Association. When asked why people give to charities, donors often cite knowing a potential beneficiary as a motive (Burgoyne, Young, & Walker, 2005; Radley & Kennedy, 1995; Sills, 1957). In a study of the March of Dimes, Sills (1957, p. 193) found that people were more likely to donate when they had experience with polio. It is likely that a similar link also exists between experience with cardiovascular diseases and donations to the Dutch Heart Association.

First of all, patients with cardiovascular diseases know the negative consequences of their disease for the quality of life from their own experience. Relatives of current or former patients and patients' friends know these consequences from their experiences with relatives and friends. From these experiences, they will feel that cardiovascular diseases are a serious problem. The study of Sills (1957) clearly revealed that volunteers for the March of Dimes were more likely to be aware of the negative consequences of polio, often from experiences with relatives or friends. Experimental studies on helping behavior have shown that people are more likely to help others who appear to be suffering from a more serious problem (Wagner & Wheeler, 1969; Levitt & Kornhaber, 1977). If people are more likely to support charitable causes that they believe fight more serious problems, they are more likely to support the Heart Association than the Fund for Rare Diseases – which is a real charity in the Netherlands that indeed raised only a marginal amount of money, €21,000 in 2005 (CBF, 2006).

Secondly, before people can donate to a health charity, they have to be aware of its existence or receive a direct solicitation. Patients themselves will be more likely to be aware of the existence of the Dutch Heart Association, because they have received information on treatment and prevention from the Association through their doctors. Relatives and friends learn about the

Association through patients. Sills (1957, pp. 86–87) reports such a link for experience with polio and volunteering for the March of Dimes. If asked for a charitable contribution to the Association, they will feel they support people like their relative or friend – even if it is not their relative or friend soliciting a contribution. One of the respondents in Sills' (1957) study of March of Dimes volunteers expressed knowing a polio patient as a motive for joining as a volunteer after a direct solicitation from someone else. In addition, people with experience with cardiovascular diseases may feel grateful for the work of the organization as a beneficiary or through the experiences of their relative or friend with a cardiovascular disease. Many people with experience with polio in Sill's (1957, p. 91) study reported reciprocity motives for their volunteer activities in the March of Dimes.

Making or Breaking the Link between Awareness of Need and Giving

This chapter deals with the question which factors moderate the relationship between experience with cardiovascular diseases and donating money. When does experience with cardiovascular diseases increase one's donations to the Heart Association? Or, in other words: when people know a patient with cardiovascular diseases, what makes them more or less likely to give to the Dutch Heart Association?

A recent review of research on philanthropy (Bekkers & Wiepking, 2007) suggests that there are many reasons why awareness of need may not lead to donations. The general argument is that not everybody who knows a heart patient will be equally likely to support the Dutch Heart Association. In the present chapter, I consider three factors that moderate the relationship between experience with cardiovascular diseases and giving to the Dutch Heart Association: dispositional empathy; the number of family ties in one's social network; and the value of social responsibility. People with a higher level of dispositional empathic concern, a stronger endorsement of the value of social responsibility and a higher number of family ties in their social networks will be more likely to donate money to the Heart Association when they know a heart patient. Those who are less empathically concerned with other people, deny responsibility for the welfare of others, and are part of social networks with weak ties are less likely to give to the Heart Association if they know a heart patient.

Networks: Networks play a key role in social control. Persons who are embedded in networks with strong ties are more likely to conform to normative expectations of others in the network because they have a higher likelihood of encountering them in the future (Coleman, 1990). Giving is guided by normative expectations (Radley & Kennedy, 1995): most people consider charitable giving as socially desirable behavior. Family ties are usually stronger and more enduring than ties to acquaintances or friends. Combining these two observations, I expect that persons with a higher number of family ties in their social network will be more likely to support the Dutch Heart Association when they know a heart patient.

Social networks are also likely to have direct effects on charitable giving. The size and composition of social networks determine how often people receive solicitations for charitable contributions. Persons with more extensive networks are more likely to receive solicitations. Obviously, those who receive more solicitations are more likely to engage in philanthropy (Bryant, Slaughter, Kang, & Tax, 2003). Networks also determine to what extent people perceive social needs. People with a more extensive social network are more likely to be aware of social problems. Through contacts with other individuals, people learn about their problems in daily life. Those who have more contacts with others will be more aware of health problems in society.

Empathy: Empathy, or more precisely, empathic concern, is the tendency to vicariously respond to the emotions of others (Davis, 1994). Individual differences in empathic concern are rather stable over long periods of time and are associated with various types of prosocial behavior (Davis, 1994; Eisenberg et al., 2002). Empathic concern is likely to be positively associated with donating to the Dutch Heart Association. Previous studies have shown that higher levels of empathic concern are associated with higher levels of charitable giving (Bennett, 2003; Bekkers, 2006; Bekkers & Wilhelm, 2007). Previous research has also revealed that empathic concern is most strongly associated with prosocial behavior when it benefits in-group members (Stürmer, Snyder, Kropp, & Siem, 2006, Stürmer, Snyder, & Omoto, 2005) or strangers who may be encountered in the future (Bekkers & Wilhelm, 2007). Given these results, it is likely that empathic concern moderates the link between knowing a person with cardiovascular diseases and giving to the Dutch Heart Association. More empathic individuals associate the Dutch Heart Association with the heart patient they know and care for. They will therefore be more likely to donate to the Dutch Heart Association than individuals with lower levels of empathic concern. Less empathic individuals will find it less problematic to ignore solicitations for contributions and will feel less guilty towards the heart patient they know when they do not contribute. Less empathic individuals will also be less likely to donate to the Dutch Heart Association if not solicited directly.

Social Responsibility: Social responsibility refers to those behaviors that 'good citizens' are expected to display (Berkowitz & Daniels, 1964; Berkowitz & Lutterman, 1968). Charitable giving is such an act of citizenship: decent citizens support charitable organizations. The norm of social responsibility prescribes that one should contribute to social needs, also if these needs are distant or abstract, long-term needs (Schuyt, Smit, & Bekkers, 2004). Unlike empathy, social responsibility is not an automatic, emotional process, but a consciously processed unconditional norm, like the 'principle of care' (Bekkers & Wilhelm, 2007).

The converse of social responsibility is responsibility denial (Schwartz & David, 1976, Schwartz & Howard, 1980). Denial of responsibility ('blaming the victim') is likely to occur when people find themselves unable to help and were not involved in creating the problem (Schwartz & David, 1976). Work by Schwartz has also shown that individual differences in responsibility exist and are associated with a lower likelihood of helping needy victims (Schwartz, 1973). When people feel that victims are themselves responsible for the needy situation these victims are in, people are less willing to donate money to relieve the need. It is likely that denial of responsibility occurs among some people who know heart patients. Cardiovascular diseases have been linked to unhealthy lifestyle choices like smoking and a high cholesterol diet.[4] And obviously, a heart patient one knows will not be cured by one's donation to the Dutch Heart Association. People who are prone to deny responsibility for the misfortune of others are less likely to donate to charities fighting specific illnesses when they know patients suffering from these illnesses. I expect that people with high levels of social responsibility are less likely to deny responsibility, and will therefore be more likely to donate to the Dutch Heart Association when they know a heart patient.

Health: It is not clear a priori whether one's own health is associated with a higher or lower likelihood of giving to health charities when one has experience with cardiovascular diseases. I offer two exploratory hypotheses: the solidarity hypothesis and the similarity hypothesis. According to the solidarity hypothesis, persons in better health themselves are more likely to donate to a health charity when they know a patient suffering from an illness. In this case, giving is a form of solidarity with the sick. Facing a patient, one may wonder 'Why does she suffer, while I'm healthy?' and feel uneasy or even guilty about being better off. Giving may alleviate such feelings of guilt (Basil, Ridgway, & Basil, 2006). As a result, healthy persons may be more likely to donate to the Dutch Heart Association when they know a heart patient.

According to the similarity hypothesis, however, people in worse health may be more likely to donate to the Dutch Heart Association when they know a heart patient. In this case, the similarity between the patient and the potential donor increases the likelihood of giving. Byrne (1971) shows that people find similar others more likeable. Lowry (1973) suggests three dimensions of communicator–recipient similarity: demographic similarity, attitudinal similarity and situational similarity. He indicates that physical similarities, such as being a heart patient or not, would be included under the demographic similarities. In many studies on helping behavior, similarity between recipient of help and a potential helper has been shown to increase the likelihood of offering assistance (Burger, Messian, Patel, Prado, & Anderson, 2004; Yinon & Sharon, 1985; Bryan & Test, 1967; Gaertner & Dovidio, 1977; Lindskold, Forte, Haake, & Schmidt, 1977; Sole, Marton, & Hornstein, 1975). Facing a patient, people who are not in perfect health themselves may be more likely to empathize with the patient, and more likely to give.

Data and Methods

To test the hypotheses, I use data from the first two waves of the Giving in the Netherlands Panel Survey (GINPS). The GINPS is a web-based computer-assisted self-interview. Respondents are drawn from a pool of approximately 70,000 individuals who regularly participate in poll surveys. The fieldwork took place in May 2002 and May 2004. The second wave of the GINPS was conducted in May 2004, five to six weeks after the deadline for tax filings. 1,557 persons received an invitation to complete an online survey. In total, 1,316 respondents (85%) completed the questionnaire. Only respondents who participated in both waves of the survey are included in the analyses ($n = 1{,}246$).[1] More details on sampling, design and questionnaires of the GINPS can be found elsewhere (Wiepking, 2008; Schuyt et al., 2007).

Measures

Donations to Dutch Heart Association: Respondents reported on charitable donations using an adaptation of the 'IU-Method + Area' module, in which first questions are asked about methods of donating followed by questions about donations to different charitable subsectors (Rooney, Steinberg, & Schervish, 2001). After the questions about giving in different sectors, respondents in GINPS03 were also prompted about their household's donation to 64 particular charitable organizations, including the Dutch Heart Association. Respondents were asked to first select those organizations (from a list displaying ten organizations per time) to which their household had donated in 2003. After that, for all positive responses the exact amount donated was asked.

Experience with cardiovascular diseases: The survey asked whether 'you or someone close to you has suffered from heart or vascular diseases in the past 12 months'. Almost one-third (30.9%) responded 'yes' to this question. A limitation of this question is that the data do not tell whether the respondent suffers from cardiovascular diseases herself or whether she knows a heart patient. Another dataset, however, shows that more than 90% of those who report knowing a person with cardiovascular health problems are not heart patients themselves.[5] So it can be assumed that in most cases a positive response means that the respondent knows a heart patient.

Social networks: In the second wave of the GINPS, a position generator instrument was included to measure the size and composition of social networks (Lin & Dumin, 1986). Fifteen occupations with a wide range of social status (from a truck driver to CEO) were listed, and respondents indicated whether they knew anyone in that occupation, and if so, whether this was a relative, friend, or acquaintance. A count of the number of occupations accessed served as a measure of the size of the social network; the proportion of all occupations accessed through relatives served as a measure of family orientation in the network.

Empathic concern: Empathic concern was measured with a Dutch translation of six items from the empathic concern scale from Davis' (1994) Interpersonal Reactivity Index. The mean of the items (Cronbach's alpha: 0.75) served as a measure of dispositional empathic concern.[6]

Social responsibility: Social responsibility was measured as the mean level of agreement on a 1 (disagree completely) to 5 (agree completely) scale with five statements reflecting social responsibility (e.g., 'We have to leave this world a better place for the next generation'). The items were developed and validated in the first wave of the Giving in the Netherlands Panel Study (Schuyt et al., 2004). The Cronbach's alpha of this scale was not optimal but sufficient (0.590).

Empathy/responsibility composite score: Empathy and social responsibility were fairly strongly correlated (0.414). Because the hypotheses on interactive effects of experience with cardiovascular diseases and empathic concern and social responsibility were in the same direction, I averaged the empathic concern and social responsibility scores into a composite score.

Joy of giving is a measure available in the second wave of the survey consisting of three items referring to the positive emotions for giving to charities (sample item: 'Giving to charities makes me happy'). All items were measured on a 1–5 scale ranging from 'completely disagree' to 'completely agree' (except the empathic concern items, which ranged from 'does not apply to me at all' to 'applies to me completely'). The reliability of the scale is 0.771.

Generalized Social Trust was measured with two items that are commonly used as two alternatives: 'In general, most people can be trusted' and 'You can't be too careful in dealing with other people'. Responses to these questions were strongly correlated ($r = -0.42$). The mean of both items – the latter recoded – served as a measure of trust.

Subjective health: Subjective health was measured with the commonly used question 'In general, how would you rate your own health?'. Response categories were 'poor' (1), 'moderate' (2), 'good' (3), 'very good' (4) and 'excellent' (5). While this seems to be a rather crude and overly simple measure, previous research has revealed that the question is a valid indicator of objective health status, and has predictive power for the development of objectively assessed illnesses and mortality (Miilunpalo, Vuori, Oja, Pasanen, & Urponen, 1997; Idler & Benyamini, 1997).

The following socio-demographic variables are included because they are related to philanthropy in the Netherlands (Bekkers, 2006; Bekkers & Wiepking, 2006): *gender* (female = 1), *age* (in years), *household income* (log-transformed, originally measured in 24 categories ranging from €2.5k to €300k, higher incomes truncated), *home ownership* (a dummy variable for owning one's home), *level of education* (seven categories, ranging from primary education to post-doctoral degree), *working status* (a dummy variable for having paid work), five dummy variables for *religious affiliation* (Catholic, Reformed Protestant ('Hervormd'), Rereformed Protestant ('Gereformeerd'), other Christian affiliation, non-Christian affiliation; no religious affiliation being the reference category) and *church attendance* (five categories, ranging from 'never' to 'once a week or more') and *town size* (in 1,000s of inhabitants). All socio-demographics were measured in the first wave.

Results

Those Who Know Heart Patients are More Likely to Support the Dutch Heart Association

The basic assumption of this chapter is that experience with cardiovascular diseases is associated with a higher likelihood of giving to the Dutch Heart

Association. This assumption is supported by the data. In the sample, 65.6% of all respondents report having made a donation to the Dutch Heart Association.[7] The likelihood of having made a donation differs considerably between those who know a heart patient and those who do not. The difference is about ten percentage points. 72.7% of those who know a heart patient had made a donation, vs. 62.4% among those who did not know a heart patient. The χ^2 statistic is 13.35, which is strongly significant ($p < 0.000$) with 1 df.

Who Has Experience with Cardiovascular Diseases?
To establish the relationship between experience with cardiovascular diseases and donations to the Dutch Heart Association accurately, it is necessary to control for variables that are associated with experience with cardiovascular diseases and with charitable giving. Therefore, I conducted an exploratory analysis of experience with cardiovascular diseases. The analysis is a probit regression analysis, which provides estimates of the change in the likelihood of experience with cardiovascular diseases given a one unit change in the predictor variables. Predictor variables in the analysis are socio-demographic variables (model 1), subjective health, empathic concern, social responsibility, and access to occupations through family, friends and acquaintances (added in model 2). Table 1 reports the results of these analyses.

Firstly, I find that those in better health are less likely to be or know heart patients (see model 2). This finding not only makes intuitive sense because heart patients will evaluate their own health as worse than non-heart patients; to the extent that the relationship is due to knowing rather than being a heart patient it may also suggest that social network formation is partly health-based. The healthy are more likely to know other healthy persons, while those in worse health are more likely to know others whose health is less than optimal.

Secondly, I find that more empathic persons are more likely to know heart patients. This is not surprising since empathic concern contributes to social skills that facilitate the formation of friendships in general and the willingness to interact with needy persons (Davis et al., 1999).

Thirdly, I find that those who have access to a higher number of occupations from the position generator through family and acquaintances (but not friends) are more likely to know a heart patient. This means that people who know more people in a variety of occupations through family ties or as an acquaintance are more likely to know a heart patient. Interestingly, having many friends does not increase the likelihood of

Table 1. Probit Regression Analysis of Experience with Cardiovascular Diseases ($n = 1{,}312$).

	Model 1	Model 2
Female	0.025	−0.006
Age (years)	0.002**	0.001
Gross household income (× 1,000)	0.000	0.000
Owns home	−0.048*	−0.049*
Level of education (1–7)	0.012	0.012
Paid work	−0.025	−0.018
Catholic	−0.058*	−0.074**
Reformed protestant	−0.002	−0.010
Rereformed protestant	−0.032	−0.025
Other religion	−0.037	−0.062
Church attendance (1–5)	−0.002	−0.011
Community size (× 1,000)	0.000	0.000
Subjective health (z)		−0.074***
Empathic concern (z)		0.039**
Social responsibility (z)		−0.015
Access to occupations through family (z)		0.058***
Access to occupations through friends (z)		0.014
Access to occupations through acquaintances (z)		0.051***

*Significant at 10%; **Significant at 5%; ***Significant at 1%.
Note: Entries are marginal effects. All variables are dichotomous unless noted otherwise; (z) indicates z-standardized variable.

experience with cardiovascular diseases. It is not clear why this is the case. One possibility is that people with cardiovascular diseases are less able to establish and maintain friendships. Another possibility is that other people are less likely to establish and maintain friendships with heart patients. But with the present data I cannot test these ideas.

Other findings in model 1 include that homeowners are less likely to have experience with cardiovascular diseases than those who rent their homes, and that Catholics are less likely to have experience with cardiovascular diseases than the non-religious.

Who Gives to the Dutch Heart Association?

Table 2 reports estimates of a tobit regression analysis of the amount donated to the Dutch Heart Association in the past year.[8] Model 1 includes as predictors socio-demographic variables, empathic concern and social responsibility and the network size and composition.

Table 2. Tobit Regression of Amount Donated to the Dutch Heart Association ($n = 1{,}312$).

	Model 1	Model 2	Model 3
Female	−0.201	−0.205	−0.206
Age (years)	0.015***	0.014***	0.014***
Gross household income (× 1,000)	0.006**	0.006**	0.006**
Owns home	0.373***	0.393***	0.385***
Education (1–7)	−0.170***	−0.174***	−0.170***
Paid work	−0.047	−0.036	−0.018
Catholic	0.076	0.116	0.114
Reformed protestant	0.122	0.130	0.124
Rereformed protestant	−0.331	−0.319	−0.344
Other religion	−1.343***	−1.314***	−1.359***
Church attendance (1–5)	0.158**	0.165**	0.169**
Community size (× 1,000)	−0.001***	−0.001***	−0.001***
Subjective health (z)	−0.062	−0.024	0.058
Empathic concern/social responsibility (z)	0.445***	0.433***	0.357***
Number of occupations accessed (z)	0.139**	0.104	0.107
% of occupations through family (z)	−0.030	−0.037	−0.051
Experience with cardiovascular diseases		0.507***	0.448***
% of family ties × experience			0.069
Empathy/responsibility × experience			0.288*
Own health × experience			−0.257*
Constant	0.839**	0.703*	0.683*

*Significant at 10%; **Significant at 5%; ***Significant at 1%.
Note: Entries are unstandardized coefficients. All variables are dichotomous unless noted otherwise; (z) indicates z-standardized variable.

The results in model 2 reveal that experience with cardiovascular diseases is positively related to donating to the Dutch Heart Association when controlling for factors associated with knowing heart patients. Because the amount donated-variable is log-transformed the effects of predictor variables can be interpreted in terms of relative changes. People who know a heart patient give about 50% more money to the Dutch Heart Association than those who do not know a heart patient. A one standard deviation increase in the empathy/responsibility composite score is associated with a 43% increase in the amount donated.

Model 3 includes interaction terms between experience with cardiovascular diseases and empathy/social responsibility, the proportion of occupations accessed through family ties and subjective health. These interaction terms test whether the relationships of empathy/social responsibility, the proportion of occupations accessed through family ties and subjective health are stronger or weaker for those who have experience with cardiovascular diseases and those who do not. A statistically significant interaction with a positive sign indicates that the relationships of these variables with donations to the Dutch Heart Association are more strongly positive among those who know a heart patient than among those who do not.

The results in model 3 support the hypothesis that experience with cardiovascular diseases is more likely to result in donations to the Dutch Heart Association when people have higher levels of empathy and social responsibility. I find a positive interaction between experience with cardiovascular diseases and the empathy/social responsibility mean score. Though the interaction term is only marginally significant, the effect is substantial. A one standard deviation increase in empathy/social responsibility is associated with a 29% higher amount donated to the Dutch Heart Association. However, no support is found for the hypothesis that experience with cardiovascular diseases is more likely to result in donations to the Dutch Heart Association when the proportion of family ties in one's network increases. The negative interaction between own health and experience with cardiovascular diseases implies that persons in worse health are donating more to the Dutch Heart Association when they have experience with cardiovascular diseases. A one standard deviation increase in subjective health is associated with a 26% lower amount donated to the Dutch Heart Association. This implies support for the similarity hypothesis, and rejects the solidarity hypothesis.

A comparison of the results in models 1 and 2 reveals that experience with cardiovascular diseases partly mediates the relationship between size of the social network and donations to the Dutch Heart Association. Table 2 also reveals that home owners donate more to the Dutch Heart Association, as well as higher income households, older persons, persons with lower levels of education, more frequent church attendees and persons living in smaller communities.

The empathic concern/social responsibility mean score retains a positive relationship to the amount donated to the Dutch Heart Association in model 2. This means that experience with cardiovascular diseases does not mediate the effect of empathic concern and social responsibility. Table 1 showed that people with higher empathic concern are more likely to have experience with cardiovascular diseases. The present results indicate that there is a sizeable direct relationship between empathic concern and social responsibility and donations to the Dutch Heart Association that is independent of knowing a heart patient.[9]

Who gives to the Dutch Heart Association Rather than to Other Health Charities?

A disadvantage of the tobit specification is that it is not clear whether relationships of predictor variables with donations are driven by the likelihood of donating at all, or by the amount donated. To explore this matter, I have also estimated a multinomial logit model of donations to the Dutch Heart Association (see Table 3). In this analysis, respondents who made a donation to the Dutch Heart Association (who are placed in the reference category) are contrasted with donors who supported other health charities and with respondents who made no charitable donations at all. Thus, the analysis reveals how the donor base of the Dutch Heart Association differs from the group of respondents who do not donate to health charities (first column of each model) and from the group of

Table 3. Multinomial Logit Regression of Health Charity Donations.

	Model 1		Model 2		Model 3	
	None	Other	None	Other	None	Other
Female	0.071	0.072	0.072	0.077	0.063	0.086
Age (years)	−0.011	0.004	−0.010	0.005	−0.010	0.006
Household income (× 1,000)	−0.003	0.002	−0.003	0.002	−0.003	0.002
Owns home	−0.735***	−0.300*	−0.754***	−0.333**	−0.760***	−0.320**
Education	0.220***	0.190***	0.224***	0.196***	0.222***	0.196***
Paid work	−0.039	0.054	−0.044	0.042	−0.054	0.036
Catholic	−0.446	−0.199	−0.46*	−0.239	−0.442	−0.239
Reformed protestant	−0.146	−0.140	−0.151	−0.148	−0.147	−0.147
Rereformed protestant	0.104	0.374	0.101	0.362	0.113	0.392
Other religion	1.374***	1.006***	1.371***	0.992***	1.424***	1.062***
Church attendance	−0.102	−0.095	−0.106	−0.105	−0.102	−0.115
Community size (× 1,000)	0.003***	0.001***	0.003***	0.001***	0.003***	0.001***
Subjective health	0.025	0.039	0.005	−0.002	−0.074	−0.073
Trust	−0.173*	−0.045	−0.172*	−0.047	−0.172*	−0.050
Joy of giving	−0.322***	0.047	−0.321***	0.052	−0.312***	0.067
Empathic concern/social responsibility	−0.577***	−0.286***	−0.575***	−0.277***	−0.591***	−0.189*
Occupations accessed (z)	−0.198*	−0.083	−0.178*	−0.045	−0.180*	−0.050
% of occupations through family (z)	0.007	0.043	0.012	0.053	−0.032	0.085
Experience with cardiovascular diseases			−0.296	−0.624***	−0.237	−0.602***
% of family ties × experience					0.178	−0.186
Empathy/responsibility × experience					0.047	−0.433**
Own health × experience					0.250	0.281*
Constant	−2.042***	−1.998***	−1.965***	−1.851***	−1.952***	−1.873***

*Significant at 10%; **Significant at 5%; ***Significant at 1%.

Note: All variables are dichotomous unless noted otherwise; (z) indicates z-standardized variable. Reference category: donation to the Dutch Heart Association.

respondents who donate to other health charities (second column of each model). I first discuss the latter group of findings.

The main findings on the contrast between donors to the Dutch Heart Association and donors to other health charities are that people are more likely to donate to the Dutch Heart Association (rather than to other health charities) when they have higher levels of empathic concern and social responsibility (model 1), when they have experience with cardiovascular diseases (model 2), and especially if these two are combined. Having experience with cardiovascular diseases is more likely to result in donations to the Dutch Heart Association rather than other health charities when people have a higher level of empathic concern and social responsibility (a negative interaction in model 3). Having experience with cardiovascular diseases is more likely to result in donations to the Dutch Heart Association (rather than other health charities) when people are in worse health. This supports the similarity hypothesis. The interaction of the proportion of family ties in the social network with experience with cardiovascular diseases is not significant.

A comparison between these findings and the findings in Table 2 tells us to what extent the results in Table 2 are driven by the mere likelihood of donating to the Dutch Heart Association rather than the amount donated. In Table 2, the interaction between experience with cardiovascular diseases and empathy/social responsibility was only marginally significant and weaker than in Table 3. This indicates that the finding in Table 2 was driven mainly by the higher likelihood of supporting the Dutch Heart Association among highly empathic persons with experience with cardiovascular diseases, and not by a higher amount donated by this group of respondents. Otherwise, these effects would have added up to a stronger effect in Table 2. The interaction of experience with cardiovascular diseases and subjective health is of similar magnitude in Tables 2 and 3, indicating that there is no such interaction effect on the amount donated to the Dutch Heart Association.

Other interesting findings on the contrast between donors to the Dutch Heart Association and other health charities are that donors to the Dutch Heart Association are more likely to be home owners, have lower levels of education, are more likely to live in smaller communities and have higher empathy/responsibility levels. Affiliation with a small Christian religious denomination (e.g., Evangelical, Jehova's Witnesses) is associated with a lower likelihood of donating to the Dutch Heart Association.

The analysis in Table 3 also reveals differences between donors to the Dutch Heart Association and the group of respondents who do not donate to health charities at all. The main differences are with respect to religious affiliation, education, home ownership, empathy/social responsibility, generalized social trust and joy of giving. Those who do not donate to health charities at all are less likely to be home owners, more highly educated, are more often affiliated with a small Christian religious denomination and have lower levels of empathy/social responsibility, trust and joy of giving. Interestingly, experience with cardiovascular diseases is not associated with a higher likelihood of donating to the Dutch Heart Association rather than not donating to health charities. This suggests that experience with cardiovascular diseases only results in donations to the Dutch Heart Association when people are attracted to health charities in the first place. If people donate to health charities and they happen to know a heart patient, they are much more likely to donate to the Dutch Heart Association rather than other health charities. But knowing a heart patient does not result in a higher likelihood of donations to other health charities (e.g., the cancer fund).

DISCUSSION AND CONCLUSION

This study showed that those who know heart patients are more likely to support the Dutch Heart Association, also when controlling for factors associated with knowing heart patients. Support was found for the hypothesis that experience with cardiovascular diseases is associated with a higher likelihood of donating to the Dutch Heart Association among people with higher levels of empathy and social responsibility. This finding is in line with the theory that empathic concern and feelings of responsibility for the welfare of others more easily manifest themselves in prosocial behavior towards beneficiaries at a closer social distance (Bekkers & Wilhelm, 2007; Stürmer et al., 2005, 2006).

I found that experience with cardiovascular diseases is associated with a lower likelihood of donating to the Dutch Heart Association among those who rate their own health as better. This result supports the similarity hypothesis, and rejects the solidarity hypothesis. Those who are more similar to heart patients because they are not in excellent health themselves are more likely to donate to the Dutch Heart Association when they know a heart patient. It may still be the case that those who have experience with cardiovascular diseases are more likely to donate when they feel more guilty for being healthy themselves. Empathic people are more likely to feel sorry for other people's misfortune. However, this tendency does not manifest itself in donations to the Dutch Heart Association among those in excellent health.

This study also shed light on the profile of donors to the Dutch Heart Association. Socio-demographic variables such as age, gross household income and owning a home have a positive relationship with the amount donated to the Dutch Heart Foundation. Remarkably, education has a negative relationship with the amount given to the Dutch Heart Foundation. In dozens of studies, education is associated with higher total giving (Bekkers & Wiepking, 2007). The analyses reveal that this higher generosity among the better educated in the Netherlands does not extend to health charities. With the current data I cannot show why this is the case. Future research is needed to clarify this issue.

No support was found for the hypothesis that experience with cardiovascular diseases leads to higher donations when the proportion of family ties in one's network increases. While having a larger social network is associated with a higher likelihood of giving to health charities, a stronger family orientation – apparent from a higher proportion of family members in one's network – is not associated with donations to health charities. It seems that family members do not differ from friends and acquaintances in their encouragement of donations to health charities. However, it should be noted that the measure included in the analysis only represents the proportion of all occupations that people have access to through family relationships. This is a far from perfect measure of the social influence of family members. Ideally, one would like to know how often people talk with family members about charitable donations, to what extent family members exert social pressure to donate and the number of solicitations to donate to charitable causes received through family members. Future research on the influence of social networks on charitable giving should include such measures.

Another issue for future research is generalization. This study deals with only one specific health charity: the Dutch Heart Association. I assume that the results for this specific case can be generalized to other health charities fighting other diseases, such as cancer. Future research should test this assumption.

My general question was to what extent donations to the Dutch Heart Association are a form of solidarity of the healthy with the sick. Historically, one can say that the Dutch Heart Association is indeed a form of solidarity. The Dutch Heart Association did not emerge as a movement of patients advocating their rights or as a self-help movement. The Dutch Heart Association was founded by a group of medical professionals who saw possibilities for improvements of treatment and prevention of cardiovascular diseases. The organization emerged from the shared perception among medical professionals that public health could be improved through the advancement of science and technology. The focus on research and technology is still apparent in the organization's programs. The largest part of all expenses of the Dutch Heart Association is allocated to scientific research. Public education and prevention programs also receive substantial shares. Internal evaluations reveal that these programs contribute an increased awareness of symptoms of cardiovascular diseases and preventive measures that people can take themselves. From the perspective of the output of the Dutch Heart Association, the organization embodies solidarity of the healthy with the sick.

However, from the perspective of input – the donor side – the Dutch Heart Association is not so much a form of solidarity of the healthy with the sick as a form of solidarity with the not-so-healthy with the sick. The results of the empirical analyses of the donor base show that the health situation of current donors to the Dutch Heart Association is somewhat below average. People are more likely to donate to the Dutch Heart Association when they know a heart patient, and those in excellent health are less likely to know a heart patient. In addition, among people who do know a heart patient, those in a below average health situation are more likely to donate to the Dutch Heart Association.

These results indicate limits to voluntary solidarity. Solidarity is not easily generalized to dissimilar others. Empathy is a source of compassion with strangers, but the effect of empathic concern on giving is limited if one does not know a heart patient. Solidarity is based on similarity and personal experiences.

From a broader policy perspective, the results can be taken as a warning sign in the debate on public vs. private funding of health care and prevention of illnesses. In the absence of public funding, private funding is more likely to come from those who have experience with the illness. Because those with higher socio-economic status are in better health, private contributions are made by those with a higher stake in future health care but with limited resources.

NOTES

1. It should be noted, however, that high private contributions may also cause government funding to remain low. To test which way the causality runs, longitudinal data on government spending and private contributions are required.

2. The largest charity in the Netherlands is the KWF Cancer Fund, with a fundraising income of €63 million in 2005 (CBF, 2006). This is 31.5% of all private contributions to health charities; total contributions to all charities fighting cancer amount to 38.5% of all contributions.

3. I also considered the number of hospitalizations and the number of ill health years as correlates of the amount donated to charities fighting specific health problems. These factors also showed some large discrepancies with total donations. For example, psychological illnesses rank 1st in the number of ill health years but rank 13th in total donations; 14.6% of all hospitalizations are related to muscular diseases, but only 4% of total donations goes to organizations fighting these diseases. An important factor that may explain some of the discrepancies is whether illnesses are perceived as avoidable health risks. The numbers of polio and HIV/AIDS patients may not have been huge, but the public's perception was that 'everyone was at risk'.

4. The degree of responsibility of patients suffering from cardiovascular diseases for their illness is likely to be perceived as higher than the degree of responsibility of cancer patients. This may explain why cancer attracts more donations than cardiovascular diseases, despite a lower 'objective need'.

5. In the Giving in the Netherlands Panel Survey 2007 several questions were asked on health problems in one's social network, and an additional set of questions on health problems among respondents themselves. 682 of the 1,474 respondents (46.3%) reported knowing someone who suffered from cardiovascular diseases in the past five years. 67 of these respondents (9.8%) reported suffering from cardiovascular diseases themselves. An additional 190 respondents reported that they suffered from cardiovascular diseases themselves, but did not know any others suffering from cardiovascular diseases. Thus, almost three quarters of all heart patients (73.9%) in the sample reported not knowing others with cardiovascular diseases. This means that our variable 'experience with cardiovascular diseases' can be interpreted mainly as 'knowing a heart patient' rather than 'being a heart patient'.

6. The seventh item ("I am a soft-hearted person") was deleted because it lowered the reliability of the scale (to 0.732).

7. This is a very high proportion. The proportion is that high because the Dutch Heart Association has an extensive network of about 75,000 volunteer fundraisers who collect money door to door.

8. The tobit regression model takes censoring of donations at zero into account. A substantial proportion of respondents does not donate to the Dutch Heart Association (34.4%). Including these respondents as zeros in an OLS would bias the parameter estimates downward.

9. Additional analyses with separate scales for empathic concern and social responsibility (available upon request) indicate that both scales have a positive relationship with donations to the Dutch Heart Association, but that the relationship of donations with social responsibility is stronger than the relationship with empathic concern.

ACKNOWLEDGMENTS

This chapter was written with financial support from the Netherlands Organization for Scientific Research, grant number 451-04-110. Thanks to

May-May Meijer and Pamala Wiepking for various contributions to this chapter. I thank the editors for useful comments and suggestions.

REFERENCES

American Heart Association & American Stroke Association. (2007). *Inspiring Change: Annual Report 07*. American Heart Association, Dallas, TX.

Basil, D. Z., Ridgway, N. M., & Basil, M. D. (2006). Guilt appeals: The mediating effect of responsibility. *Psychology and Marketing*, *23*, 1035–1054.

Bekkers, R. (2006). Traditional and health related philanthropy: The role of resources and personality. *Social Psychology Quarterly*, *68*, 349–366.

Bekkers, R., & Wiepking, P. (2006). To give or not to give, that's the question. How methodology is destiny in Dutch data. *Nonprofit and Voluntary Sector Quarterly*, *35*, 533–540.

Bekkers, R., & Wiepking, P. (2007). *Generosity and philanthropy: A literature review*. Report commissioned by the John Templeton Foundation. SSRN Working Paper, 1015507.

Bekkers, R., & Wilhelm, M. O. (2007). Helping behavior, dispositional empathic concern, and the principle of care. Paper presented at the 36th Arnova conference, Atlanta, November 16, 2007.

Bennett, R. (2003). Factors underlying the inclination to donate to particular types of charity. *International Journal of Nonprofit and Voluntary Sector Marketing*, *8*, 12–29.

Berkowitz, L., & Daniels, L. R. (1964). Affecting the salience of the social responsibility norm: Effects of past help on the response to dependency relationships. *Journal of Abnormal and Social Psychology*, *68*, 275–281.

Berkowitz, L., & Lutterman, K. G. (1968). The traditional socially responsible personality. *The Public Opinion Quarterly*, *32*, 169–185.

Bryan, J. H., & Test, M. A. (1967). Models and helping: Naturalistic studies in aiding behavior. *Journal of Personality and Social Psychology*, *6*, 400–407.

Bryant, W. K., Slaughter, H. J., Kang, H., & Tax, A. (2003). Participating in philanthropic activities: Donating money and time. *Journal of Consumer Policy*, *26*, 43–73.

Burger, J. M., Messian, N., Patel, S., Prado, A. D., & Anderson, C. (2004). What a coincidence! The effects of incidental similarity on compliance. *Personality and Social Psychology Bulletin*, *30*, 35–43.

Burgoyne, C. B., Young, B., & Walker, C. M. (2005). Deciding to give to charity: A focus group study in the context of the household economy. *Journal of Community and Applied Social Psychology*, *15*, 383–405.

Byrne, D. (1971). *The attraction paradigm*. New York: Academic Press.

CBF. (2006). *Fondsenwerving in Nederland 2005*. Amsterdam: Stichting Centraal Bureau Fondsenwerving.

CBS. (2007). Causes of death and hospitalization statistics 2005. Downloaded from statline.cbs.nl on June 19, 2007.

Coleman, J. S. (1990). *Foundations of social theory*. Cambridge, MA: Belknap Press.

Davis, M. H. (1994). *Empathy: A social psychological approach*. Madison, WI: Brown & Benchmark Publishers.

Davis, M. H., Mitchell, K. V., Hall, J. A., Lothert, J., Snapp, T., & Meyer, M. (1999). Empathy, expectations, and situational preferences: Personality influences on the decision to participate in volunteer helping behaviors. *Journal of Personality*, *67*(3), 469–503.

Durlauf, S. N. (2002). Bowling alone: A review essay. *Journal of Economic Behavior and Organization*, *47*, 259–273.

Eisenberg, N., Guthrie, I. K., Cumberland, A., Murphy, B. C., Shepard, S. A., Zhou, Q., & Carlo, G. (2002). Prosocial development in early adulthood: A longitudinal study. *Journal of Personality and Social Psychology*, *82*, 993–1006.

Gaertner, S. L., & Dovidio, J. F. (1977). The subtlety of white racism, arousal, and helping behaviour. *Journal of Personality and Social Psychology*, *35*, 691–708.

Giving USA. (2007). *Giving USA 2007: The annual report on philanthropy for the year 2006*. Glenview, IL: Giving USA Foundation.

Haug, M. R., & Lavin, B. (1979). Public challenge of physician authority. *Medical Care*, *17*, 844–856.

Haug, M. R., & Lavin, B. (1981). Practitioner or patient – Who's in charge? *Journal of Health and Social Behavior*, *22*, 212–229.

Hoeymans, N., & Poos, M. J. J. C. (2006). Ziektelast in DALY's: Wat zijn wegingsfactoren en hoe zijn ze bepaald? In: R. Rivm (Ed.), *Volksgezondheid Toekomst Verkenning, Nationaal Kompas Volksgezondheid*. Bilthoven: RIVM.

Idler, E. L., & Benyamini, Y. (1997). Self-rated health and mortality: A review of twenty-seven community studies. *Journal of Health and Social Behavior*, *38*, 21–37.

Levitt, L., & Kornhaber, R. C. (1977). Stigma and compliance: A re-examination. *Journal of Social Psychology*, *103*, 13–18.

Lin, N., & Dumin, M. (1986). Access to occupations through social ties. *Social Networks*, *8*, 365–385.

Lindskold, S., Forte, R. A., Haake, C. S., & Schmidt, E. K. (1977). The effects of directness of face-to-face requests and sex of solicitor on streetcorner donations. *Journal of Social Psychology*, *101*, 45–51.

Lowry, D. (1973). Demographic similarity, attitudinal similarity, and attitude change. *Public Opinion Quarterly*, *37*, 192–208.

Miilunpalo, S., Vuori, I., Oja, P., Pasanen, M., & Urponen, H. (1997). Self-rated health status as a health measure: The predictive value of self-reported health status on the use of physician services and on mortality in the working-age population. *Journal of Clinical Epidemiology*, *50*, 517–528.

Milofsky, C., & Blades, S. D. (1991). Issues of accountability in health charities: A case study of accountability problems among nonprofit organizations. *Nonprofit and Voluntary Sector Quarterly*, *20*, 371–393.

Nederlandse Hartstichting. (2005). *Jaarverslag 2005*. Den Haag: Hartstichting.

Putnam, R. D. (2000). *Bowling alone. The collapse and revival of American community*. New York: Simon & Schuster.

Radley, A., & Kennedy, M. (1995). Charitable giving by individuals: A study of attitudes and practice. *Human Relations*, *48*, 685–709.

Rooney, P. M., Steinberg, K., & Schervish, P. G. (2001). A methodological comparison of giving surveys: Indiana as a test case. *Nonprofit and Voluntary Sector Quarterly*, *30*, 551–568.

Schuyt, T. N. M., Gouwenberg, B. M., Bekkers, R., Meijer, M. M., & Wiepking, P. (2007). *Geven in nederland 2007: Giften, Legaten, Sponsoring en Vrijwilligerswerk*. Amsterdam: Reed Business.

Schuyt, T. N. M., Smit, J., & Bekkers, R. (2004). Constructing a philanthropy-scale: Social responsibility and philanthropy. 33d Arnova Conference, Los Angeles.

Schwartz, S., & David, A. B. (1976). Responsibility and helping in an emergency: Effects of blame, ability and denial of responsibility. *Sociometry*, *39*, 406–415.

Schwartz, S. H. (1973). Normative explanations of helping behavior: A critique, proposal, and empirical test. *Journal of Experimental Social Psychology*, *9*, 349–364.

Schwartz, S. H., & Howard, J. A. (1980). Explanations of the moderating effect of responsibility denial on the personal norm–behavior relationship. *Social Psychology Quarterly*, *43*, 441–446.

Sills, D. L. (1957). *The volunteers: Means and ends in a national organization*. Glencoe, IL: Free Press.

Sole, K., Marton, J., & Hornstein, H. A. (1975). Opinion similarity and helping: Three field experiments investigating the bases of promotive tension. *Journal of Experimental Social Psychology*, *11*, 1–13.

Stürmer, S., Snyder, M., Kropp, A., & Siem, B. (2006). Empathy-motivated helping: The moderating role of group membership. *Personality and Social Psychology Bulletin*, *32*, 943–956.

Stürmer, S., Snyder, M., & Omoto, A. M. (2005). Prosocial emotions and helping: The moderating role of group membership. *Journal of Personality and Social Psychology*, *88*, 532–546.

Wagner, C., & Wheeler, L. (1969). Model, need, and cost effects in helping behaviour. *Journal of Personality and Social Psychology*, *12*, 111–116.

Wiepking, P. (2008). *For the love of mankind*. Ph.D. Thesis, Vrije Universiteit, Amsterdam.

Yinon, Y., & Sharon, I. (1985). Similarity in religiousness of the solicitor, the potential helper, and the recipient as determinants of donating behavior. *Journal of Applied Social Psychology*, *15*, 726–734.

PART III
THEORETICAL AND POLICY IMPLICATIONS

SPEAKING FOR STEM CELLS: BIOMEDICAL ACTIVISM AND EMERGING FORMS OF PATIENTHOOD

Chris Ganchoff

ABSTRACT

Purpose – *Recent research on the modes of patient activism has displaced older notions of patients as passive, compliant subjects of biomedical power. This chapter expands analyses of patient activism to examine the intersections between the processes of identity formation, the emergence of a new scientific field (human stem cell research), and political institutions.*

Methodology – *This chapter uses in-depth interviews, ethnographic techniques, and textual analyses to collect data regarding California's 2004 ballot initiative, Proposition 71, The California Stem Cell Research and Cures Act. Data were analyzed using a situational analysis approach. Situational analysis is a variant of grounded theory that organizes data in the form of maps of connections between actors and social worlds.*

Findings – *This chapter examines the content and significance of this event through the construction of a collective identity among supporters of Proposition 71, what I call "stem cell activists." The construction of this*

Patients, Consumers and Civil Society
Advances in Medical Sociology, Volume 10, 225–245

ISSN: 1057-6290/doi:10.1016/S1057-6290(08)10011-0

collective identity serves as an important ground from which individuals and groups carve out political claims of self-representation. Stem cell activists also helped pass a controversial initiative through the efforts in publicly supporting Prop 71 and human stem cell research.

Research limitations – *This research is limited in that it only examined individuals who became stem cell activists, and not individuals from whom this identity failed to gain salience. More research is needed to understand the conditions under which this identity becomes incorporated within a person's political repertoire.*

Value of chapter – *This chapter brings together theoretical perspectives on the symbolic aspects of identity construction and the political economy of biomedical science. This chapter will be of interest to scholars in medical sociology, science and technology studies, and social movement researchers.*

INTRODUCTION

There has been a recent explosion in the literature covering the dynamics, organizational forms, and implications of the activism found in and around the biomedical sciences (Epstein, 1996; Kroll-Smith & Hugh Floyd, 1997; Klawiter, 1999; Brouwer, 2001; Brown, Zavestoski, McCormick, & Mandelbaum, 2001; Rapp, Heath & Taussig, 2001; Barbot & Dodier, 2002; Callon & Rabeharisoa, 2003; Crossley, 2003; Rapp, 2003; Callon & Rabeharisoa, 2004; Brown et al., 2004; Hess, 2004; Barbot, 2006; Dumit, 2006; Morris & Balmer, 2006; Mykytyn, 2006). It would be an impossible task to reduce the vast diversities of groups, ideologies, strategies, conflicts, and affinities to even a loosely bounded set of concepts or theories that can account for the ranges of differences found in empirical cases. However, patient advocacy organizations and health social movements have now become critical actors addressing a wide variety of diseases and conditions, such as HIV/AIDS, breast cancer, as well as issues in health policy including health care inequalities and affordable health insurance.

The concepts of patient advocacy organizations and health social movements have become indispensable tools for understanding health disparities and the attempts to ameliorate the problems caused by institutional inequalities found around the world. Their theoretical force is bolstered by connections with social movement theory, from which theorists who employ the concepts of patient advocacy organizations and health social movements draw resources. One of the critical junction points in organizations and movements, for both activists and theorists, is the first contact between a person and a social movement. That is, the question is under what conditions do individuals join a movement or an organization that is pressing for social change? More specifically, what are the processes that push and pull individuals into becoming part of patient advocacy organizations or health social movements?

Social movement theorists have long been interested in the successes, failures, and outcomes involving recruitment processes. Some have pointed to the importance of existing networks of friends and acquaintances that can be drawn upon for support (Mueller, 1994; McAdam, 1999; Mansbridge & Morris, 2001). Some have attempted to overcome the interest/altruism distinction by pointing towards activism as a style of life (Teske, 1997). Others have highlighted the importance of framing techniques to provide acceptable and legitimate representations of some aspect of social struggle (Snow, Rochford, Worden, & Benford, 1986; Snow & Benford, 1992; Johnston & Noakes, 2005). Finally, some have emphasized "moral shocks" that draw in individuals and groups of actors to the action (Jasper & Poulsen, 1995).

This chapter addresses this question through the concept of collective identities. It has been argued that patienthood can act like a collective identity. It functions as a ground state or principle from which broader political or moral claims can be articulated, similar to what some have termed "biological citizenship" (Petryna, 2002; Rose & Novas, 2005). What is interesting in the case of patienthood is that it does not automatically produce something like a collective identity. While standardized diagnoses produce populations of people, individuals and groups within any focal population will have very different understandings and expectations about their diagnosis, available treatment modalities, and potential outcomes. Rose and Novas (2005, p. 441) refer to this diagnostic classification as simultaneously "dividing" or setting the parameters of who gets treatment or who does not, and "unifying" individuals under a diagnostic category in the face of other social differences. However, despite the power of unification that diagnostic procedures possess, a "politicized collective illness identity" (Brown et al., 2004, p. 60) will not be isomorphic with the population that has the disease or condition. Thus, the collective identities that emerge in the fields of biomedicine are neither transparent nor automatic signifiers of the focal population that they represent. Rather, the formation of collective identities in and around diagnostic categories is consequential for the forms of activism that take shape over time.

This chapter examines the collective identity of *stem cell activist*, and activists support of California's Proposition 71, the California Stem Cell Research and Cures Initiative (henceforth Prop 71), which passed with 59% of the popular vote in the November 2004 general election. Prop 71 created a new state agency, the California Institute for Regenerative Medicine (CIRM), as well as altered the state's constitution. Prop 71 emerged from the actions of several groups of actors, including state politicians who supported human stem cell research, patient activists dismayed over the Bush administration's policies towards funding human embryonic stem cell research, and scientists looking for new sources of sponsorship. Different segments of this coalition had been active on multiple fronts, including federal and state legislatures, since the Bush administration's announcement regarding NIH funding of human embryonic stem cell research in August 2001. Prop 71 stipulated that grant money would go to both non-profit and for-profit institutions, after the scoring of proposals by a "study section" of scientists from outside of California, a process modeled after the NIH system. In addition to experimental and clinical projects, grant money would also be used for the construction of new research facilities (such as laboratories, cell and tissue banks, and other research cores), an important consideration given the restrictions placed on the use of NIH grant money and human embryonic stem cell research. Specifically, Prop 71 set up the California Institute for Regenerative Medicine (CIRM), which is the agency that conducts all these activities, including developing operational guidelines, formulating requests for proposals, monitoring funding streams, and promoting stem cell research. The CIRM is directed by a 29-member board of directors, called the Independent Citizens Oversight Committee (ICOC). Prop 71 specified the eligibility criteria for ICOC members, who were subsequently appointed by state government officials.

The collective identity of stem cell activist was not constructed directly in opposition to a counter-identity framing, or economic injustice, or even state-sanctioned repression or violence. Rather, I want to highlight this collective identity's connections to a controversial biomedical technology. Working through the concept of collective identity, I argue that stem cell activists have created dense networks and affiliations that are sustaining activism in different formats. First, stem cell activists are in close contact with other groups of actors interested in that technology as well, including bench scientists, biotechnology advocates, university officials, policy makers, and government regulators. Stem cell activists do not operate in only one domain of social life, but travel across social worlds, and produce multiple effects within and across these worlds. Second, like HIV/AIDS treatment activists and others before them, stem cell activists have become a visible presence in the spaces of public representation, including the Internet (web-based activism, home pages, and listservs), government (committee and sub-committee hearings), and civil society (public meetings and debates). By operating across a range of different social spaces, stem cell activists deploy and re-signify multiple discourses within and outside of biomedical institutions. Testimonies by patients in public venues do critical kinds of rhetorical and political work. Finally, the work of stem cell activists is redefining aspects of contemporary patienthood in liberal capitalist societies. In the United States at the beginning of the 21st century, identity politics generally operate through claims to static and monolithic identity categories, such as claims based or racial or gender phenotypes. While these claims are important provisional tactics for marginalized groups, they carry potential dangers as well. For example, insistence on the authenticity of a particular racialized experience can be used as an organizing principle for both progressive and reactionary racial projects. This chapter expands these insights into the politics of biomedical identities, and how controversial technologies both reinforce and destabilize identity projects that have taken shape over the last 20 years in North America.

THEORIZING COLLECTIVE IDENTITIES AND THE BIOMEDICAL SCIENCES

In the conclusion to *Impure Science*, Steven Epstein (1996) pointed out the upsurge in patient activism in late 20th century United States that focused on the construction of identities as the basis for collective organizing. This work has paid off for many groups, as patients have brought attention to their conditions, successfully lobbied for greater support for disease research, and garnered important positions within biomedical institutions. This has led some to argue for an emerging "partnership" model (Rabeharisoa, 2003) between patient activists and bench researchers, for example, in helping to steer experimental and clinical research decisions and priorities. This work has revealed interesting dimensions in the relationships between patient activism and biomedical research, and highlighted the often unrecognized roles that lay experts (Brown, 1992; Arksey, 1994; Epstein, 1996) have played (and continue to play) in the production of biomedical knowledge. In addition, lay experts have been critical in affecting health and science policies at both the state and federal levels, including raising awareness of legislators and regulators in terms of political support for patient advocacy, and increasing funding for research and clinical care.

In terms of human stem cell research, the testimonies of patients with various afflictions have become a central discourse in the unfolding of the public forms of this research. Human stem cell research remains at a very early stage, and is far from a unified discipline or scientific program. The research is occurring in many different labs around the globe, from molecular neuroscience to endocrinology to developmental reproductive biology, each with its own protocols and standards. Patients are active in many venues, from legislative forums to scientific conferences, representing themselves and loved ones in pushing for the scientific and policy-based elaboration of human stem cell research. This work is not coordinated by a single organization, but rather by a loose coalition of various actors that share information, strategies, and rhetorics of action. This coalition has recently called itself the "pro-cures" movement, and is a lively group of people with spinal cord injuries, Parkinson's disease, diabetes, and other conditions, their friends and supporters, as well as political professionals, scientists and physicians, and representatives of universities and research centers. Members and supporters of the pro-cures movement were central actors on the Prop 71 campaign. Before looking at this campaign, I want to briefly outline the theoretical strands that this chapter draws from, and the assumptions behind my claims.

The concept of collective identities has long interested scholars and activists attempting to understand social movements. It is certainly true that various identity categories have been imposed upon populations and groups for different ideological and institutional purposes. The divergent typologies of racial classifications, which themselves have temporal and regional differences, are pernicious examples of the enduring connections between forms of power and collective identities (from a vast literature, see Deacon, 1999; Gilroy, 2001; Magubane, 2003; Hacking, 2005). Indeed this coerced aspect of some collective identities has unsettled discussions regarding how freely one chooses an identity, or if identity is even a choice in the first place. Arguments about the "gay gene" or the "female brain" abound (Hamer & Copeland, 1995; Brizendine, 2006), and even though some of the spokespeople for these objects are opposed to the exclusions or inequalities associated with sexual or gender categorization, questions remain about the "degrees of freedom" that an individual has from his or her focal identity.

Nonetheless, much work has shown that collective identities, including race, gender, and sexuality are flexible identity categories that are (re)interpreted and altered by groups and individuals according to both institutional necessities and tactical opportunities. The concept of collective identities has been especially useful for understanding the individual's range of participation in the phases of social movements. That is, individuals have different degrees of participation over time, and some completely drop out from movement activities. Polletta and Jasper (2001, p. 285) define a collective identity as, "an individual's cognitive, moral and emotional connection with a broader community, category, practice or institution. It is a perception of a shared status or relation, which may be imagined rather than experienced directly, and it is distinct from personal identities, although it may form part of a personal identity." As scholars have pointed out, collective identities are the products of active renegotiation over time, and they are both constructed and deconstructed (Gamson, 1989; Taylor & Whittier, 1992; Gamson, 1995). For example, *technoscientific identities* emerge around biomedical practices and techniques, diagnostic and therapeutic categories, and discourses of risk and health (Clarke, Mamo, Shim, Fishman, & Fosket, 2003). The pro-cures movement has produced a technoscientific identity, what I am calling a stem cell activist. I turn now to a closer look at that identity category during the Prop 71 campaign.

STEM CELL ACTIVISM AND COLLECTIVE IDENTITIES

I am arguing that the category of stem cell activist can be thought of as a collective identity because, at a general level, it provides a space from which political claims can be articulated. That is, following Polletta and Jasper's (2001) emphasis on the relational and perspectival attributes of collective identities, becoming a stem cell activist involves making public arguments that stem cell research would benefit actors with various conditions, despite the early stage of the research, the moral complexities of the materials involved, and the uncertain therapeutic future.

At first glance, this seems like an awkward identity category. It does not appear to share the same assumptions involved in thinking about other identity categories, such as race, gender, or sexuality. The category of "stem cell activist" carries neither uniform phenotypical markers, nor the historical resonances or institutional consequences of identification, whether through consent or coercion, that both serve as the conditions of possibility for, and the normative bases of, the resulting social structures built up around a category like race, for example. While stem cell activist is certainly an achieved, rather than ascribed, identity category, it is connected to a politics of the body and "modes of disclosure" (Charmaz, 1993; see also Klawiter, 1999 on embodied protests) about corporeal states.

In what follows, I argue that stem cell activism is an important lens to view the processes through which individuals and groups enact the emerging politics of patienthood that are taking shape in the United States and elsewhere. This chapter is based on a larger project that tracked the development of Prop 71 in California, and the forms of activism associated with this initiative.

Data were collected from a multitude of social positions, and analyzed using a situational analysis mode of inquiry (Clarke, 2005). Situational analysis is a variant of grounded theory that organizes data in the form of maps of connections between actors and social worlds. I interviewed a total of 40 subjects for this project from a variety of social worlds (membership is described in Table 1). Interviews were conducted in 2003–2004, and lasted from 60–120 min, and were selected from a convenience sample based on subject's public participation in Prop 71 events. Interviews were taped and transcribed. In addition, I attended multiple conferences, public meetings, and debates about Prop 71 and human stem cell research during the campaign season. Field notes from these events were transcribed and coded. In addition, I reviewed several reports from federal and state agencies covering human stem cell research, as well as campaign literature and DVDs produced by the Yes on 71 campaign.

The data presented here draw from textual analyses of media documents and reports, ethnographic observations from activity primarily in northern California, and interviews with stem cell activists who worked in support of the Yes on 71 campaign. Table 2 lists the activists interviewed, their (or other's) diagnoses, and the dates of diagnosis or injury. These activists

Table 1. Interviewee Backgrounds.

Social World Membership	Number of Interviews Conducted
Patient activists	17
Scientists (PhD)	10
Opponents of Prop 71	4
Biotechnology representatives	3
Professional organizations	3
Science movements	2
Governmental officials	1

Table 2. Interview Subjects.

Name (All Names are Pseudonyms)	Subject of Injury	Diagnosis	Date of Diagnosis/Injury
Ed	Son	Type I diabetes	1999
Victoria	Grandson	Type I diabetes	1999
Susan	Daughter	Type I diabetes	Unknown
Carol	Self	Parkinson's disease	1995
John	Self	Parkinson's disease	Unknown
Paul	Self	Parkinson's disease	1998
Sarah	Self	Parkinson's disease	Unknown
Steve	Self	Parkinson's disease	Unknown
Patricia	Self	Parkinson's disease	1990
Julie	Self	Parkinson's disease	1988
Jackie	Self	Parkinson's disease	1994
Betty	Self	Multiple sclerosis	1978
Craig	Son	Spinal cord injury	1994
Monica	Self	Spinal cord injury	1992
Rachel	Self	Spinal cord injury	1992
Walter	Self	AIDS	Unknown

suffered from various conditions, or had loved ones with the condition, including Parkinson's disease, Type I (juvenile) diabetes, and spinal cord injuries.

In what follows, I briefly describe what Prop 71 was, and the efforts of the Yes on 71 campaign to position patient activism on behalf of the campaign. Second, I turn to the processes of becoming a stem cell activist during the Prop 71 campaign, and the public enactments of this identity category. Finally, I distinguish stem cell activism from other kinds of biomedical activism, and the effects that this activism is having on emergent forms of patienthood in the United States and elsewhere.

The Event: Proposition 71 and Stem Cell Activism

Prop 71 emerged in part out of the uncertainty around federal funding of human embryonic stem cell research. Groups of actors supporting this research had already sprung to action prior to the Bush administration's August 2001 decision to restrict NIH funding to a set of approved cell lines. This included politicians in the state legislature, as well as groups outside of formal political institutions. One important group of actors, including Hollywood producers, bench scientists, leaders of patient advocacy organizations, and state politicians were responsible for the creation and drafting of Prop 71 (Ganchoff, 2007). This group eventually hired a skeleton staff to help with running a proposition campaign, which is an expensive and demanding operation in a state as large as California. This staff became a non-profit known as Californians for Stem Cell Research and Cures, and once the initiative qualified for the ballot, became the core staff for the Yes on 71 campaign, and eventually the CIRM. Here I am going to focus on activity following ballot qualification that occurred in June 2004.

The Yes on 71 campaign had two field offices that coordinated campaign activity in northern and southern California. Patient advocacy organizations and activists were involved in all stages and aspects of the Yes on 71 campaign. Campaign staffers would meet with organizations, sometimes with a stem cell scientist, and attempt to persuade the organization to endorse the campaign. Staffers also coordinated with local activists, distributed literature, crafted email alerts, and promoted letter and editorial writing to local newspapers. These local contacts were exceedingly important, as they were generally patient activists who were well known and respected within local- and state-level patient advocacy organizations.

Becoming a Stem Cell Activist

I argue that during the Prop 71 campaign, patient activists from different backgrounds came together and forged a collective identity, that of stem cell activist. Here, I foreground the processes and practices that patient activists themselves saw as meaningful. These practices of self-redefinition were critical in terms of human stem cell research and Prop 71. Human stem cell research is a technically complex field in formation, and fraught with multiple controversies, including scientific, moral, and commercial dilemmas and arguments. How did patient activists before and during the Prop 71 campaign make sense of these problems?

First, the stem cell activists I interviewed had long histories of involvement in biomedicine, given that they and their loved ones had gone through the processes of diagnosis and treatment. All were part of some patient advocacy organization, and many supported multiple organizations. These experiences gave activists different perspectives on the development and use of biomedical technologies, as well as the health care system in general. For example, several stem cell activists with family members with juvenile (Type I) diabetes spoke about the often intense, on-going relationships with medical professionals in terms of training in monitoring blood sugar levels, injection schedules, and diet management.

Second, these interactions with health care providers and institutions lead stem cell activists to view biomedical technologies in generally positive ways, although not unreflectively. That is, rather than seeing human stem cell research in terms of "slippery slopes" or affronts to human dignity that dominate Western bioethical discourse, stem cell activists drew upon their experiences to see stem cells as another kind of biomedical technology. In opposing this form of technological or instrumental determinism, activists used pre-existing frames from other domains of life to argue in support of Prop 71. For example, I asked one activist how she understood her involvement in the Yes on 71 campaign

> To me that means when you see an area where you can have an impact to help someone in getting there, you do it. You take an active role, like in organizing – it is called 'Tikkun Olam'. It's Hebrew for 'heal the world.' When I was getting involved with this thing, for some reason, that all of a sudden it just spring to me that there is the meaning, and I particularly feel that's true with this stem cell research. It's not just for diabetics that I'm here, but it's for all these people who suffer from these diseases, that there is a miracle out there waiting to happen, and we need to move it forward.

This activist framed human stem cell research through an understanding of biomedical technologies not as dominating, but as pragmatic. By pragmatic, I mean it was a framing that was derived from being confronted with a problem. There is an idealist strand to this understanding, but the idealism comes from engagement with the world, not from a rejection or separation from empirical life. This was not uncommon among patient activists, given their extensive connections and entanglements with biomedical institutions. However, I do not want to imply that this view is universal. For example, disability rights activists have criticized discourses of curing and healing as masking new forms of exclusion and misrecognition (Oliver, 1990; Shapiro, 1993; Barnartt & Scotch, 2001). Therefore it is important for any analysis of these forms of representation to underscore the multiplicity of positions within biomedical fields. Stem cell activism is one form of the collective identities possible, and as I have argued, far from an automatic or transparent signifier of whole populations.

Finally, stem cell activists cultivated their collective identities through interactions with other experts in scientific and political worlds. For example, one patient activist described to me how, following his diagnosis with Parkinson's disease (PD), he became interested in how many people in California had PD as well. As luck would have it, his neurologist was located at UCLA. When he repeated his thinking about tracking rates of PD in the state to his neurologist, the neurologist said that what would be really helpful is some form of systemized collection of data in the form of a confidential registry. The neurologist directed the PD activist to a colleague in the School of Public Health who is an epidemiologist researching the incidence of PD in the San Joaquin Valley of central California. The epidemiologist corroborated the activist's ideas that what is needed is some kind of method to collect the profiles of PD patients across the state, and that this could be best coordinated not by an individual university researcher but by the state. Paul's luck would continue

> So, I lived 4 doors away from my state assembly member, who happened to be chair of the health committee. And one day I was out washing my car, and he drove by, and we stopped and chatted, and I suggested that he sponsor the registry bill. Using the contacts I made at [patient advocacy organization], and the involvement of the Parkinson's Institute, we successfully lobbied the bill through the state legislature, and the governor did sign it, over the objections of his staff. (Interview, 8/17/05)

The registry is being set up at the time of this writing. It is only the second PD registry in the United States. These rich biographies of activism provided not only frames for action, but also interactions with various kinds of experts. These interactions bolstered the stocks of knowledge of stem cell activists, but also introduced them to the norms of communication that operate within expert enclaves. This positioned stem cell activists as important boundary actors between their local parent's groups and organizations, and the worlds of biomedicine and politics.

Stem Cell Activism in Public

These interactions with other actors served as the conditions within which the collective identity of stem cell activist was forged. A crucial step in the process was the public affirmation of this identity. Scholars from a wide array of disciplines have become increasingly interested in the organization of publics and counterpublics. Michael Warner (2002, p. 90) argues that publics have several distinguishing elements, including the "reflexive circulation of discourse." At a general level, Warner is referring to the mutually constituting relationships between individual speakers, their local attachments, and broader "publics." These complex, interlacing connections produce publics, in the sense that arguments and discussion "in public" enlarge the field of argumentation to include more actors, as well as novel forms of enunciation and interpretation (2002, p. 91). That is, Warner highlights that while discourses travel with different temporal modes, they must be "artfully" reproduced in different contexts (2002, p. 102).

Stem cell activists drew from pre-existing frames and rhetorics, as well as transformed shared meanings of these frames during the processes of constituting a public. These included "rhetorics of curing" (Ganchoff, 2007), or claims that human stem cell research will provide relief from suffering. The official Prop 71 campaign slogan was "Save Lives with Stem Cells." There were also moral claims about the necessity and urgency of human stem cell research. Finally, there were economic claims framing Prop 71 as a biomedical development project that would bring jobs and tax revenue to California. During the Prop 71 campaign, there were three central formats of activity. First, activists engaged in myriad informal conversations and debates regarding human stem cell research. Human stem cell research offers curative promises to many. This may be accomplished by getting human stem cells (embryonic and adult) to differentiate into other kinds of cells (neurons, cardiac muscle, or pancreatic islet cells) through various forms of biochemical or genetic manipulation. Additionally, human embryonic stem cells can be used as a tool to study disease progression in experimental conditions, by looking at the development of a disease in a human cell as it changes over time. Activists used the public scripts of the benefits of human stem cell research (such as "saving lives" and "helping the economy") and deployed them in private settings. The worlds of patient activism are filled with the particularly dense affiliations around pain and suffering (as well as transcendence), giving deep salience to the public scripts of the Prop 71 campaign. In living rooms and parent's groups, patient activists engaged in the active rearticulation of human stem cell research and the production of hope.

Second, activists spoke at formal events, including debates, conferences, and public hearings. They represented their embodied selves as persons demanding recognition. For example, one PD activist testified about the "chemical costume" of medications that he wears in order to counteract the effects of neurodegeneration. Without these medications, the activist argued that the "real me" emerges: "a man unable to walk without assistance, unable to stand without falling over." This production of authenticity relied on the disclosure of the real self as marked, and inverted the logics of stigma. Stem cell activists did not hide their disease identities, but publicly affirmed them as the grounds for supporting a political initiative.

Finally, activists made use of virtual formats, such as the Internet, to express themselves and transmit information in the broadest sense possible. One activist in Southern California compiled and organized the information related to PD organizations in her local area into an email that she sent out to a list she had created. Her list is "hand-made," in that the information she collects is produced by other organizations, but she formats all the text, and has rules for its operation, such as inclusion and exclusion criteria

> I try to keep my bulletin with the range of [names area] county and vicinity, and I don't put anything that has to do with for-profit, money gaining things. I just have this certain skepticism. It doesn't make any sense because some people do have speakers who are doing long-term planning, insurance, that kind of stuff. And that's fine. But I don't like to do ads. I don't want to have any strings. The whole point in what I'm doing is to try to be neutral but helpful. Parkinson's is, I think, unusual in that it has several different factions in terms of patient support and research support. They have little turfdoms.

This list is not simply a technical object; it also reflects the politics of its designer. Specifically, the activist excluded messages from for-profit enterprises. However, she included messages from the Yes on 71 campaign. This activist drew upon a shared sensibility regarding the politics of health and illness as part of her communication strategies.

Stem cell activists were not uncritical supporters of Prop 71. While they backed the campaign, they articulated clear understandings that treatments derived from human stem cells were very far away, and possibly unaffordable. Some activists included critiques of market-based health care as a major obstacle to the development of stem cell therapeutics, and argued that Prop 71 did not go far enough in addressing this issue. In a larger sense, they also recognized larger concerns about the manipulation of human biological life, often expressed by the opponents of Prop 71, as having unforeseen negative consequences (Ganchoff, 2007). Despite these critiques, stem cell activists worked to, in Michael Warner's (2002) words, expand the field of argumentation through interdigitating concerns about the delivery of health care in the United States with the politics of hope. In this sense, stem cell activists took up multiple positions vis-à-vis Prop 71. They worked for its passage, and continue to support human stem cell research. But they also offered important criticisms of the political economy of drug development, and possible negative outcomes of technical interventions into human biologies.

These three forms of stem cell activism are contiguous, and open up interesting questions regarding the public/private distinction. That is, as the body, health, and illness have become sites of intense conflict over the past century, the politics of representation regarding life and death are transforming. Stem cell activism is one example of this reformulation of stigma and identity within and around the worlds of biomedicine. The formation of this collective identity thus affords us an important view upon not only the effects of social movement mobilization, but also the different ways through which the public and private valences of collective identities are mediated by participation across social worlds.

DISCUSSION: EMERGENT FORMS OF PATIENTHOOD

Proposition 71 passed in November 2004 with 59% of the popular vote. The stem cell activists that supported Prop 71 came from different patient advocacy organizations and health social movements and have provisionally unified into a larger movement. The identity category of stem cell activist that undergirds the pro-cures movement was certainly given shape by elites, as well as interpreted and inhabited by patient activists before and during the campaign. The frontal rhetorical move by the Yes on 71 campaign was to highlight the hope for cures to benefit a population of individuals. However the ambiguities and complexities of this research produced difficulties for the supporters of Prop 71, and a shared view of human stem cell research was not guaranteed. These social processes extend across different domains. For example, Sulik and Eich-Krohm (2008) argue that becoming a medical consumer involves syntheses of lay, embodied, and professional forms of knowledge. However, while stem cell activists drew upon consumerist discourses, they were not uncritical of these positions. Since consumption is stratified by social categories, such as race, class, and gender, there are different ways to be a consumer. Political events can and do interrupt the consumption process, and in the case of Prop 71, activate new health social movements.

It is well documented that rhetorical appeals alone are insufficient to produce a social movement, let alone a collective identity (Teske, 1997; McAdam, 1999; Polletta & Jasper, 2001). My empirical data reveal that many stem cell activists have at best a qualified hope in human stem cell research as a therapeutic modality, even in the distant future. This situation gets more complicated when the costs of publicly disclosing one's illness are taken into consideration. For activists oriented towards a single disease or condition, the formation of collective identities will be refracted through the development of "lay expertise" as others have documented (Brown, 1992; Arksey, 1994; Epstein, 1996). Lay expertise develops as a function of activist involvement and engagement with varieties of scientific, political, and economic discourses and practices, and is of course not without its own pitfalls and dilemmas, including dissention and fragmentation of health social movements in the face of internal disagreements (Epstein, 1996; Klawiter, 1999).

Stem cell activism differs from patient activism around a single disease in two ways that are consequential for the public claims of representation that activists deploy. First, human stem cell research is deeply controversial in multiple ways. There are the politics of research materials, which are themselves of different species, depending on where one makes the ethical cut, so to speak. That is, the research materials of human stem cell research is shot through with conflicts at every phase, from gametes to zygotes to embryos to fetuses to children to adults, through controversies regarding the status of the object, techniques of procurement and/or treatment, and claims to ownership and usage in terms of intellectual property, and questions of distributive justice and potential access to treatments. Some of these controversies, such as the status of strong ownership claims to research materials, may be closed by the authority of the judicial system, for example. Others, like debates around the metaphysical qualities of research materials, will likely never end.

Second, the organization of the pro-cures coalition is around a scientific field that is itself in the process of formation. The procurement of research materials, namely human gametes and embryos, remains thorny for groups across the political spectrum, from left to right. In vitro, hESCs tend to differentiate down lineage pathways, and thus require various interventions to keep them in an undifferentiated state. This has raised concerns about their suitability for human transplantation. Some scientists have expressed concern with the speed at which hESC-based treatments are moving towards clinical trials, and fear a repeat of the catastrophes of gene therapy clinical trials, for example.

These structural limits appear in the forms of stem cell activism currently taking shape. For example, the "political economy of hope" model (Rose & Novas, 2005; Rose, 2007) takes on added complexity when the scientific bases for the hope are themselves contested or in the process of formation. As Rose (2007) articulates, this model relies on activists' beliefs in the efficacy of new biotechnological interventions, as well as the speculative hopes of others, such as biotech companies, venture capitalists, and scientists, each group with its own sets of investments. Together, these hopes produce arguments in support of more research. In the case of Prop 71, hope itself became an object of discourse. Some actors were accused of having too much hope, or of being naïve about the possibility of a cure. In turn, others are charged with losing hope, or of not having any.

The embodied politics of stem cell activism, which combine biomedical and political discourses into claims for recognition, are amplified through their connections within the fields of regenerative medicine. Opponents of this research have been successful in turning failures, ambiguities, missteps, and outright frauds into spectacular events signifying deep problems. Stem cell activists' claims to recognition must take into account these counter-framings; indeed they have, as activists have presented their immediate suffering as a moral counterweight to the framing of the human blastocyst as a human subject.

CONCLUSION

The emerging contours of "biological citizenship" (Petryna, 2002; Rose & Novas, 2005) are provoking a range of associations and affinities, as well as frictions and differences, among the groups of actors within contemporary patient advocacy organizations and health social movements. Patient activists, bench researchers, university officials, biotech and pharma entrepreneurs, and governmental actors are being brought into close proximity in the unfolding of contemporary biomedical politics. Prop 71 was an exemplar of this provisional grouping.

During the campaign, patient activists became stem cell activists through their enrollment on the Yes on 71 campaign. However this collective identity is far from a transparent or unmediated marker of a population. This chapter brings analyses on collective identities and current research on health activism to bear on the construction of technoscientific identities. Stem cell activism certainly shares commonalities with other patient activism; however, its proximity to controversial biomedical objects and a scientific field that is in the early stages of formation, intersects the kinds of lay expertises that are mobilizing around state- and federal-level movements and policies.

Stem cell activism as an identity category is certainly being promoted by elite groups. Some authors have pointed out the problems with this promotion, especially in its neoliberal forms. For example, Fisher and Ronald (2008) point out how pharmaceutical companies use discourses of patient empowerment in order to further their commercial interests. Similarly, both Sulik and Eich-Krohm (2008) and Holster (2008) argue that the strategies of different organizations within health care markets, coupled with the Internet, serve to transform patients into consumers. At the same time, this identity category is a strategically useful tool for patient activists to form provisional unities across different patient advocacy organizations and health social movements. This chapter argues that continued research on the biomedical sciences and biotechnology should track the interlaced formation of scientific fields and practices, and activist fields and practices, and deepen the concept of lay expertise to take into account the production and reception of recognition claims and collective identities of patient activists by heterogeneous publics.

ACKNOWLEDGMENTS

The author would like to thank Adele Clarke, Susan Chambré, Melinda Goldner, and the anonymous reviewers for their close readings and insightful comments.

REFERENCES

Arksey, H. (1994). Expert and lay participation in the construction of medical knowledge. *Sociology of Health and Illness*, *16*, 448–468.

Barbot, J. (2006). How to build an 'Active' patient? The work of AIDS associations in France. *Social Science and Medicine*, *62*, 538–551.

Barbot, J., & Dodier, N. (2002). Multiplicity in scientific medicine: The experience of HIV positive patients. *Science, Technology and Human Values*, *27*, 404–440.

Barnartt, S., & Scotch, R. (2001). *Disability protests: Contentious politics 1970–1999*. Washington, DC: Gallaudet University Press.

Brizendine, L. (2006). *The female brain*. New York, NY: Morgan Road Books.

Brouwer, D. (2001). ACT-Ing up in congressional hearings. In: R. Asen & D. Brouwer (Eds), *Counterpublics and the state* (pp. 87–110). Albany, NY: State University of New York Press.

Brown, P. (1992). Popular epidemiology and toxic waste contamination: Lay and professional ways of knowing. *Journal of Health and Social Behavior*, *33*, 267–281.

Brown, P., Zavestoski, S., McCormick, S., & Mandelbaum, J. (2001). Print media coverage of environmental causation of breast cancer. *Sociology of Health and Illness*, *23*, 747–775.

Brown, P., Zavestoski, S., McCormick, S., Mayer, B., Morello-Frosch, R., & Gaisor, R. (2004). Embodied health movements: Uncharted territory in social movement research. *Sociology of Health and Illness*, *26*, 1–31.

Callon, M., & Rabeharisoa, V. (2003). Research 'In the Wild' and the shaping of new social identities. *Technology in Society*, *25*, 193–204.

Callon, M., & Rabeharisoa, V. (2004). Gino's lesson on humanity: Genetics, mutual entanglements and the sociologist's role. *Economy and Society*, *33*, 1–27.

Charmaz, K. (1993). *Good days, bad days: The self in chronic illness and time*. New Brunswick, NJ: Rutgers University Press.

Clarke, A. (2005). *Situational analysis: Grounded theory after the postmodern turn*. Thousand Oaks, CA: Sage Publications.

Clarke, A., Mamo, L., Shim, J., Fishman, J., & Fosket, J. (2003). Biomedicalization: Technoscientific transformations of health, illness, and U.S. biomedicine. *American Sociological Review*, *68*, 161–194.

Crossley, N. (2003). From reproduction to transformation: Social movement fields and the radical habitus. *Theory, Culture and Society*, *20*, 43–68.

Deacon, H. (1999). Racial categories and pyschiatry in Africa: The asylum on Robben Island in the nineteenth century. In: W. Ernst & B. Harris (Eds), *Race, science and medicine, 1700–1960* (pp. 101–122). New York, NY: Routledge.

Dumit, J. (2006). Illnesses you have to fight to get: Facts as forces in uncertain, emergent illnesses. *Social Science and Medicine*, *62*, 577–590.

Epstein, S. (1996). *Impure science: AIDS, activism, and the politics of knowledge*. Berkeley, CA: University of California Press.

Fisher, J. A., & Ronald, L. M. (2008). Direct to consumer responsibility: Medical neoliberalism in pharmaceutical advertising and drug development. In: S. Chambré & M. Goldner (Eds), *Advances in medical sociology: Patients, consumers and civil society* (pp. 29–51). Bingley, UK: Emerald Group Publishing Limited.

Gamson, J. (1989). Silence, death, and the invisible enemy: AIDS activism and social movement 'Newness'. *Social Problems*, *36*, 351–367.

Gamson, J. (1995). Must identity movements self-destruct? A queer dilemma. *Social Problems*, *42*, 390–407.

Ganchoff, C. (2007). *Regenerating movements: Human stem cells and the politics of potentiality*. Ph.D. dissertation, University of California, San Francisco.

Gilroy, P. (2001). *Against race: Imagining political culture beyond the color line*. Cambridge, MA: Harvard University Press.

Hacking, I. (2005). Why race still matters. *Daedalus*, *Winter*, 102–116.

Hamer, D., & Copeland, P. (1995). *The science of desire: The search for the gay gene and the biology of behaviour*. New York, NY: Simon and Shuster.

Hess, D. (2004). Guest editorial: Health, the environment and social movements. *Science as Culture*, *13*, 421–427.

Holster, K. (2008). Making connections: Egg donation, the Internet, and the new reproductive technology marketplace. In: S. Chambré & M. Goldner (Eds), *Advances in medical sociology: Patients, consumers and civil society* (pp. 53–73). Bingley, UK: Emerald Group Publishing Limited.

Jasper, J., & Poulsen, J. (1995). Recruiting strangers and friends: Moral shocks and social networks in animal rights and anti-nuclear protests. *Social Problems*, *42*, 493–512.

Johnston, H., & Noakes, J. (Eds). (2005). *Frames of protest: Social movements and the framing perspective*. Lanham, MD: Roman and Littlefield Publishing Group.

Klawiter, M. (1999). Racing for the cure, walking women, and toxic turing: Mapping cultures of action within the Bay Area terrain of breast cancer. *Social Problems*, *46*, 104–126.

Kroll-Smith, S., & Hugh Floyd, H. (1997). *Bodies in protest: Environmental illness and the struggle over medical knowledge*. New York, NY: New York University Press.

Magubane, Z. (2003). Simian, savages, skulls, and sex: Science and colonial militarism in nineteenth-century South Africa. In: D. Moore, J. Kosek & A. Pandian (Eds), *Race, nature, and the politics of difference*. Durham, NC: Duke University Press.

Mansbridge, J., & Morris, A. (2001). *Oppositional consciousness: The subjective roots of social protest*. Chicago, IL: University of Chicago Press.

McAdam, D. (1999). *Political process and the development of black insurgency, 1930–1970*. Chicago, IL: University of Chicago Press.

Morris, N., & Balmer, B. (2006). Volunteer human subjects' understandings of their participation in a biomedical research experiment. *Social Science and Medicine*, *62*, 998–1008.

Mueller, C. (1994). Conflict networks and the origins of women's liberation. In: E. Laraña, H. Johnston & J. Gusfield (Eds), *New social movements: From ideology to identity* (pp. 234–266). Philadelphia, PA: Temple University Press.

Mykytyn, C. (2006). Anti-aging medicine: A patient/practitioner movement to redefine aging. *Social Science and Medicine*, *62*, 643–653.

Oliver, M. (1990). *The politics of disablement: A sociological approach*. New York, NY: St. Martin's Press.

Petryna, A. (2002). *Life exposed: Biological citizens after Chernobyl*. Princeton, NJ: Princeton University Press.

Polletta, F., & Jasper, J. (2001). Collective identity and social movements. *Annual Reviews of Sociology*, *27*, 283–305.

Rabeharisoa, V. (2003). The struggle against neuromuscular diseases in France and the emergence of the 'Partnership Model' of patient organisation. *Social Science and Medicine*, *57*, 2127–2136.

Rapp, R. (2003). Cell life and death, child life and death: Genomic horizons, genetic disease, family stories. In: S. Franklin & M. Lock (Eds), *Remaking life and death: Toward an anthropology of the biosciences* (pp. 129–164). Santa Fe, NM: School of American Research Press.

Rapp, R., Heath, D., & Taussig, K. S. (2001). Genealogical dis-ease: Where hereditary abnormality, biomedical explanation, and family responsibility meet. In: S. Franklin & S. McKinnon (Eds), *Relative values: Reconfiguring kinship studies* (pp. 384–412). Durham, NC: Duke University Press.

Rose, N., & Novas, C. (2005). Biological citizenship. In: A. Ong & S. Collier (Eds), *Global assemblages: Technology, politics, and ethics as anthropological problems* (pp. 439–463). Malden, MA: Blackwell Publishing.

Rose, R. (2007). *The politics of life itself: Biomedicine, power, and subjectivity in the twenty-first century*. Princeton, NJ: Princeton University Press.

Shapiro, J. (1993). *No pity: People with disabilities forging a new civil rights movement*. New York, NY: Random House, Inc.

Snow, D., & Benford, R. (1992). Master frames and cycles of protest. In: A. Morris & C. Mueller (Eds), *Frontiers in social movement theory* (pp. 133–155). New Haven, CT: Yale University Press.

Snow, D., Rochford, E., Jr., Worden, S., & Benford, R. (1986). Frame alignment processes, mobilization, and movement participation. *American Sociological Review*, *51*, 464–481.

Sulik, G., & Eich-Krohm, A. (2008). No longer a patient: The social construction of the medical consumer. In: S. Chambré & M. Goldner (Eds), *Advances in medical sociology: Patients, consumers and civil society* (pp. 3–28). Bingley, UK: Emerald Group Publishing Limited.

Taylor, V., & Whittier, N. (1992). Collective identity in social movement communities: Lesbian feminist mobilization. In: A. Morris & C. Mueller (Eds), *Frontiers in social movement theory* (pp. 104–130). New Haven, CT: Yale University Press.

Teske, N. (1997). *Political activists in America: The identity construction model of political participation*. New York, NY: Cambridge University Press.

Warner, M. (2002). *Publics and counterpublics*. Cambridge, MA: The MIT Press.

FORGING A NEW COMMONS: SELF-HELP ASSOCIATIONS IN SLOVENIA AND CROATIA

Ann Dill and Joanne Coury

ABSTRACT

Purpose – *This chapter assesses the role of self-help groups within the emerging civil society in two transitional economies, Croatia and Slovenia, focusing on the impact of relationships with health or social care professionals and the state.*

Methodology – *Methods include participant observation, interviews, and document analysis of 31 groups studied intermittently from 2001 to 2007.*

Findings – *Self-help groups range from those three decades old to those dealing with "new social problems." Groups, and the third sector generally, remain essentially dependent on the state. Few exist separately from formal service organizations. Those closely linked with medical institutions are challenged by state retrenchment and privatization. Others contend with funding instability, and Western models of non-profit development are expanding. Relationships with professionals are neither subservient nor independent; instead, groups act as corollaries and educators to the professional realm.*

Implications, limitations, and value – *Findings suggest more nuances in self-help groups' relations with the state and professionals than found in*

Patients, Consumers and Civil Society
Advances in Medical Sociology, Volume 10, 247–271

ISSN: 1057-6290/doi:10.1016/S1057-6290(08)10012-2

Western settings. This may illustrate both the potential and the limits of citizen involvement in new non-governmental sectors. It also demonstrates how relations between professionals and self-help groups depend on social and material relations well beyond the domain of systems of care. While specific findings cannot be generalized beyond the research settings, the study shows the importance of understanding such groups within social and political contexts. Contributions to civil society here included re-making public meanings, identities, and relations with professionalized systems. Further comparative assessment of self-help associations is essential to theory on the third sector in civil society.

The third sector plays an important role in the growth of civil society in post-socialist countries. Voluntary associations, in particular, have assumed increased salience following economic and political transitions, both as a means of promoting civic participation and values and as a "safety net" protecting against the worst outcomes of the decentralization of the welfare state. There is both theoretical and empirical consensus that grassroots and non-governmental organizations can mediate between civil society and the state, enabling the latter to promote civil society development, ideally without promoting corporatist domination (Svetlik, 1991; CIVICUS, 1997; Osborne & Kaposvari, 1997; Powell & Guerin, 1997; Brown, 1998; Fisher, 1998; Gittell & Vidal, 1998).

There has yet, however, to be a focus specifically on self-help and mutual aid associations in these transitional settings, nor has there been acknowledgement of their potential contribution to the evolution of human services or civil society more broadly. Commonly viewed as depicting an arena for voluntary collective action intermediate between the state and private life, the concept of civil society played a major role motivating the transformation of socialist societies (Madison, 1998; Deacon, 2001). As noted by Madison (1998, p. 9), "the struggle against socialist totalitarianism *was* the struggle for civil society, as the activists involved themselves clearly realized." Achieving freedom from state control implied individual as well as collective autonomy, a citizenship based on universal human rights, and unfettered association (Wesolowski, 1995; Madison, *op. cit.*). The accountability of democratic government and self-rule of the market were understood as essential to civil society. At the same time, civil society was an acknowledged precondition for the legitimacy of the public sphere and civic institutions (Pérez-Díaz, 1993, 1995; Deacon, 2001). While the rebirth of civil society in Central and Eastern Europe had different origins and trajectories in each country, it was commonly accompanied by the creation of a wide range of grassroots and formal associations, including the type of self-help groups studied here.

As in the United States and Western Europe, attributes of such groups mirror the essential elements of the third sector that Lohmann (1992) terms "the commons": voluntary participation, shared resources, shared purposes, a sense of mutuality, and standards of fairness. These elements can in turn reinforce the foundations of civil society, given supportive cultural, institutional, and political contexts. Works by Borkman and Munn-Giddings (2008) and Staples and Stein (2008), both in this volume, demonstrate the significant political role and structural change produced by the actions of self-help groups and organizations in Western settings. The role of self-help and mutual aid associations in promoting civil society, is, however, likely to vary depending on their social and political environments and the extent to which those environments facilitate or circumscribe voluntary activity.

Of particular relevance for this volume, examining self-help groups in the context of diverse voluntary sectors is also essential to understanding the evolving nature of health consumerism (Borkman & Munn-Giddings, 2008). A multidimensional construct, consumerism typically implies an activist role for the patient, who challenges medical dominance, negotiates treatment options, develops knowledge and self-care, and asserts the expertise of embodied experience (Haug & Lavin, 1979, 1981; Hibbard & Weeks, 1987; Zadoroznyj, 2001). Public attitudes in the United States have long favored such patient empowerment; however, as found early on, "consumerist attitudes are not explanatory of consumerist behavior" (Haug & Lavin, 1981, p. 222). Moreover, the manifestation and extent of consumerism are likely to vary within different health care systems (Borkman & Munn-Giddings, 2008). To the extent that the health care system has been part of the state apparatus, consumerist approaches might be expected to rise alongside challenges to state legitimacy. In contrast, attempts to privatize health care might engender resistance by those concerned with human rights, as with the women's movement's struggle against such restructuring in El Salvador described by Almeida and Delgado (2008). Comparative study of the changing contexts of care is thus essential in order to theorize consumer behavior at both the individual and collective levels.

This chapter examines self-help and mutual aid initiatives related to health and social welfare in Slovenia and Croatia. Examples include groups for people with hypertension, diabetes, breast cancer, mental illness, and eating disorders, as well as family members of mental health consumers and parents with disabled children. The study explores the relationships of such groups to professional providers and institutions, showing how such relationships are shaped by the historical, social, and political economic contexts in which they evolve. Contextual factors such as policy legacies, cultural values, the role of the state, and globalization fundamentally affect the role of self-help relative to the health care system and the place of self-help groups in the third sector more broadly. The analysis demonstrates that relations between professional care and self-help cannot be gauged solely in terms of the extent of professional dominance or group autonomy; both may, in turn and independently, be contingent on social and material relations well beyond the domain of systems of care.

This study follows Gidron and Chesler's (1994, p. 3) definition of self-help groups, devised for international analysis, in terms of certain paradigmatic elements: "the recruitment and mobilization of peers in an informal and non-hierarchical setting, and the sharing of their common experiences." This definition includes elements most analysts of self-help emphasize: voluntary interaction among peers who take on responsibility for the concerns they have in common and support one another through sharing knowledge and experience (cf. Hasenfeld & Gidron, 1993; Borkman, 1999; Staples & Stein, 2008). On the other hand, Gidron and Chesler leave for empirical determination the focus, organization, and context of specific groups. In particular, their definition leaves open to question the extent to which self-help groups are autonomous, "governed by and for the people with the shared experience, not ... professionals or outsiders," definitional aspects used in the study of self-help by Borkman & Munn-Giddings (2008) in this volume and typically found in accounts based in Western societies (cf. Katz, 1984; Humphreys & Ribisl, 1999; Staples & Stein, 2008). We assert that bracketing the question of group autonomy is essential when working in settings where there has been little independence of action beyond structures provided or condoned by the state.

Slovenia and Croatia are appropriate sites for this study because, while self-help groups have been active there since the 1970s, the transition to democratic, capitalist regimes opened up new possibilities for civic organization. With that, self-help and mutual aid associations of diverse types began to form in many sectors, and especially within health care. Some of the groups studied here pre-date the war of Yugoslav dissolution, and post-war self-help initiatives are now swelling their ranks.

Both older and newer self-help efforts face a political paradox. On the one hand, their ability to claim and frame their condition as a social problem – i.e., to develop and assert their own "meaning perspective"

(Borkman, 1999, p. 7) on the nature of their shared situation – has increased with the opening up of opportunities for collective organizing. On the other, the economic and political resources available to them have constricted with the retrenchment of the welfare state, while competition for those resources has expanded in proportion to the emergence of the third sector. These groups thus have greater potential political and social legitimacy, but must struggle to find the means to convert those into organizational stability and social or political clout. This chapter assesses the strategies self-help groups develop in response to this dilemma and the shaping of those strategies by more macro-level interests of the state.

Nowhere are the roots of this paradox more evident than for those groups concerned with health-related conditions. Even before the war of Yugoslav dissolution, health ministries in Slovenia and Croatia had devised plans to bring health care under (then Republic-level) centralized control and to introduce supplementary insurance plans – both indicators of the retrenchment in public coverage that would follow (Dill, 1993). As laws in the 1990s subsequently enabled the privatization of medical practice and institutions, physicians developed a parallel system of care more readily accessible than that of the state, but only for those able to afford it. Within the same decade, laws enabled the formation of member-based and public benefit organizations and their registration as Non-Governmental Organizations (NGOs). By the middle of the first decade of the new century, there would be hundreds of NGOs related to health and social welfare issues throughout both countries, and each would have public bodies assigned to support and govern such activity. Even more recent or prospective legislation aims at facilitating and regulating NGO formation, charitable donations, volunteer activity, and the formation of community foundations.

Among the new health-related NGOs are the groups examined in this chapter. First are long-standing self-help groups that formally became NGOs but remained closely connected with the institutions in which they had originated. This was true for groups in ambulatory care centers as well as organizations for people with cancer. Second are newer entities now empowered to act independently of state or institutional settings; examples are groups consisting of mental health consumers, women with eating disorders, and individuals with diverse physical disabilities. Third are groups representing a variety of situations for which there had not been state-controlled or institutionally sponsored collective action; for example, couples dealing with infertility, parents of children with special needs, and people both deaf and blind. All of these NGOs claim to advocate both on the level of individual members and on that of public awareness and policy.

This is particularly true of those in the third category, the claims of which have thus come to signify "new social problems."

Both newer groups and those dating from the 1970s show mixed patterns of connections with professionals. While those in ambulatory care centers were initiated by health professionals, many of the groups, as well as the "cancer clubs," operated under member leadership. Analysis of the ambulatory care groups indicated that none achieved complete autonomy from those professionals, but many established control over their own structures and agendas. (Sokolovsky, Sošić, & Pavleković, 1991) Newer groups tend to be member-originated and driven, though some have professionals at their head or as consultants.

On the surface, the structural connection of many groups with professionals appears more like what would be considered "support groups" in US settings; this, however, fails to acknowledge the extent of members' autonomy or to assess the nature of their goals. It is thus essential to ask further questions: To what extent do groups accept or contest biomedical models and assumptions? In what ways do they collectively develop perspectives other than those of biomedicine? In what ways do they cultivate "consumerist" attitudes among members, or encourage members to adopt alternative understandings to those of their physicians? Overall, to what extent do they define themselves in relation to care professionals, and what is the nature of that relationship?

Such questions have long been the topic of research on self-help groups in Western and American settings, examining the relationship of self-help to professional care and gauging the sources and impact of professionalism on self-help activity. (see, e.g., Borkman, 1990; Hasenfeld & Gidron, 1993; Borkman, 1997; Gartner, 1997; Humphreys & Ribisl, 1999; Shepherd et al., 1999; Adamsen & Rasmussen, 2001). While it is beyond the scope of this chapter to compare the self-help movement in the West with that in the study settings, the analysis here will suggest the need to re-focus from questions of the relationships between groups and professionals, to an examination of the political and social contexts within which such relations occur.

METHODOLOGY

The study reported here is part of an ongoing research project examining the role of the third sector in the transformation of health care and social welfare in countries formerly part of Yugoslavia (Coury & Lučanin, 1996; Coury & Dill, 2000a, 2000b; Dill & Coury, 1999; Coury & Štambuk, 2002).

This work began with an examination of health, social welfare, and social services for the Yugoslav elderly before the war of dissolution (Dill, 1993) and thus builds upon long-standing contacts now within third sector programs.

For the purposes of this chapter, Slovenian and Croatian groups are treated together, as distinctions between older and newer groups were found more significant than those of national boundaries. To locate self-help groups, a "snowball" sampling technique began with individuals at the Andrija Štampar School of Public Health and the Cancer League known to have been instrumental in the development and analysis of groups established in the 1970s and 1980s. Their leads identified groups for people with hypertension, diabetes, and various cancer diagnoses. Newer groups were found through various means; these included directories of NGOs in each country, people instrumental in the development of those directories, quasi-public officials familiar with NGO developments, and professionals (psychiatrists and psychologists, sociologists, and social work faculty) connected with, or knowledgeable about, a variety of groups. Interviews took place during the summer of 2001 with members of 24 organizations (some of which ran multiple groups) identified through these means, and five group meetings were observed. Follow-up of targeted groups and discussions with members from an additional seven took place during 2003, 2005, and 2007 (see the Appendix). Groups named in this chapter are those from whom explicit permission was obtained in the most recent contact; identities of others are obscured in order to maintain confidentiality.

Most interviewees were leaders of their respective groups, which might have biased our results towards the "official" version of the group's ideology and agenda. To counteract that possibility, views of different groups addressing the same problem area were elicited, as were those of individuals knowledgeable about the field in general. The majority of groups were in and around the capital cities of Zagreb and Ljubljana. Information on groups in other areas was obtained from respondents, as well as through Internet sources.

Interviews followed a semi-structured format responsive to the context and concerns of each interviewee. All interviews covered the following core elements: a review of the origins, history, and mission of the group; a description of its current membership, structure, and activities; views regarding the impact on the group of the war (for those whose creation predated or shortly followed it); relations to service agencies, professional providers, and other institutional players; extent, forms, and sources of support; connections with other groups and NGOs; connections with public agencies and ministries; and factors perceived as facilitating or impeding group goals. Interviews were conducted in English or in Croatian, at times with simultaneous translation. Notes were transcribed and qualitative data analysis conducted both in the field and subsequently.

THE HISTORICAL CONTEXTS OF SELF-HELP IN EX-YUGOSLAVIA

Self-help approaches have an extensive history in this region. Indeed, the first International Conference on the Role of Self Help and Mutual Aid in Contemporary Society, with participants from 16 countries and four continents, was held in Dubrovnik, Yugoslavia (now Croatia) in 1979 (Katz, 1984). Following changes to the Yugoslav constitution in 1974 that liberalized the process of creating voluntary associations, physicians from the Andrija Štampar School of Public Health (in Zagreb) founded clubs for self-care and mutual help of patients with hypertension. Groups for diabetics and alcoholics followed, in Slovenia as well as Croatia. While informed by existing knowledge of self-help approaches in Europe and the United States, these efforts also took deliberate account of the constitutionally defined duty and right of citizens to participate in the management of both community and work affairs, institutionalized in the system of "self-management" organizations at federal, republic, and local levels (Barath, 1990; Sokolovsky et al., 1991).

While linked to doctors and nurses at health centers that formed the backbone of primary medical care at the community level, organizationally these groups belonged to the self-management structures of local or work communities. Self-management, or *Solidarnost*, governed all industry, health and social welfare, and civil association in former Yugoslavia. Self-management councils existed at state, regional, workplace, and community (or "commune") levels, charged with making administrative and resource allocation decisions that were relatively autonomous of central state control and attuned to local needs (the extent to which these councils were truly independent from party control has been contested; see Parmalee, 1985; Saric & Rodwin, 1993). In health care and social services, consumers, or "users," had councils parallel to those of "providers" (professionals and administrators). Self-help groups would have had representation in user councils.

Little information is available about these early self-help groups and their development, but those in ambulatory (or primary) care centers appear to have been the first to claim the title "self-help" (*Samo Pomoć*). By the early 1980s there were more than 1,000 members of then 25 hypertension groups, and newer groups for diabetics (Barath, 1990). Groups governed themselves and, to a variable extent, set their own agendas. The vast majority of groups operated in connection with physicians and nurses, however, and biomedical treatment models heavily shaped group agendas (Sokolovsky et al., 1991).

Around the same time, the Yugoslav Cancer League founded clubs for people who had received laryngectomies. Subsequently the League established clubs for women who had surgery for breast cancer, colon cancer patients, and people receiving chemotherapy. These clubs were intended to assist with psychosocial rehabilitation and, though professionally facilitated, were governed by members.

Prior to the war of Yugoslav dissolution in the early 1990s, both government and service systems were moving in directions that would further promote the expansion of voluntary associations. For example, nearly 50 percent of the more than 12,000 Slovenian voluntary organizations registered in 1998 had been founded between the second half of the 1970s and the end of the 1980s (Kolarić, 1998). All were membership organizations, primarily sports clubs and professional associations. The first Yugoslav Congress of Volunteer Work was held in 1986, bringing together indigenous societies not connected with socio-political organizations; these would have included health care organizations such as self-help groups and cancer clubs. In Slovenia during the 1970s and 1980s, some mental health care recipients and providers defied the dominance of institutional care, developing the first community-based support groups and services (cf. Švab & Tomori, 2002). Throughout Yugoslavia, legal and bureaucratic movement towards privatization (including third sector provision) of health care and social welfare was evident, as was increased openness within those sectors to initiatives of non-professionals (Dill, 1993).

The war and the attendant transition towards a market economy fueled an explosion of NGO involvement in Slovenia and Croatia, involving both international aid agencies and the stimulation of domestic NGOs focused on the needs of war victims, refugees and displaced people, traumatized children, and vulnerable elders, among others. The system of self-management that had organized all public institutions was effectively abolished, and the newly independent countries first centralized the provision of health care and social welfare services, then retrenched on the scope and extent of entitlements through mechanisms such as increased co-payments and secondary insurance.

Laws permitting the creation, and governing the operation, of autonomous NGOs began to be enacted in the 1990s and are still under construction and revision. The differences between these NGOs and earlier voluntary societies lie primarily in the lack of state and party control; it is also now possible to create foundations and non-profit service providers, absent under former regimes. While formally independent of the state, in order to qualify for any type of public support (whether at national or local levels) organizations are required to register as NGOs. These legal changes thus promoted the institutionalization, i.e., the creation of a legal organizational structure, of new grassroots movements.

New self-help groups emerged within this context of political and economic transformation. While only a few began directly through aid from a foreign government or INGO, others had been stimulated by leaders' experiences in NGOs dealing with war-related and post-war issues. Some organizations took advantage of the new possibilities for NGO registration to change their structures in ways that promoted self-help activities. For example, while remaining part of a parent "umbrella" association, Croatian associations for people with disabilities split apart into NGOs centered on more specific diagnostic categories, which then operated as self-help groups focused on the specific needs of their members.

Almost all of the newer groups exist as part of NGO service agencies; that is, either the group itself is a service offered to constituents served by other programs within the agency, or the group overlaps, in membership and administration, with related programs. A self-help group for domestic abuse victims in Slovenia is an example of the former, since the parent organization also runs a shelter and other services. NGOs for women with breast cancer include "cancer clubs," which operate on a self-help basis, branches of Europa Donna, a Europe-wide breast cancer advocacy organization, and Reach-to-Recovery, a one-to-one support program. While these are separately registered, their memberships heavily overlap, and for the most part they share the same leaders, many of whom are themselves cancer survivors.

Regardless of the historical development of the groups in relation to NGOs, many of the associations studied fall somewhere between what the West might consider professionally developed or "support" groups and those more strictly "self-help" in nature. The primary care groups and some of the newer ones fall more on the "support" side, as they are organized by those working in professional capacities. Even in these cases, however, members choose their own leaders, decide on the agenda for meetings, and use the term "self-help" in referring to their purposes. The newer groups with grassroots origins remain more autonomous of professionals, (though their leaders tend to come from the educated elite with the ability to develop professional connections of their own choosing). Moreover, all groups develop, over time, a shared set of connections and understandings – a "meaning perspective" – that goes beyond the provision of mutual psychological support for members (Borkman, 1999).

It should be evident that the act of registering as an NGO is a pivotal point in self-help group development, particularly for those that begin as more "pure" grassroots self-help associations and, subsequent to registration, develop into service agencies. To register requires a certain minimal membership, a code of by-laws, and officers and executive board; increasingly, it also implies a certain level of scrutiny from the state as well as the public. Respondents noted that to get any support (private or public) and even "to be taken seriously" it was essential to register as an NGO, thus moving towards a more formal organizational status. Becoming an NGO is necessary in order to secure meeting space, program, and operating funds, the ability to solicit public support – in short, the lifeblood of every group. Moreover, since newer groups often have formed around issues not accommodated in current service systems, they use NGO registration as a stepping-stone towards program development.

Self-help groups in Slovenia and Croatia thus comprise a rich array of organizations, from those with a three-decade history to those newly minted in the 21st century. As noted for self-help groups in Eastern Europe more generally (Barath, 1991), the older groups *tend* to be more professionally controlled than newer ones, that is, to have their existences validated, their structures determined, and their agendas set by professional service providers or organizations closely affiliated with professionally controlled domains. Their objectives are generally oriented at changing aspects of members' lives (i.e., personal change) and organizing group activities. Newer groups *tend* to be more "member owned" (cf. Borkman, 1999, pp. 80–81ff.) directed outwards towards social change, and deliberate in their development of new collective identities (cf. Ganchoff, 2008). There are exceptions in each category, however, and relations between groups on the one hand and service professionals or agencies on the other, are more complex than such description suggests.

RELATIONS WITH THE PROFESSIONAL REALM

By all accounts, relations of self-help groups with health care professionals have varied from their beginnings in former Yugoslavia, with some of the initial groups reportedly taking more control over their own structures and agendas than others (Sokolovsky et al., 1991). The groups of this type in the present study remain focused on medical aspects of their conditions, and their meetings are facilitated by nurses, who keep medical records on members (e.g., blood sugar levels) generated during group meetings. During meetings that were observed, members of these groups discussed medically relevant issues, such as control of their conditions through diet, exercise, and stress reduction.

These long-standing self-help groups may thus be termed medically focused *regardless* of their relationships with particular professionals. As well, they have not and do not challenge medical providers or institutions. There are several contextual factors that appear responsible for this. Until recently these groups existed within a state apparatus that guaranteed the provision of health care and, moreover, provided vehicles for non-professional participation in governance within the self-management system. (Of course, that system may have functioned as much to vitiate broader protest as to facilitate popular participation, and the extent to which the state discouraged dissent should not be underestimated.) The relatively small scale and tight networks of both societies must also be considered as a factor that could muffle conflict of groups with professionals; as one NGO advisor put it, "today I might see a doctor on behalf of this group; but tomorrow I'll see him as a patient."

Relations between doctors and patients in these settings provide further explanation for the reluctance of self-help groups to confront medical professionals. As stated by analysts from the University of Zagreb, "The traditional medical-paternalistic approach still dominates between doctors and patients [in Croatia], where the doctor is dominant and, implicitly or explicitly, disputes the autonomy of the patient. It should be emphasized that the vast majority of patients accept this kind of asymmetrical power, as they themselves were raised with the mindset of the omnipotence of doctors and their own incompetence in matters of treatment" (Babič-Bosanac & Dzakula, 2006, pp. 409–410).

A final contextual matter is that questions of patient rights and bioethics have yet to be addressed to the extent that paralleled the consumerist movement in health care in the US from the late 1960s through the 1970's (Weitz, 2006; cf. Borkman & Munn-Giddings, 2009). For example, the Croatian Association for Patients' Rights lobbied for five years in order to achieve the enactment by the Croatian Parliament of a Law for the Protection of the Patients' Rights (http://www.waml.ws/pages/newsletters.asp; cf. Dula & Maja, n.d.), legislation that has yet to impact the provision of health care fully (Babič-Bosanac & Dzakula, 2006). Issues such as informed consent and confidentiality were just being introduced into the curricula of future health professionals in 2005. For self-help groups to challenge professional dominance would thus have required them to be on the forefront of much wider social and institutional issues, while in many cases they were simply struggling to find a place to meet.

Older self-help groups have survived in part by crafting for themselves a role of "adjunct" reinforcing or augmenting biomedicine, instead of contesting it. Although most of the newer groups have not emerged in the same adjunct capacity, the issues they address tend to be medicalized issues – that is, their members are people who require (or are presumed to require) medical or rehabilitative services. To the extent that groups take a critical stance, it is towards the type of care that is provided, and specifically the failure of professionals to consider their knowledge and needs. Groups for both adults and children with disabilities, for instance, reported that primary care physicians lack knowledge critical to their treatment. They further resented the type of treatment often encountered from specialists, for example, "I don't want to be a therapist; I am a mother, I am expert for my child. I want partnerships with professionals. Professionals must help me with my child, but not in (such) a way that they're gods."

Even groups more critical of professional control did not necessarily want to claim jurisdiction for themselves. For example, mental health consumer groups in Slovenia formed as part of a broad social movement against institutional care, roughly 20 years following the de-institutionalization movement in America (cf. Švab & Tomori, 2002; Švab, 2003). Community mental health services are scarce in both countries, which still rely on mental hospitals for short- and long-term care despite careful movement towards de-institutionalization. Self-help group leaders, who generally are also "users" albeit some have advanced psychological training, are critical of the hierarchy between consumers and providers; one, holding both hands at the same height, noted "We're equal here [at the group] … they [members] feel that. With psychiatrists, they're here [one hand held high] and we're here [other hand held low]." Nonetheless, groups are divided internally as well as amongst themselves about whether complete consumer control over group activities and other services would be desirable. Only one completely consumer-owned service program was identified.

For the most part, newer groups take it as their mission to educate professionals about their perspectives and the needs of their members. A variety of group leaders deliver lectures for faculty and students at medical and social work schools. Some groups offer internship placements for social work students. One has taken steps to "grow our own professionals" by mentoring young members towards professional careers. A professor involved with NGOs summed up the situation, "Our problem is first to develop professionalism ... We regard it as good ... but there is also a movement towards independence from professionalism."

SELF-HELP GROUPS AND THE CHANGING ROLE OF THE STATE

While political and economic developments have in many ways nurtured the emergence of self-help groups in these countries, related trends have inhibited their growth. This is primarily because of their dependence on the state for legitimacy and public resources. Beyond registration requirements, groups are dependent on public auspices for essential resources such as space and program funding. Still extant hypertension and diabetes groups retain meeting space in social community centers, shared with groups meeting at other times. (One meeting of a newer group attended took place in a small community center room during a time when, unbeknownst to either, another new group had also arranged a meeting. Jokingly re-naming itself the "Outdoors Group," the latter decided to meet on the stairs outside the building.) Cancer clubs have lost claims on space in hospitals and clinics as those institutions have closed, become private, or restricted use of rooms to paying renters. Newer groups that are connected with service programs have typically received some office space – generally one or two relatively small rooms – from the town government; the space was generally in great need of repair as well as furnishings. With one exception, none had obtained a dedicated meeting space from organizations that might provide it in the United States, such as churches, libraries, schools, or universities; and only one had managed to secure some rooms through a private donation. For decorations, furnishings, utilities, program development, and miscellaneous expenses, all groups relied on dues (generally quite small), outside sponsors, and their own contributions of labor. Less than a handful had managed to develop a base of support both stable and diversified.

Dependency on the state appears most problematic for those self-help groups with the longest connection to public auspices, and in particular, to the health care sector. Even though physicians are (and were) less directly involved with these groups than public health nurses, the groups draw from physicians' registries, and the nurses are tied to and responsible for specific primary care practices. Thus, it becomes harder, if not impossible, to maintain the group when doctors are unavailable or uncooperative. Changes in the structure of health care reimbursement and the movement of doctors into private practice appear to have vitiated the availability of physicians and with it the numbers and activities of medical self-help groups. Shifts in the health care system towards cost-savings, which might have enhanced the groups' salience, aim at screenings and preventive equipment rather than secondary support functions. These trends also under-cut the clubs for cancer survivors, which had been used to a greater level of support than currently received from the Cancer League. Commenting ironically on current economic strictures, one leader lamented that members used to visit other clubs in Hungary and Poland, but were now confined to trips to Bosnia and Bulgaria.

State support has provided greater opportunities for expansion by newer groups, which tend to address problems and populations under-served by the public systems. Examples include mental health consumers and their families, people with eating disorders, people with multiple sensory impairments, parents of children with special needs, and people who stutter. Beyond space, these groups receive program grants from state resources (mostly lottery-derived) and two types of temporary staff: "civil service workers" (men completing community service as an alternative to the military), and women completing the equivalent to workfare programs (in Slovenia only). None of these resources is provided permanently, however, and the lottery funding is allocated differently from year to year.

A more global issue derives from the fact that the problems these groups address are subject to social stigmatization and misunderstanding, which is part of the reason they had not been part of the former state regime of services. Respondents stated that it is still considered shameful to see (or have a family member see) a psychiatrist; that neither the public nor physicians understand problems like eating disorders; and that issues like infertility or sexual abuse are simply not openly acknowledged. One group dealing with such a taboo issue quoted the government minister arranging space for them in a remote part of town as saying he wanted them to be "where no one can see you."

Changes in the health care sector are only one way in which the state (or its devolution) has affected self-help groups. Over the period of this study, Slovenia became a member of the European Union, while Croatia edged, if irregularly, towards the same outcome. Efforts to achieve social and political standards required for EU membership have molded both state policy and its financing of third sector organizations in both countries. Self-help groups that build on areas related to EU standards for health and social care have thus had some advantage.

The World Bank, USAID, and international foundations have also affected NGOs directly and through their sponsorship of state restructuring. The World Bank recently provided grants for eight "civic engagement projects" in Croatia (www.worldbank.hr). Several groups reported European foundations as sources of small grants as well as training. USAID, through its Academy for Educational Development (AED), funded a program termed "CroNGO," which from 2002 to 2004 sponsored capacity-building programs for nine NGOs as "Partners for NGO Sector Sustainability." (www.aed.hr/en/crongo.asp). One of these partner organizations was the "Club of Women Suffering from Breast Cancer" in Split, which was to provide "strategic planning and capacity-building support to the National Network of Clubs of Women Suffering from Breast Cancer" as well as "develop models and pilot projects for NGO-government collaboration on the local level (*ibid.*)." Given that the capacity of the clubs had indeed suffered from the state withdrawing its prior support, such activities are both ironic and essential for these groups to survive.

Through leadership training and "capacity development" programs, these international bodies are transmitting models of NGO operation informed by Western third sector organizations. For example, AED recently held a conference in Zagreb about "self-financing activities and social enterprise in the non-profit sector ... including both mission-related and non-mission-related enterprises (http://www.aed.hr/en/Default.asp)." "Vision, mission, and strategy" have been so drilled into one self-help association leader as the essentials of NGO development, that she says them almost as one word. Translating Western models, and the issues they address, into these new settings does not always proceed smoothly, however. A particularly jarring example came in one respondent's description of a planned "cultural competency" program for schoolteachers as focused on Serbian and Roma children. Before the war, it can be argued, the children of Croatian citizens of Serbian descent would not have been deemed culturally "different"; while the Roma often reject the symbolic inclusion such "cultural competency" programs imply.

The most pervasive international impact on Slovenian and Croatian NGOs still comes, however, from broader trends in the globalized economy: the introduction of capitalism and the privatization of formerly state domains. These at once made the third sector both possible and essential. Human services, in particular health care, went from complete public control to a mix of the state and the market. Access to health care has become a property not of "citizens," but of "consumers." The relationship of self-help groups to health care professionals and institutions must thus be seen in the context of both sets of actors coming to terms with these conditions.

SELF-HELP GROUPS NOW: CONSUMERS WITHOUT CONSUMERISM

To summarize the situation of self-help groups in this study, the older groups, remnants of the Yugoslav regime and still most linked to state-provided care, face extreme challenges. Competition for resources, even that as basic as meeting space, forecloses expansion and threatens continued operation. One option is to find alternate sources of support, but these too are highly sought by all third sector players. Patients and their families *by default* have become "consumers," but not "consumerist." That is, it has become the norm to use any funds available through family networks to pay for private care, especially (but not exclusively) for life-threatening conditions. Such care is available in private clinics, but also from the same physicians who operate in the public sphere. Choice severely limited by resources can hardly be called "consumerism," but even for those able to pay, seeking second opinions or "shopping around" for health care is not common. As described, notions of patient rights are only now entering the discourse of health care, and professional dominance is rarely challenged either by individuals or by groups. The support and advocacy provided by these groups has become more critical as care within the public domain has constricted.

More recently founded groups encounter the same state strictures as older groups, but have been more adept at securing private and international support. These associations also do not contest professional models and commonly have professionals as co-leaders or consultants. Their own leaders also act as instructors to health professionals-in-training, informing them about the social dimensions of the illness. The nature of their relationship with the health professions was summed up by one leader, "They have started to count on us as a real resource which can be powerful (to help them learn how to) work with families in a proper way."

These groups focus on achieving as "normal" a life as possible, with normalcy still medically bracketed. Some mental health clubs, for example, require members to contract to remain on their medication; this is framed as for the good of the club meetings as well as that of the individual.

Their broader objectives, as one group leader put it, are not framed by Western concepts of human rights and freedom: "Our motto has always been not to make all people equal ... but our battle is to try to minimize all the inequality." Whether members will achieve full social inclusion hinges, of course, on the very economic conditions that limit their options for care.

Newer groups that deal with "new social problems" are the least under biomedical control, but accordingly have less automatic entry or voice within institutional settings. Their impact has hinged on building reputations, member bases, and support as part of broader networks of associations. Indeed, these were the only groups found to develop formal collaboration with other associations not directly in their domain. Like the other new groups, these have developed relationships with professional workers and associations that they see as alliances or partnerships. The tone of this work has been more activist, but as much to assert the importance of patient activation as to question professional authority. As described by a member of *PUŽ* (an association of parents of children with special needs), "Parents must be active not just six times a year when they go to the doctor, but must search for new methods, approaches, and partnerships with professionals. When you have a group started by a professional, people expect them to solve their problems. We cooperate with professionals very much, but in a different way."

It is also among these recently formed groups that both organizational and identity-related models truly alternate to those of biomedicine are developing, however. Alcoholics Anonymous, with its 12-step approach, has gained a quick foothold as an alternative to institutionally based treatment groups. *Dodir*, an association for people both deaf and blind, has broadened its reach to those with only hearing impairment, in the process taking on the mantle of "Deaf culture" (Croatian Association of Deafblind Persons Dodir, 2004). Its leader made clear her personal commitment to this "social" rather than "pathological" model when she said, "God took away my hearing, but gave me Deafness." *PUŽ* is now developing programs to educate parents of their rights, making them more "activated" consumers. It is also applying for funding for a social enterprise project training aides to support young adults in independent living. These examples reflect Western models, and to some extent represent the transplantation of those models through deliberate action by interests such as the World Bank and AED. For these member associations, however, they are logical extensions of self-help approaches in a context where making systems work in one's favor has always been, and remains, a major challenge. The development of self-help independent of professional care, or more broadly of an autonomous "third sector" is quite simply not possible, given the dynamics at play between market and state.

DISCUSSION: SELF-HELP, PROFESSIONALISM, AND THE STATE

While similar in objectives, Croatian and Slovenian self-help groups differ in critical ways from those in the United States and Western Europe. These include the formation of hybrid self-help/service organizations and the building of collaborative links with professionals and professional groups. Each of these is found in American and European self-help settings, but not with the same uniformity or urgency. This suggests, in turn, even greater blurring between the efforts of formal voluntary organizations and self-help grassroots initiatives, as well as between professional and member-owned associations, than has typified American and Western European self-help efforts (cf. Borkman, 1999; Landzelius, 2006). Further work is needed to disclose the permutations of these different structures and their implications for the definition and consequences of "self help."

As well, the groups we studied neither wish to be, nor want to be, considered as independent from state support, as opposed to the stance common to self-help groups in the United States (cf. Gidron & Chesler, 1994). Ivan Svetlik (1991), a Slovenian expert on the third sector and social welfare, concluded early in the post-Socialist transition that only the state could provide the supportive environment essential to third sector growth. Interestingly, Grønbjerg and Salamon (2002) point to a similar dynamic relationship between the state and civil society organizations that exists under conditions of state retrenchment.

As has been suggested of self-help in other parts of Europe with developed social welfare systems, these groups exert more of a social change agenda than historically true in the United States (Katz, 1984). These agendas also take the newer groups, particularly, far beyond the limited, more professionalized focus of earlier self-help movements in Yugoslavia. At the same time, the agenda is more one of social inclusion than of radical change; that is, groups seek to work within societal and professional systems to promote better services, greater access to public goods, and increased social acceptance.

CONCLUSION

Seen within the context of political and economic systems, the expansion of self-help groups in Croatia and Slovenia might be interpreted as, first, a reaction to the retrenchment by the state to provide only basic levels of care and second, a pawn to transnational capitalism. While exaggerations, these views reflect the most fundamental trends in the first and second sectors. On the other hand, self-help has always been the most pragmatic option for citizens in these settings: if individuals did not organize to help themselves, no one – no agency, no institution, no profession – would do it for them. The challenge for the third sector has been to generate such activity beyond the bounds of kin networks, not to achieve autonomy from state and market forces. Similarly, autonomy from professional dominance is neither an option nor sought at this time.

Nonetheless, this examination identifies several ways in which self-help group members benefit from participation and, as well, turn towards broader engagement in a new civic arena. As they work together on common problems based on a shared ideology, members begin to think about themselves in new ways. This transformation of worldview becomes mirrored in the groups' educational and advocacy activities. Members develop organizational skills by the securing space and official status, as well as through "in the trenches" training in fund-raising and consensual decision-making. These skills then transcend organizational boundaries through the creation of allied service programs, overlapping memberships, and cooperative efforts, linking groups to external sources of power and resources. The bridges they build to professional and international organizations may themselves constitute the "weak links" some think critical to civic development.

Taken alone, these factors would be only as powerful as the aggregate sum of members and groups. As Borkman and Munn-Giddings (2008) demonstrate, however, at the community level self-help groups can achieve significant structural changes through empowerment and advocacy activities. Groups in our study sites were not seeking such change through the challenge of professional dominance found in the United Kingdom or United States. Moreover, it is critical that both their actions and limitations been understood within a context in which there has not be a strong, independent third sector, nor a tradition of consumer choice, volunteerism, or even generalized civic trust. As has been found for charitable giving, it is not easy to generate voluntary solidarity among those who are dissimilar from one another (Bekkers, 2008); thus, groups based on shared experience and experiential sharing may be more potent than their numbers suggest.

Self-help groups in these settings should therefore be understood not so much as building civil society directly, as contributing to the capacity for civil society through a symbolic, as well as material, re-making of the public space. It is not, for example, an exaggeration for groups to consider "building professionals," given that the public space occupied by particular professional groups has been dismantled and is currently under re-construction. While the privatization of health care is the largest scale example of this, such change is evident as well in areas such as the training of social work students for NGO leadership, or the on-going movement for de-institutionalization in mental health.

In addition, these groups seek to transform not merely individual, but also collective and public identities. Achieving individual empowerment is, in this approach, accompanied by the development of civic agency. Particularly important in this regard is the lack of separation between self-help efforts and more organized, service-oriented programs. One of the main contributions of self-help groups may thus be to the legitimacy of the non-governmental sector at large, as well as to the notion of altruistic voluntarism (Dill & Fink, 2002).

Further contributing to the transformation of civic space is the groups' ability to put forward new meaning perspectives without necessarily challenging professional paradigms. Particularly for those groups stigmatized by society (as well as by professional cultures), self-help participation provides the opportunity to "create a social space and explore new and different ways of being with their problem than is otherwise available" (Borkman, 1999, p. 43). As self-help groups engage their members in meaning-making activities, they generate trust and shared understandings that in turn build social capital. As groups generate and disseminate these perspectives through their activities and their members' own changed identities, they may also, if gradually, transform the wider culture.

The challenges faced by these groups are well known by third sector organizations in other contexts. It is likely that the structure and functions of self-help groups in Slovenia and Croatia will continue to be different from those in the United States and Western Europe because of their different social contexts and policy legacies. Their contributions to civil society may nonetheless be the same, insofar as they provide arenas for the contestation of social problems, the re-definition of identity, and the expansion of voluntary association.

REFERENCES

Adamsen, L., & Rasmussen, J. M. (2001). Sociological perspectives on self-help groups: Reflections on conceptualization and social processes. *Journal of Advanced Nursing*, *35*, 909–917.

Almeida, P., & Delgado, R. (2008). Gendered networks and health care privatization. In: S. Chambré & M. Goldner (Eds), *Advances in medical sociology: Patients, consumers and civil society* (pp. 273–299). Bingley, UK: Emerald Group Publishing Limited.

Babić-Bosanac, S., & Dzakula, A. (2006). Patients' rights in the Republic of Croatia. *European Journal of Health Law*, *13*(4), 399–411.

Barath, A. (1990). Hypertension clubs in Croatia, Yugoslavia. In: A. H. Katz & E. I. Bender (Eds), *Helping one another: Self-help groups in a changing world* (pp. 205–214). Oakland, CA: Third Party Publishing Company.

Barath, A. (1991). Self-help in Europe 1979–1989. A critical review. *Health Promotion International*, *6*, 73–80.

Bekkers, R. (2008). Straight from the heart. In: S. Chambré & M. Goldner (Eds), *Advances in medical sociology: Patients, consumers and civil society* (pp. 197–221). Bingley, UK: Emerald Group Publishing Limited.

Borkman, T. (1990). Self-help groups at the turning point: Emerging egalitarian alliances with the formal health care system? *American Journal of Community Psychology*, *18*, 321–332.

Borkman, T. (1997). A selective look at self-help groups in the United States. *Health and Social Care in the Community*, *5*, 357–364.

Borkman, T. (1999). *Understanding self-help/mutual aid.* New Brunswick, NJ: Rutgers University Press.

Borkman, T., & Munn-Giddings, C. (2008). Self-help groups challenge health care systems in the US and UK. In: S. Chambré & M. Goldner (Eds), *Advances in medical sociology: Patients, consumers and civil society* (pp. 125–150). Bingley, UK: Emerald Group Publishing Limited.

Brown, L. D. (1998). Creating social capital: Nongovernmental development organizations and intersectoral problem solving. In: W. W. Powell & E. S. Clemens (Eds), *Private action and the public good* (pp. 228–244). New Haven, CT: Yale University Press.

CIVICUS. (1997). *Building a civil society worldwide: Strategies for successful communications.* Washington, DC: A series of Case Studies, Civicus.

Coury, J., & Dill, A. E. P. (2000a). Between state, market and community: Welfare retrenchment and third sector development in Croatia and Slovenia. Presented at the 4th International Conference of the International Society for Third Sector Research, Dublin, Ireland.

Coury, J., & Dill, A. E. P. (2000b). A new civic voice: How Croatian and Slovenian nonprofit hospice organizations are reshaping the public space. Presented at the Annual Meeting of the Association for Research on Nonprofit Organizations and Voluntary Action, New Orleans.

Coury, J. M., & Despot Lućanin, J. (1996). Mending the social safety net after state socialism: 'Dobrobit' – One nongovernmental organization in Zagreb, Croatia. *Nonprofit and Voluntary Sector Quarterly*, *25*, 283–301.

Coury, J. M., & Štambuk, A. (2002). Uvodna riječ: tematski broj ćasopisa o socijalnoj politici, hospiciju I palijativnoj skrbj (Introduction to the special double number on end-of-life care policy issues). *Revija za Socialnu Politiku*, *9*(3), 241–244.

Croatian Association of Deafblind Persons Dodir. (2004). *1994–2004 10 years with you.* Zagreb, Croatia: Croatian Association of Deafblind Persons Dodir.

Deacon, N. (2001). *In search of civil society.* New York: Palgrave.

Dill, A., & Coury, J. (1999). The role of the non-profit sector in open society development: Case studies from Croatia. Presented at the Annual Meeting of the Society for the Study of Social Problems, Chicago.

Dill, A. E. P. (1993). *Transformation of social policy for the elderly in former Yugoslavia.* Washington, DC: National Council For Soviet and East European Research.

Dill, A. E. P., & Fink, T. (2002). Između tržišta, države i zajednice: smanjenje troškova unutar socijalne skrbi i razvoj hospicija u Sloveniji. (Between market, state and community: welfare retrenchment and hospice development in Slovenia). *Revija za Socialnu Politiku, 9*(3), 281–292.

Dula, R.-S., & Maja, P. (n.d.). Legal issues of the protection on patients rights in Croatia. Available at http://www.pravapacijenata.hr/pdf/Stradovi/LegalIssuesPPRightsCro.pdf

Fisher, J. (1998). *Nongovernments: NGOs and political development in the third world.* West Hartford, CT: Kumarian Press.

Gartner, A. (1997). Professionals and self-help: The uses of creative tension. *Social Policy, 27*, 47–52.

Gidron, B., & Chesler, M. (1994). Universal and particular attributes of self-help: A framework for international and intranational analysis. In: F. Lavoie, T. Borkman & B. Gidron (Eds), *Self-help and mutual aid groups: International and multicultural perspectives* (pp. 1–44). New York: The Haworth Press, Inc.

Gittell, R., & Vidal, A. (1998). *Community organizing: Building social capital as a development strategy.* Thousand Oaks, CA: SAGE Publications.

Grønbjerg, K. A., & Salamon, L. M. (2002). Devolution, marketization, and the changing shape of government-non-profit relations. In: Salamon, L. M. (Ed.), *The changing state of nonprofit America* (pp. 447–470). Washington, DC: Brookings Institution Press.

Hasenfeld, Y., & Gidron, B. (1993). Self-help groups and human service organizations: An interorganizational perspective. *Social Service Review, 67*, 217–236.

Haug, M. R., & Lavin, B. (1979). Public challenge of physician authority. *Medical Care, XVII*(8), 844–858.

Haug, M. R., & Lavin, B. (1981). Practitioner or patient – Who's in charge? *Journal of Health and Social Behavior, 22*(3), 212–229.

Hibbard, J. H., & Weeks, E. C. (1987). Consumerism in health care: Prevalence and predictors. *Medical Care, 25*(11), 1019–1032.

Humphreys, K., & Ribisl, K. M. (1999). The case for a partnership with self-help groups. *Public Health Reports, 114*, 322–329.

Katz, A. (1984). Self-help groups: An international perspective. In: A. Gartner & F. Riessman (Eds), *The self-help revolution* (pp. 233–242). New York: Human Sciences Press, Inc.

Kolarić, Z. (1998). The non-profit-voluntary sector in Slovenia (country profile). Paper presented at Johns Hopkins University, Baltimore, MD.

Landzelius, K. (2006). Introduction: Patient organization movements and new metamorphoses in patients. *Social Science and Medicine, 62*(3), 529–537.

Lohmann, R. A. (1992). *The commons: New perspectives on nonprofit organizations and voluntary action.* San Francisco: Jossey-Bass.

Madison, G. B. (1998). *The political economy of civil society and human rights.* London: Routledge.

Osborne, S. P., & Kaposvari, A. (1997). Towards a civil society? Exploring its meanings in the context of post-communist Hungary. *Journal of European Social Policy*, *7*, 209–222.

Parmalee, D. E. (1985). Whither the state in Yugoslav health care? *Social Science and Medicine*, *21*, 719–732.

Pérez-Díaz, V. (1993). Cambridge, MA: Harvard University Press.

Pérez-Díaz, V. (1995). The possibility of civil society: Traditions, character and challenges. In: J. A. Hall (Ed.), *Civil society theory history, comparison* (pp. 80–109). Cambridge, UK: Polity Press.

Powell, F., & Guerin, D. (1997). *Civil society and social policy*. Dublin: A. & A. Farmer.

Saric, M., & Rodwin, V. G. (1993). The once and future health system in the former Yugoslavia: Myths and realities. *Journal of Public Health Policy*, *14*(2), 220–237.

Shepherd, M. D., Schoenberg, M., Slavich, S., Wituk, S., Warren, M., & Meissen, G. (1999). Continuum of professional involvement in self-help groups. *Journal of Community Psychology*, *27*, 39–53.

Sokolovsky, J., Sošić, Z., & Pavleković, G. (1991). Self-help hypertensive groups and the elderly in Yugoslavia. *Journal of Cross-Cultural Gerontology*, *6*, 319–330.

Staples, L., & Stein, R. (2008). The clubhouse model: Mental health consumer-provider partnerships for recovery. In: S. M. Chambré & M. Goldner (Eds), *Advances in medical sociology: Patients, consumers and civil society* (pp. 177–196). Bingley, UK: Emerald Group Publishing Limited.

Švab, V. (2003). Preparing mental health reform in Slovenia. *International Journal of Psychosocial Rehabilitation*, *8*, 5–9.

Švab, V., & Tomori, M. (2002). Mental health services in Slovenia. *International Journal of Social Psychiatry*, *48*, 177–188.

Svetlik, I. (1991). The future of welfare pluralism in the postcommunist countries. In: A. Evers & I. Svetlik, (Eds), *New welfare mixes in care for the elderly* (Vol. 40, No. 1, pp. 13–23). Eurosocial Report, European Centre for Social Welfare Policy and Research, Vienna.

Weitz, R. (2006). Issues in Bioethics. In: R. Weitz (Ed.), *The sociology of health, illness, and health care* (4th ed., chapter 13, pp. 396–421). Belmont, CA: Thomson Wadsworth.

Wesolowski, W. (1995). The nature of social ties. In: J. A. Hall (Ed.), *Civil society theory, history, comparison* (pp. 110–135). Cambridge, UK: Polity Press.

Zadoroznyj, M. (2001). Birth and the 'reflexive consumer': Trust, risk and medical dominance in obstetric encounters. *Journal of Sociology*, *37*, 117–139.

APPENDIX. SELF-HELP ASSOCIATIONS INCLUDED IN STUDY, BY COUNTRY, DATE OF INTERVIEWS, AND FOCAL AREA

Focal Area	Slovenia	Croatia
Cancer clubs	2001, 2005	2001, 2003, 2005, 2007
Eating disorders	2001	2001, 2005
Mental health	2001, 2005, 2007	2001, 2005, 2007
Hospice (including, groups for volunteers)	2001, 2003, 2005	2001, 2003, 2005
Care for children	2001	2001, 2003, 2005, 2007
Disability, elders	2001	2001, 2003, 2007
Other medical conditions	2001, 2007	2001, 2007
Alcoholism	2001, 2005	2001, 2007
Other	2001	2005

GENDERED NETWORKS AND HEALTH CARE PRIVATIZATION

Paul Almeida and Roxana Delgado

ABSTRACT

Purpose – *This study identifies the multiple contributions of the Salvadoran women's movement in sustaining mass mobilization under the threat of public health care privatization.*

Methodology/approach – *A case study methodological approach shows how the emergence of an autonomous women's movement in El Salvador in the late 1980s and early 1990s "spilled over" (Meyer & Whittier, 1994) to assist in the maintenance of the health care campaigns in the late 1990s and early 2000s.*

Findings – *We observed three arenas in which the women's movement played pivotal roles in the anti-health care privatization struggle: (1) women-based organizations; (2) leadership positions within larger coalitions brokering the participation of diverse social sectors; and (3) key advocacy roles inside the state. These three contributions of the women's movement increased the overall level of mobilization and success against health care privatization.*

Research limitations – *The study centered on one major group of health care consumers. The role of other civic organizations should be examined in future research.*

Patients, Consumers and Civil Society
Advances in Medical Sociology, Volume 10, 273–299

ISSN: 1057-6290/doi:10.1016/S1057-6290(08)10013-4

Originality/value of chapter – *The study demonstrates that in the era of globalization, women's movements form a critical part of the social movement sector facilitating the construction of large coalitions protecting consumers from neoliberal restructuring in areas such as public health care.*

INTRODUCTION

Between 1999 and 2003 Salvadoran civil society organizations launched two massive protest campaigns to prevent the privatization and outsourcing of part of the public health care system (the Instituto Salvadoreño del Seguro Social). The first campaign lasted five months while the second campaign endured for nine months. On both occasions the health care movement averted the privatization of the Social Security hospitals. The campaigns involved multitudinous street marches and protest actions in all 14 departments of the country, including the creative *marchas blancas* (white marches) which drew up to 150,000 demonstrators dressed in white (or painted themselves white) to show their solidarity with the public health care profession. Some estimates place the largest *marchas blancas* with 250,000 participants (Meza, 2002). The latest census figures calculate the national population at 5.7 million people. Hence, the *marchas blancas* incorporated potentially up to 4 percent of the entire populace.

The movement is one of the largest and most successful in Latin America in preventing a neoliberal reform measure (of any type) from implementation. Table 1 summarizes the two anti-health care privatization campaigns. The anti-privatization conflicts in El Salvador provide exemplars of "health activism" (Landzelius, 2006) and health social movements (Borkman & Munn-Giddings, 2008; Ganchoff, 2008) in that they clearly manifested major "collective challenges to medical policy, public health policy and politics" (Brown & Zavestoski, 2004, p. 679).

This study analyzes the multifaceted contributions of the Salvadoran women's movement in sustaining mass mobilization under the threat of public health care privatization. Special attention is given to demonstrating how the emergence of an autonomous women's movement in El Salvador in the late 1980s and early 1990s "spilled over" (Meyer & Whittier, 1994) to assist in the maintenance of the health care campaigns in the late 1990s and early 2000s. Three areas in which the women's movement played pivotal roles in the anti-health care privatization struggle include: (1) women-based nongovernmental organizations (NGOs); (2) leadership positions within larger coalitions brokering the participation of diverse social sectors; and

Table 1. Summary of Anti-Health Care Privatization Campaigns.

	Anti-Health Care Privatization Campaign No. 1 (November 1999–March 2000)	Anti-Health Care Privatization Campaign No. 2 (September 2002–June 2003)
Major grievances	Partial privatization of Salvadoran Social Security hospitals and services, failure of government to enforce collective labor contract of ISSS employees	Privatization of the public health care system
Groups participating in protest coalition	Health care unions, public sector labor, women's organizations, students, NGOs	Health care unions, public sector labor, women's organizations, students, NGOs
Forms of protest	Strikes, mass marches (of 10,000–50,000), solidarity work-stoppages, sit-ins	Strikes, mass marches (of 10,000–200,000), roadblocks, sit-ins, vigils, hunger strikes
Consequences for health care consumers and patients	Increasing medical costs, less access	Increasing medical costs, less access, exclusion from health care policy-making
Campaign outcome	Impeded privatization	Impeded privatization

(3) key advocacy roles inside the state (Banaszak, 2005), especially in opposition political parties and state agencies (Stearns & Almeida, 2004). Without the pre-existing women's movement, the mobilizations against public health care restructuring would have been much smaller in scale and less efficacious in achieving its goals.

SPECIFYING MOBILIZING STRUCTURES AND EXTERNAL ALLIES IN HEALTH CARE MOVEMENTS

Recent surveys of resource mobilization and political process perspectives of collective action (McCarthy & Zald, 2002; Edwards & McCarthy, 2004) point to the need to specify more precisely the mobilizing structures (McCarthy, 1996) and influential allies (Tarrow, 1998) most likely to contribute to producing large-scale movement activity. We suggest that in the case of health care privatization in El Salvador, women provided key resources of organizations, leaders/brokers, and political allies inside the state.

Nongovernmental organizations (NGOs): While often taken for granted in advanced capitalist societies, the ability of civil society groups to establish organizations in lesser-developed countries (LDCs) provides a major upward shift in scale to launch collective action (Tilly & Tarrow, 2006). Organizations raise the level of mutual awareness and social interaction between individuals and groups (Gould, 1995). A variety of NGOs have accompanied the spread of democratization in LDCs over the past 30 years. One subset of NGOs that has grown substantially throughout the developing world in recent decades is women-based organizations (Paxton & Hughes, 2007). Such organizations provide fungible resources such as money, organizing skills, social networks, leaders, and members that can be mobilized for campaigns against unwanted social policies (Andrews, 2004; Edwards & McCarthy, 2004), including women's associations (Minkoff, 1995; McCammon et al., 2008).

In the late 19th and early 20th centuries the formation of women-based associations and maternal organizations played key advocacy roles in constructing a nascent welfare state in the United States (Skocpol, 1992). In the current period of global economic integration and welfare state retrenchment, women's organizations often perform strategic functions in confronting the weakening of social protections guaranteed by national governments (Naples, 2002). Moghadam (2005, p. 199) observes an upsurge in feminist activism against neoliberal policies in the developing world. She contends that "the state matters because of women's stakes in the areas of reproductive rights, family law, and social policy." For example, during the massive demonstrations triggered by the international debt crisis in Argentina in the early 2000s, women reportedly constituted between 50 and 75 percent of the protest participants (Borland & Sutton, 2007). In particular, health policy is a major arena in which women have serious concerns and interests, especially in terms of rising costs and loss of access due to privatization (Desai, 2002). Women engage in the public health care system as consumers more than men and women's groups are more likely to participate collectively in issues relating to health policy than other issues perceived to be less germane to their everyday lives (Machado, 1988).

Leaders and brokers: Brokers connect groups and organizations that otherwise would not be related to each other (Diani, 2003, p. 107). In particular social movements, female leaders have served as bridges between different constituencies in supporting social mobilization. Such a structural location in a field of organizations and social movements helps piece together powerful coalitions of multiple social groupings that can address major national issues such as public health care policy (Diani, 2003).

Robnett's (1996, p. 1688) study of African American women in the U.S. civil rights movements demonstrated the crucial structural role of women's positions as an "intermediate layer of leadership" in mobilizing multiple groups against racial segregation. Female leaders have been particularly prominent in issues over threats to public health, such as the local grassroots movements that constitute the environmental justice movement (Cable, 1992; Brown & Ferguson, 1995).

Allies inside the state: Women serving in prominent positions inside government and quasi-governmental bodies such as state agencies, parliament, universities, and state-sponsored commissions may also provide a critical ally for consumer groups trying to turn back unfavorable policies such as health care spending cuts. These "institutional activists" advocating on behalf of social movements inside the polity assist by raising success expectations of achieving movement goals, therefore, broadening mobilization (Santoro & McGuire, 1997; Stearns & Almeida, 2004). The women's movement in a variety of national contexts has placed sympathetic actors inside state institutions that support causes important to women (Banaszak, 2005).

In sum, specifying more precisely key *mobilizing structures* and *external allies* most conducive to consumer-based movements, such as those in defense of public health care, increases our understanding to when large-scale mobilization is most likely to arise. Women-based NGOs and leaders that act as brokers represent two specific components of a movement infrastructure that may especially contribute to consumer-based health activism.[1] McAdam (1996), Tarrow (1998), and Meyer (2004) have consistently contended that external allies constitute a fundamental feature of the political environment encouraging expanded collective action, especially in cases affecting public health (Almeida & Stearns, 1998). We argue that women inside the state (Banaszak, 2005) may be an especially crucial external ally to movements confronting unwanted policy changes in the public's access to health care.

METHODS

We reconstruct two sequential campaigns in defense of consumers' access to state-funded health care in El Salvador between 1999 and 2003 in order to explain the level of mobilization. Data on women's organizations, public opinion, interviews with movement participants, and secondary sources (including newspaper coverage) are used to demonstrate the multiple contributions of Salvadoran women and the women's movement in producing large-scale collective action against health care privatization via nongovernmental organizations, brokers, and allies inside the polity. The case study design allows for an in-depth analysis of central actors (NGOs, brokers, and institutional activists) and their relationships to one another and the state in policy conflicts (Snow & Trom, 2002). These processes would be difficult to capture in a large sample quantitative-type analysis. The case study offers important lessons and strategies for other consumer-based movements currently struggling against neoliberal health care policy reforms that reduce access to state-subsidized medical services.

HEALTH CARE PRIVATIZATION IN EL SALVADOR

El Salvador's experience with health care privatization is rooted in the region's larger neoliberal trajectory in the wake of the Third World foreign debt crisis. During the 1980s, El Salvador was embroiled in a civil war and the economy was partially subsidized by foreign assistance from the United States.[2] However, by the mid-1980s the government of José Napoleón Duarte initiated a number of austerity policies, including wage freezes in the public sector and the devaluation of the national currency. The public health care sector employees union, the Sindicato de Trabajadores del Instituto Salvadoreño del Seguro Social (STISSS) acted as one of the prominent public sector unions in the 1980s leading the resistance to the early austerity policies (Estudios Centroamericanos, 1987). These economic stabilization policies are consistent with the first generation of structural adjustment programs encouraged by the International Monetary Fund, the World Bank, and the Inter-American Development Bank (IADB) throughout the developing world.

In 1989, a more pro-neoliberal government took power in El Salvador – the National Republican Alliance Party (ARENA). ARENA initiated a series of privatizations and layoffs in the public sector in the early 1990s. The ARENA government also began to negotiate structural adjustment loans with the World Bank and other international financial institutes (El Salvador Information Project, 1994). Similar to the marketization of health services in the global North (Fisher & Ronald, 2008), by the mid-1990s, neoliberal policy-makers inside the state targeted the Salvadoran public health care system for restructuring, which included more private provision of health services and selling off parts of the state-run health system (from entire hospitals to services such as security, cooking, and sanitation). In particular, in 1993, the Salvadoran government set up a national commission, with guidance and assistance from the World Bank, IADB, and the Pan-American Health Organization, to develop structural reforms in El Salvador's public health care systems.

The commission suggested a series of changes that involved greater private sector participation in government-administered hospitals and medical services (Colegio Médico de El Salvador, 2002). These proposed adjustments were aimed at both the Ministry of Public Health and Social Assistance (MSPAS) and the Social Security Institute (ISSS) (El Salvador's two main public health systems). The proposals were met with mild opposition by the doctors and medical workers in the two state health structures (Schuld, 2003). Physicians employed in the two public hospital systems perceived these restructurings as part of the conditionality on loan agreements with international financial institutions such as the IADB and World Bank.[3] Similar processes of privatization of health and social services were enacted throughout the region in the 1990s as second stage economic reforms (Kaufman & Nelson, 2004), especially in Argentina, Chile, and Colombia.

As is the case for most of Latin America, the majority of Salvadorans rely on the public health care systems for basic health services (i.e., primary care and preventative health). With high rates of poverty, informalization of the economy, and the majority of the population working at minimum wage or less, average Salvadorans cannot afford private medical care and services. The MSPAS provides very basic medical coverage to up to 75 percent of the population (the poorest sectors not covered by a formal employer health insurance program).[4] The ISSS provides medical support to about 15–20 percent of the population (about one million people). The ISSS offers state-administered health coverage for workers in the formal sector that participate in a health care insurance plan (with employer and employee contributions) and maintains the best-equipped hospitals and services. Slightly more than the remaining 5 percent of the population receive health care from private hospitals and clinics or are covered by special plans for teachers and military personnel. These segmented health care systems fit the general pattern for Latin America – a social security system (i.e., health care) for salaried workers, their dependents, and retirees in the formal sector of the economy and a general public health system for everyone else (Nelson, 2004). These types of public health care systems strived to achieve universal coverage in the developing world in the post-World War II era of state-led development and formed a defining component of the welfare state in poorer countries. The notion that such public health systems would compete with private medical services was largely "unthinkable" until the 1990s (Sen, 2003, p. 2).

During the mid-1990s, the medical workers, nurses, doctors, and patients/clients of both public health care systems (MSPAS and ISSS) felt left out of the restructuring process being negotiated within elite policy networks of business groups, the executive branch, and the international financial institutions. The general public hospital system began to charge user fees to impoverished clients as well as initiated outsourcing of some hospital services. These exclusionary actions led physicians in the ISSS to form their own labor union in October 1997 – the Sindicato de Médicos Trabajadores del Instituto del Seguro Social (SIMETRISSS)[5] – and for nongovernmental organizations working on health issues to take up health care reform as a major issue for civil society debate. Once founding their labor organization, and after spending seven months trying to negotiate with public health system officials, SIMETRISSS and doctors from the MSPAS (the general public health system) launched a number of strike actions in the first half of 1998 over their exclusion from the restructuring of the public health care system, better services for patients, as well as salary demands (Funes, Rivera, Hernández, & Zelada, 1998).

The Ministry of Labor declared the strikes illegal and ordered the arrests of the leadership of the physicians' labor union (Vargas Escolero, 1998). However, the doctors responded with more mobilizations and high levels of internal solidarity with 80–90 percent of all doctors in the MSPAS and ISSS system participating actively in the movement.[6] These work stoppages and demonstrations impressed scholarly observers as some of the most successful protests in postwar El Salvador (Vargas Escolero, 1998) (even before the major campaigns against health care privatization discussed later). The direct actions by the public sector doctors forced the government to negotiate and concede to some of their key salary demands in an epoch of overall decline for Salvadoran labor. Most importantly, in the 1998 accords the government promised to improve the quality of both public health care systems (ISSS and MSPAS) for patients and integrate the striking physicians into the commissions planning the national restructuring of the public hospital systems (Funes et al., 1998).

In late 1999, the Salvadoran government ignored the agreements of the previous health care conflict and unilaterally initiated a trial program of outsourcing the ISSS hospital units and services without consulting medical professionals, staff, or clients. That is, the ARENA administration and upper level management of the ISSS began to set up pilot experiments in ISSS hospitals where medical services and procedures were subcontracted out to private medical firms, laboratories, and individual doctors as well as secondary operations such as security, cleaning, and cooking. This led the health workers and doctors unions to launch a major five-month strike against health care privatization between November 1999 and March 2000.

The health care workers could not resist the creeping privatization process alone; they needed the assistance of other sectors in civil society. SIMETRISSS reached out to nongovernmental organizations (especially those working on community health issues) and the university community while STISSS garnered the support of other state sector labor unions. The 1999–2000 strike involved work stoppages in hospitals, solidarity strikes by sympathetic unions, several mass marches and demonstrations in the major cities and towns of the country, and sit-ins by doctors and staff on major streets in San Salvador. The momentum of the movement had reached such force that the government negotiated an accord with the public health sector unions in March 2000 in which the President promised to end the privatization process and the health care movement agreed to end social movement and strike activities (SIMETRISSS, 2000).

Another outcome of the negotiations involved the formation of a national commission on health care reform, the Consejo de Reforma del Sector Salud, which included the public medical associations, the business community, health care patients, and the nongovernmental associations working in health care. Having key stakeholders involved in the public health system reform debate was a major goal since the mid-1990s for doctors and NGOs working in public health (e.g., the demands of Acción para la Salud en El Salvador (APSAL)) in that the restructuring process resulted in better quality health services for clients. In December of 2000, the Consejo de Reforma presented its proposal to President Flores. The President subsequently ignored the recommendations of the Consejo, creating the potential for future rounds of conflict over the distribution of public health services. SIMETRISSS and STISSS, after holding workshops with ISSS patients and nongovernmental organizations (including women's organizations), both advocated in the proposal for increased ISSS health care coverage to informal sector and rural workers and against privatization. They also demanded that ISSS clients hold positions on the ISSS Executive Council as well as be represented on the boards of individual ISSS hospitals where they had been historically excluded (SIMETRISSS, 2000).

Following over two years of relative political calm (and two major earthquakes in 2001), in July of 2002, the business community and the ARENA government came up with a new legislative proposal calling once again for the outsourcing of ISSS medical services and units. The new initiative for health care privatization disregarded the recommendations of the national committee set up after the 1999–2000 strike, which represented the interests of patients, workers, doctors, and civil society. By September of 2002, the new proposals for health care privatization sponsored by the business community and the ARENA government began to work their way through the legislative pipeline. The new privatization policy threats pushed not only for greater subcontracting of medical services to the private sector in the ISSS hospital system, but also for the creation of a voucher program where ISSS clients could select between private and public medical treatment. Opponents viewed these new policies as threatening public access to health care in general and a slow creeping privatization where the state would eventually completely disinvest from the public health infrastructure. They also regarded the new policy proposals as an infringement of political rights whereby the Salvadoran Constitution stipulates public administration of health care and guarantees citizens' access to medical treatment.

As they acted in the previous episode of conflict, the health care workers and doctors associations coalesced into a coalition to resist the privatization efforts. This time, the public sector labor unions appeared much weaker after a series of privatizations in several government institutions that dismissed thousands of state employees. In order to make up for this loss in the social movement sector, the health care unions called out even more groups from civil society to assist them in their struggle. Women leaders and women's associations answered the mobilization appeal.

A new health care strike was launched in September of 2002 that lasted until June of 2003, the longest strike campaign in the country's history. The 2002–2003 strike involved immense mass marches of over 100,000 participants as well as roadblocks on the country's major highways and border crossings. Striking doctors attended patients in make shift encampments in front of the public hospitals as well as dispatched special medical brigades into rural communities to treat clients. The campaign ended with a negotiated settlement in June 2003. The government again promised not to privatize the public health system and the medical workers and doctors returned to work. The agreement also called for the revival of the Consejo de Reforma del Sector Salud as the primary force in recommending health care reform. The health care conflict may be one of the largest campaigns against privatization in Latin America, and certainly against market-based health care reforms. Women's roles and networks linked to the larger campaign played a decisive role in the struggles to defend public health care for consumers in El Salvador. We next identify the key contributions of Salvadoran women and the women's movement in producing these large and successful multi-group mobilizations against neoliberal health care restructuring.

THE SALVADORAN WOMEN'S MOVEMENT

Salvadoran women participated in social movement-type activities throughout the 20th century. In the late 1920s and early 1930s women played an integral role in the most important labor organization in the country, the Federación Regional de Trabajadores (FRT) (Gould & Lauria-Santiago, 2004). In the early 1940s they protested against the Hernández Martínez military regime. In 1957, the Communist Party established one of the first women-based organizations – the Fraternidad de Mujeres Salvadoreñas that advocated for greater female representation in labor unions (Griffith & Gates, 2004).[7] Later in the 1960s, women participated in large numbers and top leadership positions in the public teachers' association (ANDES-21 de Junio), the most powerful movement of the decade (Almeida, 2008). In the 1970s, women organized in the workplace as market vendors and in their neighborhoods and schools (Herrera, 1983; Navas Turcios, 1987). As social conflict escalated in the late 1970s, each political faction challenging the authoritarian regime organized a women's organization within its revolutionary structure (Shayne, 2004). During the civil war of the 1980s, women's organizations supported displaced war refugees and victims of state repression, while women formed up to 30 percent of the insurgent FMLN army (Viterna, 2006).

By the end of the civil war in the early 1990s, the women's movement in El Salvador had come into existence as its own autonomous force (i.e., not controlled by male-dominated leftist political factions). Women now headed NGOs, formed their own autonomous organizations (Navas, Orellana, & Domínguez, 2000), and demanded leadership positions inside the state. The emergence of the Salvadoran women's movement in the early 1990s occupied a pivotal role in creating the mass mobilization to protect the Salvadoran health care system.

Parallel to women's health movements in the United States (Rutherford & Gallo-Cruz, 2008; Sulik & Eich-Krohm, 2008), health care provided one of the major everyday life issues that the nascent Salvadoran women's movement could effectively mobilize a constituency. Traditionally in El Salvador, women are responsible for meeting children's health requirements, interacting directly with public health care system officials and staff when bringing their children to clinics and hospitals (FESAL, 2004, p. 439). Salvadoran women as consumers use the public health system for contraception and reproductive health needs more than any other source or institute (FESAL, 2004). Various maternity health needs are also among the three most common causes for patients entering ISSS public hospitals (SIMETRISSS, 2000, p. 71). Table 2 presents information on the public opinion of Salvadoran men and women regarding the public health care system from nationally representative surveys conducted between 1997 and 2002. A majority of women report the desire not to privatize the ISSS or MSPAS public hospital systems. Though both sexes show a majority against privatization, women demonstrate a moderately higher preference than men that public health remains under governmental jurisdiction.

Table 2. National Public Opinion Data on Health Care Privatization in El Salvador.

Date	Question	In Agreement (%)	In Disagreement (%)	Do not Know/No Response (%)	*N*
November 1997	Would you be in agreement or disagreement if the government were to privatize the ISSS Hospital System?	Women 19.3 Men 27.8	Women 57.4 Men 53.4	Women 23.3 Men 18.7	1,202
November 1997	Would you be in agreement or disagreement if the government were to privatize the Ministry of Public Health?	Women 15.0 Men 20.4	Women 66.2 Men 64.3	Women 18.8 Men 15.5	1,202
December 1999	Would you be in agreement or disagreement if the ISSS were privatized?	Women 14.7 Men 18.5	Women 74.3 Men 74.2	Women 11.0 Men 7.3	1,326
December 1999	Would you be in agreement or disagreement if some of the ISSS hospitals were privatized?	Women 15.9 Men 21.2	Women 73.0 Men 72.2	Women 11.1 Men 6.6	1,326
December 2002	Do you agree or disagree with the Parliament's decision to Pass Decree 1024 which *prevents* health care privatization?	Women 78.0 Men 78.8	Women 11.8 Men 14.5	Women 10.2 Men 6.7	1,256

Source: Compiled from Universidad Centromericana "José Simeón Cañas" University Institute for Public Opinion Surveys (1997–2002).

Women's networks, organizations, and leadership positions were able to represent these public sentiments against health care privatization by coordinating with the larger social and consumer movement in defense of public access to medical services. The growing *intensity* of the movement along with public opinion over time, as witnessed in growing displeasure with the idea of privatization along with diminishing numbers responding "don't know," placed even greater pressure for policy-makers to act (see Table 2).

One of the largest coordinating attempts of the early women's movement, *Mujeres 94*, a coalition of dozens of women's groups mobilized between 1993 and 1994, challenged presidential candidates to agree to take up a pro-women and pro-feminist platform (Viterna and Fallon, 2008). Several of the central planks of the platform included health care issues such as more and better public hospitals, comprehensive sex education, and free and voluntary motherhood (Kampwirth, 2004, pp. 92–93). Additionally, *Mujeres 94* insisted that 50 percent of leadership positions in political parties be held by women. The coalition presented this petition to representatives of major political parties following a historic mass march of 5,000–6,000 women in the capital in August 1993 (Kampwirth, 2004, p. 92). In summary, the public health care systems constituted an important part of women's everyday experiences in El Salvador. When public health care came under the threat of privatization, the women's movement viewed it as harming women's interests as consumers and patients and pooled critical resources and personnel into supporting the anti-privatization campaigns.

WOMEN-BASED NONGOVERNMENTAL ORGANIZATIONS

By the early 1990s, several women's organizations entered the political scene that focused primarily on defending and extending women's rights. These NGOs included ADEMUSA, ORMUSA, Las DIGNAS, Las Mélidas, CEMUJER, and several others (see Kampwirth, 2004 for an exhaustive listing). The organizations participated in social projects with women in rural zones and created a large social network based on women's issues. The majority of women's organizations originate from the revolutionary organizations that made up the FMLN in the 1980s (Shayne, 2004). The experience of participation in political mobilizing provided women valuable and transferable organizational skills in the 1990s when they broke off from their male-dominated revolutionary organizations (Ready, Stephen, & Cosgrove, 2001; Shayne, 2004). In addition, participation in the revolutionary movement in the 1980s provided women with social networks across much of the national territory to help build the new autonomous social movement in the following decade (Kampwirth, 2004).

One of the main issues the women-based organizations focused on involved health needs of poor urban and rural women (Ready et al., 2001). At minimum, one quarter of all women-based organizations in El Salvador work on health care issues.[8] Hence, women's associations enlisted the support of doctors and health care professionals in various projects, while prominent female physicians participated as members and in the leadership of some of the main organizations working on gender-related issues. Women's associations such as Las DIGNAS frequently give workshops on gender discrimination to labor unions and employees in the public health care systems (STISSS, 2000). The overlap between women's NGOs and employees of the public medical care system facilitated the involvement of the women's organizations in the two anti-health care privatization campaigns between 1999 and 2003.

Very early in the first strike in 1999, one of the most prominent feminist organizations in El Salvador, Las DIGNAS, paid for advertisements against health care privatization in nationally circulating newspapers. Las Mélidas (MAM), another major women's organization, encouraged its members to participate in several of the mass marches between December 1999 and March 2000. Several other feminist organizations contributed resources and volunteers (e.g., ORMUSA) to the first anti-privatization campaign in 1999–2000. The role of women's NGOs became even more pronounced in the 2002–2003 campaign to make up for the relative decline in the public sector labor movement.

The two major coalitions that supported the 2002–2003 anti-health care privatization campaign were the Foro de la Sociedad Civil and the Alianza Ciudadana Contra la Privatización (ACCP). The Foro emerged in early 1999 as a multi-community response to reconstruction efforts after Hurricane Mitch while the ACCP formed early in the second health care campaign. The Mesa Permanente de Mujeres, Las Mélidas (MAM), and PROCOMES (specializing in micro-credit for women) played an integral part of the Foro. The ACCP was composed of several women's organizations, including MAM, DIGNAS, Instituto de Investigación, Capacitación y Desarrollo de la Mujer (IMU), CEMUJER, and associations of market vendors. In addition, several nongovernmental organizations maintain special programs dedicated to women's rights, such as CORDES, CRIPDES, FUNSALPRODESE, and FUNPROCOOP, enlisted in the ACCP.

Even local-based women's organizations in rural regions provided participants in the health care demonstrations such as the Asociación para el Desarrollo Integral de la Mujer (ADIM) from repopulated communities in the remote province of Morazán. Women's organizations continued to contribute vital resources to the health care movement in early 2003 as the strike dragged on. During solidarity festivals with striking health workers held in Apopa, Santa Tecla, downtown San Salvador, and in the University of El Salvador, women's organizations raised money, donated food, and gathered school supplies for public health system employees (and their children) that had not received a paycheck in months.

WOMEN AS BROKERS AND LEADERS

Not only did women's organizations play a major role in providing members and resources to the anti-privatization campaigns, key female leaders served as critical nodes in the larger network of opposition to public health privatization. Previous research has shown that Salvadoran women served as critical "bridges" in organizing the revolutionary movement of the 1970s and 1980s by their social ties between different groups (Shayne, 1999). An analogous process also took place during the health care campaigns. The leaders of Comunidades Rurales para el Desarollo de El Salvador (CRIPDES) and ACCP were both women ((Kampwirth, 2004, p. 78) also lists CRIPDES' women's program as a major organization in the women's movement).[9] These female leaders linked together several organizations into coalitions in their role as broker (Diani, 2003). For example, in the 1999–2000 campaign, the female leader of CRIPDES spoke out early in the campaign against the government's intransigence in negotiating with health care workers (López, 1999). This same leader organized publicity caravans through San Salvador, Chalatenango, San Vicente, and La Libertad of over two dozen civil society organizations (Medrano, 2000a). The caravans informed the larger population, including rural peasants, on the need to participate in a major upcoming anti-health care privatization street demonstration on January 14, 2000 sponsored by the Movimiento de la Sociedad Civil Contra la Privatización (MSCCP). The caravans and other organizing efforts led by women appear to have paid off as the January 14 demonstration in defense of public health was described by reporters as "multitudinous" and drew rural participants into the capital from more distant regions such as San Vicente, Chalatenango, Usulután, Aguilares, Sonsonate, and Santa Ana (Medrano, 2000b).

In the 2002–2003 health care conflict, the ACCP was led by a woman who had decades of experience working with rural communities in popular health care. The ACCP acted as a coalition of dozens of NGOs, labor unions, and student associations and played a determinant part in organizing the *marchas blancas* and coordinating demonstrations on a national scale. Early in the second campaign, the leader of ACCP personally visited several social sectors, ranging from coffee farmers to bus drivers, to inform them of the health care campaign and their need to participate.[10] Female leaders in STISSS and SIMETRISSS focused their efforts on raising awareness among ISSS patients and clients, especially nurses affiliated with STISSS.

In addition, women served in key leadership positions of the patients' movement in the Asociación Nacional de Derechohabientes del Instituto Salvadoreño del Seguro Social (ANDHISSS) – the main organization of ISSS clients (Domínguez, 2002). The Association of Social Security health patients (ANDHISSS) formed in April of 2002 to improve medical services in the ISSS for the over one million beneficiaries. A female leader headed ANDHISSS during the 2002–2003 campaign. She along with other leaders met and organized ISSS clients on a national scale, educating health care patients on the need to resist outsourcing of medical services and the consequences of privatization. Both the female leaders of the ACCP and ANDHISSS were featured speakers at the March 2003 International Women's Day demonstration in San Salvador – a major annual event organized by the Salvadoran women's movement (Las DIGNAS, 2003). During the movement campaigns, the women's movement also pushed for increased representation of women in the labor unions and NGOs comprising the large coalition against health care privatization.[11]

WOMEN AS ALLIES INSIDE THE STATE

Individual women and women-based associations not only mobilized in the streets against health care reform, but also inside the state. One key actor was Dr Violeta Menjívar, a medical physician and parliamentary representative for the oppositional political party FMLN.[12] In the 1999–2003 period, Dr Menjívar served as the chair of the parliamentary commission on Health and the Environment – the legislative committee that oversees public health care issues and policy. She vehemently opposed health care privatization. She acted as an outspoken critic of Legislative Decree 131 passed in 2001, which provided the government with a legal precedent to begin subcontracting various public services such as health care. In September of 2002, Dr Menjívar led the fight to overturn the concessions law (Decree 131), in order to impede the privatization of government services and utilities (Escobar, 2002a). This legislative battle inside the legislature raised success expectations for the health care movement on the streets just as the second major strike was beginning to take place against privatization. When Salvadoran President Francisco Flores (of the ARENA party) vetoed these attempts, new legislation was introduced protecting health care provision as a governmental responsibility enshrined in the Salvadoran Constitution. This legislation originated in early October 2002 from STISSS and SIMETRISSS as well as a petition presented to Dr Menjívar's Commission in the legislative assembly following a mass march of over 50 NGOs led by the female leader of Alianza Ciudadana (Escobar, 2002b).

The petitions eventuated in Legislative Decree 1024, which guaranteed that public health care (both the ISSS and the MSPAS) would remain a government responsibility and prohibit privatization of the national health care infrastructure and services. Dr Menjívar guided this piece of legislation from the Health and Environment Commission into legislative debate, where it passed on two separate occasions (in October and November 2002) in a rare unification of oppositional political parties against the dominant ruling ARENA party. After ARENA successfully re-united with a smaller conservative party, it overturned the anti-privatization law in December of 2002. However, Dr Menjívar continued to work arduously on anti-health care privatization legislation inside the parliament well into 2003 as the protest campaign endured.

Dr Menjívar also served as a board member of MAM's program on women and public policy and her sister, Dr Zoila Aminta Menjívar, was active in SIMETRISSS. Violeta delivered speeches in the *Tribuna Abierta* (a weekly public gathering of FMLN supporters) along with another female FMLN parliamentary representative (Lilian Coto) encouraging the population to support the social movement on the streets against health care privatization just as the legislative assembly was discussing the privatization of health care in early October of 2002 (Leiva, 2002). Dr Menjívar also led a legislative delegation to visit SIMETRISSS doctors on a hunger strike in April 2003, giving legitimacy and encouragement to the movement in the seventh month of the prolonged strike. Having female representatives in the legislative assembly was a major demand and relative gain of the Salvadoran women's movement (Luciak, 2001), as witnessed by the platform of *Mujeres 94*. These hard-won advancements have translated at times, after difficult uphill struggles, in women legislators acting decisively to get laws favorable to women passed in the National Assembly, such as alimony legislation (Shayne, 2004). Women legislators can influence their male homologues to change their way of thinking about issues that affect women's lives (Shayne, 2004). Dr Menjívar followed this trend as an advocate inside the parliament during the campaigns against health care privatization.

Dr Beatrice Alamanni de Carrillo, the Human Rights Ombudswomen (Procuradora) of the Salvadoran government, took office in 2001 and serves as another example of a movement ally inside the state and institutional advocate. Dr Carrillo, a lawyer, is also active in women's associations such as the Association for University Women. The Governmental Human Rights office was created out of the peace negotiations ending the civil war in 1992. The mission of the office centers on reporting, documenting, and denouncing human rights violations. During the health care protests, Dr Carrillo sent squadrons of staff to report on police abuses and protect the demonstrators. This included observing roadblocks and sit-ins to document police misconduct. Women leaders in the health care movement trusted Carrillo to the point of reporting to the Ombudswoman's office where nonviolent protest actions would take place in advance in order for her to dispatch her staff to serve as witnesses to thwart or document police abuse.[13]

Carrillo also intervened when the national civilian police tried to prevent busloads of peasants from entering the capital to attend the *marchas blancas*. The police set up check points on the country's major highways and attempted to detain buses that appeared on route to health care demonstrations in the capital. Through negotiations by Dr Carrillo's office, the buses were eventually allowed to proceed to the capital. In addition, the Procuradora's agency helped release jailed protestors from incarceration (including 11 female unionists in STISSS in January 2003).

The Procuradora's office also published reports on the health care crisis, reinforcing the movement's collective action frame that public health care is a basic human right (not a commodity) and that the Salvadoran constitution stipulates health care as the state's responsibility (Mesa Permanente sobre El Derecho Humano a la Salud en El Salvador, 2004). In early October 2002, as the second strike campaign gained vigor, Dr Carrillo publicly condemned the General Director of the ISSS for failing to negotiate with the health care unions and provide services to clients (Procuraduría para la Defensa de los Derechos Humanos, 2002). She also publicly chastised President Flores for vetoing legislation passed by the majority of the parliament that attempted to resolve the health conflict. The actions of Dr Carrillo went well beyond all previous officeholders of the Human Rights bureau and provided the health care movement with an important advocate within the polity. In appreciation of her work, several prominent organizations in the women's movement (e.g., Las DIGNAS and MAM) petitioned the parliament in 2004 for a three-year renewal of her appointment as Human Rights Ombudswoman (Orellana, 2004).

These strategic positions inside the state for the women's movement encouraged the health care mobilization process and its successful outcomes. Having women in leadership positions inside of government bureaus and in political parties acted as a central demand for the women's movement throughout the early 1990s. Dr Menjívar and Dr Carrillo represent these victories by the women's movement that subsequently supported the campaigns to defend public health care.[14] In May of 2003, the Mélida Anaya Montes (MAM) women's organization honored both Dr Carrillo and Dr Menjívar in a special ceremony of recognition for their valuable work in protecting human rights during the second health campaign. These findings are consistent with other studies that demonstrate the role of women inside the state allying with social movements (Banaszak, 2005) and the need for health-based movements to find partners within the government such as political parties and state agencies (Stearns & Almeida, 2004).

SUMMARY OF WOMEN'S CONTRIBUTIONS TO PROTECTING PUBLIC HEALTH CARE

It is hard to imagine how Salvadoran civil society would have sustained opposition to health care privatization without the involvement of the women's movement. From the early to late 1990s, collective efforts at stemming privatization in telecommunications, food pricing and regulation, electrical power distribution, banking, pensions, and other sectors all failed before the health care campaigns. These earlier movements against privatization, at best, only organized public workers in the affected sectors and, at worst, failed to mobilize a campaign of any significance. The unsuccessful movements lacked the ability to reach out to other groups in civil society. At the same time, in the early to mid-1990s, the autonomous women's movement was just getting off the ground, setting priorities around issues of political representation, male responsibility, reproductive health, and improvements of the public health system, among other issues.

By the mid-1990s, the women's movement had become an integral part of the Salvadoran social movement sector (McCarthy & Zald, 1977). It provided a rich array of divisible resources that it could contribute to the movement to prevent health care privatization in the late 1990s and early 2000s. The women's movement supplied organizational assets in terms of financial resources for paid advertisements against health privatization and encouraged its rank-and-file members to participate in social movement activities against the outsourcing of public hospital units. Organizations such as Las DIGNAS encouraged affiliates to participate in the *marchas blancas* in the crucial remaining months of the 2003 campaign to re-infuse the movement before it showed signs of waning. The women's movement and NGOs also supplied key leaders that brokered the involvement of dozens of civil society associations in the health campaign, including dozens of rural communities.

The women's movement also pressured the national government and political parties throughout the early and mid-1990s for more female representation in the state (Luciak, 2001). These efforts resulted in the FMLN party promoting more women as parliamentary representatives and high-level appointments in legislative committees such as the head of the Health and Environment Commission of the national legislature than other parties. This hard work also eventuated in women serving as the heads of state agencies such as the Human Rights Ombudsmen's Office. These women inside the polity would champion the cause of defending public health care provision.

DISCUSSION AND CONCLUSION

In mid-2004, a year after the major health care demonstrations terminated, one of the authors asked a female nurse and leader in the STISSS health care workers' union which social sectors were more most important in demonstrating solidarity during the 2002–2003 health care strikes? She responded, "the general population, women's organizations and the FMLN political party."[15] The goal of the interview was to probe into the major civil society actors involved in organizing the health care mobilizations from the viewpoint of key activists for a larger study on the social movement. It is interesting to note that the only civic organization the respondent mentioned was "women's organizations." We have argued throughout this investigation the reasons why women proved so important in mobilizing the campaigns.

In 2007, public health privatization reemerged as a major social issue, especially in the form of outsourcing of medical units and water services. The Legislative Assembly returned to debating major legislative initiatives on public health care left over from the 2003 strike negotiations. Each side in the conflict has presented its own legislative proposals. Doctors, clients, and women's organizations prefer that medical services continue to be administered by the state, ensuring greater social equity of health care access. The ARENA party, international financial institutions, and large business groups in El Salvador demand more private sector participation and investment. On June 16, 2007, the health care movement mobilized its first major *marcha blanca* since 2003 to show support for the anti-privatization proposal. The march drew up to 15,000 participants with major representation from the women's movement, health care professionals, and clients.

With only 30,000 employees in the two public health care systems (10,000 in the ISSS), the movement needed allies to prevent an unfavorable, elite-led restructuring of the health system. Health care workers and doctors are concentrated in the largest cities, especially the capital. In order to launch a nationwide campaign to defend the public's access to health care, they needed the solidarity of other groups and institutional advocates. As Salvadoran women would be the most affected by the impending health care reforms as the system's major consumers and clients, the women's movement entered into a coalition with the public health sector employees. The women's movement participation in the health care campaigns assisted in creating the historic *marchas blancas* of over 100,000 demonstrators on multiple occasions and achieving a relatively favorable outcome by supplying personnel, networks, and actors inside the state.

For health care-based movements in the developing world, specifying major civil society actors and processes of movement articulation are central to understanding when widespread mobilization is likely to materialize. In societies where a strong women's movement emerges, consumer groups and public health care staff and professionals may be able to construct formidable coalitions in order to turn back unfavorable policies such as attempted privatization of the medical infrastructure. Women's interests in maintaining access to low cost public health motivates organizations and leaders working on women's issues to link to other groups interested in protecting the public health care system.

In the current period of neoliberal restructuring, struggles to protect the environment, water, and public health will likely demand coalitions of multiple social sectors. Whereas during the previous period of state-led development, traditional social sectors such as the labor movement and trade unions played a major role in expanding and protecting social security and access to health care, the contemporary epoch of globalization has altered the character of the social movement sector. Labor flexibility laws, state downsizing, and internationally mobile capital have reduced the political power of labor unions. New social movements and nongovernmental organizations, often led by women, play vital roles in attempting to piece together broad coalitions of public sector labor unions, environmentalists, students, opposition political parties, and sympathetic individuals inside the state to turn back threats to consumer protection such as the commoditization of public health care systems.

NOTES

1. Other types of NGOs would also be important to consumer and health policy campaigns such as environmental and community-based organizations. Our focus in this study is on women's contributions.

2. The Salvadoran Civil War took place between 1981 and 1992. Nearly 80,000 Salvadorans died in the conflict with over 80 percent of the deaths attributed to the government military, paramilitary and security forces. The war was rooted in El Salvador's authoritarian political structure (see Almeida, 2008). In January 1992 the United Nations negotiated peace negotiations between the rebel FMLN guerrilla army and the Salvadoran government. The peace accords allowed for the democratization of the Salvadoran polity and the legalization of the FMLN as an electoral political party.

3. First author interview with a leader of SIMETRISSS doctor's union. May 5, 2003, San Salvador.

4. However, within this 75 percent covered under the MSPAS, the poorest rural strata often lack access to the general public health system with the largest hospitals concentrated in the cities. Rural public health clinics are often only open a few days a week with very minimal services. Hence, for the poorest segments of the rural population it is difficult to use the public hospital system because of resource constraints and geographical isolation.

5. Before this time some doctors in the ISSS participated in the STISSS labor union that formed back in 1966. The formation of a doctor's labor union was unprecedented in the country and demonstrated how severe the crisis had become in the Social Security system in that a public sector labor union was formed by a professional group in a period of absolute decline for labor unions in general in Latin America and El Salvador. The doctors in the MSPAS formed a labor association in the late 1990s – the Asociación de Médicos Nacionales (AMENA) – and gained legal recognition in early 2001. Because, the MSPAS constitutes a government ministry, labor unions are not permitted, only occupational associations. The doctors that initiated the formation of AMENA were very active along with ISSS doctors in confronting the public health restructuring process since the mid 1990s. Workers in the MSPAS founded a labor association in rhe early 1970s, the Asociación Nacional de Trabajadores del Ministerio de la Salud Pública y Asistencia Social (ANTMSPAS).

6. First author interview with SIMETRISSS leader, May 24, 2004, San Salvador.

7. See "Sobre Mujer Salvadoreña" *Voz Popular*, March 13, 1980, p. 2.

8. At least nine of the 30 women-based nongovernmental organizations listed by Kampwirth (2004) work on health care issues.

9. The CRIPDES program working exclusively with rural women is called Programa de Desarrollo de la Mujer de CRIPDES and was founded in the early 1990s.

10. Interview with leader of Alianza Ciudadana contra la Privatización, May 19, 2004, San Salvador.

11. Women leaders also emerged in other NGOs during the health care protest campaigns. For example, three female leaders in the Unidad Ecológica Salvadoreña (UNES) – a prominent environmental NGO – incorporated many local communities into the 2002–2003 health care campaign via bicycle caravans and other public events throughout western El Salvador.

12. FMLN is the acronym for the Farabundo Martí Front for National Liberation, the largest oppositional political party in El Salvador.

13. Interview with leader of Alianza Ciudadana contra la Privatización, May 19, 2004, San Salvador.

14. Another example of a female institutional advocate that assisted the health care campaign was the work of Dr. María Isabel Rodríguez. Dr. Rodríguez is trained as a medical doctor and served as the Rector of the University of El Salvador from 1999 to 2007. She encouraged the university community (students, faculty, and staff) to participate in the *marchas blancas* and denounced the privatization process.

15. Interview with first author, San Salvador, May 23, 2004.

ACKNOWLEDGMENTS

The authors appreciate the detailed comments and insights provided by Susan Chambré and Melinda Goldner on early drafts of this chapter and data made available by José Miguel Cruz.

REFERENCES

Almeida, P. D. (2008). *Waves of protest: Popular struggle in El Salvador, 1925–2005*. Minneapolis: University of Minnesota Press.

Almeida, P. D., & Stearns, L. B. (1998). Political opportunities and local grassroots environmental movements: The case of Minamata. *Social Problems*, *45*(1), 37–60.

Andrews, K. (2004). *Freedom is a constant struggle: The Mississippi civil rights movement and its legacy*. Chicago: University of Chicago Press.

Banaszak, L. A. (2005). Inside and outside the state: Movement insider status, tactics, and public policy achievements. In: D. Meyer, V. Jenness & H. Ingram (Eds), *Routing the opposition: Social movements, public policy, and democracy* (pp. 149–176). Minneapolis: University of Minnesota Press.

Borkman, T., & Munn-Giddings, C. (2008). Self-help groups challenge health care systems in the U.S. and U.K. In: S. Chambré & M. Gouldner (Eds), *Advances in medical sociology: Patients, consumers and civil society* (Vol. 10, pp. 127–150). Bingley, UK: Emerald Group Publishing Limited.

Borland, E., & Sutton, B. (2007). Quotidian disruption and women's activism in times of crisis, Argentina 2002–2003. *Gender and Society*, *21*(5), 700–722.

Brown, P., & Ferguson, F. (1995). 'Making a Big Stink': Women's work, women's relationships, and toxic waste activism. *Gender and Society*, *9*, 145–172.

Brown, P., & Zavestoski, S. (2004). Social movements in health: An introduction. *Sociology of Health and Illness*, *26*(6), 679–694.

Cable, S. (1992). Women's social movement involvement: The role of structural availability in recruitment and participation processes. *The Sociological Quarterly*, *33*(1), 35–50.

Colegio Médico de El Salvador. (2002). ENADE 2002: Ofensiva Privatizadora de la Salud de ANEP y ARENA. *Boletín Colmed*, *4*, 1–2.

Desai, M. (2002). Transnational solidarity: Women's agency, structural adjustment, and globalization. In: N. Naples & M. Desai (Eds), *Women's activism and globalization: Linking local struggles and transnational politics* (pp. 15–33). New York: Routledge.

Diani, M. (2003). 'Leaders' or brokers? Positions and influence in social movement networks. In: M. Diani & D. McAdam (Eds), *Social movements and networks: Relational approaches to collective action* (pp. 105–122). Oxford: Oxford University Press.

Domínguez, D. (2002). Derechohabientes dispuestos a respaldar huelgas de STISSS y SIMETRISSS. *Co Latino*, September 9, p. 4.

Edwards, B., & McCarthy, J. D. (2004). Resources and social movement mobilization. In: D. Snow, S. Soule & H. Kriesi (Eds), *The Blackwell companion to social movements* (pp. 116–152). Oxford: Blackwell.

El Salvador Information Project. (1994). Privatization report #1. San Salvador: El Salvador Information Project (August).

Escobar, I. (2002a). FMLN pide eliminar las concesiones de servicios públicos. *Co Latino*, September 12, p. 3.

Escobar, I. (2002b). ONGs presentan propuesta de decreto para frenar privatización de la Salud. *Co Latino*, October 8, p. 2.

Estudios Centroamericanos. (1987). La Batalla Desigual: Gobierno Vrs. STISSS. *Estudios Centroamericanos*, *42*(7), 483–486.

FESAL. (2004). *Encuesta Nacional de Salud Familiar: Informe Final.* San Salvador: United States Agency for International Development.

Fisher, J. A., & Ronald, L. M. (2008). Direct to consumer responsibility: Medical neoliberalism in pharmaceutical advertising and drug development. In: S. Chambré & M. Gouldner (Eds), *Advances in medical sociology: Patients, consumers and civil society* (Vol. 10, pp. 29–51). Bingley, UK: Emerald Group Publishing Limited.

Funes, M. I., Rivera, C., Hernández, A., & Zelada, B. (1998). Finaliza Conflicto en Salud. *La Prensa Gráfica* (May 22), 4–5.

Ganchoff, C. (2008). Speaking for stem cells: Biomedical activism and emerging forms of patienthood. In: S. Chambré & M. Gouldner (Eds), *Advances in medical sociology: Patients, consumers and civil society* (Vol. 10, pp. 225–245). Bingley, UK: Emerald Group Publishing Limited.

Gould, J., & Lauria-Santiago, A. (2004). They call us thieves and steal our wage: Toward a reinterpretation of the Salvadoran rural mobilization, 1929–1931. *Hispanic American Historical Review, 84*(2), 191–237.

Gould, R. V. (1995). *Insurgent identities: Class, community, and protest in Paris from 1848 to the commune*. Chicago: University of Chicago Press.

Griffith, K., & Gates, L. (2004). Colonels and industrial workers in El Salvador, 1944–1972; seeking societal reform through gendered labor reforms. In: A. Lauria-Santiago & L. Binford (Eds), *Landscapes of struggle: Politics, society, and community in El Salvador* (pp. 71–84). Pittsburgh: University of Pittsburgh Press.

Herrera, N. (1983). *La mujer en la revolución salvadoreña*. Mexico City: COPEC.

Kampwirth, K. (2004). *Feminism and the legacy of revolution: Nicaragua, El Salvador, Chiapas*. Athens, OH: Ohio University Press.

Kaufman, R., & Nelson, J. (2004). Introduction: The political challenges of social sector reform. In: R. Kaufman & J. Nelson (Eds), *Crucial needs, weak incentives: Social sector reform, democratization, and globalization in Latin America* (pp. 1–19). Baltimore: Johns Hopkins University Press.

Landzelius, K. (2006). Introduction: Patient organization movements and new metamorphoses in patienthood. *Social Science and Medicine, 62*, 524–537.

Las DIGNAS. (2003). 8 de marzo, las salvadoreñas salieron a las calles. *Dignas Solidarias*, Boletín, 31, (Marzo).

Leiva, S. (2002). Ya no basta decir que malo es. *Co Latino*, October 12, p. 3.

López, I. (1999). Organizaciones de la Sociedad Civil llaman al Gobierno a dialogar frente a conflictos laborales. *Co Latino*, December 6, p. 3.

Luciak, I. A. (2001). *After the revolution: Gender and democracy in El Salvador, Nicaragua, and Guatemala*. Baltimore: Johns Hopkins University Press.

Machado, L. (1988). The participation of women in the health movement of Jardim Nordeste, in the Eastern Zone of São Paulo, Brazil: 1976–1985. *Bulletin of Latin American Research, 7*(1), 47–63.

McAdam, D. (1996). Conceptual origins, current problems, future directions. In: D. McAdam, J. D. McCarthy & M. Zald (Eds), *Comparative perspectives on social movements: Political opportunities, mobilizing structures, and cultural framings* (pp. 23–40). Cambridge: Cambridge University Press.

McCammon, H., Chaudhuri, S., Hewitt, L., Muse, C. S., Newman, H. D., Lee Smith, C., & Terrell, T. M. (2008). Becoming full citizens: The U.S. women's jury rights campaigns, the pace of reform, and strategic adaptation. *American Journal of Sociology, 113*(4), 1104–1147.

McCarthy, J. D. (1996). Constraints and opportunities in adopting, adapting, and inventing. In: D. McAdam, J. D. McCarthy & M. N. Zald (Eds), *Comparative perspectives on social movements: Political opportunities, mobilizing structures, and cultural framings* (pp. 141–151). Cambridge: Cambridge University Press.

McCarthy, J. D., & Zald, M. (1977). Resource mobilization and social movements: A partial theory. *American Journal of Sociology, 82*(6), 1212–1241.

McCarthy, J. D., & Zald, M. (2002). The enduring vitality of the resource mobilization theory of social movements. In: J. H. Turner (Ed.), *Handbook of sociological theory* (pp. 533–565). New York: Kluwer.

Medrano, J. (2000a). Caravana vehicular organiza movimiento civil. *Co Latino*, January 11, p. 4.

Medrano, J. (2000b). Trabajadores públicos marchan contra la Privatización. *Co Latino*, January 14, p. 3.

Mesa Permanente sobre el Derecho Humano a la Salud en El Salvador. (2004). *Fundamentos del Proceso de Reforma del Sector Salud en El Salvador*. San Salvador: La Procuraduría para la Defensa de los Derechos Humanos (PDDH).

Meyer, D. S. (2004). Protest and political opportunity. *Annual Review of Sociology*, *30*, 125–145.

Meyer, D. S., & Whittier, N. (1994). Social movement spillover. *Social Problems*, *41*, 277–298.

Meza, P. (2002). Comisión Tripartita Satisfecha con Segunda Marcha Blanca. *Co Latino*, October 24, p. 4.

Minkoff, D. (1995). *Organizing for equality: The evolution of women's and racial-ethnic organizations in America, 1955–1985*. New Brunswick: Rutgers University Press.

Moghadam, V. M. (2005). *Globalizing women: Transnational feminist networks*. Baltimore: Johns Hopkins University Press.

Naples, N. (2002). Changing the terms: Community activism, globalization, and the dilemmas of transnational feminist praxis. In: N. Naples & M. Desai (Eds), *Women's activism and globalization: Linking local struggles and transnational politics* (pp. 3–14). New York: Routledge.

Navas, C. M., Orellana, N., & Domínguez, L. (2000). *La experiencia organizativa de mujeres rurales en la transición post-guerra (1992–1999)*. San Salvador: FUNDE.

Navas Turcios, C. (1987). *Las Organizaciones de Mujeres en El Salvador: 1975–1985* (Masters thesis in Latin American Studies, Universidad Nacional Autónoma de México).

Nelson, J. M. (2004). The politics of health sector reform: Cross-national comparisons. In: R. Kaufman & J. Nelson (Eds), *Crucial needs, weak incentives: Social sector reform, democratization, and globalization in Latin America* (pp. 23–64). Baltimore: Johns Hopkins University Press.

Orellana, G. S. (2004). Procuradora cerca de su reelección por segundo mandato. *Co Latino*, June 22.

Paxton, P., & Hughes, M. M. (2007). *Women, politics, and power: A global perspective*. Los Angles: Pine Forge.

Procuraduría para la Defensa de los Derechos Humanos. (2002). Censura Pública. *Co Latino*, October 3, p. 9.

Ready, K., Stephen, L., & Cosgrove, S. (2001). Women's organizations in El Salvador: History, accomplishments, and international support. In: K. Kumar (Ed.), *Women and civil war: Impact, organizations, and action* (pp. 183–203). Boulder: Lynne Rienner Publishers.

Robnett, B. (1996). African-American women in the civil rights movement, 1954–1965: Gender, leadership, and micromobilization. *American Journal of Sociology*, *101*(6), 1661–1693.

Rutherford, M., & Gallo-Cruz, S. (2008). Selling the ideal birth: Rationalization and re-enchantment in the marketing of maternity care. In: S. Chambré & M. Gouldner (Eds), *Advances in medical sociology: Patients, consumers and civil society* (Vol. 10, pp. 75–98). Bingley, UK: Emerald Group Publishing Limited.

Santoro, W., & McGuire, G. (1997). Social movement insiders: The impact of institutional activists on affirmative action and comparable worth policies. *Social Problems*, *44*(4), 503–519.

Schuld, L. (2003). El Salvador: Who will have the hospitals. *NACLA Report on the Americas*, *21*(4), 42–45.

Sen, K. (2003). Introduction: Restructuring health services – Public subsidy of private provision. In: K. Sen (Ed.), *Restructuring health services: Changing contexts and comparative perspectives* (pp. 1–17). London: Zed Books.

Shayne, J. (1999). Gendered revolutionary bridges: Women in the Salvadoran resistance movement (1979–1992). *Latin American Perspectives*, *26*(3), 85–102.

Shayne, J. (2004). *The revolution question: Feminisms in El Salvador, Chile, and Cuba.* New Brunswick, NJ: Rutgers University Press.

SIMETRISSS. (2000). *Propuesta: Modelo de Modernización Hospitalaria basado en la Participación del/la Derechohabiente y del/la Trabajador/a.* San Salvador: SIMETRISSS y AGEPYM.

Skocpol, T. (1992). *Protecting soldiers and mothers: The political origins of social policy in the United States.* Cambridge: Harvard University Press.

Snow, D., & Trom, D. (2002). Case study and the study of social movements. In: B. Klandermans & S. Staggenborg (Eds), *Methods of social movement research* (pp. 146–172). Minneapolis: University of Minnesota Press.

Stearns, L. B., & Almeida, P. D. (2004). The formation of state actor–social movement coalitions and favorable policy outcomes. *Social Problems*, *51*, 478–504.

STISSS. (2000). *Memoria de Labores STISSS 1999–2000.* San Salvador: STISSS.

Sulik, G., & Eich-Krohm, A. (2008). No longer a patient: The social construction of the medical consumer. In: S. Chambré & M. Gouldner (Eds), *Advances in medical sociology: Patients, consumers and civil society* (Vol. 10, pp. 3–28). Bingley, UK: Emerald Group Publishing Limited.

Tarrow, S. (1998). *Power in movement* (2nd ed.). Cambridge: Cambridge University Press.

Tilly, C., & Tarrow, S. (2006). *Contentious politics.* Boulder: Paradigm.

Vargas Escolero, M. (1998). Reflexiones en torno a la lucha sindical de SIMETRISSS. *Estudios Centroamericanos*, *53*, 233–236.

Viterna, J. (2006). Pulled, pushed, and persuaded: Explaining women's mobilization into the Salvadoran guerrilla army. *American Journal of Sociology*, *112*(1), 1–45.

Viterna, J., & Fallon, K. (2008). Democratization, women's movements, and gender-equitable states: A framework for comparison. *American Sociological Review*, *73*, 668–689.